# (Re)structuring Copyright

For Daphné and Sophie

ELGAR MONOGRAPHS IN INTELLECTUAL PROPERTY LAW

**Series Editors:** Graeme B. Dinwoodie, *University of Oxford Faculty of Law, UK,* Rochelle Dreyfuss, *New York University School of Law, USA* and Annette Kur, *Max Planck Institute for Innovation and Competition, Germany*

This monograph series provides an important forum for authoritative scholarly works in the field of intellectual property law. It represents a showcase for original research that is theoretically rigorous and analytically precise, but above all meets the highest academic standards – setting the benchmark for scholarship in IP.

Whether considering the most pressing issues in the field of intellectual property or offering a fresh take on well-worn ground, books in the series cover the full array of rights and issues, from trade marks, copyright, and patents to trade secrets, TRIPS and design rights, and from traditional knowledge and development issues to geographical indications. Sometimes critical, often challenging, and always global in outlook, the series seeks books that engage with new and previously under-developed themes in the field, draw on other disciplines in order to further thinking in the field, or alternatively attempt to redefine or to offer a definitive statement on areas of uncertainty in the existing law.

The primary mission of the series is the development of original thinking in intellectual property law. It fosters the best theoretical and empirical work from both well-established authors and the next generation of scholars.

# (Re)structuring Copyright

## A Comprehensive Path to International Copyright Reform

Daniel J. Gervais

*Milton R. Underwood Chair in Law, Vanderbilt University, USA and Professor of Information Law, University of Amsterdam, the Netherlands*

ELGAR MONOGRAPHS IN INTELLECTUAL PROPERTY LAW

 Edward Elgar
PUBLISHING

Cheltenham, UK • Northampton, MA, USA

Published by
Edward Elgar Publishing Limited
The Lypiatts
15 Lansdown Road
Cheltenham
Glos GL50 2JA
UK

Edward Elgar Publishing, Inc.
William Pratt House
9 Dewey Court
Northampton
Massachusetts 01060
USA

Paperback edition 2019

A catalogue record for this book
is available from the British Library

Library of Congress Control Number: 2016957237

This book is available electronically in the **Elgar**online
Law subject collection
DOI 10.4337/9781785369506

ISBN 978 1 78536 949 0 (cased)
ISBN 978 1 78536 950 6 (eBook)
ISBN 978 1 78990 214 3 (paperback)

Typeset by Servis Filmsetting Ltd, Stockport, Cheshire
Printed and bound by CPI Group (UK) Ltd, Croydon, CR0 4YY

# Contents

# Figures

# Tables

# About the author

Daniel J. Gervais is Professor of Law at Vanderbilt University Law School and Director of the Vanderbilt Intellectual Property Program. He is also Professor of Information Law at the Institute for Information Law (IViR) at the University of Amsterdam, Editor-in-Chief of the *Journal of World Intellectual Property* and editor of www.tripsagreement.net. Prior to joining Vanderbilt, he was the Acting Dean, University Research Chair in Intellectual Property at the Faculty of Law at the University of Ottawa (Common Law Section). Before he joined the Academy, Professor Gervais was successively Legal Officer at the GATT (now WTO); Head of Section at WIPO; and Vice-President of Copyright Clearance Center, Inc. (CCC). Professor Gervais studied computer science and law at McGill University and the University of Montreal, where he obtained LL.B. and LL.M. degrees, and received several awards. He also received a Diploma *summa cum laude* from the Institute of Advanced International Studies in Geneva and a doctorate *magna cum laude* from the University of Nantes, France. In 2012, he became the first law professor in North America elected to the Academy of Europe. Professor Gervais is a member of the American Law Institute and Associate Reporter of the Restatement of Copyright (First) project. In 2017–2019, he is President of the International Association for the Advancement of Teaching and Research in Intellectual Property (ATRIP).

# Preface

This book aims to inform the debate about the future of copyright and its influence on human creativity. It is possible that, in a few years, all books will be the product of artificial intelligence and a version of Bob Dylan's songs will be written by the son or daughter of IBM's Watson. We are not quite there. Copyright has been, and is still, linked to many forms of (human) literary and artistic creation. Literature and art are perhaps the most vivid mirror of a society, its deepest aspirations and fears, its horrors and its magnificence. How policy affects that creation is, therefore, crucial to future human progress.

In common parlance, 'artists' create Art. In copyright, we call artists 'authors'. We could call them 'creators'. Art is used and often owned by those who distribute, disseminate, package, and sell it, to be enjoyed or used in one form or another by all of us. Art then enters a cycle of appropriation, use, reuse and transformation, sometimes leading to more creation. Creation has a very broad meaning in the copyright realm. It includes 'art' proper but also non-fiction writing and many more utilitarian forms of creation such as maps and (certain) computer programs. Some quality contributions to human progress are created by amateurs, from deeply influential essays to child prodigy music composers. Talent—however that term is defined—seems not to have been distributed evenly; yet even abundant talent needs to be honed, nurtured and developed. Mozart started composing as a child but few of the works he wrote before the age of 21 are among the ones people listen to on a regular basis two and half centuries later. That nurturing is a key function that copyright, properly structured, can accomplish. This book proposes a way to structure copyright internationally to achieve this aim. There are no doubt many other ways to get there, but I can think of no higher policy objective. There is a fundamental 'anthropological' aspect to the quest for human development and policies that support it, although there is a sheer economic argument to be made as well: in the 'knowledge economy', creativity replaces material goods. Immaterial capital displaces physical capital. Knowledge is a commodity in itself; it is increasingly produced not to support the production of material goods (e.g., an improvement on a physical device) but for its own exchange value. As a matter of human *and* economic development, policy must ensure that those who can, and will, push their creative limits, including in developing new knowledge, can do so.

True, technological changes make the policy work ahead harder. Those changes will alter in unforeseeable ways the interaction between humans and machine. Whether humans adapt to the machine (think of all the people walking with their heads down looking at a small screen) or whether the machine helps human creativity and potential flourish is the next great question. Law and policy can only influence the course of events up to a certain point, in part because regulatory interventions are so often educated guessing at best. Yet the outcome that André Gorz and others have described—the economy serving humans rather than the other way around—is the best possible one.

Good policy can maximize our chances of getting there. Copyright is not the only tool in the policy toolbox of course. It forms part of a broader set of policies known as intellectual property (IP) and IP itself is part of an array of cultural and economic levers available to policy makers, from tax credits and subsidies (*ex ante* tools) to awards and prizes (*ex post* tools). The copyright system remains front and centre in this discussion, however. Yet it is a broken system. Not surprisingly, many voices have called for copyright (and sometimes all of IP) to be jettisoned as an obsolete industrial revolution era policy dinosaur. The early days of the Internet led the Grateful Dead's John Perry Barlow to declare copyright dead. It is not. Others have made it their task to reduce copyright to its simplest expression, reflecting an underlying assumption that copyright is a negative—as little copyright as possible is necessarily a better outcome. Perhaps such calls for reduction are merely a reluctant acknowledgment that it is unrealistic in this era of trade rules to think that copyright can be scrapped entirely.

There are two other ways to see such recent developments. One is a cynical view. Many major commercial 'intermediaries' whose business is to sell advertisements need 'content' in myriad forms to draw users to their apps, sites and services. Whether it be a cat video or a Fellini movie, a recording of a high school band or a Puccini opera, a blog-post or a Jane Austen book matters not to them. I submit that it should matter to us all. Indeed, this concern *must* inform proper copyright policy. The other way to see recent developments is to embrace them, because they do lead to progress in a number of areas. The idea that entire libraries of paper books can be word-searched online is clearly a positive development, leaving aside for now the idea that those who write those books need not be remunerated for the uses of their works. The power of the Internet to disseminate new creations worldwide at little or no cost is a powerful tool to level the distribution playing field (for example by allowing anyone to publish an ebook) and potentially bringing all cultures, not just major players, to 'users' worldwide. Digital tools that allow amateurs *and* professionals to create, modify and add their own creativity to existing works can allow new creations to emerge and flourish, although it can also lead to 'lazy' creation by copying. Imitation has always been a part of the human creative process and this has now been raised to immeasurably higher levels, for both good and bad.

More 'content' is a good thing. More good 'content' is a far better thing. By 'good' I mean the type of work that alters our perceptual filters, forces us to think and rethink our world, moves us, and hopefully can make us better humans. Sometimes it is hard to know which is which. The initial failure of many new forms of art, including the famous rejection of the Impressionists by the bourgeois Parisian elites, come to mind. It is clear, however, that to achieve those aims new 'content' must not only be created, it must be made available. Current policy efforts aimed at providing new and stronger ways to take down unauthorized content are thus often misguided, although not in cases of straight piracy that add no value. We should aim not to take content down but to put more good content up, but all of that cannot and should not happen at the expense of those who have spent their lives honing their craft and/or by preventing new creators to do so. An equilibrium must be established—it can be done.

The current lack of equilibrium and the deficient structure of copyright results, in part, from a process of historical changes and accretions to the list of copyright 'rights' and, in part, from a lack of clarity as to its purpose. Indeed, very few national laws state one or more purposes of copyright. European Union Directives often mention several aims in their recitals. Efforts to define a purpose is often seen as a binary exercise. I have been asked so many times what 'side' of copyright I was on. Must one side win? This book takes the view that we can all 'win'.

The United States Constitution is a helpful guide. It is unique in that it states the purpose (Progress of Science and Useful Arts), beneficiaries (Authors) and mode of implementation (Exclusive Rights in 'Writings', for Limited Times) of copyright. Copyright should promote 'progress'. Words matter. This means that copyright is not needed to promote mere 'change'. Change happens no matter what. Progress, not necessarily so. In his 1974 Invitation to Jurisprudence Professor Harry Jones noted that not all forms of change are progress. Change that is not progress means moving sideways or going backwards. Change is merely a difference between two points (A and B) on a timeline. Progress is an improvement at point B.

Progress does not mean that there is an end-state that we must identify, such as Fukuyama's initial description of an End of History. But human progress, its emancipation, through science and the arts, is surely progress. That said, governments, courts and policy makers cannot and should not dictate the direction of societal and technological change. Cultural memes and economic forces are too powerful to resist, and often they lead change that does constitute progress. But I submit that it is the role of all branches of government to *promote* progress by ensuring that a larger proportion of change is progress. It is the role of academics (among others) to illuminate the economic, sociological, philosophical, and historical underpinnings that can then inform the thinking about how policies can affect the degree to which change will lead to progress.

# Acknowledgements

The author is grateful to the editors of the series, Professors Graeme Dinwoodie, Rochelle Dreyfuss and Annette Kur. I also wish to thank all participants at the IIP Roundtable hosted by professors Jerome Reichman and Irene Calboli at Duke University Law School (April 30–May 1, 2015) for comments on Chapter 8, in particular Professors James Boyle, Margaret Chon, Terry Fisher, Susy Frankel, Peter Jaszi, Ruth Okediji, Lisa Ramsey and Marketa Trimble. Special thanks to my Vanderbilt colleague Chris Serkin for his willingness to read and discuss the manuscript. Thanks to co-authors of articles used in the preparation of this project (identified on pages xvi and xvii), Professors Christophe Geiger, Elizabeth Judge, Alana Maurushat, Martin Senftleben, and Dashiell Renaud. I am grateful also to my colleagues on the Restatement of Copyright (ALI) Project, Professors Christopher Sprigman, Lydia Pallas Loren, R. Anthony Reese and Molly van Houweling. Last but not least thanks to the Vanderbilt students who worked with me on various parts of this long project, in particular Ann Mikkelsen, PhD, whose work on the history of authorship was most useful, and my research assistants Chelsea Fitzgerald, Rebecka Manis, Maciel Salazar and JP Sauer. All errors in the text are entirely mine.

# How to use this book

Although copyright is a complex and technical subject, it impacts each and every one of us. Hence, the book is designed to be as user-friendly as possible for non-experts. Part I explains most of the key aspects of international copyright law and policy. Many chapters in Part I present the concepts and doctrines of international copyright law. Readers already familiar with one or more of the chapter topics may want to skip or only skim those chapters. My hope, however, is that readers who already have a degree of familiarity with the subject matter will learn something new or find some new perspectives. Part II contains a series of concrete policy prescriptions. It first proposes structural changes to copyright law, whether in national legislation or international instruments. It also tackles administrate changes that can be effected even without changing the structure of legislation. In the Epilogue, a new text of major provisions of a Berne Convention is proposed. The book also contains appendices that may be useful for some readers. The first explains the notions of fair use and fair dealing as forms of open-ended permitted uses. The second examines the little known exceptions contained in the Appendix to the Berne Convention.

There are some minor repetitions in the book. In almost every case when something was discussed elsewhere in the book a cross-reference was added. To avoid sending the reader back and risk breaking the flow for a minor reason, however, I decided to repeat some of the information (typically one or two paragraphs) where I felt this would make it easier to use the book.

# Previous publications

Some of the chapters in the book are based on previous publications, although in each case those chapters have been modified and updated.

The foreword and introduction draw on themes discussed in the Introduction to the book *The Evolution and Equilibrium of Copyright in the Digital Age* (Cambridge Univ. Press, 2014)—co-edited with Professor Susy Frankel.

Chapter 1 is based in part on 'Fragmented Copyright, Fragmented Management: Proposals to Defrag Copyright Management' (2003) 2 *Canadian Journal of Law & Technology* 15–34 (with Professor Alana Maurushat).

Chapter 3 is based in part on 'The Three-Step Test Revisited: How to Use the Test's Flexibility in National Copyright Law' (2014) 29:3 *American University International Law Review* 581 (with Christophe Geiger and Martin Senftleben).

Chapter 4 is based in part on 'Of Silos and Constellations: Comparing Notions of Originality in Copyright Law' (2009) 27:2 *Cardozo Arts & Entertainment Law Journal* 375 (with Professor Elizabeth Judge); and 'Feist Goes Global: A Comparative Analysis of the Notion of Originality in Copyright Law' (2003) 49:4 *Journal of the Copyright Society of the USA* 949.

Chapter 5 is based in part on 'The Derivative Right, or Why Copyright Protects Foxes Better than Hedgehogs' (2013) 15:4 *Vanderbilt Journal of Entertainment & Technology Law* 785; and 'The Tangled Web of User-Generated Content' (2009) 11:4 *Vanderbilt Journal of Entertainment & Technology Law* 841.

Chapter 9 is based in part on 'Towards a New Core International Copyright Norm: The Reverse Three-Step Test' (2005) 9 *Marquette Intellectual Property Law Review* 1.

Chapter 10 is based in part on 'Making Copyright Whole: A Principled Approach to Copyright Exceptions and Limitations' (2008) 5:1/2 *University of Ottawa Law & Technology Journal* 1.

Chapter 11 is based in part on 'Collective Management of Copyright and Related Rights in the Digital Age', in D. Gervais (ed.), *Collective Management of Copyright and Related Rights*, 3rd edn (Kluwer Law International, 2015); and 'The Landscape of Collective Management' (2011) 24:4 *Columbia Journal of Law & the Arts* 423.

Chapter 12 is based in part on 'The Future of United States Copyright Formalities: Why We Should Prioritize Recordation, and How To Do It' (2013) 28:3 *Berkeley Technology Law Journal* 1460 (with Dashiell Renaud).

Chapter 13 is based in part on 'TRIPS and Development', in D. Halbert and M. David (eds), *The SAGE Handbook of Intellectual Property* (Sage, 2014), 95–112; and D. Gervais (ed.), *IP Calibration, in Intellectual Property, Trade and Development*, 2d edn (Oxford University Press, 2014) 86–114.

# Introduction

> More and more third parties jump on board to help the artists, or labels,
> navigate and collect feedback or money, but it just adds to the noise and
> confusion, further widening the gap between fan and artist and the journey
> of their music. I feel digitally torn apart; and in the data-driven era, the
> movement of music, money and feedback should be frictionless. A total
> rethink is in order.[1]

This is how Imogen Heap, the British singer-songwriter, creator among
other successful projects of the 2009 album *Ellipse*, described the woes of
music copyright. It is not just music. The entire copyright-based system of
production of entertainment and informational works is in disarray. She
is right that a 'rethink' is called for. Instead of trying to change what is *in*
the box of copyright, however, this book argues that the *box itself* needs
to be restructured.

The book's main premise—and the explanation of its title—is that
copyright is either poorly structured (one can always try to impose a structure ex post) or, as I see it, unstructured. The inadequacy or absence of the
*structure* of the current copyright system is due to two main factors, both
of which are linked to the transition of almost everything to the digital
realm.

First, copyright evolved from a system mostly meant to control certain
uses of physical products to a major regulatory vector for the online
environment. Initially, it was created for and traded by and between professionals (authors, publishers, producers, various distributors, etc.), who
could typically afford greater transaction costs, including understanding
sometimes arcane copyright rules. This also afforded policy makers the
'luxury of expediency' in defining copyright rights not in terms of actual
market or other impacts but by focusing on the technical nature of the
use made of a protected work (reproduction, adaptation, performance in
pubic, communication to a public at a distance, etc.). In the 'bricks and
mortar' environment, the poor structure of copyright could thus often be

---

[1]   Jamie Bartlett, 'Imogen Heap: Saviour of the Music Industry?' *The Guardian*
(London, 6 September 2015) <http://www.theguardian.com/music/2015/sep/06/
imogen-heap-saviour-of-music-industry> accessed 24 September 2015.

*1*

remedied in contracts among copyright 'professionals'. Private ordering stepped in where the statute created unnecessary complexity or did not map well onto *actual* uses of protected material. This is no longer the case. The shift from a professional or 'one-to-many' distribution infrastructure in which copyright was managed mostly by professionals to a 'many-to-many' infrastructure means that individuals users are at once authors, users and reusers of material and hence in the crosshairs of copyright. Contractual patches no longer work well or make matters worse, such as lengthy End User Licensing Agreements (EULAs), those contracts of adhesion in which users are often asked to give up the right to use statutory flexibilities.

Second, the size and might of online intermediaries (right holders and/ or users) pulling policy decisions in their direction, without any obvious desire to compromise, eclipse discussions focusing on actual authors and users of copyright material. The result is an increasing distance between authors, individual users and copyright policy—that is the gap described by Imogen Heap in her quote at the beginning of this introduction. This is making it much harder to see—and for many users to accept—a justification for copyright. Yet, justifications, properly recast, do exist and should inform appropriately structured policy choices.

I do not believe that there is a perfect or essential copyright law somewhere in a platonic policy cave.[2] Policy is imperfect and contingent. Changes in technological tools and the social norms that develop around them make optimal policy design a moving target. Indeed that 'movement' (of the target) is best viewed as part of the equation, thus favouring a (more) dynamic copyright system. That said, dynamism and discombobulation are not synonyms. Copyright should always strive to achieve normative equilibrium. In this sense, one can agree with Plato's direction to the legislator to bring about a result that is the closest possible to the 'most noble and most true'. As discussed in the Preface, I can hardly think of anything nobler and truer than policy objective fostering human creativity.[3]

Against this backdrop, this book has two specific objectives. First, it aims to identify structural and other deficiencies within the current system. Part I of the book is thus diagnostic in nature. Part II offers detailed and concrete pathways to improve the current system and articulates a

---

[2]  I am perhaps more Aristotelian because I do not start from that premise, I get there primarily from observation of human history. Art and creativity have played and continue to play a key role in human evolution and development.

[3]  Plato, *Laws*, V 746 (Basic Books, 1980), 134.

*structured approach to international copyright reform.* A comprehensive reform is not only necessary to ensure that copyright meets its needs in the future; it is also a far better alternative than the current path to a patchwork of regional and bilateral trade agreements, sometimes not compatible with one another, evolving in parallel with myriad new multilateral copyright treaties often ratified only by a fairly small number of countries, and then only years after the treaty's adoption.

The key point I wish to demonstrate in Part I is that there is a lack of, or a deficiency in, copyright's structure and that remedying it will increase the relevance, usability and user-friendliness of copyright. Yet that is the way most laws and national treaties read: a series of exclusive rights on the one hand, and a series of exceptions and limitations, on the other.

My proposal, in very quick summary, *is to rebalance the expression of copyright rights to align them with their purpose, therefore reducing the perceived need to fight copyright, including by introducing more and more exceptions and limitations.* The economic component of copyright should be a *right to prohibit uses that demonstrably interfere with actual or predictable commercial exploitation.* This would of course be subject to limitations and exceptions (L&Es), but the objective is to *build intrinsic limits in the scope of the right itself* and make it *independent of the technical nature of the use* made (copy, performance, etc.). In order to comply with international norms, which this book considers an essential part of the solution, the right should be interpreted by defining 'use' to encompass current technical uses (reproduction, performance, communication). A restructured right would greatly reduce cumbersome interfaces between the various L&Es (say, between fair use and a library exception) because the right itself would be more focused. The proposal includes, in the Epilogue, a partial new draft of the Berne Convention, still today the most important copyright treaty—at least in terms of global membership, with 176 member states as of September 2018 but also one that remains compatible with the obligations undertaken by Members of the World Trade Organization (WTO).

The book uses a creator-user dialogic approach to facilitate analysis, but uses a systemic approach to structure rights themselves. In other words, rights, exceptions and remedies must be viewed in this 'systemic' light. Building a key limitation in the formulation of economic rights is not an entirely new idea. For example, the right of public performance is inherently limited by the notion of 'public'.

The task at hand is to balance the protection of authors of 'works',[4] on the one hand, and 'access' to such works by users and reusers, on the other

---

[4] Internationally, the most important treaty in the fields of copyright (in

hand. While efforts to seek a balanced level of protection are not new,[5] translating this high-level balancing act into a structured approach and deriving actual policy objectives, levers and decisions has proven elusive. Reform proposals, including the restructuring suggested in this book, should be based on the public interest. Unlike a number of commentators, however, I do not believe that the public interest is always best served by eliminating or attempting to reduce copyright.[6] The public interest is best served neither by over-production nor by under-protection. In short, the level, mode and type of enforceability of copyright must all be balanced to achieve something as close to a systemic equilibrium.

That does not mean that the opposite is true of course, namely that *more* copyright leads to better outcomes. The problem is *structural*. Current copyright law is 'one-size-fits-all', yet at the same time highly fragmented, regime. This means that every copyright holder gets more or less the same package of 'right fragments' (reproduction, performance, adaptation, etc.), which can then be split by country, language, etc. But then copyright protects one thing, and one thing only, namely 'works',[7] provides a single set of rights and exceptions and the term of protection is typically the

---

terms of membership at least), is Berne Convention for the Protection of Literary and Artistic Works (adopted 9 September 1886, as last revised at Paris on July 24, 1971) 1161 UNTS 30 (Berne Convention). The importance and contents of the Convention are explained in Chapter 2. Article 2 of the Convention defines (by enumeration), the object of protection under the Convention, namely 'literary and artistic works.' In the United States, the statute refers to 'works of authorship'. See the US Copyright Act 1976 (Copyright Act) ss 101 and 102(a), 17 USC s 102 (2010) ('Copyright protection subsists, in accordance with this title, in original works of authorship fixed in any tangible medium of expression. . .').

[5]    As will be shown in Chapter 2, they can be traced back at least as far as the (original) text of the Berne Convention (1886).

[6]    See Lothar Determann, 'Dangerous Liaisons-Software Combinations as Derivative Works? Distribution, Installation, and Execution of Linked Programs under Copyright Law, Commercial Licenses, and the Gpl' (2006) 21 *Berkeley Technology Law Journal* 1421, 1438.

[7]    In the US, sound recordings are works but they have a special regime, not having the public performance right and instead having a limited right in digital transmissions (Copyright Act 1976, s. 106(6)). That is due in large part to the fact that sound recordings have 'copyright' and not, as in other countries, a related or neighbouring right. See Tyler T. Ochoa, 'Is The Copyright Public Domain Irrevocable? An Introduction to Golan v. Holder' (2011) 64 *Vanderbilt Law Review En Banc* 123, 141. This in turn begs the question of the originality of sound recordings, since originality is a constitutional requirement to obtain federal copyright protection. See Melville B. Nimmer and David Nimmer, *Nimmer on Copyright*, vol. 1 (Matthew Bender 1963) s. 2.10[A][2][b] (discussing record producers' originality requirement for copyright in the sound recording); and William F. Patry,

same for all works.[8] Copyright, simply put, is both highly fragmented and unstructured. The current system rests on the assumption that a single set of rights, limitations and exceptions works optimally to serve the interests of authors and those of the people who use and reuse their works. That is simply not so.

The book gives authors and users at least as much normative space as the intermediaries that currently dominate the discourse. After all, we *need* authors to create and users to enjoy their creations. Intermediaries, in contrast, are contingent. Yet they capture the policy debates, often to gain market advantage. In doing so, they distance copyright from its normative foundations.

The most common legal metaphor to describe a balancing process is probably that of a scale with two pans. In copyright policy terms, the scale used to construct this book weighs the interests of authors, in one pan, and those of users, in the other, without tipping the normative scale unfairly in one direction. It is worth noting that this approach reflects human rights norms: Article 27 of the Universal Declaration on Human Rights (UDHR)[9] protects *both* the rights of authors (to the protection of the moral and material interests resulting from and scientific, literary or artistic production) and the rights of users (freely to participate in the cultural life of the community, to enjoy the arts and to share in scientific advancement and its benefits).

The book explores basic structural deficiencies in the current copyright system based on the Berne Convention and its successive revisions until 1971. This will demonstrate that: (a) the protection of authors was instituted in the public interest; (b) there is no contradiction between adequate protection of authors and the public interest; and (c) the public interest requires appropriate limitations and exceptions for the benefit of (other) authors and users. It should indeed be self-evident that not all 'authors' are in the same situation. The harder and more interesting inquiry is whether one can push the analysis beyond merely acknowledging the existence of this diversity. Structuring copyright implies abandoning the fiction of homogeneity of authorship that pervades current policy and instead develop a taxonomy of authorship, with direct policy effects.

---

*Patry on Copyright*, vol. 1 (Thompson West 2007) s. 3:161; and Jon M. Garon, 'Entertainment Law' (2002) 76 *Tulane Law Review* 559, 619.

[8]   The Berne Convention does limit certain rights to specific categories of works. For example, art. 11*ter* provides a right of public recitation only to literary works, which seems logical enough.

[9]   Universal Declaration of Human Rights (adopted 10 December 1948) UNGA Res 217 A(III) (UDHR) art. 27.

To structure the proposed taxonomy, the book explores changes in the notion of authorship. It has evolved throughout the twentieth century and has now been replaced with that of a 'twenty-first century author'. This author, who could be referred to as 'post post-modern',[10] is often happy to reuse pre-existing material and to cooperate with others, but also insists on attribution (that is, recognition of her authorship). Of those authors who seek protection of their interests, some, not all, also expect financial returns when their works are used in commerce. For those who do not, it is often because they are otherwise compensated (academics and scientists for example).

Unlike distributors and commercial entities that aggregate rights and content, most authors (whether or not they seek financial gain) have a limited interest in trying to *control* the dissemination of their works. Simply put, most authors want attribution and wide dissemination, at least once a work has been made publicly available. Some want payment, but very few want (or think they can or should exert) control over what individual non-professional users do. This matters in policy analysis because, while the major commercial intermediaries who often own copyright and who *do* want (some) control over dissemination networks are only a part of the copyright picture, copyright policy often seems entirely articulated around their interests. The current system provides full protection by default, that is, without *intentionality*. A vast amount of material is protected by copyright by default due to the absence of formalities. This issue is ripe for a fresh debate.

The other pan of the scale weighs the interests of *users*.[11] Users can make mere consumptive uses of commercial copyrighted material, such as watching a movie or reading a book. They can do more, however. They can add comments (and social media 'likes'). They may want to re-disseminate the material with these 'additions'. Some users will go beyond this. They will copy or derive from pre-existing works and sometimes genuinely transform and re-contextualize them, and become authors in their own

---

[10]    See Umberto Eco, '*Innovation and Repetition: Between Modern and Post-Modern Aesthetics*' (1985) 114 *Daedalus* 161, 180–81.

[11]    In a WIPO study undertaken by Sam Ricketson, it is suggested that the term 'exceptions' be used for rules which 'grant immunity from infringement proceedings for particular kinds of use' (i.e., the 'quotation-type' of rules), whereas 'provisions that exclude, or allow for the exclusion of, particular categories of works' should be called 'limitations.' Sam Ricketson, 'WIPO Study on Limitations and Exceptions of Copyright and Related Rights in the Digital Environment' (5 April 2003) SCCR/9/7 <www.wipo.int/meetings/en/doc_details.jsp?doc_id=16805> accessed 11 May 2015.

right. Others may only be looking for ideas or information contained in copyrighted material, for example as part of a research project (here defined very broadly). For them, searching, accessing and being able to quote and reuse is essential to their ability to engage with existing material.

The book proceeds as follows. Part I begins by exploring major structural problems with copyright and explores applicable constraints contained in relevant international instruments, including the Berne Convention, the TRIPS Agreement, and the 'three-step test', the most significant limit to a state's ability to create limitations and exceptions to copyright in international law. While as a theoretical matter one could suggest that reform proposals ignore existing treaties, the book takes the view that countries are unlikely to pull out of WIPO and the WTO. The book does not take all existing constraints as a permanent feature of the system, however, and suggests, in the last chapters of Part II, a more realistic way to improve international copyright. It suggests a *structured reform of the rights, exceptions and limitations*, and, as noted above, the indispensable look at the regulation of their application, specifically via formalities and collective management. The book then turns to developing nations and the specific challenges they face in calibrating their copyright regime. The Epilogue proposes a concrete set of reforms, and suggests that they be enshrined in a revised Berne Convention, without leaving the WTO entirely out of the reform picture. A first Appendix explaining fair use and fair dealing follows for readers who may have an interest in learning more about open-ended statutory formulations of permitted uses. Another Appendix unpacks another important international set of limitations, namely those contained in the Berne Convention Appendix.

# PART I

# Identifying structural issues

# 1. Copyright in common law jurisdictions

## 1.1 INTRODUCTION

There are, as noted in the Introduction, several problems that explain the inglorious predicament of copyright law and policy.

First is the fact that a system used to regulate mostly trade in, and use of, physical products (books, records, copies of motion pictures on 35mm film, etc.), the production and distribution of which was managed by professionals (professional authors, record companies, film producers, broadcasters, etc.) whose business included dealing with and transacting over copyright (in the same way that corporations deal with complex tax and employment laws as a matter of necessity if not exactly jubilation), has had a *dual change of target*. The first facet of the change is that the nature of the technology used to create and disseminate copyright works has changed radically. Most of it is now done online, and controlled by a host of players who do not see themselves as copyright holders but rather as providing or enhancing access to 'content', often in exchange not for monetary payment but for pushing targeted ads on users. The second facet of the change is that the technology allows users to engage in a much more proactive way with copyright content, by making it available to others (e.g., via social media), modifying it, commenting on it, etc. In other words, the regulatory vehicle has barely evolved but it is not used on the paved roads for which it was conceived but rather on a rocky path of rapid technological evolution.

A second set of problem is more technical in nature, yet is it also a fundamental aspect in need of reform. It is the fact that copyright is not truly a right but rather a complex bundle of 'right fragments' that differ from country to country in number, scope and nature despite the existence of binding international norms that have led to some degree of harmonization. The rights fragments are generally expressed in terms of the *technical nature of the use* made of the work, not its purpose or whether the use has any value. For example, the right of reproduction, which lies at the core of the copyright edifice, is often read as implying that any *copy* of copyright material is prima facie infringing. Lawmakers and courts have long recognized that this makes no sense and have carved out many forms of reproductions that happen by the billions every day, such as temporary or transient copies made when a work is transmitted online.

A great—if perhaps not very serious—illustration of this is the 'Kopimashin' created by the The Pirate Bay's co-founder. The machines made 100 copies per second of Gnarls Barkley's 'Crazy' but then deleted them even as they were created. As Cory Doctorow put it, the machine has 'an LCD screen that calculates a running tally of the damages [. . .] inflicted upon the record industry through its use. The 8,000,000 copies it makes every day costs the record industry $10m/day in losses'.[12] It is quite obvious that this activity causes not a penny of losses for anyone. Yet it would likely be considered 'massive copying' under current copyright laws.

This is a symptom of a much greater malaise, namely that the way in which rights are formulated is no longer well-connected to *actually relevant forms of use*. It is like using a surgeon's scalpel to open a can of tuna. You can get there, but there are better ways. Making matters worse, the rights fragments expressed in terms of technical uses (reproduction or copying, performance in public, adaptation, communication to the public, etc.) do not map over the exceptions and limitations (E&Ls), which are often expressed either as purpose-specific (e.g., libraries may make copies for preservation purposes) or as open-ended tests left for courts to define a range of permitted uses (e.g., fair dealing and fair use).

This first chapter explores these deficiencies against the backdrop of the evolution of copyright in common law jurisdictions, such as Australia, Canada, New Zealand, South Africa, the UK and the US to name just a few. This chapter presents two structural problems using mostly common law jurisdictions as exemplars. Chapter 2 will continue the analysis from a broader geographic approach.

## 1.2  THE STATUTE OF ANNE

Let us begin with a bit of history. For common law countries, it is generally thought that the first copyright statute is the Statute of Anne (1709–10). There is a debate surrounding the exact intentions of the British Parliament when it was enacted. On the one hand, the statement: 'for the

---

[12]  Cory Doctorow, Pirate Bay co-founder invents an infernal device that will utterly bankrupt the music industry, Boingboing.net, 22 December 2015 (available at <http://bit.ly/1Seczn3> accessed 23 December 2015).

Encouragement of learned Men to compose and write useful Books. . .' in the Statute's title suggests that it was partly enacted with the public good in mind. Some scholars even go so far as to argue this was the primary intention.[13] On the other hand, the enactment was clearly in reaction to pressure from publishers seeking to legitimize their self-regulation, combined with the government's quest to maintain some sort of monopolistic publishing market.[14]

This dual objective had previously been achieved by combining a ban on the importation of foreign books (in 1534[15]) and the grant by Queen Mary of a Charter to the Stationer's Company (in 1556). The Stationers' (publishers) Charter allowed them to search out and destroy any book printed in contravention of the Statute of Proclamation. Because entries in the Company's register were restricted to Company members, only books licensed by the Stationers could be registered and legally printed in the UK. This served both the interests of publishers and of the Crown, which maintained a degree of control over new publications. The system was enforced both through the Star Chamber and, for Elizabeth and her Stuart successors, with assistance from the Church, no doubt a reflection of the deep religious struggles of that period.[16] The Stationers' privileges lapsed in 1679. While King James revived it for seven years in 1685, it could not last long in the political climate of his dethronement. Parliament finally refused to renew it in 1694.

The policy discussions that led to the adoption of the Statute of Anne were informed by the work of authors and scholars such as John Milton[17] (English poet, best known for his epic, *Paradise Lost*) and John Locke (English philosopher and physician regarded as one of the most influential thinkers of the Enlightenment) who were instrumental in the fight to put

---

[13] Ronan Deazley, *On the Origin of the Right to Copy, Charting the Movement of Copyright Law in Eighteenth-Century Britain (1695–1775)* (Hart Publishing 2004) 226.

[14] L Ray Patterson, *Copyright in Historical Perspective* (Vanderbilt UP 1968) 8, 143.

[15] As a point of reference, Caxton introduced the printing press into England in 1476, 26 years after its invention by Gutenberg.

[16] James I also issued 'printing patents', in the same form as letters patent concerning 'inventions' to certain publishers, but most were issued to Company members. But those patents were limited in time and thus much less important than the unlimited stationers 'copyright'. The censorship element was reinforced by various decrees of the Star Chamber issued in 1566, 1586 and 1637. See Patterson (n 14) 6.

[17] See his *Areopagitica* (1644) reprinted in *Areopagitica: A Speech of Mr. John Milton for the Liberty of Unlicensed Printing, to the Parliament of England* (New York, Grolier Club 1890).

an end to the Stationers' 'licensing' regime, which they considered as a form of prepublication censorship.[18] Milton's name is often used in the history of copyright to refer to the contract by which he transferred all rights to *Paradise Lost* for £20. That contract is used as evidence both that authors were entitled to proprietorship in their work and that publishers were treating authors unfairly.

Locke's name is used to justify extensive copyright protection as a natural property right flowing from an author's labour. Locke favoured a temporary exclusive right for authors in literary works for the life of the author plus 50 or 70 years.[19] He seemed to have less sympathy toward the publishers' monopoly.[20] He was also aware of the need for new material to enrich the public domain:

> I know not why a man should not have liberty to print whatever he would speak. . .
> That any person or company should have patents for the sole printing of ancient authors is very unreasonable and injurious to learning; and for those who purchase copies from authors that now live and write, it may be reasonable to limit their property to a certain number of years after the death of the author, or the first printing of the book, as, suppose, fifty or seventy years. This I am sure, it is very absurd and ridiculous that any one now living should pretend to have a propriety in, or power to dispose of the propriety of any copy or writings of authors who lived before printing was known or used in Europe.

Locke died in 1704 as new proposals for a first 'copyright' statute were being discussed. The Statute of Anne, which granted 'authors and their

---

[18]   Mark Rose, *Authors and Owners: The Invention of Copyright* (Harvard UP, 1995) 28–32.

[19]   John Locke, *Memorandum*, King, 203, 208–9.

[20]   In a letter to a member of Parliament, B Rand, Correspondence of John Locke and Edward Clarke, at 39 (org.1927 rep.1975), he wrote:

> By this monopoly also of those ancient authors, nobody here, that would publish any of them anew with comments, or any other advantage, can do it without the leave of the learned, judicious stationers. For if they will not print it themselves nor let any other, by your labour about it never so useful, and you have permission to print it from the Archbishop and all the other licencers, it is to no purpose. If the company of stationers so please it must not be printed. An instance you have of this in Æsop's Fables. Pray talk with A. Churchill concerning this who I believe will be able to show you other great inconveniences of that act, and if they can possibly, I wish they could be remedied. And particularly, I think, that clause, where printing and importation of any books, to which any have a right by patent is prohibited, should be at least thus far restrained that it should be lawful for anyone to print or import any Latin book whose author lived above a thousand years since.

assigns' the sole right and liberty of printing books for a period of 14 years from first publication,[21] was finally granted Royal Assent on 5 April 1710. The fact that the Statute granted the right not only to the Stationers but also to the authors—a major difference from the Stationers' monopoly that was in place until 1694—was the direct result of the Stationers' reliance in their petition to Parliament on a 'natural' right of authors in their works. This was part of a pan-European strategy of publishers at the time.[22] Focusing the attention on authors allowed booksellers to achieve their aims while avoiding the problem of defending their unpopular trade monopoly.[23] That said, to see the author merely as an excuse to grant an exclusive right on books would be an oversimplification.[24] Authors did want rights they could enforce themselves, even though many of them were reasonably happy to work with the publishers. An argument that authors used at the time was that if they had an *obligation* not to write defamatory or otherwise 'unacceptable' (in the eyes of the authorities) material, then authors should have a coextensive antipodal *right* in their writings.

Put differently, there was a timely convergence of interests between authors and publishers. On the one hand, authors were basking in the sun of the Enlightenment, stroked by the rays of individualism.[25] On the other,

---

[21]   A second term of 14 years was possible if the author was still alive.

[22]   See Roger Chartier, 'Figures of the Author', in Brad Sherman and Alain Strowel (eds), *Of Authors and Origins: Essays on Copyright Law* (OUP 1994).

[23]   See Patterson, (n 14) 169; and Jon M Garon, 'Normative Copyright: A Conceptual Framework for Copyright Philosophy and Ethics' (2002) 88 *Cornell Law Review* 1278, 1298.

[24]   As Professor Bently cautioned:

> . . .it is often said that a natural-rights-based justification for copyright inevitably produces a different conception of copyright than is produced by an incentive argument. More specifically, it is argued that a natural rights conception of copyright leads to longer and stronger protection for authors (and copyright holders) than an incentive-based conception. This is because a natural rights argument for copyright is assumed to result in a form of property that is perpetual and unqualified. In contrast, an incentive-based argument only justifies the grant of the minimum level of protection necessary to induce the right-holder to create and release the work. [. . .]
> While it is understandable that lobby groups use (or abuse) the various justifications to further their ends, more problems arise when people begin to believe the rhetoric. . . .

Lionel Bently and Brad Sherman, *Intellectual Property Law*, (OUP 2001) 33–4.

[25]   Michel Foucault commented that the modern concept of author 'constitutes a privileged moment of individualism in the history of ideas'. Michel Foucault, 'What is an Author?', in J Harari (ed.) *Textual Strategies: Perspectives in*

the Stationers advocated in favour of a right for authors of which they would be the assignees, through the then-prevailing patronage arrangements. They understood that they needed a justificatory theory other than greed or, indeed, their desire to survive to convince both Parliament and the public.

The Statute of Anne was not the first recognition of 'author's rights' in the United Kingdom. A common law right had been recognized decades earlier. Nor was it the first appearance of authors' rights internationally. The role of the author as holder of a 'right' in the products of her intellectual work had emerged in France almost a century earlier. A French court granted the equivalent of an injunction to prevent an almanac being sold without the consent of its author.[26] The court's reasoning was close to modern trade-mark/passing off principles in that it was afraid the author's reputation might suffer if a book with his name on it was published without his consent. Yet this case, and the many cases that would follow, support Mark Rose's observation that:

> [In] the early modern period, in connection with the individualization of authorship. . ., there developed a general sense that it was improper to publish an author's text without permission. The acknowledgement of an author's interest in controlling the publication of his texts is not necessarily the same as the acknowledgment of a property right in the sense of an economic interest in an alienable commodity.[27]

One might speak more of *propriety than property* in such a context. Chapter 2 continues this discussion by presenting the emergence of author's rights internationally.

## 1.3  IMPACT OF THE STATUTE

The entry into force of the Statute in 1710 raised the question whether it abolished or superseded extant common law copyright. Before the Statute, common law copyright had been used mostly to prevent the *first* publication of a work without the author's consent, which was also the law in civil law jurisdictions. Only after its first publication did the book enter the (different) realm of commercial exploitation. Authors and publish-

---

*Post-Structuralist Criticism* (Cornell UP 1979) 141. See also Peter Jaszi, 'On the Author Effect: Contemporary Copyright and Collective Creativity' (1992) 10 *Cardozo Arts and Entertainment Law Journal* 293.

[26]  Rose (n 18) 17–19.
[27]  Ibid., 18.

ers tried to convince various courts that the Statute had not superseded the pre-existing, perpetual common law copyright. Scottish booksellers who were happy to reprint 'public domain' English titles[28] argued that, if common law copyright ever existed, it could not no longer be enforced after the expiry of the statutory monopoly.

But authors had strong supporters. The Stationers supported efforts by authors to have perpetual property rights vested in authors recognized— provided those rights would be assigned to them. Alexander Pope, the famous British poet and translator of Homer's *Iliad* and *Odyssey*, was also one of most active advocates for the English author community at the time. His famous court case against the controversial English publisher Edmund Curll[29] (in part because he published a few books considered pornographic) is considered a major precedent still today.[30] Curll had published a series of letters he had bought on various subjects written by several authors, including Pope. This publication was unauthorized. Quite importantly for our purposes, it was probably the first case that clearly separated as a legal matter the tangible property in the letter (belonging to the recipient) and the author's property in the (intangible) content, an important abstraction. After doing so, the Court was able to rule in Pope's favour.

The case highlighted the divide between those who advocated authorial rights in the broadest sense and those who preferred to limit common law rights to unpublished content.[31] Indeed, a number of injunctions had been issued in the Chancery to stop unpublished manuscripts from being published.[32] The question was whether common law judges could be convinced to go in the same direction.

---

[28]  See *Millar v Kinkaid* (1750), 4 Burr 2319, 98 ER 210.

[29]  *Pope v Curll* (1741) 1 Ark 341.

[30]  See Pat Rogers, 'The Case Pope v Curll' (1972) The Library: Transactions of the Bibliographical Society 27, 326–31.

[31]  To further demonstrate the importance of British copyright history on US (state) common law copyright, one could cite s 985 of the California Civil Code, which is directly inspired by *Pope v Curll*. It provides as follows: 'Letters and other private communications in writing belong to the person to whom they are addressed and delivered; but they cannot be published against the will of the writer, except by authority of law.' It is fairly apparent that the writer's right to prohibit is not a 'property' right.

[32]  As noted by Professor Patterson, several orders of the Court of Assistants made it clear that the stationers had to show they had the author's consent. See Patterson (n 14) 69. However, authors themselves could not copyright. With respect to published works, it was a publisher's right only until the Statute of 1709. See ibid., 5.

In *Tonson v Collins*,[33] Benjamin Collins, a bookseller, tried to prevent the defendant from reprinting copies of a work he owned. The case was heard *en banc* (by all available common law judges).[34] There was agreement among the parties that authors were protected at common law (without the intervention of the Statute, therefore) from any unauthorized first publication of their work. The disagreement focused squarely on whether common law copyright in published works survived the enactment of the Statute of Anne and if so, to what extent. The outcome of the case was inconclusive[35] but it allowed Lord Mansfield, who acted as barrister on behalf of plaintiffs, to enunciate pro-copyright views. This is important because Lord Mansfield became Chief Justice of King's Bench a few years later, and authored a key opinion in the famous *Millar v Taylor*[36] case. He ruled that the author's common law copyright existed in perpetuity both in published and unpublished works, 'it is just that an author should reap the pecuniary profits of his own ingenuity and labour.[37] It is just, that another should not use his name, without his consent. It is fit that he should judge when to publish, or whether he will ever publish'.[38] In this brief quote, we find *three of the four components* of modern copyright, namely: the right to control economic exploitation of the work; the right to prevent its publication; and the 'moral right' not to see one's name used without consent.

The question of common law copyright surviving the Statute of Anne did not die until *Donaldson v Becket*.[39] Thomas Becket (not to be confused with the twelfth century Archbishop of Canterbury) and a group of booksellers who had obtained the rights to *The Seasons* and other poems obtained an injunction in Chancery against Edinburgh bookseller Alexander Donaldson, who had reprinted the poems after the expiration of statutory protection. The case made its way to the peers, who ended up overturning the injunction and deciding that no common law copyright in published works had survived the Statute of Anne. But a narrow victory it was. On the question of whether the common law copyright survived

---

[33]   1 Black W 301(1761), 96 ER 169.

[34]   King's Bench, Common Pleas and Exchequer.

[35]   In fact, the case was dismissed for collusion between the parties. Apparently, a pact had been made to get the court to recognize the author's perpetual common law right. See Patterson (n 14), 165–7.

[36]   (1769) 4 Burr 2303, 98 ER 201.

[37]   Terms which will reappear in the early twentieth century, when the notion of 'originality' will be defined by UK courts.

[38]   98 ER 201, 252.

[39]   (1813) 2 Brown's Parliamentary Cases (2nd edn) 129, 1 ER 837; 4 Burr 2408, 98 ER 257.

authorized publication, the common law judges—who had been asked to provide their opinion to the peers (who, in those days, all voted, lawyers and laymen alike)—voted six to five *against* the right.[40] By 1770, it was thus clear that there was a common law right only to prevent first publication, and a separate statutory right that prevented reprinting of a book for 14 years—a term which would eventually be extended. In reaching this conclusion, arguments based on moral impropriety had at least as much weight in swaying Parliament and the courts as labour-based narratives. Professor Brad Sherman's work has shown[41] that the subsequent evolution of copyright law in the UK during the nineteenth century[42] was that of a system open to influences of emerging international norms[43] and developments in Prussia, Saxony and France.

## 1.4   MORE RECENT EVOLUTION OF COPYRIGHT IN COMMON LAW JURISDICTIONS

Copyright in this 'original' version was a right to prevent copying for limited times. Authors and publishers of theatrical plays and music were at disadvantage because most of the economic value of their material was created when the play was performed, not when it was copied. Thus a parallel right to prevent the performance in public was eventually added. What followed between the mid-eighteenth century and the early 1990s, i.e., approximately 250 years, is a process of haphazard historical accretions: each time a new form of creation (i.e, cinema) or dissemination (i.e., radio, television, cable, satellite) was invented, copyright was adapted through court decisions, amendments to national laws and new international treaties, such as the 1994 TRIPS Agreement concluded as a part of WTO Uruguay Round of global trade talks (1986–94). New 'rights fragments' were added to the 'bundle' of rights, which now includes reproduction, public performance/communication to the public, adaptation and translation (a rough equivalent of the right to 'make derivative

---

[40]   According to Professor Rose, the vote was actually six top five in favour of the authors but was not reported correctly. See Rose, (n 18) 98–111.
[41]   See Brad Sherman, 'Remembering and Forgetting: The Birth of Modern Copyright Law' (1995) 10 IPJ 1.
[42]   If it ever was. Authorial advocates were fully aware of Kantian and natural rights justifications used on the Continent, as is apparent in Defoe's writings, among others.
[43]   Including both bilateral treaties and the Berne Convention. See Sherman (n 41) 8–12.

works' in the US statute), rental, sometimes a lending right and a *droit de suite* (resale right for works of fine art). Not all such fragments exist in all countries, nor are they identical in scope or called the same way. Very often, each rights fragment is owned by or licensed to a different 'rights holder', and each fragment may itself be assigned or licensed often for each territory, langue, etc. The result is a complex matrix of rights, which itself changes through time.

While one could discuss whether each such change to the initial framework of copyright was adequate (such as the addition of computer programs to the category of 'literary works'—a form of protection now mostly viewed as inadequate both doctrinally and normatively), which is easier to do *a posteriori*, the fact remains that for 300 years or so copyright was designed as a mechanism to regulate relations among professionals (authors, publishers, distributors and professional users) who could handle a certain degree of complexity. More importantly perhaps, prior to 1995, most users only needed *one* right fragment for example, the reproduction right to make copies of books or CDs, or the right of public performance to perform a play or music in public. Absent an exception, on the Internet one needs at least two fragments: reproduction (on the computer/server) and communication to the public (part of the right of public performance in the United States). If an adaptation or translation is required, a third right fragment is required. If multiple territories are involved (which is the default case of the Internet), one may need to license or acquire multiple rights fragments in each territory. This will typically involve multiple licensing transactions. Each transaction will necessarily involve costs (for all parties). In addition, the owner (or licensee) of each fragment may try to get the lion's share economic value of the entire licensed operation, even though the fragment owned or exclusively licensed to that person is only one of many needed.

A case in point is the licensing of radio broadcasting. In the past broadcasters only needed to license the communication to the public fragment and many national laws allowed them to make unlicensed 'ephemeral recordings' without a separate reproduction license. The law recognized the *dominant fragment* as being the performance/communication, as it were, and paid little heed to the temporary copy that may be made by the broadcaster. But in the age of digital broadcasting, more or less permanent copies of songs are made on servers operated by or for the broadcaster and owners of the reproduction fragment of musical works in many countries are now trying to license the copying of music by broadcasters, at a price which would be added to the existing broadcasting (communication) licenses.

To explain this key point from a different perspective, prior to 1995 copyright was a right used by and between professionals, with discrete rights fragments corresponding (more or less) to identifiable uses or users. End uses and users did not matter. For example, no one had to sign a license agreement when buying or borrowing a book or a CD. Indeed, many countries had specific exceptions for end-user use, such as private copying and this inapplicability of copyright, recognized by law, was often 'compensated' by levies on blank media or recording equipment or blanket licenses used for, e.g., photocopying. That is no longer the case. Copyright is now a tool used against individual end-users, trying to prevent them from using copyrighted material beyond boundaries set by right holders. Users who access online material must click-accept licensing terms in contracts of adhesion that often run 10, 20, 30 pages or more and often limit their right to use the material, and may contain waivers of exceptions such as fair use, fair dealing or private copying. Technology, in the form of Digital Rights Management, is sometimes used to enforce those restrictions technologically. In a fundamental change to the nature of copyright (at least to the extent that this right is clearly designed to target end-users), laws have been adopted in the United States (the 1998 Digital Millennium Copyright Act or DMCA), Europe (as part of 'Information Society' or InfoSoc Directive) and many other countries to prevent the circumvention of technological locks, a legislative backing of the private, non-negotiable, ordering contained in license agreements. These laws were adopted in the wake of the two WIPO treaties adopted on 20 December 1996, the WIPO Copyright Treaty and the WIPO Performances and Phonograms Treaty. Many copyright industries, in particular music and film, are understandably troubled by the unauthorized online availability of 'content'. They are thus trying to find other measures, including criminal enforcement (which implies the use of state resources) and denial of access.

The arguments of those right holders are simple and straightforward: copyright is property and by using that property without paying for it, users are 'trespassing' as it were, or, in economic terms, getting value without paying for it. Clearly, copyright industries need revenue to continue to do what they do. Interestingly, numbers published by the Recording Industry Association of America (RIAA) show that after a significant drop, revenues increased in 2003, even though unauthorized use of music doubled over the same period. RIAA numbers show that the industry had continued year-over-year increases in both wholesale and retail revenue in 2015, 2017 and 2018. A number of studies—including a detailed 2018 report by the Institute for Information Law of the University of Amsterdam (IvIR)—have also tended to demonstrate that file-sharers and other unauthorized users still buy CDs and that for some types of music and other categories of copyright material at least, unauthorized use is a form of viral advertising. Independently of the validity of those findings, there are <u>no</u> studies that show that a download equals a lost sale in every case. It is more realistic to say that some downloads are lost sales, some have no effect on sales (e.g., the user listens for a few seconds and realizes she does not like the music) and some have a positive effect. In the area of scientific and technical publishing, making content available online and cross-linking publications (including those of competitors) seems to have led to an increase in both use and revenues.

The new models upend the very notion of *scarcity* that had been a paradigmatic justification for many IP rights (rights to exclude meant to create scarcity). Available empirical and anecdotal data made available in recent years has confirmed my initial intuition and led me to one fairly solid conclusion: the evolution of the Internet as a market for information is counter-intuitive: value does not come from scarcity; it comes from exposure. As I wrote back in 2005, *information does not have or acquire commercial value because it is scarce, but because it is found by those who value it.* The corollary of this axiom is that 'content' must be available, including to those for whom it may not have value. In this scenario, thinking of copyright material as property and interpreting any access to such property as some form of trespass is clearly inappropriate. Yet, too often that is still the stated purpose of copyright policy.

The unauthoritized availability of music and video files has demonstrated beyond a doubt the inadequacy both as a matter of revenue increase for copyright holders and as a matter of privacy and personal data protection of trying to count or limit 'copies' online. Legal and technical efforts to stop to reduce file-sharing, for example, have reduced some unauthoritized activity (though often the effect was short-lived) but they often failed to increase income for right holders and also had significant public relations costs. Unauthorized use is effectively reduced only when the content was available legally online without undue use restrictions.

It is also necessary going forward to recognize the myriad ways in which consumers *decide for themselves* whether to pay (reducing the incentive by having a fair but paying option is useful here) by hiding technologically using USENET, proxies, TOR, etc. They may decide to get something for free to 'try' and pay later once they have determined that the object has value. This represents a shift from paying up front or *ex ante*, before knowing how much actual value the object has, to paying after the fact, that is, *ex post* valuation by individual users. This is not a song that some right holders like to hear but ignoring reality is a poor basis for policy making.

The next wave of change is three-dimensional printing. The sharing of files containing instructions to print objects protected by design rights, copyright and/or patents will induce dramatic changes. As with music and video file-sharing, however, the end of physical scarcity does not *have to* mean the end of IP, an issue other scholars have also discussed.[44] The lesson is that the use and enforcement of the right must change in fundamental ways, from a power to limit or control copies to the establishment of fair remuneration flows.

Naturally, efforts to reduce copyright (and patents some might add) and—ultimately to get rid of it entirely—find favour in the world of online intermediaries. Companies that provide access to links to file-sharing sites now can provide links to sites that provide 3D printing files and sell ads in the process, without having to share profits with those who created this 'content'. This book takes the view that there are huge societal risks in allowing them to continue to do so.

Yet it is undeniable that the valuations of online intermediaries reflect the ability of Internet users to find information that one values (most). Old and new intermediaries are front and centre. Both Internet-only entities such as Google/Alphabet and ISPs, and more traditional ones (though using new tools) such as libraries and information intermediaries, have an ever greater role to play. They are information locators but also choke points, the link between millions of websites, on the one hand, and billions of users on the other. They empower new information business models. They are also an easy policy target because, if one cannot stop the Internet end-user, then why not stop the intermediary? In the US, the liability of many online intermediaries, including ISPs, was limited as part of the DMCA 'deal'. They are under various obligations to block access to infringing material ('notice and take-down') and may have to respond to right holder-issued subpoenas. Right holders have also attacked makers of software that allows Internet users to share material and individual end-users.[45] Yet by targeting end-users and intermediaries, copyright holders are attacking their consumers and business partners, respectively. This is not necessarily what they teach in business schools.

This strategy had pernicious unintended effects. Widespread disregard for copyright, and the law more generally, in online behaviour patterns has led to cynicism. It may have damaged respect for the rule of law itself. Social norms justify end-users who use software that makes copyright enforcement harder to detect and enforce. Napster was a centralized database; In contrast, peer-to-peer (P2P) technologies were only programs

---

[44] Mark A Lemley, 'IP in a World without Scarcity' (2015) 90 *New York University Law Review* 460.

[45] Napster was based on well-identified servers which were easy to identify and shut down once the injunction issued. File-sharing services such as Grokster are based on a decentralized architecture that gets parts of files from the computers of network users and are thus much harder to locate and shut down.

that located data on the PCs of network users; and newer technology such as proxy-based sharing and even the use of the old USENET protocol make users almost untraceable on the network. This means that more and more Internet users are shielding themselves not only from copyright law, but other laws as well, which may even have consequences for national security.

In retrospect, recent changes to copyright laws may have been rushes to judgment. In fact, countries that have not changed their laws are not doing any 'worse'. The short answer lies in *occupying the information space, rather than limiting it*; abandoning the property paradigm, and, yes, allowing users to 'share'. This may be done through a combination of voluntary licensing (assuming all right holders can agree), some form of collective licensing and appropriate limitations and exceptions.

## 1.5   DRAWING LESSONS FROM COPYRIGHT'S HISTORY

The brief look at history in the previous pages shows a haphazard evolution, adding new rights and subject matter and, not always in parallel, new exceptions and limitations. The history of copyright law is indeed one of progressive fragmentation along two axes. First, along a *'work' axis*, to bring under the copyright umbrella new forms of creation (photography, cinematography, computer programs); second, along a *right axis* to create rights in respect of new uses of copyright material (radio and then television broadcasting, cable and satellite transmission, now the Internet).[46] Initially, each type of use fitted rather nicely under one right (or fragment of the copyright 'bundle'): reproduction was the right for books,[47] records and even compact discs; communication to the public for broadcasters,[48] adaptation for novels made into movies, etc. But the Internet changed all that: making a protected work available on an Internet server is a reproduction (on the server) and a communication to the public. Holders of the 'reproduction fragment' of the copyright bundle in respect of musical works are asking for a tariff to be paid because

---

[46]   See Daniel Gervais, *La notion d'œuvre dans la Convention de Berne et en droit comparé* (Droz 1998).

[47]   Of course, each fragment can itself be split. The owner of the right for the hardcover edition may not be the same as for paperback.

[48]   Interestingly, because they needed to make temporary copies of material to be broadcast and this involved another right, legislators in several countries opted for so-called 'ephemeral recordings'.

broadcasters are making copies that go beyond the ephemeral recording exception. Exceptions to rights are being challenged. Not only can the right be exploited differently, and different fragments grouped ('sub-bundles'), as in the broadcasting and Internet examples above, but each of these 'rights' may be further subdivided based on language and the market where the work will be used.

Copyright is, as just noted, a bundle of rights (reproduction, public performance, communication to the public, translation, adaptation, etc.). Right fragments[49] such as 'reproduction' or 'public performance' are a source of frustration for users because they no longer map out discrete uses, especially on the Internet. Put differently, a single use of a copyright work or object of a related right (e.g., performance, recording) often requires multiple authorizations (right fragments) from several different right holders. *The way in which right fragments are expressed no longer matches who does what, and for which purpose,* with a work or object of a related right.

As we saw in the previous section, fragmentation has its roots in the pre-Internet history of copyright (from the late seventeenth century until the 1990s—approximately 300 years), which was essentially that of the adaptation to new forms of creation (e.g., cinema, computer programs) and dissemination of copyright works (radio, then television broadcasting, cable and satellite). Copyright adapted and was able successfully to regulate new markets made possible by these new technologies because they were created by *professionals* who were willing and able to live with a certain degree of complexity as part of their compliance efforts. However, many of these new technologies added layers of complexity because the right fragments in the copyright bundle grew, usually by analogy, to bring new forms of use under the copyright umbrella. For example, playwrights and music composers were able to obtain rights in respect to the live performance of their works by arguing that this was their main economic use. When radio was invented, those same live performances (mostly of opera and music) were then broadcast directly to the homes of listeners. People did not attend the live performance, and the existing exclusive right of live public performance did not apply. Broadcasters were making a commercial use of the material similar to the use made by theatre or concert hall operators. It was quite logical then, to extend the right of public performance to the communication of the performance of a work

---

[49] Fragment or fragmentation is derived from the Latin adjective 'fractus.' See Kimberly Wertenberger, 'Fractals, Mandelbrot Sets & Julia Sets' (available at <http://www.ms.uky.edu/~lee/ma502/fractals/FRACTALS.html> last accessed 22 November 2015).

at a distance by radio (or 'Hertzian' waves). It was only a small step after
that to add television and later communication by cable, satellite and the
Internet. The result of this historical process is the bundle composed of
'copyright rights' we find in most national copyright laws. The complexity
of transactions required for the exploitation of several types of copyright
works can be illustrated as shown in Figure 1.1.

The fragmentation of copyright occurs on many different levels—of
rights stemming from national laws, which recognize several economic
rights (reproduction, communication to the public, adaptation, rental, etc.)
within market structures, within licensing practices, within a repertory of
works, within different markets (language, territory) and through the inter-
operability (or lack thereof) of rights clearance systems. Fragmentation
has a direct impact on all affected parties, whether they be right holders,
users of copyright works or regulatory authorities that oversee the process.

The inherent difficulty is perhaps best illustrated by way of examples.
If a hypothetical broadcaster wanted to put music on the Internet, at least
five right fragments could be involved, namely:

- reproduction on the emission server;[50]
- authorization of communication to the public in territory of
  emission;
- communication to the public in territory of reception;
- 'making available';[51] and
- reproduction on another computer in the territory of reception.[52]

In fact, this rights matrix is more complex because there are three levels of
rights involved in music:

- composers, songwriters and lyricists;
- performing artists; and
- makers (producers) of the sound recording.

The rights matrix is demonstrated in Table 1.1.

In short, 15 different rights analyses are required if one considers both
offline and online uses. Actually, if the composer and lyricist's rights

---

[50]  Unless, at the time the copy is made, it is a 'private copy'. Even then theories
based on the right of destination might apply.

[51]  Assuming this is considered a separate right implementing art 8 of the WIPO
Copyright Treaty (1996), and arts 10 and 14 of the WIPO Performances and
Phonograms Treaty (1996). This is discussed further in Chapter 5.

[52]  Which is also potentially a 'private copy'.

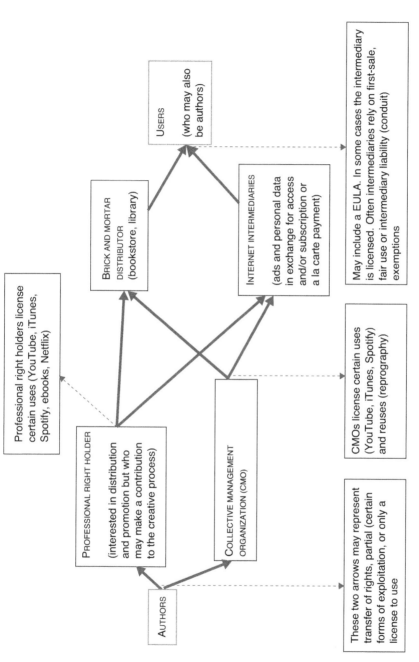

*Figure 1.1  Transactions required for the exploitation of copyright works*

*Table 1.1*    *Rights matrix to license a point-to-point Internet*
               *communication of a sound recording containing a performance*
               *of a protected musical work*

| Right →<br>Right holder ↓ | Composer/<br>Lyricist | Performer | Producer |
|---|---|---|---|
| Reproduction on emission server | C/PC? | C/PC? | PC? |
| Authorization of communication in<br>  territory of emission | C | C/R | C/R |
| Communication to the public in<br>  territory of reception | C | C/R | C/R |
| [Making available] | C | C | C |
| Reproduction in territory of reception | C/PC? | C/PC? | PC? |

*Notes:*
C—right likely to be administered by a collective.
PC—use possibly covered by private copying regime.
R—right is only to remuneration (as opposed to exclusive).

are administered separately or if multiple authors and performers are
involved, the matrix would be even more complex. Naturally, there are
ways in which the situation could be simplified, notably by agreements
among Collective Management Organization (CMOs—see Chapter 11)
that allow one participating CMO to grant a worldwide license on behalf
of all other participating entities, especially with respect to the right of
communication to the public. Still, one must proceed with each of the
rights analyses in Table 1.1 to avoid a potential finding of infringement. In
other words, the rights clearance process involves multiple layers of rights
and clearing each of these rights can be a labyrinthine process even if each
such process is in itself efficient. Because rights ownership and licensing
arrangements change through time, the matrix becomes four-dimensional.

Rights analyses concerning audiovisual works add yet another layer of
complexity to the analysis. A film might include rights to a screenplay,
a book on which the screenplay was based, musical works incorporated
in the film, any art or photographs used in the setting, as well as the end
product of the film itself. Each of the works[53] in turn involve several
different rights fragments and, consequently, multiple right holders and
systems of rights clearance and possibly also guilds or unions. Some right
holders may have moved or died. And of course any one of the right
holders who has an exclusive right may prevent the use and stop or force

---

[53]    Or object of a related right such as a sound recording.

a rearrangement of the entire project. Each holder of a right fragment has a potential veto.

When it comes to cloud-based software, matters are even worse. The technology may in some cases reduce the number of technical uses but give some of them enormous economic importance. As Determann and Nimmer explain:

> [I]n the cloud context, the one RAM copy can be accessed by multiple users— very much unlike the desktop scenario. In the usage phase, once the cloud solution is up and running, users make access requests from remote computers. Each time the software is executed, numerous fractional excerpts of the RAM copy are reproduced in cache memory spaces and the CPU of the cloud provider's server. [. . ..] Thus, cloud scenarios permit a far greater number of users to utilise one software copy.[54]

In sum, copyright fragments have lost their meaning to users and right holders alike. This is reflected in the fact that contracts and licensing arrangements for copyright works do not usually refer to the specific rights enumerated in this section or if they do, it is an afterthought.[55] Contracts define the 'use' that should be allowed, and not which fragments of rights are needed. This is not borne from any malicious intent but stems from how the rights within a particular market develop over time factoring into the equation the evolution of technology.

Copyright's current structure uses an (old) regulatory model for the (new) target of online uses and of fragmented rights form the backdrop for the analysis in the chapters that follow. But first, let us take a look at the international context and applicable norms.

---

[54] Lothar Determannn and David Nimmer, 'Software Copyright's *Oracle from the Cloud*' (2015) 30 *Berkeley Technology Law Journal* 161, 196–7.

[55] A contract to allow webcasting normally refers to the function of broadcasting, independently of whether a communication to the public, one or more reproductions, or adaptations may take place. The problem is that right ownership is still by and large, especially in the area of collective management, owned by different entities based on right fragments, not actual uses of the work. While a single economic transaction should take place, several legal transactions are involved. See Al and Bob Kohn, *Kohn on Music Licensing: 2000 Supplement* (2nd edn, Aspen Law & Bus 2000) 398–9.

# 2. The international emergence of author's rights

## 2.1 INTRODUCTION

The Berne Convention for the Protection of Literary and Artistic Works[56] is the most important copyright treaty in the world, both in terms of geographic coverage (176 countries as of September 2018) and history (its first text dates back to 1886). Its weight increased even more when it was partially incorporated into the WTO Agreement on Trade-Related Aspects of Intellectual Property Rights (TRIPS),[57] and its applicability made subject to trade sanctions for WTO members who are found not to be in compliance with Berne. Any reform effort must take account of the constraints that Berne and TRIPS might impose on policy makers. This chapter reviews the history and contents of the Convention. In doing so it offers additional guidance on copyright's deficiencies and possible paths to reform and thus continues the analysis contained in the previous chapter.

## 2.2 PRE-1860

One could go back to the Bible—and even before—when discussing the emergence of authors' rights. Let us start a bit closer in time to the current era, namely with medieval Europe. That is the epoch during which authors' rights (more or less as we know them today) emerged. But things were very different then. Texts were living documents. Authors would work using previously published material and often not think of mentioning the name of the author of that work or else would do so only in allusive fashion. Well-known examples such as *Percival* and the *Romance of the Rose* were

---

[56] Berne Convention for the Protection of Literary and Artistic Works, (9 September 1886, as last revised at Paris 24 July 1971) 1161 UNTS 30 (Berne Convention).
[57] TRIPS is not a self-standing treaty of course. It is part of treaty, as Annex 1C of the Agreement Establishing the World Trade Organization (1994) 1869 UNTS 299, 33 ILM 1197.

'co-authored' over time. Shakespeare himself paraphrased previous works, and rewrote and modified many of his plays. "Shakespeare was, in modern terms, a plagiarist on a vast scale. According to Malone, out of 6,033 lines of parts I, II, and III of Henry VI, Shakespeare copied 1,771 verbatim and paraphrased 2,373. Whole passages of Antony and Cleopatra, to take just one example, were line-by-line versifications of prose historical works."[58] In what may have been an early form of crowdsourcing, Jean Wauquelin (a fifteenth century author who worked for the Duchy of Burgundy) asked his readers to add to his incomplete biography of Alexander the Great, which he had produced at the request of Philip the Good.[59]

What we might more naturally refer to today as the 'author' of a work had already begun to appear, however, as early as the thirteenth century. I am referring here to the first books published in the first person, books in which the author claimed that his art and knowledge, and the subjectivity of the work, are what created the value in the work.[60] Divine inspiration gave way to the lyrical 'I' as the source of 'truth' and, in doing so, allowed a new aesthetics to emerge. That distinction in turn led to a separation between objective and subjective truth, *between history and story*.

This evolution would be felt in philosophical texts as well soon after the fall of Constantinople—often used as a milestone for the end of the Middle Ages. A number of humanist philosophers would focus on human creativity and identify wisdom and erudition acquired through classic (pre-medieval) texts, in what may be seen as a rebirth of the *studia humanitatis* advocated by Cicero.[61] The introduction of the printing press across Europe was a powerful catalyst that affected those changes both qualitatively and quantitatively. Texts could be distributed and read much more widely, and more new texts could be published. This reinforced the emphasis on authorship and increased the social status of authors. Even before there were laws regulating this matter there were interesting debates on intertextuality and what constituted acceptable 'borrowing' from previous texts. To quote Montaigne's *Essays*:

> So of peeces borrowed of others, he may lawfully alter, transforme, and confound them, to shape out of them a perfect peece of worke, altogether his

---

[58] Giancarlo Frosio, Rediscovering Cumulative Creativity from the Oral Formulaic Tradition to Digital Remix: Can I Get a Witness? (2014) 13 J. Marshall Rev. of Intell. Prop. Law 344, 368.

[59] See Isabelle Diu et Élisabeth Parinet, Histoire des auteurs (Perrin, 2013), 37.

[60] See Michel Zink, La subjectivité littéraire: Autour du siècle de Saint Louis (Paris, Presses universitaires de France, 1985).

[61] Diu et Parinet (n 59), 44.

owne; alwaies provided his judgement, his travell, studie, and institution tend to nothing, but to frame the same perfect. Let him hardily conceale where or whence he hath had any helpe, and make no shew of anything, but of that which he hath made himselfe. Pirates, pilchers, and borrowers, make a shew of their purchases and buildings, but not of that which they have taken from others.[62]

*Naming* the authors of books was far from obvious. Until the sixteenth century in many European countries there was no fully developed onomastic system. The author's 'name'—so central to the notion of attribution—was a fluctuating notion. Once the model of a first name and family name (surname) had been more firmly established, the author's name began appearing on the title page of books.[63] The idea of paternity or authorship (as a matter that one could 'claim') emerged. Erasmus wanted his name on his translation of the New Testament.[64] A book published in Florence in the second half of the sixteenth century, entitled *Lives of the Most Excellent Painters, Sculptors and Architects*, and which focused on Michelangelo and other Renaissance artists, is considered a 'charter text of Renaissance individualism'.[65] It drew deep lines between author and work. Clearly, the narrative of the individual author and his 'genius' found fertile soil in the Renaissance.

The seventeenth century would take for granted that identified individuals would publish books under their own name and be recognized as 'authors'. Galileo's *Dialogo* (1632) and Descartes' *Discourse on the Method* (1637) are prime examples. Galileo chose to write his opus in Italian, not Latin, probably desiring to facilitate its access by the 'masses'.[66] Descartes added not just his name but a central philosophical stone to the edifice of individualism. *Cogito ergo sum*: the individual's ability to think as proof of her existence. This idea would of course survive for centuries as a central tenet of Western philosophy and its ripples are still felt today (phenomenologists would add a wrinkle to Descartes by stating in essence that the individual does not doubt that she doubts, and therefore, she is).[67] This did not diminish the focus on individual 'genius', quite the opposite. The recognition of authorship also meant that many sixteenth century authors made a decent living as professional authors, often for 'entertainment' (Corneille in French theatre for example).

---

[62]  See e.g., Montainge, *Essays*, I, 26.
[63]  Diu et Parinet, (n 3) 48.
[64]  Ibid., 49.
[65]  Marco Ruffini, *Art Without an Author* (Fordham University Press 2011) 1.
[66]  Diu and Parinet (n 3) 55.
[67]  I am thinking here e.g., of Husserl—more or less three centuries later.

The next steps were taken in the eighteenth century in the wake of Locke's work, and a few years later, Hume's empiricist philosophies and the centrality of human experience. This evolution did not depart from individualism. Indeed, it meshed rather well with the growing importance attached to individuals as authors of works. The author was once and for all enfranchised from historical constraints or obligations to claim religious or objective inspiration. The author as owner of her person could naturally claim ownership of her work. That said, as shown in Chapter 1, Locke did not necessarily support or advocate a form of property in intellectual labour.

A fairly common feature of the protection of authors at the time was a quid pro quo for disclosure: in publishing a text, an author took a risk (of being sued for libel or of being prosecuted for disseminating ideas 'disliked' by authorities). The reward was an exclusive right. We see this quid pro quo very clearly for example in a 1758 *mémoire* prepared by Malesherbes (while he was President of the Court of Aids, a very rough equivalent of which might be the Exchequer Court in England[68]) on the rights of authors, which stated that authors 'should be allowed to sell their works when their name is printed in it'.[69] This intellectual process allowed the idea of a *right* in literary and artistic creations to emerge. This happened for example in England in the 1709–10 Statute of Anne, discussed in the previous chapter, which mentioned authors but was particularly friendly to the stationers (publishers) and in France well before the 1789 Revolution.

The next step was to internationalize the protection.

## 2.3   1860–1895

The most obvious way to obtain international protection is to adopt a new treaty. The eighteenth and first part of the nineteenth centuries saw a flurry of bilateral copyright treaties guaranteeing national treatment but providing very little in terms of minimum standards of protection. The situation became rather messy. The need for a multilateral solution arose.

The seed of the Berne Convention was sown in the 1870s by the Paris-based *Association littéraire et artistique internationale* (ALAI).[70] ALAI's

---

[68]   American readers may be more familiar with Malesherbes' great grandson, Alexis de Tocqueville.

[69]   David Peeperkorn, 'Malesherbes on the Rights of Authors', in J C Kabel (ed.), *Intellectual Property and Information Law* (Kluwer Academic, 1998) 231.

[70]   The United States joined the Berne Convention in 1989. (See <www.wipo.

first president was the famous French author and human rights campaigner Victor Hugo,[71] perhaps best known today for *Les Misérables* but in his day famous also as an advocate for the Romantic Movement so closely associated with the natural rights foundation of authors' rights.[72]

The prototypical 'Romantic Author' is the model on which much of the early international copyright edifice was built.[73] Romantics saw creative works as extensions of their authors, but they also believed in the power of individuals to influence and shape events. Victor Hugo wrote that 'literature was the government of humankind by the human spirit'.[74] If a conflict should arise between the rights of the author and those of 'the human spirit', he wrote, the latter should prevail.[75] This meant that, in the same vein as utilitarian analyses that conclude that copyright protection should stop once the goal of maximizing welfare—by ensuring that new works are created without stifling unnecessarily the potential for new ones (i.e., should go no further than is required to 'promote the progress of science and useful arts'[76])—or economic analyses of copyright that look for a (measurable) optimal protection point at which creation and dissemination of new works is not negated by deadweight and other welfare losses, Hugo's understanding of what was to become the Berne Convention clearly incorporated the public interest as part of its framework but from a different angle.[77] In his defence of the public interest, Hugo also

---

int/treaties/en/ShowResults.jsp?lang=en&treaty_id=15> last accessed 26 August 2015). On ALAI (see <www.alai.org> last accessed 27 August 2015).

[71]   As President of ALAI, Hugo was instrumental in the early draft of the Berne Convention. One should note to offer a more accurate picture that Hugo's views changed over time, see Calvin D Peeler, 'From the Providence of Kings to Copyrighted Things (and French Moral Rights)' (1999) 9 *Indiana International & Comparative Law Review* 423, 450–51.

[72]   See Matthew Josephson, *Victor Hugo: A Realistic Biography of the Great Romantic* (Jorge Pinto Books, 2006) 95.

[73]   Romanticism is considered to have started in the eighteenth century and peaked during the first half of the nineteenth century. The Berne Convention was signed in 1866, based on negotiations that started in the 1850s in the wake of the Romantic wave. For a detailed history of that Convention, see Sam Ricketson and Jane C Ginsburg, *International Copyright and Neighbouring Rights: The Berne Convention and Beyond*, vol 1 (2nd edn, OUP 2006).

[74]   In the original text: 'La littérature, c'est le gouvernement du genre humain par l'esprit humain'. < http://www.gilles-jobin.org/jobineries/index.php?2005/10/29/290-victor-hugo-en-1878>.

[75]   Ibid.

[76]   US Constitution, art. 1, s. 8, cl. 8.

[77]   Victor Hugo, 'Discours d'ouverture du Congrès littéraire international de 1878', 3 (available at <http://www.inlibroveritas.net/lire/oeuvre1923.html> last accessed 29 March 2015).

referred to the *exclusion of ideas* from the scope of copyright protection, a notion now well established in Western legal systems and in the TRIPS Agreement.[78] Two quick examples should suffice. First, the US Copyright Act[79] excludes from the scope of protection ideas, procedures, processes, systems, methods of operation, concepts, principles, and discoveries. Second, French treatises on copyright/authors' rights (or 'literary and artistic property') typically mention that ideas should circulate freely as a fundamental principle of copyright protection.[80]

The operational translation of this foundational role of the public interest was to protect authors *in exchange or as recognition for* the personal contribution they make to humankind and the development of 'human intelligence', with limits to such protection when the public interest (as the sole foundational consideration) no longer supports protecting an author's rights in her creation.[81] Romanticism's view of authors' rights was, therefore, not intrinsically unbalanced. Indeed, the (fairly basic) original 1886 text of the Berne Convention reflected an equilibrium, in large part because of its simplicity. The basic premise of the 1886 text was to ensure that authors who were nationals of countries that would accede to the new treaty (and form the 'Berne Union') would be protected in all countries of the Union without discrimination, a principle known as *national treatment*.[82] Otherwise, the original Convention only contained a few rights: translation,[83] public representation for dramatic and dramatico-musical works,[84]

---

[78] Agreement on Trade-Related Aspects of Intellectual Property Rights, Including Trade in Counterfeit Goods: General Agreement on Tariffs and Trade-Multilateral Trade Negotiations (The Uruguay Round), art. 9.2, 33 ILM 81 (15 December 1993) <http://www.wto.int/english/docs_e/legal_e/27-trips.pdf>.

[79] 17 USC s. 102(b).

[80] *Les idées sont de libre parcours*. See e.g., André Lucas, Henri-Jacques Lucas and Agnès Lucas-Schloetter, '*Traité de propriété littéraire et artistique*' (4th edn, LiTec 2012). As the authors explain: 'C'est un principe fondamental du droit de la propriété intellectuelle que les idées sont en elles-mêmes de libre parcours. La règle a été présentée comme une concession à l'intérêt de la société', para. 30.

[81] Ibid., 3. In rough translation (by the author), Hugo stated that '[i]f either the right of the writer or the right of the human spirit must be forfeited ('sacrificed'), it is assuredly the right of the writer that must be, because public interest is the sole preoccupation and must come before everything else'.

[82] WIPO, *1886–1986: Berne Convention Centenary* (Geneva, WIPO, 1986), 119. [Hereinafter 'Berne Convention Centenary'].

[83] Berne Convention (1886), arts 5, 6 and 9(2). See Berne Convention Centenary ibid., 228. The term of protection was ten years.

[84] Ibid., arts 5–6. The term of protection was ten years.

and a limited right of reproduction,[85] which the 1886 text implicitly recognized.[86] The initial text of the Convention also contained some exceptions and limitations, including one for the reproduction of 'articles of political discussion, news of the day or miscellaneous facts', which could not be prohibited,[87] and one for 'use in publication for teaching or scientific purposes'.[88] Those exceptions and limitations for news of the day, facts and 'articles of political discussion' reflected public interest considerations, particularly freedom of information and of the press. In a precursor to current debates about the manufacture of tools to circumvent Technical Protection Measures (TPMs), a Protocol to the 1886 text also provided that the manufacture and sale of 'instruments for the mechanical reproduction of musical works in which copyright subsists should not be considered as constituting an infringement of musical copyright'.[89]

Balance was not just on *Hugo's* mind. For American authors at the time, fostering creative genius did not have to be a goal at odds with concurrent interests in preserving and maintaining a cultural commons.[90]

---

[85]  The most fundamental right, the right of reproduction, was mostly taken for granted as it were, because it was only incorporated in the Stockholm Convention Revision (Act) of 1967. Act of Stockholm of July 14, 1967. Berne Convention Centenary (n 26) 232–4. It was also at the 1967 Revision Conference that the three-step test, to which I return below, was included in the Convention. It had existed in national laws for decades before that, starting with the (English) Statute of Anne of 1710 (8 Anne c. 19).

[86]  First, it referred to 'infringing *copies*', which were 'liable to seizure on importation'. Berne Convention (1886), art. 12(1). Berne Convention Centenary (n 26) 228. It also contained an explicit, though conditional, right of reproduction for newspapers or periodicals, which applied only if specifically asserted by the author, ibid., art. 7. More importantly, the 1886 text contained a partial definition of 'unlawful reproductions to which this Convention applies', which, interestingly, included 'unauthorized indirect appropriations of a literary or artistic work, of various kinds, such as adaptations, musical arrangements, etc., when they are only the reproduction of a particular work, in the same form, or in another form, without essential alterations, additions, or abridgements, so as not to present the character of a new original work'. ibid.

[87]  Berne Convention (1886), art. 7(2). Berne Convention Centenary (n 26) 228.

[88]  Ibid., art. 8. This exception only allowed countries to maintain existing exceptions.

[89]  Final Protocol of September 9, 1886, art. 3. Berne Convention Centenary (n 26) 228.

[90]  As legal scholars such as L Ray Patterson have pointed out, the language of the Constitution suggests, in order of priority, that copyright first promote learning, then preserve the public domain, and—only thirdly—encourage creation by benefiting the author. See L Ray Patterson and Stanley W Lindberg, *The Nature of Copyright* (Athens, University of Georgia Press, 1991) 49.

Late eighteenth- and early nineteenth-century American thinkers and authors sought to articulate and codify competing visions of selfhood in the increasingly important print culture. Thomas Jefferson espoused a 'natural' authorial voice that was 'harmonious, vatic', its agenda to 'blot out authorial innovation, to ventriloquize common sense and sensibility, and to "harmonize" the wisdom of previous texts and voices', producing documents such as the United States Constitution itself.[91]

As Modernism slowly started to push Romanticism out of the normative spotlight used to delineate author interests, Modernist writers (British and American alike) made use of an array of literary materials and of texts written by others in their work, embracing techniques such as collage, pastiche, and complex patterns of allusions even as they continued to pay homage to the author as 'original genius'.[92] Ezra Pound, probably the most prominent and public of the Moderns when it came to politics, engaged in extended meditations on copyright and its relation to the creative process, and in doing so explicitly and implicitly acknowledged the importance of *balancing financial benefit to the author with future artists' needs for prior cultural materials*. Pound's international copyright view suggested protecting authors' intellectual labour while ensuring that it was made available and affordable to the public. Specifically, it proposed perpetual and automatic copyright yet included provisions designed to make all published works publicly accessible. Key provisions included *compulsory licenses* that would apply if heirs allowed a work to go out of print, or if someone wished to import or translate a foreign work for publication in the United States, and an exception for the concurrent publication of cheap editions of highly successful works after a certain number of copies were sold.[93] Pound also would have required that the author place copies of his book at the National Library and public libraries of four major American cities.[94] These requirements for public access foreshadow the contemporary debate as to whether works made available online should be 'controlled'. In Poundian terms, it would seem fair to suggest that dissemination with few use restrictions (within monetized systems for certain categories of works like music) produces better outcomes.

---

[91]  Jay Fliegelman, *Declaring Language: Jefferson, Natural Language and the Culture of Performance* (Stanford UP 1993) 65.
[92]  See Paul Saint-Amour, Introduction in *Modernism and Copyright* (OUP 2011) 31.
[93]  Ibid., 50–53.
[94]  Ibid., 48–9.

## 2.4    1896–1967

The text of the Berne Convention was revised and made more complex by the addition of new right fragments (a notion discussed in the previous chapter) at successive revision conferences (1896, 1908, 1928, 1948, and 1967).[95] When exceptions or limitations were provided with such new rights, they were often expressed as unspecified possibilities available to national legislators.[96] In other cases limitations took the form of possible compulsory licenses.[97] In a few cases a right fragment was introduced into the Convention 'in principle'[98] but essentially made optional and, therefore, no exception was needed in the Convention.[99] Countries could then decide both whether to introduce the right and then how to modulate it.

Table 2.1 shows the principle milestones of this evolution during which a number of new rights were added to the Convention to recognize the fact that some works (especially theatrical, musical and cinematographic) derive most of their commercial value from their public performance (live) or communication (distance). When exceptions or limitations were provided together with the new rights, they were often expressed as *unspecified possibilities offered national legislators,* though not always. In certain cases (e.g., arts 11*bis*(2) and 13), limitations took the form of a compulsory licensing system. In other cases (e.g., the *droit de suite,* or resale right in works of fine art[100]), a right was only introduced into the Convention 'in principle' and, therefore, no exception was needed in the text of the Convention itself.[101] The underlying assumption was that national legis-

---

[95]   For a detailed list of rights added to the Berne Convention at each revision conference, see Daniel Gervais, 'Making Copyright Whole: A Principled Approach to Copyright Exceptions and Limitations' (2008) 5(1/2) *University of Ottawa Law & Technology Journal* 1, 8–9.

[96]   See ibid.

[97]   Berne Convention, arts 11*bis*(2) and 13.

[98]   See e.g., the *droit de suite,* an optional resale right in works of fine arts. Berne Convention, art. 14*ter*.

[99]   The same technique was used in the TRIPS Agreement, which provides, e.g., a right for broadcasting organizations (as a related or neighboring right) in art. 14 but the last sentence of that article then makes it optional. See Daniel Gervais, *TRIPS Agreement,* (4th edn, Sweet & Maxwell 2012).

[100]   A resale right in works of fine arts. Paris Act Relating to the Berne Convention for the Protection of Literary and Artistic Works, 24 July 1971, 1161 UNTS 18388, art. 14*ter* [hereinafter Berne Convention (1971)].

[101]   The same technique was used in the TRIPS Agreement, which provides, e.g., a right for broadcasting organizations (as a related or neighboring right) in art. 14 but the last sentence of that article then makes it optional. See Gervais (n 98) 306–7.

*Table 2.1   Evolution of rights, limitations and exceptions in the Berne Convention (1886–1971)*

| Revision or Protocol (year) | New rights (Article) | New limitations or exceptions (Article) |
| --- | --- | --- |
| Paris (1896) | Extension of reproduction right to serial novels (must be asserted, IV)<br>Right of adaptation applied specifically to transformation of a novel into a theatrical play and vice versa | |
| Berlin (1908) | Term of protection of life + 50 years (7)<br>Broader translation right (8)<br>Removal of need to assert reproduction right in serial novels and short stories<br>New right of adaption for mechanical reproduction and public performance using such reproductions (13)<br>Extension of right to obtain seizure to such adaptations (13(4))<br>New right of reproduction and public performance by cinematography (14) | Possible conditions and restrictions on mechanical reproduction right (13) |
| Rome (1928) | Moral right (6*bis*, 9(2), 11*bis*(2))<br>New exclusive right of communication by broadcasting (11*bis*(1)) | Possible exclusion from protection of political speeches and speeches in legal proceedings (2*bis*(1))<br>Possible limit on right of reproduction of lectures, addresses and sermons (2*bis*(2))<br>Possible limit on the right of communication by broadcasting, including compulsory licenses (11*bis*(2)) |
| Brussels (1948) | Broader right of translation (8)<br>Broader moral right (in quotations, 10(3)) | Mandatory right of quotation (10(1)) |

*Table 2.1*   (continued)

| Revision or Protocol (year) | New rights (Article) | New limitations or exceptions (Article) |
|---|---|---|
| | Extension of public performance right to communications to the public of the performance (11(1))<br>Extension of communication right to broadcasting or communication by any other means of wireless diffusion of signs, sounds and images; any communication to the public by wire (cable) or rebroadcasting; and public communication by loudspeaker (11*bis*(1))<br>New right of public recitation (11*ter*)<br>Broader right of adaptation, arrangement and other alteration (elimination of reference to new original work as being excluded, 12)<br>Broader right in cinematographic adaptations (now includes distribution as well as public performance, 14)<br>New *droit de suite* (resale right, 14*bis*(1)) | Possible exception to use excerpts in educational and scientific publications (10(2)); replaces previous possibility of maintaining existing exceptions<br>Possible exception for the recording, reproduction and public communication of short extracts for the purpose of reporting current events (10*bis*)<br>Possible conditions (incl. compulsory license) on broader communication right (11*bis*(2))<br>Possible exception for ephemeral recoding and official archiving (11*bis*(3))<br>Possible limit on resale right (14*bis*(2)) |
| Stockholm (1967) | New / broader right of reproduction (all categories of works, 9(1))<br>News reporting reproduction exception may be excluded by right holder (10*bis*(1))<br>Broader right of public performance and communication (reservations no longer mentioned, 11) | Three-step test (9(2))<br>Possible limits on protection of official texts (2(4))<br>Right of quotation extended to all works but must be compatible with fair practice and the extent of use must be justified by purpose (10(1))<br>Modification of educational exception, limited to 'by way of illustration' and |

*Table 2.1*

| Revision or Protocol (year) | New rights (Article) | New limitations or exceptions (Article) |
| --- | --- | --- |
| | New right of public communication of a recitation; right extended to translations (11*ter*)<br>Right of performance for cinematographic works extended to communication by wire (14*bis*) | compatibility with 'fair practice' but applied also to broadcasts and recordings (not just publications, 10(2))<br>Newspaper / periodicals reproduction exception now applies to broadcasting and communication and to publications on 'economic, political or religious topics' (10*bis*(1))<br>Exception for reporting current events by photography, cinematography, broadcasting or communication to the public limited to 'the extent justified by the informatory purpose' (10*bis*(2))<br>Protocol for developing countries* |
| Paris (1971) | | New Appendix (providing developing countries with the possibility of issuing compulsory reproduction and translation licenses, subject to a complex administrative machinery)** |

*Notes:*

Not included in this table are: (a) extensions of the protection to new types of works (photography, works of applied art, cinematography, etc.); (b) definitional changes (what is 'published' etc.); (c) dispute-settlement (incl. a limited right to retaliate for failure to protect); and (d) administrative provisions.
* Discussed in section 1.2 in Appendix 2 below.
** See section 1.3 of Appendix 2, below.

lators would develop their own balanced approach when implementing a new right. Hence, while the evolution of the domain of *rights* in the Convention between 1886 and 1967 was linear, the same cannot be said of the domain of exceptions and limitations. Still today, exceptions and limitations appear mostly as *unregulated policy space* in the Convention. The pinnacle of this development was the adoption of the *three-step test* in 1967, which is the subject of the next chapter. The test began its international career as a political compromise designed to allow, within limited confines, exceptions to be made by Berne member countries to the right of reproduction, a full version of which was only introduced, as Table 2.1 shows, only in the 1967 text. The three-step test has since become the cornerstone of exceptions to all copyright rights due to its broad use in the TRIPS Agreement.[102] To this rather vague test (as we will see in the next chapter), the 1967 revision also included a reference to 'fair practice'[103] in the exception for education, and references to the 'extent justified by the purpose' in relation to the exceptions thus arguably adding an evidentiary burden on users.

As just mentioned, the only exception expressed in mandatory terms in the current text of the Convention is the right of quotation.[104] Other important exceptions, which have been part of the Convention from its inception and through all revisions, namely those that relate to news reporting and political discussion, are optional. In that sense, and without entering here into the debate as to whether free expression is already fully factored into copyright norms[105] or whether protection of free expression[106] might force copyright holders to yield beyond exceptions provided

---

[102]   TRIPS Agreement, arts 13 (all copyright rights), 26(2) (industrial designs) and 30 (patents).
[103]   Berne Convention, art. 10 (1) and (2).
[104]   Berne Convention, art. 10, which indeed reads like a user *right*:

*It shall be permissible* to make quotations from a work which has already been lawfully made available to the public, provided that their making is compatible with fair practice, and their extent does not exceed that justified by the purpose, including quotations from newspaper articles and periodicals in the form of press summaries.

[105]   Michael Birnhack, 'Global Copyright, Local Speech' (2006) 24 *Cardozo Arts & Entertainment Law Journal* 491; by the same author, 'Copyrighting Speech: A Trans-Atlantic View' in Paul L C Torremans (ed.), *Copyright and Human Rights* (Kluwer L Int'l 2004) 37–62 (available at <http://ssrn.com/abstract=905216> accessed 20 November 2015); Neil W Netanel, 'Copyright and a Democratic Civil Society' (1996) 106 *Yale Law Journal* 283.
[106]   See L Ray Patterson, 'Free Speech, Copyright and Fair Use' (1987) 40 *Vanderbilt Law Review* 3.

for in national laws and international texts,[107] there is a sense throughout the Convention that public interest considerations related to information and the press trump exclusive copyright rights.

In sum, while rights are generally well delineated in the Convention, exceptions other than those related to 'public information' and the right of quotation are mostly *unregulated space*, often subject only to the three-step test. Normatively, the incremental elevation of the level of protection to encompass new forms of commercial exploitation of individual human creativity with unclear or unspecified exceptions have made it difficult to define proper boundaries for those rights in a globalized world. The impact of this policy vacuum has been felt very palpably on the Internet, where social norms are interfacing with exceptions that are often unclear at the national level and unspecified at the international level.

## 2.5   THE 1971 APPENDIX

The history of the 1971 Appendix to the Berne Convention is interesting for at least two reasons. First, politically it provides a backdrop for the negotiation of broad public interest-based exceptions (here to facilitate economic and cultural development). Second, as a technical legal matter, it provides an example of how the drafting of exceptions and limitations in international instruments is likely to correlate to the extent they will actually be used.

For most of the early history of the Convention, developing countries were mostly members as colonies, for example India as part of the United Kingdom. Very few independent Berne Union members belonged to the category.[108] Concerns that some of the developing countries had with the growth of the international trade in books, mostly about availability of copies and translation in national languages, were shared by many of the industrialized nations as well, however, as the history of the translation right in the Convention tends to demonstrate.[109]

The formal part of the story begins with an important seminar held in

---

[107]   See Daniel Gervais, 'The Role of International Treaties in the Interpretation of Canadian Intellectual Property Statutes' in O Fitzgerald (ed.), *The Globalized Rule of Law: Relationships between International and Domestic Law* (Irwin Law 2006), 549–72 (available at <http://works.bepress.com/daniel_gervais/15/> accessed 20 November 2015).
[108]   Haiti and Tunisia participated from early on.
[109]   Ricketson and Ginsburg (n 17) s. 14.04.

Brazzaville in 1963 in which 23 African countries participated.[110] While its purpose was mostly educational, the seminar adopted a number of recommendations that might still find echoes in more recent demands formulated by those countries. The recommendations focused on a reduced term of protection, better access to protected works for education, and the protection of folklore.[111] Those recommendations were taken up by a Group of Experts on the Berne Convention, which led to the publication of a report by a Study Group in 1964 convened by BIRPI, the institutional predecessor of the World Intellectual Property Organization (WIPO).[112] The Study Group report noted that copyright should be adapted to the 'social, technical and economic conditions of the contemporary community'.[113] It proposed specific rules, including a new Article 25*bis*, on translation (limitation on the exclusive right); a possible shorter term of protection; a simpler exclusive right for broadcasting; an exception for education uses; and a possibility accorded developing countries to make regional arrangements in derogation of the Convention.[114] The 1964 report was followed by a report from a committee of governmental experts a year later.[115] Between the release of the two reports, groups representing a number of authors and other right holders voiced opposition to the flexibilities sought by developing countries.[116]

Then in 1967 at the major international intellectual property Conference held in Stockholm, which adopted new acts to both the Berne and Paris Conventions and led to the establishment of WIPO, another step forward was taken. A total of 24 developing countries, many of them freshly minted members of the United Nations, had joined the Berne Union. A number of them participated in the discussions and voiced concerns about

---

[110] There had obviously been calls for special and differential treatment and other exceptions and limitations before that meeting, which explains its outcome. For a description of the pre-1963 history, see Irwin A Olian Jr., 'International Copyright and the Needs of Developing Countries: The Awakening at Stockholm and Paris' (1974) 7 *Cornell International Law Journal* 81, 95–101.

[111] Ricketson and Ginsburg (n 17) s. 14.08.

[112] United International Bureaux for the Protection of Intellectual Property, *General Report of the Swedish/BIRPI Study Group*, (Geneva, BIRPI DA/22/2, 1 July 1964).

[113] Ibid., 5.

[114] Ibid.

[115] United International Bureaux for the Protection of Intellectual Property, Committee of Governmental Experts, 1 Copyright 9 (Geneva, BIRPI DA/22/33, 1965) 194.

[116] Ricketson and Ginsburg (n 17) s. 14.11.

the evolution of the Convention.[117] India, for example, was participating for the first time in its own right in a Berne Revision Conference.

The Conference considered a possible protocol to the Berne Convention regarding developing countries. The five exceptions and limitations which the protocol would have allowed were as follows:

1. shorter term of protection (25-year minimum for most works);
2. possible limits to the translation right (possible limit of the exclusive right to ten years under certain conditions; compulsory license allowed subject to a detailed set of conditions and procedures);
3. possible reproduction licenses for educational or cultural purposes (similar to those that already existed in Article V of the UCC);
4. possible restriction of the broadcasting right to a compulsory license in the case of non-profit communications; and
5. possible compulsory licenses for teaching. Unlike the limitation at 3 above, this last possibility was not subject to an obligation to provide just compensation, but rather to conform to 'standards of payments made to national authors', a form of price discrimination imposed by the buyer, as it were.[118]

The proposed protocol resembled the 1963 recommendations, though without the reservation concerning Article 20 (special arrangements) and with more precise language for example as to which countries could benefit from the kind of special and differential treatment allowed under it.[119] The protocol failed, as is illuminated by rapporteur Vojtěch Strnad in his detailed report.[120] It was referred to as 'grossly defective' in meetings the needs of developing countries.[121] Some participants opined that access to too few works would become easier under a rule limiting the term of protection to 25 years, a term which exceeds the commercial life of the vast majority of copyrighted works. The same could be said for the translation right for teaching. Most textbooks would be outdated after such a long period of time—which in practice was in fact longer due to the formalities necessary before a translation license could be issued.[122] A well-known

---

[117]  Ibid. S. 14.05.
[118]  For a discussion, see ibid. s. 14.25.
[119]  The solution chosen here was to refer to the list generated by the United Nations. See ibid., s. 14.51.
[120]  International Bureau for Intellectual Property, 'Report on the Work of Main Committee II', reproduced in Berne Convention Centenary (n 26) 212–14. The report was also published at 3 Copyright 222–4 (1967).
[121]  Olian (n 110) 101.
[122]  See ibid.

German copyright scholar also noted that the translation license would not be useful owing to a 'lack of qualified translators, editors, composers, and printers [in many developing countries]'.[123] Most industrialized countries were also reluctant to go along with the Protocol but for different reasons. As Olian put it:

> From the point of view of the advanced countries, the Protocol represented:
> a substantial threat to the existence of copyright protection as it had evolved
> over a period of several hundred years, as well as a confiscation of the rights of
> individual authors, composers, and publishers.[124]

The ALAI, the 'author' of the first unofficial draft of the Berne Convention in the 1880s, also opposed the protocol, noting that 'influenced by considerations foreign to the Berne Convention, it went beyond limits previously considered as "insurmountable" ("*infranchissables*")' and thus called on Berne Union members postpone any decision to ratify or acceded to the protocol, at least until further fact-finding by BIRPI.[125] The International Publishers' Association adopted a resolution asking 'its [national] member associations to urge their governments to provide such technical and economic aid as would eliminate any need to ratify or implement the Stockholm Protocol'.[126] In the end, only Senegal ratified the protocol.[127] That failure left a bitter taste, a fate foreshadowed by the atmosphere of hostility and suspicion at the Stockholm Conference itself.[128]

A number of Berne Union members turned their disappointment into a desire to work on the Universal Copyright Convention (UCC) framework instead.[129] Indeed, discussions surrounding the possible protocol to Berne

---

[123]    Erich Schulze, 'Advancement of World Copyright through Aid to Developing Countries' (1970) 44 Internationale Gesellschaft für Urheberrecht (INTERGU) 59, 68.

[124]    Olian (n 110) 102.

[125]    Association Littéraire et Artistique Internationale, Assemblée générale, reprinted (in French) 4 Copyright 151 (23 April 1968).

[126]    International Publishers Association, 18th Congress (June 9 to 15, 1968) reprinted at 4 Copyright 188–9. The resolution does note, however, the Association's 'willingness to cooperate within the existing international law of copyright to facilitate such publication by making available to local publishers the necessary publishing rights for reprints and translations'. ibid.

[127]    Schulze (n 122) 68.

[128]    See Ricketson and Ginsburg (n 17) s. 14.39.

[129]    In a way, this institutional shift is also what happened in the 1980s when, disillusioned with the prospect of revising the Berne Convention (this time to increase the level of rights and protection), a number of Berne Union members shifted the debate to the GATT, which later became the World Trade Organization (WTO).

reflected the fact that, between the Brussels (1948) and Stockholm (1967) meetings, a new international copyright instrument had emerged, namely the UCC which it contained less strict rules on several important issues such as term of protection and formalities and in allowing exceptions and limitations.[130]

The renewed interest in the UCC and the perceived need to address the concerns of developing countries led the Director of BIRPI/WIPO, Georg H C Bodenhausen, to issue a report suggesting common rules under Berne and the UCC for developing countries' exceptions and limitations.[131] When discussed at an extraordinary session of the Permanent Committee of the Berne union in 1969, experts made it clear that they did *not* favour a merger of the two Conventions, but Bodenhausen did insist that the two instruments be revised simultaneously.[132] This meeting was followed by a meeting of the UCC Intergovernmental Committee and, then in the autumn of 1969, by a Joint Study Group meeting in Washington.[133] That meeting provided a set of recommendations and a framework for a joint revision of Berne and the UCC. With respect to Berne specifically, the recommendations were:

● to create a separate protocol from the Stockholm Act;
● to include a provision allowing developing countries to apply the revised UCC; and
● as a 'counterbalance', to raise the level of protection in the UCC.

The last step in this process was the joint Revision Conferences held in Paris in July 1971, where the current Appendix was adopted and made part of the Convention.[134] A detailed review of the operation of the Berne Appendix is contained in Appendix 2 to this book.

## 2.6 A DETAILED LOOK AT THE PROHIBITION AGAINST FORMALITIES

Formalities may play a part in a restructured copyright system. The two main normative impulses that led to the adoption of the prohibition against formalities in the Berne Convention were that nineteenth and

---

[130] See Ricketson and Ginsburg (n 17) ss. 18.20–18.30.
[131] See Ricketson and Ginsburg (n 17) s. 14.40. The report is published [1969] Copyright 146.
[132] See ibid.
[133] 5 Copyright 214 (1969).
[134] Under Berne Convention art. 21(1)

early twentieth century authors could not be expected to comply with formalities around the world, and that author's rights were of a nature that should not, unlike patents for example, be subject to government-imposed formalities. The second argument remains valid although not uncontroversial. The first is much less true today, if one considers both the major network of copyright 'collectives' (see Chapter 11) and the changes in technology, including the possibility of complying with formalities online and across national boundaries. Let us take a more detailed look.

As noted in section 2.1 above, the Berne Convention was the brainchild of the *Association Littéraire Internationale*, the predecessor of present-day ALAI.[135] Many Berne signatories took a *'droit d'auteur'* (the term *'auteur'* is used in the sense of the actual creator of a work and not, as is the US work-for-hire context, as the owner of the means of production) approach that recognized natural and moral rights of authors in their creative works.[136] Under a natural rights regime, requiring compliance with a set of state-prescribed formalities as a precondition to the exercise of rights seems difficult to justify.[137] To take a close example, one does not register one's right of free expression. Hence, when Berne was first signed in 1886, it introduced the principle that creators need only comply with the formalities of their country of origin.[138] In 1908, this rule was abandoned in favour of the rule of formality-free protection.[139] It has survived until now.[140] The relevant part reads as follows:

> Authors shall enjoy, in respect of works for which they are protected under this Convention, in countries of the Union other than the country of origin, the

---

[135] See M Ficsor, *Guide to the Copyright and Related Rights Treaties Administered by WIPO and Glossary of Copyright and Related Rights Terms* (Geneva, WIPO 2004) 41 [hereinafter WIPO Guide] paras 9–10:

The preparatory work necessary for the establishment of a convention to satisfy these requirements was started and brought very close to conclusion by [ALAI]. It was at the request of ALAI that the Swiss Confederation convened three subsequent Diplomatic Conferences in Berne in 1884, 1885 and 1886.

[136] See Locke (n 19).
[137] See Jane C Ginsburg, "With Untired Spirits and Formal Constancy": Berne Compatibility of Formal Declaratory Measures to Enhance Copyright Title-Searching" (2013) 28(3) *Berkeley Technology Law Journal* 1583–622; Stef van Gompel, 'Formalities in the Digital Era: An Obstacle or Opportunity?' in L Bently, U Suthersanen and P Torremans (eds), *Global Copyright: Three Hundred Years Since the Statute of Anne, from 1709 to Cyberspace* (Edward Elgar Publishing 2010).
[138] Berne Convention art. 2(2).
[139] Ibid., art. 4(2). The text of the old and new rules are discussed below.
[140] Berne Convention (1971) art. 5(2).

rights which their respective laws do now or may hereafter grant to their nationals, as well as the rights specially granted by this Convention.[141]

The enjoyment and the exercise of these rights shall not be subject to any formality; such enjoyment and such exercise are independent of the existence of protection in the country of origin of the work. Consequently, apart from the provisions of this Convention, the extent of protection, as well as the means of redress afforded to the author to protect his rights, shall be governed exclusively by the laws of the country where protection is claimed.[142]

The expression 'these rights' in Article 5(2) of the Berne Convention (1971) refers to the 'the rights which their respective laws do now or may hereafter grant to their nationals, as well as the rights specially granted by this Convention'.[143] The Convention thus imposes: (a) an obligation to grant national treatment—that is, to treat foreign rights holders no less favourably than nationals—and (b) an obligation to provide the 'rights specially granted by the Convention'.[144] The formalities prohibited under Article 5(2) are thus those that are (a) imposed by law and (b) copyright-specific.[145] Examples of such are registration with a governmental authority and any other state-prescribed, copyright-specific requirement that an author must comply with in order to bring a suit for copyright infringement, such as deposit of a copy of the work.[146]

As used in the Convention, 'enjoyment' refers to the existence and scope of the right while 'exercise' refers to enforcement.[147] Article 5(2) does not prevent authors from having to comply with ordinary (non-copyright-specific) formalities such as a court's rules of procedure or evidence.[148]

---

[141]  Ibid., art. 5(1).

[142]  Berne Convention Centenary (n 75) 149.

[143]  See WIPO Guide (n 82) para. BC-5.6.

[144]  See ibid. paras BC-5.1–5.2.

[145]  See Ricketson and Ginsburg (n 17) 325–6.

[146]  Formal requirements existing at the time essentially involved registration, deposit (in national libraries) and, in rare cases, translation in a national language within a predetermined period of time, ibid.

[147]  See WIPO Guide (n 82) para. BC-5.8.

[148]  After a detailed analysis, Professors Ricketson and Ginsburg conclude that the prohibition contained in art. 5(2) applies, with respect to the existence of copyright, to 'everything which must be complied with in order to ensure that the rights of the author with regard to his work may come into existence', including a registration requirement. They note that the addition of 'exercise' to the prohibition was meant to address the other half of the problem: 'An author may be vested with copyright, but unable to enforce her rights unless she complies with a variety of prerequisites to suit.' See Ricketson and Ginsburg, (n 17) 325 (quoting in part German delegate Meyer).

Article 5(2) came into being in the early days of the Berne Convention. It was then, and remains, part of the Convention's provisions dealing with the treatment of foreign authors (i.e., national treatment) and place of (first) publication. In the first draft of the Convention published in 1884[149] the relevant part of Article 2 read as follows:

> Authors who are nationals of one of the countries of the Contracting Countries shall enjoy in all the other countries of the Union, in respect of their works, whether in manuscript or unpublished form or published in one of those countries, such advantages as the laws concerned do now or will hereafter grant to nationals. The enjoyment of the above rights shall be subject to compliance with the conditions of form and substance prescribed by the legislation of the country of origin of the work or, in the case of a manuscript or unpublished work, by the legislation of the country to which the author belongs.[150]

It is clear from the above that the principal intent was to grant to foreign authors the same rights as nationals. This was confirmed by the Drafting Committee, which also clarified the meaning of the expression 'conditions of forms and substance', originally a German proposal, which was changed to 'formalities and conditions'. The Minutes of the First Conference held in Berne in 1884 are very useful to illuminate the meaning and purpose of the expression:

> Dr. Meyer said the following: 'It is merely a question of noting that the wording proposed by the German Delegation, *"conditions of form and substance"* has been replaced by the words *"formalities and conditions"*, and that the word *"formalities"* being taken as a synonym of the term *"conditions of form"*, included, for instance, registration, deposit, etc.; whereas the expression *"conditions"*, being in our view synonymous with *"conditions of **substance**"*, includes, for instance, the completion of a translation within the prescribed period. Thus the words *"formalities and conditions"* cover all that has to be observed for the author's rights in relation to his work to come into being, whereas the effects and consequences of protection, notably with respect to the extent of protection have to remain subject to the principle of treatment on the same footing as nationals.
> The President noted that the Conference agreed with Dr. Meyer on the scope of the words *"formalities and conditions"*.[151]

The Report of 1896 Paris Conference contains the following:

> Under the text of the Convention, the enjoyment of copyright shall be subject to the accomplishment of the *conditions and formalities prescribed by law in the*

---

[149]  See Berne Convention Centenary (n 26) 94.
[150]  Ibid.
[151]  Ibid., 94–5.

*country of origin of the work.* The meaning of this provision does not seem to be seriously debatable. As a result of it, the author needs only to have complied with the legislation of the country of origin, to have completed in that country the conditions and formalities which may be required there. He does not have to complete formalities in the other countries where he wished to claim protection. This interpretation, which is in keeping with the text, was certainly in the minds of the authors of the 1886 Convention. (Emphasis in original.)[152]

Clearly, the conditions and formalities are those mentioned in 1884, namely registration, deposit, mandatory translation or publication etc., not the need to sign contracts, file statements of claims in courts, join or otherwise deal with copyright agencies, etc. This was further reinforced at the 1908 Berlin Conference, at which a slightly different version of Article 2, which from 1908 until 1967 became 4(2)—now Article 5(2)—was adopted. There it was very clear that the provision is related to publication and similar requirements. The relevant part reads as follows:

Authors who are nationals of any of the countries of the Union shall enjoy in countries other than the country of origin of the work, for their works, whether unpublished or first published in a country of the Union, the rights which the respective laws do now or may hereafter grant to their nationals as well as the rights specially granted by this Convention. The enjoyment and the exercise of these rights shall not be subject to any formality; such enjoyment and exercise are independent of the existence of protection in the country of origin of the work. Consequently, apart from the provisions of this Convention, the extent of protection, as well as the means of redress afforded to the author to protect his rights, shall be governed exclusively by the laws of the country where protection is claimed.[153]

The Report of the 1908 Conference is worth quoting *in extenso* on this point. It begins with a statement that the provision does not apply to domestic authors and then explains the shift from the single formality requirement (in the country of origin) to the no formality formulation we have in the Convention text today:

*The enjoyment and exercise of these rights shall not be subject to any formal-ity.* It should be noted that it is exclusively the rights claimed by virtue of the Convention that are involved here. The legislation of the country in which the work is published and in which it is nationalized by the very fact of publica-tion continues to be absolutely free to subject the existence or the exercise of the right to protection in the country to whatever conditions and formalities it thinks fit; it is a pure question of domestic law. Outside the country of

[152] Ibid., 137.
[153] Ibid., 149.

publication, protection may be requested in the other countries of the Union not only without having to complete any formalities in them, but even without being obliged to justify that the formalities in the country of origin have been accomplished. This is what results, on the one hand, from a general principle which is going to be stated and explained and, on the other, from the deletion of the third paragraph of Article 11 of the 1886 Convention. This paragraph provides that:

> 'It is, nevertheless, agreed that the courts may, if necessary, require the production of a certificate from the competent authority to the effect that the formalities prescribed by law in the country of origin have been accomplished, in accordance with Article 2.'

That Article does indeed state, at the beginning of its paragraph 2, that 'the enjoyment of these rights shall be subject to the accomplishment of the conditions and formalities prescribed by law in the country of origin of the work' and, to remove difficulties which had arisen in certain countries, the Paris Interpretative Declaration had emphasized the idea – which was evidently that of the authors of the 1886 Convention – that the protection depends solely on the accomplishment, in the country of origin, of the conditions and formalities which may be required by the legislation of that country. This was already a great simplification which will be appreciated if it is recalled that there was a time not so long ago when, to guarantee a work protection in a foreign country, even by virtue of an international convention, it was necessary to register and often even to deposit that work in the foreign country within a certain time limit. The new Convention simplifies matters still further since it requires no justification. Difficulties had arisen with regard to the production of a certificate from the authority of the country of origin – this production having been considered, occasionally, as the preliminary to infringement action, which caused delays. The new provision means that a person who acts by virtue of the Convention does not have to provide proof that the formalities in the country of origin have been accomplished, as the accomplishment or non-accomplishment of these formalities must not exert any influence. However, if it is in his interest to produce a certificate to establish a particular fact, he cannot be prevented from doing so (the Article in the draft only refers to *formalities*, but it is meant to cover the *conditions and formalities* to which the 1886 Convention refers.)[154] (Emphasis in original.)

Unquestionably, in light of the above, the formalities that are prohibited under Article 5(2) are registration with a governmental authority, deposit of a copy of the work and similar formalities are linked to the existence of copyright or its exercise, especially in enforcement proceedings.

Interestingly, in its pre-1908 incarnation, the provision was arguably derogating from national treatment, though it was clearly not intended as such. Rather, Convention drafters saw it as a simplification of the multiple

---

[154]  Ibid., 148.

registration/deposit requirements.[155] If 'pure' national treatment had been applied, it would have been sufficient to grant protection to foreign authors on the condition of accomplishing the same formalities as nationals in every country. In 1908, the provision was realigned along the principle of national treatment by making it a provision against mandatory formalities while maintaining the meaning of the expression 'conditions and formalities' defined in 1884–1886. Formal requirement in existence at the time essentially involved registration, deposit (in national libraries) and, in rare cases, translation. For many reasons, although it was necessary to respect each country's ability to impose such requirements, they had to be decoupled from copyright. Deposit is still required for published works in many countries, but the sanction for failure to provide free copies to the national library cannot be the removal of copyright. The issue of mandatory translation is similarly separate from copyright, though its political importance led to the adoption of the Appendix to the Paris Act in 1971 allowing developing countries to impose compulsory translation licenses (see Appendix 2). The provision does not prevent requirements of other types.

This is further confirmed in World Intellectual Property Organizations (WIPO's) latest commentary on the Convention:

> Formalities are any conditions or measures – independent from those that relate to the creation of the work (such as the substantive condition that a production must be original in order to qualify as a protected work) or the fixation thereof (where it is a condition under national law) – without the fulfilment of which the work is not protected or loses protection. Registration, deposit of the original or a copy, and the indication of a notice are the most typical examples.[156]

'Enjoyment' is thus the very existence of the right, whereas exercise refers in particular to enforcement.[157] It would be incongruous to read Article 5(2) as preventing the mandatory doing of 'anything' to enforce their rights. Should authors just have to walk into a courtroom (itself a 'formality') without having to file a statement of claim? Not have to deal with foreign publishers and distributors because those are 'formalities'? Not have to deal with foreign tax authorities to avoid deductions at source in a foreign country? Not have to deal with foreign Collective Management Organizations (CMOs) to ensure the protection of their rights in cases in which they cannot or do not want to join a worldwide system through

---

[155] Ibid.
[156] WIPO Guide (n 82) 41. See also WIPO, WIPO *Intellectual Property Handbook* (Geneva, WIPO 2004) 262.
[157] See WIPO Guide (ibid.) 42.

54 *(Re)structuring copyright*

their national CMO, if any? That is clearly not the intent or meaning of Article 5(2). Those are all normal acts of exploitation that authors and other copyright holders must perform routinely to exploit their copyright works and not—as was made abundantly clear during the adoption and revision of the Convention, 'formalities' prohibited under Article 5(2).

In sum, the application of Article 5(2) hinges on whether the formability is (a) copyright-specific and (b) government-related. On the first element, as examples above show, it is self-evident that authors are not somehow free of all civic or judicial formalities. The second element is a distillate of the drafting history of Article 5(2).

## 2.7  POST-BERNE (1971) DEVELOPMENTS

The pendulum started swinging in favour of *proprietary copyright* towards the end of the twentieth century as copyright industries began to express their own interests, not or no longer instrumentalizing the author as copyright's *raison d'être*. The latest step of this process is the current 'assetization' of copyright and other forms of intellectual property in investment provisions of trade and investment agreements.[158] In response, several scholars and authors proposed explicit statutory provisions and ideal practices that would help to correct a copyright regime so proprietary that it endangers the future of the very cultural materials that it purports to protect. The concerns expressed by those scholars provide a basis for undermining the kinds of claims made by 'authors' affiliated with corporate copyright holders, such as the Disney songwriter who argued for perpetual copyright during Congressional hearings prior to the enactment of the Sonny Bono Copyright Term Extension Act of 1998 in the United States.[159] Creators who operate in this work made for hire environment are often anonymous craftsmen, not named creators.[160]

---

[158]  See, e.g., Switzerland-Uruguay Agreement on the Promotion and Protection of Foreign Investments, 7 October 1988, art. 1(2)(d); and Agreement between the Government of Hong Kong and the Government of Australia for the Promotion and Protection of Investments, 15 October 1993, art. 1(e)(iv), <http://bit.ly/1KtMZmR> accessed 20 November 2015.
[159]  See Martha Woodmansee, 'The Cultural Work of Copyright: Legislating Authorship in Britain, 1837–1843' in Austin Sarat and Thomas Kearns (eds), *Law and the Domains of Culture* (University of Michigan Press 1998) 66.
[160]  This resembles patronage in medieval Europe where skilled craftsmen would create what today would be copyrighted works, from small-scale and possible individual works such as poems, *chansons*, and paintings of cherubs for the Church to grand collective works such as the Chartres Cathedral, for which typically

Corporate owners may consider works not as products of author-ship but first and foremost as commercial assets, often far removed from human creative inputs. Unfortunately, not only does the current, unstructured system *not* distinguish among types of authors (in the sense that authors of works of all categories have the same rights[161]), it does not distinguish between authors and professional 'right holders'—often referred to as the 'copyright industries'—whose task is to maximize and to some extent control commercial exploitation of certain categories of copyrighted works. Yet corporate owners both drive the copyright policy discourse and drown out the voices of authors who do not need the full arsenal of rights and remedies that a record label or movie studio might.[162] Sometimes corporate owners actually argue against authorship. For example, movie studios in the United States have steadfastly opposed a right of attribution for authors recognized by law, demonstrating interests diametrically opposed to authors' desire for recognition and attribution.[163]

Even before the current wave of assetization had begun matters had not become much clearer for exceptions and limitations in the years since Berne was last revised. The 1996 WIPO Copyright Treaty (WCT)[164] refers to the need for 'balance', including in its preamble, which refers back to the Berne Convention: '*Recognizing* the need to maintain a balance between the rights of authors and the larger public interest, particularly education, research and access to information, as reflected in the Berne Convention.'[165] Beyond this rhetorical nod to the goal of maintaining 'balance', however, the WCT incorporates the three-step test as a limit to permitted limitations and exceptions.[166] An

---

no individual attribution was given. See Michael W Carroll, 'Whose Music Is It Anyway?: How We Came to View Musical Expression As A Form of Property' (2004) 72 *University of Cincinnatti Law Review* 1405, 1450. See also Max W Thomas, 'Reading and Writing the Renaissance Commonplace Book: A Question of Authorship?' (1992) 10 *Cardozo Arts & Entertainment Law Journal* 665.

[161] With the already mentioned exception of the moral right in 107 USC s. 106A.

[162] See Nicolas Suzor Access, 'Progress, And Fairness: Rethinking Exclusivity In Copyright' (2013) 15 *Vanderbilt Journal of Entertainment & Technology Law* 297, 315.

[163] See Roberta Rosenthal Kwall, *The Soul of Creativity: Forging a Moral Rights Law for the United States* (Stanford UP 2010) 28; and David Goldberg and Robert J Bernstein, 'Legislation by the 101st Congress' (1991) *New York Law Journal* 3, 3 ('[T]here is intense and extensive opposition to extending specific moral rights protection to audiovisual and other works').

[164] S Treaty Doc No 105-17 (1997); 36 ILM 65 (1997).

[165] 36 ILM 65 (1997), preamble.

[166] Ibid., art. 10(2).

Agreed Statement to that Article further provides that it 'neither reduces
nor extends the scope of applicability of the limitations and exceptions
permitted by the Berne Convention.'[167] This statement supports the
view that the three-step test does not constitute an *additional* limit on
limitations and exceptions. It may, however, serve as a guide to interpret
limitations and exceptions.

A second set of questions arises from this lack of clarity with regard
to exceptions and limitations in international copyright norms. For the
first time in copyright's 300-year-old history,[168] individual end-users,
who until recently rarely had encounters with copyright law (no one
needs to sign a license when buying a copy of a book at a bookstore or
a CD at a record store[169]) suddenly must learn rules about what they can
and cannot do (legally) with digital pictures, music, etc. to avoid liability or even prosecution.[170] Several users feel that restrictions on use of
copyright material on the Internet are at odds with established practices
of non-commercial 'sharing' and reusing of content, often to create
something new—a phenomenon sometimes referred to as the 'remix
culture' and a form of which is user-generated content.[171] Educators,
who draw considerable benefits from the great global library that is the
Internet, are pointing to the lack of clarity or technological adaptability
of exceptions.

## 2.8   THE TRIPS AGREEMENT

The 1994 TRIPS Agreement does not provide much additional normative
guidance on which copyright exceptions and limitations are required or
appropriate in each WTO member. If one looks at the Agreement, one

---

[167]   Ibid., Agreed Statement 9 (to art. 10(2)), para. 2.
[168]   Counted from the Statute of Anne. See (n 85).
[169]   A sales contract takes place, however.
[170]   Although in January 2008 the recording industry announced it would no
longer be filing massive amounts of lawsuits against individual end-users, ongoing
lawsuits. See Sarah McBride and Ethan Smith, 'Music Industry to Abandon
Mass Suits' (2008) *Wall Street Journal*, (available at http://online.wsj.com/article/
SB122966038836021137.html last accessed 22 November 2015).
[171]   On the notion of remix culture, see Chapter 5 and Lawrence Lessig, *Remix:
Making Art And Commerce Thrive In The Hybrid Economy* (Penguin Press 2008).
I take issue—but it is not the focus of this volume—with that term, user-generated
content. See Daniel Gervais, 'The Tangled Web of UGC: Making Copyright
Sense of User-Generated Content' (2009) 11 *Vanderbilt Journal of Entertainment
& Technology Law* 841.

finds a mention of technology transfer to the developing world, but not much beyond that—other than the three-step test, which was mentioned above and is discussed in the next section.[172]

The assumption in TRIPS seems to be that rights are essential but exceptions and limitations are not required for intellectual property to work (see the next chapter for a more detailed explanation). Like TRIPS, bilateral and regional trade agreements rarely impose exceptions and limitations, but they do impose minimum rights of course. One may of course question this assumption.[173] A more cynical view suggests that some Western powers want to protect the intellectual property of their nationals used in the developing world to secure new markets and revenues for ideational goods and services and even perhaps to slow the emergence of new competitors in innovation-driven fields. This view is contradicted in part by the relative 'flatness' of the world and the fact that multinational corporations increasingly outsource manufacturing *and research*.[174]

Be that as it may, the TRIPS Agreement contains little on copyright exceptions and limitations, other than what seems a mandatory exclusion of ideas, procedures, methods of operation or mathematical concepts as such. This exception to copyrightable subject matter, modelled after section 102(b) of the United States Copyright Act, was a recognition of an accepted part of copyright policy, namely that copyright attaches to the 'form' of a work, or its 'expression,' not to the ideas embodied in a work.[175] Beyond that, the Agreement (a) incorporates the Berne Convention and the E&Ls contained in that Convention, including the Appendix; (b) incorporates a version of the three-step test that, unlike its Berne parent, is not limited to the right of reproduction but applies to all rights. The test was used by a WTO dispute-settlement panel to cabin the so-called 'small exceptions' mentioned not in the Convention but rather in diplomatic records of revision conferences.[176] The Agreement also includes:

---

[172] See, e.g., art. 66.2 of the TRIPS Agreement. There is also arguably a mandatory limitation, however, namely that copyright shall not protect 'ideas, procedures, methods of operation or mathematical concepts as such'. TRIPS Agreement, art. 9.2. More on this below.

[173] See Daniel Gervais, 'Of Clusters and Assumptions: Innovation as Part of a Full TRIPS Implementation' (2009) 77(5) *Fordham Law Review* 2353, 2353–77.

[174] I am using Thomas Friedman's well-known terminology. See Thomas L Friedman, *The World is Flat* (Picador 2007).

[175] See Boleslaw Nawrocki, 'Electronic Machines and Intellectual Creation' (1970) 5 *Copyright* 29, 33.

[176] See Gervais (n 99) 280.

(a) the possibility of having no exclusive rental rights on audiovisual works (unless rental gives rise to widespread copying);[177]
(b) an exclusion of moral rights, officially because they are not 'trade-related' rights, but in reality due to US opposition;[178] and
(c) in the area of related rights: the possibility of not providing exclusive rights to broadcasters in their signal;[179] a limitation of the exclusive rental right in sound recordings to a right to remuneration (grandfathered);[180] and the application of limitations, exceptions and reservations to the extent permitted by the 1961 Rome Convention.[181]

Beyond those specific exceptions and limitations, the Agreement provides principles and objectives in its Articles 7 and 8 which may be relevant in informing the interpretation of copyright-specific provisions. Article 7 is worth quoting here:

> The protection and enforcement of intellectual property rights should contribute to the promotion of technological innovation and to the transfer and dissemination of technology, to the mutual advantage of producers and users of technological knowledge and in a manner conducive to social and economic welfare, and to a balance of rights and obligations.

A final point that bears emphasis is that TRIPS gives the WTO, and its dispute-settlement system, a significant role in determining the legality exceptions and limitations (under TRIPS but also the Berne Convention, which was incorporated into TRIPS). One of the main areas of past and probably future disputes is the three-step test.

---

[177] TRIPS Agreement, art. 11.
[178] Ibid., art. 9.1.
[179] Ibid., art. 14.3.
[180] Ibid., art. 14.4.
[181] Ibid., art. 14.6.

# 3.   The three-step test

## 3.1   INTRODUCTION

The proposals in this book, including the partial draft new Act of the Berne Convention contained in the Epilogue, aim to comply with major international norms. As a theoretical matter it is of course possible to ignore international law or to suggest that countries should adopt norms in conflict with international rules. One may also suggest that countries should leave the World Trade Organization (WTO) and other intergovernmental organizations. That is not the approach taken here. This has impacts on several levels, most notably perhaps the ability to implement outcomes of democratic processes which may be constrained by trade rules.

The reality is that the ability of governments to take measures to adapt intellectual property and other rules to their own situation and changing technological dynamics is indeed increasingly constrained by norms and standards contained in trade agreements. First among them for most nations is the TRIPS Agreement (see Chapter 2).

The rule that perhaps most directly constrains the ability of policy makers to craft a more properly delineated copyright right—or in designing new exceptions and limitations' is known as the *three-step test*. It is thus necessary to take a detailed look at the constraints it imposes on the proposals made later on.

Although it exists in various versions, the test, as expressed in the WTO TRIPS Agreement, provides that WTO members (that is, most countries around the world) must confine limitations or exceptions to exclusive rights to (1) certain special cases which (2) do not conflict with a normal exploitation of the work and (3) do not unreasonably prejudice the legitimate interests of the right holder. As one can readily see, this looks like language invented by and for lawyers.

## 3.2   HISTORICAL BACKGROUND

At the 1967 Stockholm Berne Convention Revision Conference (discussed in the previous chapter), a general rule known as the 'three-step test' was

added to the Berne Convention. It now forms an essential part of international copyright law and as such features prominently in discussions
surrounding copyright reform, notably in terms of constraints that the
test may impose on norm-setting processes. Violations of the test may
be brought to the WTO for adjudication as part of that organization's
dispute-settlement process.

A full understanding of the test's import requires some historical
background. The purpose of the initial (1967) version of the three-step test
was to allow, but also limit, exceptions to the right of reproduction—a
right fragment added in its full version to the Convention at the same
Revision Conference.[182] According to the Study Group set up by BIRPI
(WIPO's predecessor) and the Swedish Government in preparation of the
Conference, adding the right of reproduction to the Convention meant
that a satisfactory formula had to be found for inevitable exceptions to
that right.[183] The Study Group noted that, while:

> it was obvious that all forms of exploiting a work which had, or were likely to
> acquire, considerable economic or practical importance must in principle be
> reserved to the authors . . . it should not be forgotten that domestic laws already
> contained a series of exceptions in favour of various public and cultural inter-
> ests and that it would be vain to suppose that countries would be ready at this
> stage to abolish these exceptions to any appreciable extent.[184]

The Study Group also recommended that exceptions should be 'made
for clearly specified purposes'[185] adding that a limitation on the exclusive
right of the author '*should not enter into economic competition with*'
protected works.[186] These considerations informed the work of the
Conference and future interpretations of the three-step test. The work
of the Study Group was handed over at the Conference to a Working
Group mandated to try to implement the findings of the Study Group
in the text of the Convention. Initially, the Working Group proposed a
text that would have allowed exceptions for: (a) private use; (b) judicial

---

[182]   Berne Convention for the Protection of Literary and Artistic Works
1979, art. 9(1). It is untrue, however, to say that the original text did not at least
implicitly recognize a right of reproduction. First, in art. 12(1) the Convention
referred to 'infringing copies', which were 'liable to seizure on importation'. It also
contained, in art. 7, a right of reproduction for newspapers or periodicals but the
right only applied if specifically asserted by the author.
[183]   Mihály Ficsor, *The Law of Copyright and the Internet: The 1996 WIPO
Treaties, Their Interpretation and Implementation* (OUP 2002) s. 5.51.
[184]   *Records of the Intellectual Property Conference of Stockholm: June 11 to
July 14, 1967* (WIPO 1971) 111–12.
[185]   Ibid., 112.
[186]   Ibid. (emphasis added).

or administrative purposes; and (c) 'in certain particular cases where the reproduction is not contrary to the legitimate interests of the author and does not conflict with a normal exploitation of the work'.[187] The debates at the Conference initially focused on the merits of adding a list of well-delineated exceptions (which included (a) and (b), but not (c), above). However, because the outcome of the debate was progressively taking the form of a long 'shopping list', the Conference opted to follow a British proposal to take out (a) and (b) entirely and to replace them with a general provision along the lines of (c).[188]

The Conference also provided guidance on the interpretation of the new test. It indicated that the first logical step (the Conference did not consider the 'special case' requirement to be a separate step, a view with which I agree and to which I return below) was to determine whether there was a *conflict with normal commercial exploitation*. If not, then either a compulsory license or a full exception could be introduced in national law. The *compulsory license (with remuneration) would then counterbalance the level of prejudice* in the last step, i.e., it would render such prejudice reasonable where this was necessary.[189] It is also important to note that the test adopted at the 1967 Convention was *intended to guide national legislators* on the proper scope of limitations and exceptions, and then, as already noted, only for the right of reproduction.[190]

## 3.3 INTERPRETATION

As just noted, the test contained in Article 9(2) of the Berne Convention provides for limitations and exceptions to the right of reproduction:

1. in certain special cases;
2. that do not conflict with the normal commercial exploitation of the work; and
3. do not unreasonably prejudice the legitimate interests of the author.

The test was found in a relatively obscure part of the international copyright landscape (namely Article 9(2) of the Berne Convention) until

---

[187] Ibid., 113.
[188] Ficsor (n 183) s 5.53.
[189] *Records* (n 184) 1145–6.
[190] Gervais (n 98) 279–92; see also Mihály Fiscor, 'How Much of What? The Three-Step Test and its Application in Two Recent WTO Dispute Settlement Cases' (2002) 192 *Revue Internationale du Droit d'Auteur* 111, 231–42.

1994 when, with the adoption of the WTO TRIPS Agreement, it became the cornerstone for almost all limitations and exceptions to all intellectual property rights in international law.[191] It is now used as the model for exceptions to *all copyright rights* in TRIPS (art. 13); Articles 10(1) and (2) of the WIPO Copyright Treaty (20 December 1996); Article 16(2) of the WIPO Performances and Phonograms Treaty (also adopted on 20 December 1996); Article 13(2) of the Beijing Treaty on Audiovisual Performances (24 June 2012); and Article 11 of the Marrakesh Treaty to Facilitate Access to Published Works for Persons who are Blind, Visually Impaired or Otherwise Print Disabled (27 June 2013). Berne and TRIPS are different, however. In Berne, the purpose of the test contained in Article 9(2) is expressed in neutral terms ('*it shall be a matter for* legislation in the [member] countries ...'). TRIPS Article 13 uses language that suggests that exceptions and limitations should be narrow ('[WTO] Members *shall confine* ...'). In both cases, the central idea is the same, however, namely that although specific exceptions and limitations (unlike rights) are not *necessary*, some exceptions and limitations are acceptable and perhaps desirable, but within the limits posed by the test. Let us look at each step separately.

### 3.3.1 'Certain Special Cases'

There are at least two different ways to interpret the 'special case' first step. Before considering those two approaches, it is worth noting that, at the 1967 Stockholm Conference this first step was seen a *last* step:

> If it is considered that reproduction[192] conflicts with the normal exploitation of the work, reproduction is not permitted at all. If it is considered that reproduction does not conflict with the normal exploitation of the work, the next step would be to consider whether it does not unreasonably prejudice the legitimate interests of the author. Only if such is not the case would it be possible in certain special cases to introduce a compulsory license, or to provide for use without payment.[193]

---

[191]    The Agreement on Trade-Related Aspects of Intellectual Property Rights 1993, art. 9(2), contains a list of material excluded for copyrightability, namely 'ideas, procedures, methods of operation or mathematical concepts as such'; see also ibid., art. 13, which extended the three-step test of the Berne Convention to cover any copyright right (including, e.g., public performance).

[192]    This quote relates to the three-step test contained in the Berne Convention (n 182) art. 9(2), where it only applies to the right of reproduction. In the TRIPS Agreement (n 191) art. 13, it was extended to all copyright rights.

[193]    *Records* (n 184) 1145.

### 3.3.1.1 Purpose-specific cases

The first approach to the interpretation of 'special case' finds its origin in the *travaux* [legislative history]. In the first edition of his seminal book on the Berne Convention, Professor Sam Ricketson opined that 'special' meant that the exception must have a purpose and be justified by public policy.[194] This purpose-oriented (or teleological) interpretation of the Convention is seemingly reinforced by the use of the phrase 'to the extent justified by the purpose' in Article 10(1) and (2) of the Convention (which allow exceptions to be made for quotation and teaching), and Article 10*bis*(2) (which allows reporting of current events). Public information is clearly the policy basis for the latter exception and for the possible exclusion from copyright of certain official texts.

The 2001 WTO dispute-settlement panel report concerning section 110(5) of the US Copyright Act,[195]—which was issued following a challenge by the European Union of a broad exemption from the music public performance right for bars, hotels, restaurants, and supermarkets in the United States—adopted a somewhat different approach to interpret the first part of the three-step test. This was the first time the test was interpreted by an international tribunal and, although the panel was aware of Professor Ricketson's view,[196] it opted to look at the *Oxford English Dictionary*:[197]

> The term 'special' connotes 'having an individual or limited application or purpose', 'containing details; precise, specific', 'exceptional in quality or degree; unusual; out of the ordinary' or 'distinctive in some way'. This term means that more is needed than a clear definition in order to meet the standard of the first condition. In addition, *an exception or limitation must be limited in its field of application or exceptional in its scope. In other words, an exception or limitation should be narrow in quantitative as well as a qualitative sense.*[198]

The approach chosen by the panel is understandable. For valid normative reasons,[199] the WTO Appellate Body has preferred to stick with the

---

[194] Sam Ricketson, *The Berne Convention for the Protection of Literary and Artistic Works: 1886–1986* (Kluwer 1987) 482.

[195] WTO Report of the Panel WT/DS160/R of 15 June 2000 on *United States – Section 110(5) of the US Copyright Act*.

[196] Ibid., fn 114.

[197] Ibid., fn 111.

[198] Ibid., para 6.109 (emphasis added) (citations omitted).

[199] Trade agreements are bargained for and should not, therefore, be 'completed' or amended by interpretation. See, e.g., WTO Appellate Body Report and Panel Report WT/DS2/AB/R of 20 May 1996 on *United States – Standards for Reformulated and Conventional Gasoline* 17 ('[A]pplying the basic principle

ordinary meaning of words, notably to avoid introducing 'unbargained for' concessions in the WTO legal framework.[200] This approach seems compatible with the Stockholm Study Group, which had requested that any exception to the right of reproduction be 'for clearly specified purposes'.[201]

Critiques of the panel's 'dictionary approach' (that is, ostensibly using the plain meaning of terms) are many.[202] However, it seems that with the WTO as arbiter of international intellectual property disputes concerning both the TRIPS Agreement and the Berne Convention (as incorporated into TRIPS), the 'dictionary approach,' is here to stay.[203] That being said, the view that there is (also) a normative element to the first step, which requires the demonstration of the existence of a valid public policy, is not incompatible with the analysis of both panel reports, especially the *Canada Pharmaceuticals* report.[204]

To summarize, most purpose-specific exceptions would pass the first step of the test. One could argue that an exception limited to a class of users is similarly limited in scope. It is less clear, however, that an open-ended 'fair use' provision would meet this part of the test.

### 3.3.1.2　Fair use cases[205]

Are open-ended exceptions such as fair use compatible with the first step of the test? Professor Ruth Okediji has suggested that fair use could be found to be incompatible with the first step of the test.[206] However,

---

of interpretation that the words of a treaty, like the *General Agreement*, are to be given their ordinary meaning, in their context and in the light of the treaty's object and purpose').

[200]　Gervais (n 98) 146.

[201]　*Records* (n 184) 112.

[202]　Daniel J Gervais, 'Towards A New Core International Copyright Norm: The Reverse Three-Step Test' (2005) 9 *Marquette Intellectual Property Law Review* 1.

[203]　In a second panel report regarding art. 30 (another instantiation of the test), which dealt with limitations contained in the Canadian Patent Act, the first step was interpreted as meaning 'limited' (e.g., for patents, limited to an area of technology). Those interpretations are more likely to guide future WTO panels called upon to apply the three-step test. See WTO Report of the Panel WT/DS114/R of 17 March 2000 on *Canada – Patent Protection of Pharmaceutical Products*.

[204]　Interestingly, Professor Ricketson agreed with this conclusion in the newer edition of his commentary, authored jointly with Professor Jane Ginsburg. See Sam Ricketson and Jane C Ginsburg, *International Copyright and Neighbouring Rights: The Berne Convention and Beyond*, vol. 1 (OUP 2006) 765–7.

[205]　See the Appendix explaining fair use and fair dealing in greater detail.

[206]　Ruth Okediji, 'Towards an International Fair Use Doctrine' (2000) 39

Professor Carlos Correa noted that the US Government has generally defended fair use as being compatible with TRIPS in TRIPS Council debates.[207] Others have suggested that fair use is best seen not as an exception or limitation per se, but rather as either a bundle of exceptions or as a *rule* allowing courts to *make* exceptions.[208] Indeed, fair use as it is found in section 107 of the US Copyright Act is a codification of case law that preceded the adoption of the 1976 Copyright Act. Seen in parallel, the test provides flexibility to WTO Members while fair use or fair dealing provide flexibility to courts.

Naturally, the US could ignore an adverse finding by the WTO, as it has done since 2000 with the ruling on the incompatibility of section 110(5)(b) of its Copyright Act.[209] However, the US Government likely prefer not to have to deal with what would surely be a significant political reaction to an anti-fair use ruling by the WTO.

Be that as it may, the arguments noted by Professor Okediji are important for our purposes. Theoretically:

> . . . today, the fair use doctrine may be directly challenged by foreign trade partners as inconsistent with [the] United States' obligations under international copyright treaties and indirectly by domestic interests which align with foreign trade partners to utilize international fora to alter the design of domestic copyright policy. . ..the fair use doctrine is inconsistent with the Berne Convention and the TRIPS Agreement because of its indeterminacy and breadth. . ..Unlike Article 9(2) of the Berne Convention and Article 13 of the TRIPS Agreement, the fair use doctrine is a broad exception to the rights granted to authors under the Copyright Act; it clearly is not limited to 'special' cases, unless one argues that special cases are of an ilk that has to do with an identified important policy objective, an argument which the Panel clearly rejected. To the contrary, Congress typically has provided exemptions from exclusive rights for 'special cases' through legislative enactments such as [the Fairness in Music Licensing Act (the Act which introduced the exception struck down by the WTO panel in the 110(5) cases)]. Further, the Panel noted that the potential scope of users of the exception is also relevant for determining whether the exception is sufficiently limited to qualify as a special case. The fair use doctrine, unlike the other legislative exemptions under the Copyright Act, is unlimited in the scope

---

*Columbia Journal of Transnational Law* 75. In the same article, however, she also argues for an international fair use doctrine.

[207] Carlos M Correa, *Trade Related Aspects of Intellectual Property Rights: A Commentary on the TRIPS Agreement* (OUP 2007) 146–8.

[208] Pamela Samuelson, 'Unbundling Fair Uses' (2009) 77 Fordham L Rev 2537; Justin Hughes, 'Fair Use and its Politics – At Home and Abroad' (2015) in Ruth Okediji (ed.) *Copyright in an Age of Exceptions and Limitations* (CUP 2015).

[209] An arbitrator ruled that the damage to European rights holders was less than $1.5MM/year—a small fee to pay to keep the exception.

of users because it is a defense potentially available to every defendant in a claim for copyright infringement.[210]

Though an open-ended permitted use provision such as the one found in the US Copyright Act may seem *semantically* incompatible with the first step of the test, it does not follow that it is normatively incompatible. It seems unlikely that a WTO panel (or, ultimately, the Appellate Body) would rule against an *abstract* rule like the four US fair use criteria even in an 'as such' challenge (that is, looking only at the text of the challenged legislative provision not to the way in which it is applied in the WTO Member concerned). A WTO panel could, however, rule on fair use as interpreted in a particular case ('as applied'), in part because of the need to show that actual economic harm resulted from the application of the exception. Professor Okediji suggests that a general finding of incompatibility of fair use with Berne/TRIPS is thus unlikely 'given the fact that the application of fair use is determined on a case-by-case basis and that results will vary with each court'.[211] In more recent work, Professors Geiger, Senftelben, and I have suggested that the test be seen as three steps forming a whole, which would make it easier to justify a legislative approach of using open-ended exceptions and limitations (E&Ls).[212]

### 3.3.2   Interference with Normal Commercial Exploitation

What is the meaning of 'exploitation' in the context of the second step of the test? It seems fairly straightforward: any use of the work by which the copyright holder tries to extract/maximize the value of her right.[213] 'Normal' is more troublesome. Does it refer to what is simply 'common' or does it refer to a normative standard? The question is particularly relevant for new forms and emerging business models that have not, thus far, been common or 'normal' in an empirical sense. As noted above, at the revision of the Berne Convention in Stockholm in 1967, the concept was used to refer to 'all forms of exploiting a work, which have, or are likely to acquire, considerable economic or practical importance'.[214]

Professor Paul Goldstein has suggested that the purpose of the second

---

[210]   Okediji (n 206) 115, 126–28.

[211]   Ibid., 131.

[212]   Christophe Geiger, Daniel Gervais, and Martin Senftleben, 'The Three-Step Test Revisited: How to Use the Test's Flexibility in National Copyright Law' (2014) 29 *American University International Law Review* 581–626.

[213]   Ficsor (n 183) s 5.56.

[214]   *Records* (n 184) 112.

step is to 'fortify authors' interests in their accustomed markets against local legislative inroads'.[215] According to his view, the condition is thus normative in nature: an exception is not allowed if it covers any form of exploitation which has, or is likely to acquire, considerable economic importance. In other words, if the exception is used to limit a commercially significant market or, a fortiori, to enter into competition with the copyright holder, the exception is prohibited.[216] The WTO panel on the *US section 110(5)* case seemed to agree with this approach. It concluded as follows:

> [I]t appears that one way of measuring the normative connotation of normal exploitation is to consider, in addition to those forms of exploitation that currently generate significant or tangible revenue, those forms of exploitation which, with a certain degree of likelihood and plausibility, could acquire considerable economic or practical importance.[217]

### 3.3.3   Unreasonable Prejudice to Legitimate Interests of Rights Holder

The third step is perhaps the most difficult to interpret. What is an 'unreasonable prejudice', and what are 'legitimate interests'?

Let us start with 'legitimate'. As with the first step, it can be interpreted in at least two different ways. 'Legitimate' can mean sanctioned or authorized by law or principle. Alternatively, it can just as well be used to denote something that is normal or regular. To put it differently, are legitimate interests only legally protected interests? If the second, broader view is preferred, the third step could reflect a systemic option to balance the rights of copyright holders and users.[218]

---

[215]   Paul Goldstein, *International Copyright: Principles, Law, and Practice* (OUP 1998) 295; see also Ficsor, (n 183) 516.

[216]   An example of the scope of an exception based on non-commercially significant use can be found in HR 3261, 108th Cong. (2003) s. 4(b), also known as the Database and Collections of Misappropriation Act, which would allow the:

> making available in commerce of a substantial part of a database by a nonprofit scientific or research institution, including an employee or agent of such institution acting within the scope of such employment or agency, for nonprofit scientific or research purposes ... if the court determines that the making available in commerce of the information in the database is reasonable under the circumstances, taking into consideration the customary practices associated with such uses of such database by nonprofit scientific or research institutions and other factors that the court determines relevant.

[217]   Panel Report (n 195) para. 6.180.

[218]   Martin Senftleben, *Copyright, Limitations and the Three-Step Test: An Analysis of the Three-Step Test in International and EC Copyright Law* (Kluwer 2004) 226–7:

At the 1967 Stockholm Conference (Berne Convention Revision), the UK took the view that 'legitimate' had the first meaning, namely 'sanctioned by law'. Other countries seemed to take a broader view of the term as meaning 'supported by social norms and relevant public policies'.[219] The WTO dispute-settlement panel report in the *US s. 110(5)* case concluded that the combination of the notion of 'prejudice' with that of 'interests' pointed clearly towards a legal-normative approach. In other words, 'legitimate interests' are those that are protected by law.[220] The interpretation might have been different if the third step of the test had been formulated as 'the reproduction not contrary to the legitimate interests of the author'. An author may be said to have noneconomic interest beyond those protected by law (that is, beyond the limited moral right contained in Article 6*bis* of the Berne Convention, which in any event is unenforceable in a WTO dispute-settlement procedure[221]). Whether this interpretation is consonant with other instantiations of the test in TRIPS is questionable. For example, in Article 30 of the Agreement, the third step refers to 'legitimate interests of the patent owner, *taking account of the legitimate interests of third parties*'. It seems difficult to argue that third parties' interests are limited to their legal rights.

---

[C]opyright law is centered round the delicate balance between grants and reservations. On one side of this balance, the economic and non-economic interests of authors of already existing works can be found. On the other side, the interests of users – a group encompassing authors wishing to build upon the work of their predecessors – are located. If a proper balance between the concerns of authors and users is to be struck, both sides must necessarily take a step towards the center. The two elements of the third criterion (legitimate interests and unreasonable prejudice) mirror these two steps. The authors cannot assert each and every concern. Instead, only legitimate interests are relevant. As a countermove, the users recognise that copyright limitations in their favor must keep within reasonable limits.

[219]    See generally, *Records* (n 184) (republished in WIPO, *1886–1986: Berne Convention Centenary* (WIPO 1986) 192–219).
[220]    Panel Report (n 195) paras 6.223–6.229. In para. 6.224 the Panel tried to reconcile the two approaches:

the term relates to lawfulness from a legal positivist perspective, but it has also the connotation of legitimacy from a more normative perspective, in the context of calling for the protection of interests that are justifiable in the light of the objectives that underlie the protection of exclusive rights.

[221]    TRIPS Agreement (n 191) art. 9(1). Although art 1–21 of the Berne Convention and its Appendix (see Chapter 2) were incorporated by reference, WTO '[m]embers shall not have rights or obligations under this Agreement in respect of the rights conferred under Article 6bis of that Convention or of the rights derived therefrom'.

Be that as it may, it leaves open one key question for the test in the copyright field: what is an 'unreasonable' prejudice?[222] The presence of the word 'unreasonable' indicates that some level or degree of prejudice is justified. For example, while a country might exempt the making of a small number of private copies entirely, it may be required to impose a compensation scheme, such as a levy, when the prejudice level becomes unjustified.[223] This meshes with the discussion over the past 35 years or so concerning private copying and use, and the 'death by 1,000 cuts' phenomenon, whereby the behaviour of a single copyright user is not an issue but it becomes one (for the right holders) when thousands of users avail themselves of the private copying exception.[224] The idea here, although not one expressly codified in any multilateral treaty, is that when a form of use becomes unstoppable—as a technical matter and/or as a normative one because it should not be stopped—normal commercial exploitation becomes difficult. A remuneration system may then (some would say must[225]) be put in place.

To buttress the view that valid normative reasons may exist to limit the reach of exclusive rights whether as a full exception or a limitation accompanied by remuneration, the French version of the Berne Convention, which governs in case of a discrepancy between the linguistic versions,[226] uses the expression '*préjudice injustifié*', which translates literally as 'unjustified prejudice'. The Convention translators opted instead for 'not unreasonable'.[227] The inclusion of a reasonableness/justifiability criterion allows legislators to establish a balance between the rights of authors and other copyright holders, and the needs and interests of users. In other words, there should be a public interest justification to limit copyright. Naturally, while the public interest may coincide with users' interests, they are not synonymous. It is also in the public interest that there be a balanced protection for authors and other rights holders.

The WTO panel concluded that 'prejudice to the legitimate interests of right holders reaches an unreasonable level if an exception or limitation

---

[222]   It is worth noting that 'not unreasonable prejudice' is not quite the same as 'reasonable prejudice'. 'Not unreasonable' connotes a slightly stricter threshold (See Panel Report (n 195) para. 6.225).

[223]   *Records* (n 184) 1145–46.

[224]   Ficsor (n 183) 310–17, 340–46.

[225]   Ricketson and Ginsberg (n 204) 317: '[R]emuneration for private copying ... is a compulsory license for the exercise of the reproduction right'. See also Ricketson and Ginsberg (n 204) Ch. 13.

[226]   Berne Convention (n 182) art. 31.

[227]   *Records* (n 184) 1145.

causes or has the potential to cause an unreasonable loss of income to the copyright holder'.[228] A public interest imperative may lead a government to impose an exception to copyright that may translate into a loss of revenue for copyright holders. It can nonetheless be 'justified'. By focusing on economic harm, the panel may have considerably expanded the scope of exceptions: it is not the fact that a user obtained value that is determinative, but rather the fact that a rights holder can show that it lost actual value (revenue), i.e., the existence of a prejudice.[229]

### 3.3.3.1 The impact on existing markets

The incontrovertible net result of the WTO panel reports is that any exception without compensation must be measured against any demonstrable loss of income for right holders. The policy tool that would seem best to embody this is to situate the exception in an income stream target. At the centre of the target are core income streams (see Figure 3.1 below). To translate this into commercial terms, would the exception significantly limit existing sales or licensing income or, under the second step, prevent the right holder from trying to sell or license (i.e., the 'trial and error' establishment of commercial exploitation)? Any exception that does is almost certainly incompatible with the second and probably also the third step of the test. Exceptions that demonstrably affect significant income streams are also interfering with normal commercial exploitation, unless

---

[228] Panel Report (n 195) para. 6.229.

[229] This is reinforced by the later finding of an arbitration panel, convened to decide the level of harm caused by the US' refusal to modify its law to bring it into conformity with the Panel's findings. Under the WTO Dispute Settlement Understanding (DSU), which governs the WTO dispute-settlement process, a party may ask for arbitration if another party fails to implement an adopted Panel (or Appellate Body) decision. Because the US failed to implement the Panel report (which is still true as of March 2004—the WTO had ordered the US to bring the exemption in line with the Panel's ruling by July 27, 2001), the EU asked for arbitration and decision on the level of harm, which was determined to be $1.1 million/year. The EU has proposed levying a fee on copyrighted material against US nationals unless the US reforms its law. See United States – Section 110(5) of the US Copyright Act: Recourse by the United States to Article 22.6 of the DSU (WT/DS160/22, WTO March 1, 2002); United States – Section 110(5) of the US Copyright Act: Recourse by the European Communities and its Member States to Article 22.6 of the DSU (WT/DS160/21, WTO February 19, 2002); United States – Section 110(5) of the US Copyright Act: Recourse by the European Communities to Article 22.2 of the DSU (WT/DS160/19 WTO January 11, 2002); United States – Section 110(5) of the US Copyright Act: Arbitration under Article 21.3(c) of the Understanding on Rules and Procedures Governing the Settlement of Disputes (WT/DS160/12, WTO January 15, 2001).

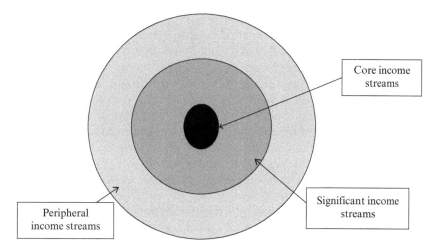

*Figure 3.1   Level of relevance of income stream for purposes of three-step-test analysis*

no commercial transaction or license is possible under the circumstances. To pass the test, an exception must, therefore, be narrowly defined (the first step) and touch essentially peripheral income streams.

Could a public interest justification 'compensate' for prima facie incompatibility with test? An exception with compensation (i.e., negating the loss of income) would probably pass the third step of the test. The second step is more difficult. If a rights holder can show that the exception prevents him from exploiting a 'market', then the normative basis for the justification would not be sufficient to compensate.

What about the public interest as overriding consideration? The public interest has been used successfully as a defence in a few UK cases, but those cases dealt with particular works (e.g., a photograph of Princess Diana on the day of her accident or the text of a ministerial briefing note[230]), though not with classes of works or users. In addition, in those cases, users had a positive right to exercise against the copyright, namely freedom of expression and information. It would be theoretically possible to add a provision to the statute that allows courts to not enforce copyright when a countervailing public interest justification supports such a decision. Others might think this unnecessary because courts can (based on equitable rules) refuse certain remedies (e.g., injunctions) and they already have some flexibility.

---

[230]   *Ashdown v Telegraph Group Ltd* [2001] EWCA Civ 1142; [2002] Ch 149; *Hyde Park Residence Ltd v Yelland*, [2000] EWCA Civ J0210-2; [2001] Ch 143.

### 3.3.3.2 The importance of prospective markets

How can a right holder demonstraté the existence of a market and thus be able to invoke incompatibility of a limitation or exception with the second step? If a market is already well-established for the form of exploitation concerned, then the burden of proof is easily met. If not, the right holder could demonstrate the existence of a market in a relevant jurisdiction. For example, if a rights holder could show that an important market is successfully exploited in other countries B, and exploitation is prevented because of an exception in country A, then prima facie incompatibility of country A's law would arguably be established.

A more difficult question is the impact on *prospective* markets, especially on the Internet. Interpreting the three-step test as applying only to established markets could stifle investment in new technology and new markets. Conversely, considering interference with any prospective market, no matter how remote, would basically render almost all limitations and exceptions incompatible with the second step. The test was not meant to go that far. First, the interference must affect an income stream (whether actual or prospective) that is sufficiently close to the centre of the target.[231] Second, the prospective market must be reasonably predictable in both time and scope.[232]

## 3.4   APPLICATION OF THE THREE-STEP TEST IN NATIONAL AND REGIONAL LEGISLATION

### 3.4.1   European Union Implementation

The European Union's Information Society ('InfoSoc') Directive[233] contains exceptions that are all purpose-specific. In other words, there is no set of criteria comparable to the US fair use doctrine.[234] However, the preamble to this Directive, which serves as a guideline for the interpretation of the operative part of the text,[235] refers to permitting

---

[231]   Figure 3.1 above.

[232]   As decided by the French Civil Supreme Court in 2006: Cass Civ 1re, 28 feb 2006, JCP 2006 II, 10084, note Lucas, Comm Com électr 2006, comm 56, note Caron, A&M 2/2006, p 177, note Dussolier, Propriété Intellectuelle 2006, p 179, obs Lucas.

[233]   European Parliament and Council Directive 2001/29/EC of 22 May 2001 on the harmonisation of certain aspects of copyright and related rights in the information society [2001] OJ L167/10.

[234]   See 17 USC § 107.

[235]   Infosoc Directive (n 233).

'exceptions or limitations in the public interest for the purpose of education and teaching' and to the need to safeguard a 'fair balance of rights and interests between the different categories of right holders, as well as between the different categories of right holders and users' through exceptions and limitations, which 'have to be reassessed in the light of the new electronic environment'.[236] The Directive also refers to the three-step test as an overarching test for exceptions. Article 5(5) reads:

> The exceptions and limitations provided for in paragraphs 1, 2, 3 and 4 shall only be applied in certain special cases which do not conflict with a normal exploitation of the work or other subject matter and do not unreasonably prejudice the legitimate interests of the right holder.

This reference to the test was described as a 'guiding principle' rather than an effective means to harmonize exceptions in the national laws of the 25 EU member states[237] because, at the level of national laws, the three-step test may be refined by enumerating certain specific cases.[238] It can also be used as a flexible test employed by courts in cases where no such specific exception exists, if domestic law permits. In implementing the Directive, a number of EU member states decided to include the test. In doing so, they usually skipped the first step, presumably because limitations and exceptions taken individually represent 'special cases' by nature. This is consonant with what I previously argued,[239] namely that, in almost every case, there are really only two *operational* steps.[240] EU countries where the second and third steps form part of national law now include

---

[236] Ibid., paras 14, 31.
[237] See Senftleben (n 218) 246–8.
[238] Bernt Hugenholtz, 'Why the Copyright Directive Is Unimportant, and Possibly Invalid' (2000) 22 *European Intellectual Property Review* 499, 501:

> What makes the Directive a total failure, in terms of harmonization, is that the exemptions allowed under article 5 are optional, not mandatory (except for 5.1). Member States are not obliged to implement the entire list, but may pick and choose at will. It is expected most Member States will prefer to keep intact their national laws as much as possible. At best, some countries will add one or two exemptions from the list, now bearing the EC's seal of approval. So much for approximation!

The University of Amsterdam made available the text of an illuminating study prepared for the European Commission on the Infosoc Directive (see <http://www.ivir.nl/publications/guibault/Infosoc_report_2007.pdf> last accessed May 11, 2015).

[239] Gervais (n 98).
[240] The Greek copyright law contains the first step as well.

at least: Croatia, France, Spain, Portugal and Greece. Australia and Mexico, among others, have also added the test to their legislative arsenal. National laws and the practices of a number of individual countries are discussed below.

The InfoSoc Directive is not the first directive to refer to the test. A version of the test is included in the Software Directive,[241] where it is used both as a guide in the preamble[242] and as a restriction on the scope of exceptions in Article 6(3).[243] It is also contained in Article 8(2) of the EU Database Directive, where it forms part of the main provisions.[244]

### 3.4.2 National Implementations

At national level, the three-step test may be applied as a binding international norm by courts in two situations, even absent a direct implementation in national law. First, courts may apply the test in any country where international treaties have direct application in the national legal order.[245] Thus, it is likely to surface in court decisions, as it did in France, for cases concerning private copying of films—discussed below.[246] Second, courts may also use the test in countries where national laws (e.g., exciting exceptions) are interpreted wherever possible in harmony with international norms.[247]

---

[241] Council Directive 91/250/EEC of 14 May 1991 on the legal protection of computer programs [1991] OJ L122/42.

[242] Ibid., 43: '[S]uch an exception to the author's exclusive rights may not be used in a way which prejudices the legitimate interests of the right holder or which conflicts with a normal exploitation of the program.'

[243] Ibid., 45: '[T]he provisions of this Article may not be interpreted in such a way as to allow its application to be used in a manner which unreasonably prejudices the right holder's legitimate interests or conflicts with a normal exploitation of the computer program.'

[244] European Parliament and Council Directive 96/9/EC of 11 March 1996 on the legal protection of databases: 'A lawful user of a database which is made available to the public in whatever manner may not perform acts which conflict with normal exploitation of the database or unreasonably prejudice the legitimate interests of the maker of the database.'

[245] See Jane C Ginsburg, 'Toward Supranational Copyright Law? The WTO Panel Decision and the "Three-Step Test" for Copyright Exceptions' (2001) 187 Revue Internationale du Droit d'Auteur 3, 7.

[246] Ibid.; see also Daniel Gervais, 'La copie privée face au test en trois étapes' (2007) 133–5 Gazette du Palais 15.

[247] Gervais (n 109).

### 3.4.2.1 Australia

In Australia, the Copyright Amendment Act 2006[248] contained the following provision:

200AB Use of works and other subject-matter for certain purposes
  (1)  The copyright in a work or other subject-matter is not infringed by a use of the work or other subject-matter if all the following conditions exist:
    (a)  the circumstances of the use (including those described in paragraphs (b), (c) and (d)) *amount to a special case*;
    (b)  the use is covered by subsection (2), (3) or (4);
    (c)  the use *does not conflict with a normal exploitation of the work* or other subject-matter;
    (d)  the use *does not unreasonably prejudice the legitimate interests of the owner of the copyright*.[249]

This provision applies to exceptions contained in that section, but not (by operation of sub-sections 200AB(1)(b) and 200AB(6)) if the use of the work is non-infringing for another reason (e.g., a reproduction of less than a substantial part, limitation on the right itself, or the making of a Braille version of a published literary work, which amounts to a compulsory license). The three-step test was not only incorporated in the Act (all three steps, contrary to most other national implementations which focus only on the last two), but was also a central consideration in preparing this Bill, partly because it was included in the Australia-US Free Trade Agreement.[250]

In addition to being addressed directly to courts in section 200AB, the three-step test was used to justify limitations in the formulation of exceptions. For example, on private copying the government declared, during the debate on the Bill, that '[t]he "one copy in each format" condition is to protect copyright owners from this exception being abused, as well as to ensure that the exception complies with the three-step test'.[251]

The Senate Committee that sought to examine the constitutionality of the Bill noted that there was 'evidence which highlighted opposing views on how the three-step test should be implemented in domestic legislation.

---

[248]  No. 158, 2006.
[249]  Ibid. (emphasis added).
[250]  Art. 17.4.10(a) (available at <http://dfat.gov.au/about-us/publications/trade-investment/australia-united-states-free-trade-agreement/Pages/chapter-seventeen-intellectual-property-rights.aspx> accessed 30 September 2015).
[251]  Submission 69A to the Senate Standing Committee on Legal and Constitutional Affairs, 3 (available at <www.aph.gov.au/Parliamentary_Business/Committees/Senate/Legal_and_Constitutional_Affairs/Completed_inquiries/2004-07/copyright06/submissions/sublist> accessed 30 September 2015).

Proposed section 200AB seeks to provide an open-ended exception in line with the US model, and to allow courts to determine if other uses should be permitted as exceptions to copyright'.[252] Critics pointed to the lack of clarity of the test and the move towards a 'lawyer-based copyright regime – a litigious model'.[253] The government's response on this key point was as follows:

> We are aware that some user interests think that it is unduly restrictive. Given that the three-step test already has to be complied with, there is an argument that should be enough, that the government should go as far as the three-step test allows. But we note in passing that the three-step test is not an obligation; you only have to go as far as you can go under the treaty obligations. The government is also aware that some copyright owner interests think that the provision is too broad and that the commercial advantage test should be narrowed even further. In the present drafting the government has sought to find a balance between those interests, recognising that this is a new exception that is different in form to some of the specific exceptions already in the Copyright Act. Therefore, the government is minded to try to balance what are reasonable interests on both sides—the copyright holders and users.

* * *

> The Government introduced the 'commercial advantage' test in recognition of concerns about the potential scope of the new exception. Indeed the Government notes arguments on behalf of some copyright holders that s 200AB is presently too wide in being potentially available to for profit schools and libraries in commercial companies and should be narrowed so that no commercial advantage, direct or indirect, can be obtained from reliance on this section.[254]

For its part, the Labour party (which, incidentally, formed the subsequent government) noted the following in the Senate report:

> Labor Senators are of the view that the particular way the Government has chosen to embody the three-step test in the Bill is problematic and an example of poor drafting that will no doubt lead to confusion and uncertainty in practice. Not only will judges be required to interpret the three-step test, but so will the users to which the exceptions apply. This is not only impractical, but also potentially costly to those user groups who may have to seek expert advice on how to properly interpret the three-step test.[255]

---

[252]  The Senate, 'Standing Committee on Legal and Constitutional Affairs: Copyright Amendment Bill 2006 [Provisions]' (Senate Printing Unit 2006) 24.

[253]  Ibid., 24–5.

[254]  Ibid., 25–6.

[255]  Ibid., 47.

The 2006 amendments limit available flexibilities but they provide an almost ironclad guarantee of TRIPS compatibility, clearly a dominant consideration in making the policy decisions that led to its adoption. Only if Australian courts were to stray too far from WTO panel interpretations would a possible case of incompatibility with TRIPS be made. This is highly unlikely because their deliberations no doubt will be guided in that respect by section 200AB(7), which defines 'conflict with a normal exploitation' and 'unreasonably prejudice the legitimate interests' as having 'the same meaning as in Article 13 of the TRIPS Agreement'. The provision must still be interpreted by higher courts to ascertain its impact.[256]

### 3.4.2.2 Belgium

In Belgium, while the three-step test was not expressly included in the amendments to the Copyright Act, it was specifically mentioned during parliamentary debates as a governing consideration.[257] As was noted in the parliamentary report, the test should serve as a *guideline for courts and tribunals when applying the law*.[258] Most copyright scholars have taken the view that Belgian courts should be able to apply the test directly.[259]

The government was initially of the view that the test should not be included *tel quel* in the Act, i.e., as an overarching provision applying to all existing exceptions, though it agreed that courts could use it as a 'guide' when the scope of application of an exception was unclear.[260] The Minister stated:

> It would be a bad signal if the legislature included the test in the statute. One could conclude that the legislature is not certain that national exceptions are

---

[256] See generally, Catherine Bond, Abi Paramaguru, and Graham Greenleaf, 'Advance Australia Fair?: The Copyright Reform Process' (2007) 10 *Journal of World Intellectual Property* 284.

[257] Document parlementaire, Législature 51 (2003-2007), 1137/013, 15, 26 (available at <http://www.lachambre.be/FLWB/PDF/51/1137/51K1137013.pdf> accessed 18 November 2016).

[258] Document parlementaire, Législature 51 (2003-2007), 1137/001, comment to art. 4 (available at <http://www.lachambre.be/FLWB/pdf/51/1137/51K1137001.pdf> accessed 18 November 2016).

[259] S Dusollier, 'Les nouvelles dispositions belges en matière de protection technique du droit d'auteur et des droits voisins' [2005] A&M 564; Alain Strowel and François Tulkens (eds), *Droit d'auteur et Liberté d'Expression* (Larcier 2006); M Buydens and S Dusollier, 'Les exceptions au droit d'auteur: évolutions dangereuses' [2001] CCE 10; Jean-Paul Triaille, 'La directive sur le droit d'auteur du 22 mai 2001 et l'acquis communautaire' [2002] A&M 11.

[260] S Dusollier, 'Le dernier tournant de l'affaire *Mulholland Drive*' [2006] A&M 178.

consistent with the three-step test. The government therefore wants to avoid creating legal uncertainty.[261]

However, in amendments to the Belgian Act, the test was used as a limit to specific new exceptions. For instance, section 22*bis*(1) allows:

> . . .the partial or complete reproduction in any medium other than on paper or similar medium, when the reproduction is made for purposes of illustration for teaching or scientific research to the extent justified by the non-profit aim and provided it does not prejudice the normal exploitation of the work.[262]

### 3.4.2.3   Croatia

In Croatia, the three-step test is part of the legislative framework. Section 80 of the Copyright Act reads as follows:

> Disclosed copyright work may be used without the author's authorization, or without the author's authorization and without payment of remuneration, only in the cases which are expressly stipulated in this Act. The provisions concerning the limitations referred to in this Chapter cover only such uses of a copyright work which *do not conflict with regular use of the work and do not unreasonably prejudice the legitimate interests of the author*.[263]

### 3.4.2.4   France

In France, the three-step test has become a central element for both lawmakers and courts. The test is included in whole or in part in several articles of the *Intellectual Property Code,* namely Article L 122-6-1 (1994—software reverse engineering), Article L 513-6 (2001—exception for teaching that applies to industrial designs), Articles L 122-5 CPI and L 211-3 (2006—exception to authors' rights and neighbouring rights, respectively), and Article L 331-9 (2006—authority set up to review the reach of anti-circumvention protection). For example, Article L 331-9 reads in part as follows:

> The provisions of this Article may, to the extent technically possible, condition the practical benefit of those exceptions on lawful access to the work or phonogram, videogram or program and ensure that they do not have the effect of undermining the normal operation and do not unreasonably

---

[261]   Joris Deene and Katrien Van der Perre, 'Nieuwe auteurswet: belang van de digitale wereld' (2005) 119 Nieuw Juridisch Weekblad 866 (quoted in the Belgian Report to the ALAI 2007 Congress (Punta del Este, November 2007)).

[262]   (Emphasis added.)

[263]   WIPO (tr), *Copyright and Related Rights Act* (O.G. 167/2003) para. 80 (emphasis added).

prejudice the legitimate interests of the rightholder in the work or the protected object.[264]

In the now famous *Mulholland Drive* case,[265] a consumer organization argued that anti-circumvention technology (TPM) prevented the making of a (lawful) private copy. A court of first instance in Paris refused to grant the relief sought. The Paris Court of Appeal disagreed and concluded that *there was no evidence* that private copying would interfere with normal commercial exploitation.[266] The Cour de cassation (civil supreme court) found that copying of digital copies of a film *could* constitute a violation of at least the second step (normal commercial exploitation):

> With respect to the normal exploitation of the work, whether this factor must be calculated to exclude the private copying exception must be assessed *in relation to the risks that the new digital environment inherently poses* to copyright and the preservation of the economic importance that the exploitation of the work in DVD format has for the amortization of the costs of film production.[267]

It remanded the case to the Court of Appeal, which found in April 2007 that the matter was moot because the consumer had no private copying *right*. In that case, the courts basically skipped over the first step of the test ('special cases') and focused on the last two steps.

### 3.4.2.5 Germany

In Germany, the test was applied by the *Bundesgerichthof* [Federal Supreme Court] *in the Kopienversandienst* case.[268] The court noted that providing adequate remuneration for the author would eliminate the unreasonableness of the prejudice to the right holders' interests and also possibly the conflict with a normal exploitation possibly caused by an exception.

---

[264] (Emphasis added.)
[265] M Stéphane P, 'UFC Que Choisir c/ SA Films Alain Sarde, SA Universal pictures video France et autres' (2004) juriscom.net (available at <http://juriscom.net/2004/04/tgi-paris-30-avril-2004-m-stephane-p-ufc-que-choisir-c-sa-films-alain-sarde-sa-universal-pictures-video-france-et-autres/> accessed 7 October 2015): Attendu que la copie d'une *œuvre filmographique éditée sur support numérique ne peut ainsi que porter atteinte à l'exploitation normale de l'œuvre . . .*' (emphasis added, note the double negative).
[266] See the commentary in Appendix 2 for full citations.
[267] (Emphasis added.)
[268] *Kopienversanddienst*, Bundesgerichthof, BGH, 29 March 2001, case I ZR 182/98, GRUR 1999, 707; GRUR Int. 2002, 170. See also *Elektronischer Pressespiegel*, Bundesgerichthof, BGH, 11 July 2002, case I ZR 255/00, GRUR 2002, 963.

### 3.4.2.6 Greece

In Greece, a number of exceptions and limitations in the Copyright Act are expressly subject to the three-step test: Article 18(2) (private use), Article 20(2) (reproduction of literary works for teaching purposes), Article 20(3) (reproduction of works of a deceased author in an anthology), Article 28(3) (public presentation of works of fine art in museums, and their reproduction in catalogues), and Article 43(3) (reverse engineering of a computer program).[269] The legislator added a new Article 28C, which applies the three-step test as a filter to all exceptions.[270]

### 3.4.2.7 Hungary

In Hungary, there was an interesting Opinion issued in 2006 by a national committee of copyright experts on the impact of the three-step test.[271] The Opinion followed a petition filed by the Public Foundation for the Protection of Copyright in Audiovisual Works (ASVA), asking whether the general rules of the Copyright Act concerning free use[272] and its specific rules concerning private copying[273] were compatible with the three-step test. The Opinion notes first the difference between copyright and neighbouring rights, stating that:

> the Stockholm diplomatic conference dealt with an explicit proposal that private copying should be recognized as an exception to the right of reproduction without any further condition whatsoever (the reason of which must have been found in the fact that, in the 1960s, the devices that now make copying so easy, perfect and massive did not exist yet), but rejected it,

while under:

---

[269] Law No. 2121/1993 on Copyright, Related Rights and Cultural Matters (as amended up to Law No. 4281/2014).

[270] 'Greek Report' in Association Littéraire et Artistique Internationale Congress, *The Author's Place in XXI Century Copyright: The Challenges of Modernization,* (ALAI 2007, CD-ROM) s 2.3.4.

[271] Council of Copyright Experts Opinion SZJSZT 17/2006 of May 11, 2006 on the copyright status of private copying from illegal sources, (text on file with author).

[272] WIPO (tr), Act No LXXVI of 1999, on Copyright, ss 33(2)–(3).

[273] Ibid., s. 35(1), which reads as follows:

A copy of the work may be made by anyone for private purpose if it is not designed for earning or increasing income even in an indirect way. This provision shall not apply to architectural works, engineering structures, software and databases operated by a computing device as well as to the fixation of the public performance of a work on video or sound carrier.

Article 15.1(a) of the Rome Convention on the protection of neighboring rights (that is, the rights of performers, producers of phonograms and broadcasting organizations), the Contracting States may introduce exceptions for private copying – and for private use in general – without any further condition.[274]

The view expressed by the Committee is reinforced by the fact that Article 13 of the TRIPS Agreement only applies to copyright proper and not to related rights (in art. 14). The Opinion distinguishes the *addressees* of the three steps. It argues that the first step is addressed to legislators (i.e., an obligation to have well-defined exceptions justified by public interest considerations), and the second and third steps, to courts. The Panel concluded, based on 'international, community and national norms on copyright that private copying from illegal sources' was not permissible 'as a free use [or] on the basis of the limitation of the exclusive right of reproduction to a mere right to remuneration'.[275]

### 3.4.2.8 Netherlands

In the Netherlands, the three-step test was incorporated in section 4 of the Dutch *Databankenwet* [Law on the Protection of Databases].[276] The possibility of including the three-step test *tel quel* in the Dutch *Auteurswet*[277] [Copyright Act] was discussed but, in the end, the legislature opted to create specific exceptions compatible with the test, together with a determination that extant exceptions were also compatible with test. Doctrinal sources seem to agree that the test may, however, be used by national courts to interpret both older and newer exceptions.[278]

---

[274] Opinion SZJSZT 17/2006 (n 271).

[275] Ibid., 19.

[276] Wet van 8 juli 1999, houdende aanpassing van de Nederlandse wetgeving aan richtlijn 96/9/EG van het Europees Parlement en de Raad van 11 maart 1996 betreffende de rechtsbescherming van databanken [Law of July 8, 1999, Adaptation of the Dutch Legislation to the Directive 96/9/EC of the European Parliament and the Council of 11 March 1996 on the Legal Protection of Databases] (available at <http://www.wipo.int/wipolex/en/details.jsp?id=9893> last accessed 17 November 2016).

[277] Wet van 23 september 1912, 'houdende nieuwe regeling van het auteursrecht' [Act of September 23, 1912, containing New Regulation for Copyright] (available at <http://www.wipo.int/wipolex/en/details.jsp?id=12810>> last accessed 17 November 2016).

[278] See H Cohen Jehoram, 'Nu de gevolgen van trouw en ontrouw aan de *Auteursrechtrichtlijn voor fair use, tijdelijke reproductie en driestappentoets*' (2005) 5 Tijdschrift voor Auteurs-, Media- en Informatierecht 153; K J Koelman, 'De nationale driestappentoets' (2003) 1 Tijdschrift voor Auteurs-, Media- en Informatierecht 6; see also Senftleben (n 218) 278–81.

Dutch courts did in fact rely on the test even before its incorporation in the InfoSoc Directive, as an applicable norm of international law. In a 1990 case known as *'Zienderogen Kunst'*, the *Hoge Raad* [Dutch Supreme Court] used the three-step test (then only contained in art. 9(2) of the Berne Convention) in holding that a quotation from a work should not unreasonably prejudice the right holder's interests in the commercial exploitation of the work concerned.[279] In 2003, the *Gerechtshof Amsterdam* [Amsterdam Court of Appeals] found that a parody did not harm the normal exploitation of the work because it was intended for a different market.[280]

In a 2005 decision concerning the making of digital press reviews for internal use in government departments, a court in *Rechtbank's-Gravenhage* [Hague Court] applied the three-step test contained in Article 5(5) of the InfoSoc Directive. The court held that the practice of scanning and reproducing newspaper articles for distribution within the department(s) in question was incompatible with the test. A previous Dutch decision had allowed the practice but only on paper.[281] The Hague Court took the view that extending this exception to the digital realm would violate the test. The finding was criticized,[282] one report noting that the court:

> took the view that 'a normal exploitation' of newspaper articles in the sense of the three-step test included their digital exploitation. It pointed out that emerging digital markets for newspaper services were becoming more and more important. Against this background, the digital government press reviews were found to 'jeopardize' the normal exploitation (second condition of the three-step test) and to unreasonably prejudice the publishers' legitimate interests (third condition). The Court added that, even if a normal exploitation was understood not to extend to digital forms of exploitation, the press reviews would still unreasonably prejudice the publishers' legitimate interest in promising future markets. Digital format, inevitably, offered enhanced possibilities of searching and archiving press articles. The extension of the analogue press review limitation to the digital environment would thus impede

---

[279]  Hoge Raad, June 22, 1990, no. 13933, Nederlandse Jurisprudentie 1991, 268, with comment by J Spoor; *Informatierecht/AMI* 1990, 202, with comment by Dommering; *Ars Aequi* 40 1991, 672, with comment by H Cohen Jehoram; cf Hoge Raad, June 26, 1992, no. 14695, Nederlandse Jurisprudentie 1993, 205, with comment by Verkade. Based on 'Dutch Report' in Association Littéraire et Artistique Internationale Congress, *The Author's Place in XXI Century Copyright: The Challenges of Modernization* (ALAI 2007, CD-ROM) s 2.3.1.
[280]  Gerechtshof Amsterdam [Amsterdam Court of Appeals], January 30, 2003, [2003] Tijdschrift voor Auteurs-, Media- en Informatierecht 94.
[281]  Hoge Raad, November 10, 1995, Nederlandse Jurisprudentie 1996, 177.
[282]  Kamiel Koelman, 'Fixing the Three-Step Test' (2006) 28 *European Intellectual Property Review* 407.

the exploitation of important additional possibilities of use. In respect of the conceptual contours of the three-step test, it can be inferred from this decision that the term 'a normal exploitation' may be understood to include potential future markets.[283]

Interestingly, none of those Dutch decisions seem to pay any attention to the first step of the test and focus instead on the last two.

The leading case post implementation of the InfoSoc Directive is ACI Adam, a decision by the Court of Justice of the European Union following a request made in 2012 for a preliminary ruling under Article 267 TFEU from the Hoge Raad (Supreme Court) of the Netherlands.[284] The Court was asked to decide whether the three-step test (referred to in the opinion as the 'three-stage test') could be used to expand the scope of an exception or only lead to the reduction of the scope of the limitation. The specific questions under consideration were the status of a private copying exception and accompanying levy, and whether it should distinguish between copies of material acquired legally or illegally. The Court opted for a restrictive interpretation of the private copying exception and for its inapplicability to unauthorized copies.

### 3.4.2.9 Spain

In Spain, the three-step test was introduced in the *Ley 22/1987 de Propiedad Intelectual* [Law on Intellectual Property][285] in Article 40*bis*, which reads as follows:

Los artículos del presente capítulo no podrán interpretarse de manera tal que permitan us aplicación de forma que causen un perjuicio injustificado a los intereses legítimos del autor o que vayan en detriment de la explotación normal de las obras a que se refieran.
[The Articles of this Chapter may not be so interpreted that they could be applied in a manner capable of unreasonably prejudicing the legitimate interests of the author or adversely affecting the normal exploitation of the works to which they refer.][286]

---

[283] Dutch Report (n 279).

[284] ACI Adam BV et al v. Stichting de Thuiskopie et al. Case C-435/12, 10 April 2014.

[285] Ley N° 22/1987, de 11 de noviembre de 1987 de Propiedad Intelectual [Law No. 22/1987 of November 11, 1987, on Intellectual Property] (available at <http://www.wipo.int/wipolex/en/text.jsp?file_id=126599> accessed 4 October 2015).

[286] Texto refundido de la Ley de Propiedad Intelectual, regularizando, aclarando y armonizando las Disposiciones Legales Vigentes sobre la Materia (aprobado por el Real Decreto legislativo N° 1/1996 de 12 de abril de 1996, y modificado por el Real Decreto N° 20/2011 de 30 de diciembre de 2011) accessed

As in many other countries, Spain considered the first step as addressed to legislators, not courts. As a result, only the last two steps were implemented in the Act. Note also that the order of the two steps does not match that of the Convention. It is, however, the order used in the EU Database Directive, the likely source of this inversion.

The effect of the introduction of the test is interesting and perhaps paradoxical:

> **It has only been used expressly in very few decisions**, of lower courts, and not as a decisive criterion but merely to 'reinforce' other prevailing arguments. It is worth mentioning that judges do not look at the *Three-Step Test* as a restrictive norm. In some cases, it has been used to 'give more space' to some limit. Paradoxically, the methodology of **'double fences'** (limits precisely defined plus the *Three-Step Test* as a safety bolt) produces such an effect. **In the hands of judges and courts, the *Three-Step Test* can lead to both strict interpretations as well as more liberal ones.** Without turning the *Three-Step-Test* into a limit, courts can feel legitimized to do flexible interpretations, provided that neither the normal exploitation of the work nor the legitimate interests of the author are damaged . . . Spanish judges do not see the *Three-Step Test* as a staircase that should be climbed one step at a time, according to a precise pre-established methodology. Rather, they look at art. 40bis . . . as a **set of criteria to be considered liberally and globally**.[287]

## 3.5 POLICY LESSONS

The first lesson to be drawn from the preceding analysis is that the three-step test is, in reality, in many cases a two-step test when the test is implemented in national legislation, because the 'special case' nature of an exception is but an instruction *addressed to lawmakers* to provide reasonably narrow and well-defined exceptions (a quantitative component), with a (preferably stated) public interest justification (the normative/qualitative component). As in the WTO Section 110(5) panel report, the first step may be used internationally (in that case by a WTO panel) to decide whether an exception is sufficiently narrow. It is harder to justify an exception when its outer limits, whether in quantity or quality, cannot be readily ascertained. Open-ended exceptions and standards designed to permit uncompensated uses (such as fair use and fair dealing) may be considered as distinct in this context.

---

4 October 2015. The 'Chapter' referred to is the set of limitations and exceptions, arts 31–40.

[287] 'Spanish Report' in Association Littéraire et Artistique Internationale Congress, *The Author's Place in XXI Century Copyright: The Challenges of Modernization* (ALAI 2007, CD-ROM) 2.3.1.2–2.3.1.3 (emphasis in original).

The second step of the test prohibits exceptions that interfere demonstrably with commercial exploitation. The focus here is akin to a finding of adverse trade impact in an antidumping case:[288] will the measure significantly prevent a rights-holder from maximizing revenue? It is clear from available interpretations of the test that normalcy of exploitation modes is *not* a purely empirical (i.e., in practice a mostly historical) notion. In other words, it is *not* simply a question of what modes are actively exploited *now*, but also of what modes are likely to become significant income streams. To recall the Stockholm Conference's phrase noted above, the test covers 'all forms of exploiting a work which had, or were likely to acquire, considerable economic or practical importance'.

Determining what is likely to acquire importance is educated guesswork at best. Courts have tended to look at market developments. They have asked rights holders to make at least a prima facie case of interference. Once the case has been made, however, it would seem that the burden shifts to the user to show that there is no demonstrable interference. This is true of most national court decisions, but also applies to law-making processes and in the aforementioned WTO panel reports.

The third step is a logical extension of the second. If there is no interference, because the rights holder's mode(s) of commercial exploitation affected by the exception are not significantly impinged upon, then perhaps the rights holders can still show a substantial loss of income. If that loss of income is unreasonable, then financial compensation should be provided.

The application of the second step by national courts resembles the 'Folsom Test' (harm to plaintiff's market), which is now codified as the fourth fair use factor in US law, as explained more fully in the Appendix. In *Folsom v March*,[289] Judge Story had to decide whether a book by March for school libraries which quoted excerpts from letters (to and from) George Washington, most of which had only been published by Folsom, was an infringement of copyright. In a famous dictum, he wrote the following:

[W]e must often, in deciding questions of this sort, look to the nature and objects of the selections made, the quantity and value of the materials used, and the degree in which the use may prejudice the sale, or diminish the profits, or *supersede the objects*, of the original work.[290]

---

[288]  I use this analogy because the incorporation of copyright rules in the WTO framework—where disputes are decided by trade experts—leads to a rapprochement of trade and intellectual rules.

[289]  9 F Cas 342 (CCD Mass 1841) (No 4901).

[290]  Ibid., 348 (emphasis added).

The huge difference of course is that the fourth US factor is precisely that, a factor in a complex equation, whereas, if one applies the three-step test in a strictly sequential fashion, failing the second step may mean that the analysis stops, leading to the conclusion that the exception does not conform.[291] The application of the third step in national legislation is also harder. Its purpose was to impose on states an obligation to provide compensation for certain exceptions (typically, moving certain exceptions to the category of compulsory licenses). It could be used to allow a court or administrative authority to impose compensation in a case where an exception causes an unreasonable loss of income. It will be interesting to see to what extent Australian and European courts, and courts in other countries where the three-step test was directly implemented in national legislation, differentiate between the second and third step,[292] and specifically whether they actually use the third step to provide compensation, and if so, how they articulate the legal basis. The risk is that they will consider the matter case by case and not systematically. Would it not then become the functional equivalent of a compulsory license? All this militates in favour of the view that the appropriate locus of the third step is not in national law but rather as a guide to policy makers. It instructs them to provide a compensation mechanism (a limitation such as a statutory license with compensation) when an unreasonable loss of income would be caused by a full exception.

Another lesson, though perhaps one that is less intuitive, is that the effect of the incorporation of the three-step test in international copyright law by the TRIPS Agreement and, more broadly, the movement of copyright from a property right based on a purported natural law of authors to a *trade-related right* given to right holders (who may be authors but are most often those who exploit the works of authors in the marketplace) has been to make it easier to provide exceptions to exclusive rights. This is because the focus is not, or no longer, on theoretical interference with the enjoyment and exploitation of a property right (by analogy, there is no need to show actual injury to justify a cause of action of trespass to land), but rather a pragmatic consideration of the actual impact on rights holders' income streams. Put differently, as a result of the paradigmatic nature of the three-

---

[291]   While I do not support a fully 'holistic' view of the test, I do, as suggested in a co-authored article, believe that the three steps can be seen as forming three parts of a single test. See Geiger (n 212).

[292]   Ibid., 618–22. Some recent CJEU cases suggest that the test in EU law is a standalone test applied in addition to the test for a given exception, thus reinforcing the fear expressed here that it will be used for a purpose quite distinct from the Berne negotiators' intent. See e.g. Stichting Brein v Wullems (t/a Filmspeler) (C-527/15) [2017] E.C.D.R. 14.

step test to gauge the validity of exceptions and limitations, the policy focus is not whether a copy or communication to the public, for example, has taken place, but on whether: (a) revenue will be (demonstrably) lost because of lost (normal, *i.e.,* reasonably expected) commercial transactions; and (b) the loss is proportionally justified on public policy grounds. Then, legislatures can look at how much revenue will be lost, and consider whether a compensation mechanism should be put in place.

Because the introduction of the test is still relatively recent in those jurisdictions where it has been 'translated' into national law (essentially Australia and Europe), there is not much in terms of empirical data to show its effects. It is thus difficult to parse the global impact of the test on innovation or the copyright industries. Econometric regressions might show correlations, but causation will take much more time to establish convincingly. This is typically the case with the adoption of any new standard of course. The farther the standard is to a known quantity or to a 'rule', however, the higher the short-term uncertainty and transaction costs that follow from having to wait for clarification by courts. Moreover, adopting a new standard in parallel use in several jurisdictions means that it likely will be interpreted in different ways.

The test has a very important positive feature, namely its dynamic nature. The second step references normalcy of commercial exploitation, which by its very nature is dynamic; markets and market practices change. The responsiveness in allowing copyright law to vibrate in tune with the evolution of market dynamics, within the bounds of treaty norms, is likely to be conducive to a more robust market for creative works, while also allowing reuses that do not interfere with this market. This should foster the development of an efficient and competitive digital marketplace (remembering that competition is 'normal') and an innovative economy. There is a risk that the test will be interpreted too strictly and cause welfare losses that do not translate into benefits that outweigh those costs. However, this uncertainty seems an unavoidable consequence of any new open-ended test.

## 3.6 APPLICATION OF THE THREE-STEP TEST TO SPECIFIC USERS OR USES

Let us apply the test to concrete fact patterns. Would a new educational exception, or an exception for research or the creation of new works be compatible with the three-step test? To pass the first step, it must be sufficiently narrow in scope. While this is generally measured in terms of the purpose (e.g., private use or non-commercial research), it could be expressed in terms of a reasonably narrow class of users. An exception for specific educational purposes, private use, 'research' (definitional issues aside—those are dealt with below), or for certain derivative uses, would likely pass the first step.

At the second step, right holders must demonstrate that the exception prevents them from trying to establish a (reasonably predictable) market (especially if such a market has been established in relevant other jurisdictions), or interferes with an established, non-peripheral market. As noted above, normalcy of commercial exploitation is a dynamic notion where technology and evolving forms of use, especially on the Internet, must be taken into account. A related factor to consider is the level of transaction costs (financially and administratively). This requires a more granular analysis.

### 3.6.1  Research and Private Use

Research and private use (whether as part of education or not) are some of the oldest exceptions to copyright, at least in Commonwealth countries.[293] Exceptions may apply in such cases in part because the uses are deemed normatively justifiable and in part because it is unlikely and/or impracticable for individual users/consumers to obtain a license. Provided those users remain 'end-users', no problem should arise. However, users can distribute copies made for private purposes to others, thus arguably abandoning their 'end-user' status. Some statutes do recognize this. For example, the Canadian exception for private use (s. 80(2)(c)) prohibits distribution of private copies. From a normative perspective, if a user makes a copy to allow someone else to perform a use that would also qualify as private, should this be prohibited? Peer-to-peer (P2P) file-sharing is the epitome of this phenomenon. It is often argued that the nature and richness of the Internet allows users to share, create social networks, etc. This is undoubtedly true, but how can any normative views derived from this type of use comply with a pre-Internet[294] set of norms, including the three-step test? How can such norms be expressed as clear legal rules? The three-step test may actually be part of the solution. Under the test, permitted uses must not necessarily be *end*-uses. If no reasonable claim to a non-peripheral sale or licensing transaction at a reasonable transaction cost can be demonstrated, then the second and third step of the test should

---

[293]  Ricketson (n 194) 485–8.
[294]  Although the three-step test is also included in the post-internet 1996 WIPO Treaties. See WIPO Copyright Treaty 1996, art. 10(2); WIPO Performances and Phonograms Treaty 1996, art. 16(2).

not be obstacles to the establishment of an exception. This could be used to justify a data mining exception, for example.[295]

There is, however, a view that an exception should not be allowed under the second step, or that compensation must be available under the third step when 'deaths by a 1,000 cuts' may occur, that is, when individual free uses are considered cumulatively. Professor Caron explained this in the context of the second step:

> [T]he judge does not decide (only) whether the use of the individual copyist affects exploitation because the actions of one person obviously almost never reach such a threshold, but whether the type the use at issue infringes the test, which involves the resurgence [in a civil system which does not apply *stare decisis*] of court opinions establishing principles for the future [*arrêts de règlement*].[296]

This seems at least facially correct. A statutory exception should not consider only the impact on an individual user; the normative question is whether the exception systematically impedes a significant, reasonably foreseeable market from developing normally (considering the type of work *and* the category of user concerned). In terms of compensation, this translates as the cumulative effect on the rights holders (that is, a demonstrable loss of income), weighed against the public interest at play, itself measured in terms of deadweight and other welfare costs. Against this backdrop, non-commercial research should not be an issue. Indeed it has long been recognized, in several national laws and international discussions, as a legitimate exception to exclusive rights.[297] Large commercial enterprises can and do obtain copyright licenses in other relevant jurisdictions for such copying. Indeed, the existence of a relatively straightforward

---

[295] 'The Hague Declaration on Knowledge Discovery in the Digital Age' Content Mine (6 May 2015) (available at <http://bit.ly/1PrN5xy> accessed 5 October 2015); see also Liat Clark, 'Report: Change European Law to Allow Scientific Data Mining' *Wired* (7 April 14) (available at <http://www.wired. co.uk/news/archive/2014-04/07/european-copyright-science-journals> accessed 5 October 2015).

[296] Caron (n 232) 3.

[297] See e.g., *CCH Canadian Ltd v Law Society of Upper Canada*, [2004] 1 SCR 339. It is unclear to what extent the decision was informed by the fact that the research (performed by or for lawyers) was used in part for judicial purposes. The decision is interpreted in some circles as allowing any research, whether commercial or not, without compensation or licensing. See Daniel Gervais, 'Le droit d'auteur au Canada après *CCH*' (2005) 203 *Revue Internationale du Droit d'Auteur* 2; Daniel Gervais, 'The Purpose of Copyright Law in Canada' (2005) 2 *University of Ottawa Law & Technology Journal* 315.

collective license was used in the US to justify findings that commercial copying even for research was not fair use.[298] To break the circularity of the argument (if license then no exception), one must consider whether licensing is reasonable and appropriate in the circumstances, weighed against the negative impact that imposing a licensing requirement may cause.

### 3.6.2   Education

To pass the first step of the test, an exception for education should be clearly delineated. If a measurable loss of income is caused, compensation should be offered under the third step. In economic terms, under that step, the exception may be viewed as displacing income from rights holders for the benefit of users, and the state may thus be called upon to establish a compensation mechanism. Because such compensation may take the form of 'rough justice' payments such as private copying, they are often not seen as highly desirable. The most problematic hurdle, however, is the second step. Would an educational exception affect core or significant income streams as defined above? A simple answer is that it depends in large part on how the exception is formulated. In terms of market(s), some of the material used in education is part of the core income stream of rights holders. For other material used, the educational market is not core but may remain very significant. In both cases, an exception would likely tread beyond the confines of the second step if a reasonable (for both parties) transaction of sale or license is available. Material that is made available under a non-commercial use license (such as many of the works licensed using Creative Commons terms and logos), and material whose use in education is occasional or peripheral, either do not require an exception or could be the subject of an exception compatible with the second step of the test. To take a simple example, an exception allowing schools to photocopy and/or scan commercially available educational textbooks and make them available for free to students (online or on paper), would be prohibited by the three-step test, specifically the second step, although developing countries might be able to use the Berne Appendix (see Appendix 2 of this book). An exception to make occasional, spontaneous copies of a few pages would not, in contrast, be incompatible with the test.

Another relevant factor in that context is the existence of demonstrable comparable markets in relevant other jurisdictions, whose rights holders

---

[298]   *Am Geophysical Union v Texaco Inc*, 60 F3d 913 (2d Cir 1994); see *also Princeton U Press v Mich Doc Servs*, No 92-CV-71029-DT, 1992 US Dist LEXIS 13257 (ED Mich Apr 6, 1992).

might ask their government to examine the TRIPS compatibility of any new exception. In both the UK and the US, licensing schemes are in place for higher education. In the US, Copyright Clearance Center, Inc. (CCC) administers the schemes, which are essentially aimed at higher education. They cover both paper (course-pack) and digital uses, including a new 'multi-use license for their institution, allowing faculty, researchers and staff to share content across campus with ease'.[299]

### 3.6.3 Scientific Research and the Three-step Test

Science and copyright can also collide.[300] Scientists are of course free to publish in open source vehicles and make their work available freely online. Copyright has never prevented this. Scientists who publish in some of the more prestigious peer-reviewed publications however (where article acceptance may make a career), do not have this same freedom, although there is evidence that changes are afoot, particularly in the UK.[301] They cannot simply scan and make available an unlimited number of articles on a publicly available site, without license or compensation. If they could, the business model of commercial science, medical, and technical (STM) publishers might collapse. Business models do collapse, and indeed they have no right to survive, but that is not to say that the business model of commercial scientific publishing *should* collapse.

To find balance, legislators and courts can limit the reach of the exclusive rights. Legislators could, for example, adopt regulation—or prod right holders to use private ordering mechanisms—allowing for a short period of exclusivity (six, 12, or 18 months are possible options), followed by either open access, or paid for, but unrestricted use license.

### 3.6.4 The Test and its Relation to Article 10(2) of the Berne Convention

The three-step test, as incorporated both in Article 9(2) of Berne and Article 13 of TRIPS is part of a broader framework, namely the Berne

---

[299] Press Release, Copyright Clearance Center, Copyright Clearance Center Announces Partnership with Amigos Library Services (available at <http://www.copyright.com/copyright-clearance-center-announces-partnership-with-amigos-library-services/> accessed 5 October 2015).

[300] Jerome H. Reichman and Ruth L Okediji, 'When Copyright Law and Science Collide: Empowering Digitally Integrated Research Methods on a Global Scale' (2012) 96 *Minnesota Law Review* 1362.

[301] Cabinet Office and Paymaster General, *Open Data White Paper: Unleashing the Potential* (Cm 8353, 2012).

Convention and the TRIPS Agreement.[302] The TRIPS Agreement incorporated by reference the provisions of the Berne Convention dealing with economic rights, including Article 10(2) of Berne. Article 10(2) is *lex specialis*, a more directly relevant provision than the general three-step test. It is relevant for the interpretation of both Berne and TRIPS. Article 10(2) of the Berne Convention (1971) provides as follows:

> It shall be a matter for legislation in the countries of the Union, and for special agreements existing or to be concluded between them, to permit the utilization, *to the extent justified by the purpose*, of literary or artistic works *by way of illustration in publications, broadcasts or sound or visual recordings for teaching*, provided such utilization is compatible with fair practice.[303]

A very brief historical perspective can contextualize this provision. In the original 1886 text of the Berne Convention, the article read only as a safeguard, based on German law, of 'special agreements existing or to be concluded between [countries of the Union]' concerning the ability to use portions from literary and artistic works in publications destined for educational or scientific purposes.[304] France tried to replace this general provision with quantitative restrictions at the 1928 Rome Convention, but failed. However, the Rome Conference adopted a resolution calling on member states to define clearly the limits for allowed borrowings.[305] Then, at the 1967 Stockholm Revision Conference, there was an interesting debate between countries that wanted to include a word such as 'borrowings' or 'excerpts' and those that preferred the more neutral 'utilization' found in the present-day version of the article. Independently of that debate, however, all countries agreed that there had to be limits to the exception. This is what led to the inclusion of the phrase 'provided such utilization is compatible with fair practice' at the end of the article. The reference to 'fair practice' is also found in Article 10(1) of the Berne Convention (concerning quotations), where it was interpreted as a reference back to the rule of reason contained in the three-step test.[306]

While this reference to 'fair practice' imposes facially vague parameters—there is certainly no predetermined quantitative limit—the use of the words 'by way of illustration' provides context to the exception. For example,

---

[302]   See Ch. 2.
[303]   (Emphasis added.)
[304]   *Berne Convention Centenary* (n 219) 233. Chrestomathies are compilations used as an aid in teaching a language.
[305]   Ibid.
[306]   Ricketson and Ginsburg. (n 204) s 13.45.

leading commentators believe that in appropriate circumstances, the use of an entire work may be appropriate if necessary for 'illustration'.[307]

Records from the successive revisions Conferences of the Convention, show that 'teaching', as used in Article 10, includes elementary as well as advanced teaching, and works intended for self-instruction.[308] There is, however, considerable debate as to the type of institution that can avail itself of the exception. The dominant view is that the exception should be limited to non-commercial teaching activities.[309]

Finally, Article 10(2) extends to the inclusion of works in a broadcast used in a school or other educational institution, but not to on-demand transmissions. The Convention treats broadcasting and transmissions (Article 11*bis*(1)) differently.[310]

To sum up, Article 10(1) and 10(2) provide latitude for Berne member states (and thus also for WTO members applying the TRIPS Agreement) to adopt exceptions that allow the use of works by way of illustration for non-commercial teaching. The exception is compatible with spontaneous, occasional use. Article 10(2) imposes a test of proportionality and, interestingly, a reference to 'fair practice'. To determine fairness, a WTO panel would likely apply a rule of reason compatible with the three-step test.[311]

---

[307] Ibid.

[308] Ibid.

[309] Ibid.; see also and Thomas Dreier and P Bernt Hugenholtz (eds), *Concise European Copyright Law* (Kluwer 2006) 45.

[310] Ricketson and Ginsburg (n 204).

[311] A WTO panel would interpret the fairness criterion against the backdrop of the three-step test, in light of Vienna Convention guidance.

# 4. Protection thresholds: originality and fixation

Together with the international rule against mandatory copyright-specific formalities[312] (such as registration) discussed in Chapter 2, another notable part of the international copyright system is the low threshold to obtain copyright protection. In most countries, the only condition for a production in the artistic or literary domain to be protected by copyright is that it be original. Some countries, including the United States, also require that the work be *fixed* in a tangible medium of expression, a topic discussed at the end of the chapter.

## 4.1 ORIGINALITY

Almost all literary and artistic 'productions'[313] can be considered original, independently of how the notion of originality is defined or which test is used to measure it. The debates surrounding originality thus relate mainly to specific types of works, such as some computer programs, factual compilations and databases. It is not this debate, which is nonetheless very interesting, that concerns us here. Rather, we are concerned with what the choice of the notion of originality as the 'filter' used to determine what is copyrightable, tells us about copyright policy itself.

Originality is expressly defined neither in the Berne Convention nor in most national laws. This means that legislators essentially have left it up to national courts to decide what makes a work original. We thus begin this chapter by looking at the US Supreme Court opinion in *Feist Publications, Inc v Rural Telephone Service Company, Inc*,[314] issued in March 1991,

---

[312] See Ch. 2.
[313] This is the neutral term used in art. 2 of the Berne Convention for the Protection of Literary and Artistic Works 1979. 'Produced' in this context refers to the fact that the creative work is not (just) in the author's mind but has been expressed in a way that is perceptible by others, or 'objectified'.
[314] 499 US 340 (1991).

which was hailed both as a landmark decision[315] and a legal 'bomb'.[316] Was *Feist* so 'original' as to deserve all the attention? After all, it did not establish a *new* originality paradigm as such but only ended a long division or split among US Federal Appellate Circuits concerning the protection under copyright of factual compilations.[317] In reality, *Feist* did much more than resolve a definitional tension: it determined that there was a constitutional requirement of creativity in US law.[318]

Not surprisingly, the decision was perceived in apocalyptic terms by the database industry: the sky had fallen, their business base would soon wither away,[319] and piracy would be free to flourish on the high seas of the database industry.[320] In sum, factual compilations would no longer be protected, and, without adequate protection, investments

---

[315] See, e.g., Tracy Lea Meade, 'Ex-Post *Feist*: Applications of a Landmark Copyright Decision' (1994) 2 *Journal of Intellectual Property Law* 245.

[316] An expression used by the former Register of Copyrights, Ralph Oman, in his testimony before the House of Representatives (quoted in Paul Goldstein, 'Copyright' (1991) 38 *Journal Copyright Society of the USA* 109, 118).

[317] Jennifer R Dowd, 'A Selective View of History: *Feist Publications, Inc. v. Rural Telephone Service Co.*' (1992) 34 *Boston College Law Review* 137, 138–9; Lea Meade (n 315) 245–6; Denise R Polivy, '*Feist* Applied: Imagination Protects, But Perspiration Persists—the Bases of Copyright Protection for Factual Compilations' (1998) 8 *Fordham Intellectual Property, Media & Entertainment Law Journal* 773, 780–81.

[318] Justin Hughes, 'The Personality Interest of Artists and Inventors in Intellectual Property' (1998) 16 *Cardozo Arts & Entertainment Law Journal* 81, 99: arguing that the court melded the notions of originality and creativity. In other cases, originality was defined as comprising both creativity and the absence of copying. This is not incorrect, but does not change our analysis. See, e.g., *Baltimore Oriole, Inc v Major League Baseball Players Ass'n*, 805 F2d 663, 668 n6 (7th Cir 1986).

[319] S Leigh Fulwood, '*Feist v. Rural*: Did the Supreme Court Give License to Reap Where One Has Not Sown?' (1991) 9(4) *Communications Lawyer* 15, 17: '[V]ast amounts of information have been ejected into the public domain, with resulting implications to all businesses for which the amassing or distribution of information is essential'.; Jessica Litman, 'After *Feist*' (1992) 17 *University of Dayton Law Review* 607. *Contra*, Paul T Sheils and Robert Penchina, 'What's All the Fuss about *Feist*? The Sky is not Falling on the Intellectual Property Rights of Online Database Proprietors' (1992) 17 *University of Dayton Law Review* 563.

[320] Daniel Davis, '*Feist Publications, Inc. v. Rural Telephone Service Co.*: Opening The Door to Information Pirates?' (1992) 36 *Saint Louis University Law Journal* 439, 440: 'This broad holding [in *Feist*] affects the economic feasibility of producing any commercially salable factual compilation, whether as a printed directory or as an automated database service, such as LEXIS, WESTLAW, Prodigy or Compuserve.'

necessary for the creation and maintenance of databases would dry up.[321] It seems, however, that the end of the database world has been postponed.[322]

The purpose of this chapter is not to re-litigate *Feist*, but rather to show that a *Feist*-like standard is now applied or is emerging in key common law countries. In a move that bridges the gap between the two major systems of copyright,[323] civil law systems have adopted a fairly similar approach.

### 4.1.1  Originality in Common Law Systems

#### 4.1.1.1  United States

The legislative history of the 1976 US Copyright Act shows that originality is required.[324] Prior to 1976, originality was not mentioned in the Act but was nonetheless required for copyright protection.[325] The question of the exact definition of the standard remained open, however.

The *Feist* Court found that *creative choices* in the selection and arrangement of the data were necessary to generate sufficient originality

---

[321]  Ibid.

[322]  Survey research of the ten years following *Feist* demonstrated that not only did the US database industry continue to grow at a consistent annual rate of approximately 6 per cent, but that the enactment of protections, such as those adopted by the EU, did not significantly impact the long-term growth of the database industry in its member nations. See European Parliament and Council Directive 96/9/EC of 11 March 1996 on the legal protection of databases; Stephen M Maurer, 'Across Two Worlds: Database Protection in the United States and Europe' in Jonathan D Putnam (ed.), *International Conference on Intellectual Property and Innovation in the Knowledge-Based Economy, May 23–24, 2001, Toronto* (Industrie Canada 2001) Ch. 13, p. 11; ibid., 48: stating that the data '*does not* show, at least so far, that the Directive has had a lasting impact on the rate at which commercial providers enter the market' (emphasis in original); see also Stephen M Maurer, P Bernt Hugenholtz, and Jarlan J Onsrud, 'Europe's Database Experiment' (2001) 294 *Science* 789.

[323]  Jane C Ginsburg, 'A Tale of Two Copyrights: Literary Property in Revolutionary France and America' (1990) 64 *Tulane Law Review* 991, 1006–14.

[324]  HR Rep No 94-1476, (1976) *reprinted in* 1976 USCCAN 5659. The Act does not define originality and this omission was apparently deliberate. See also William Patry, 'Copyright in Collections of Facts: A Reply' (1984) 6(5) *Communications and the Law* 11, 18.

[325]  Julia Reytblat, 'Is Originality in Copyright Law A "Question Of Law" Or A "Question Of Fact?": The Fact Solution' (1999) 17 *Cardozo Arts & Entertainment Law Journal* 181, 183.

to warrant copyright protection.[326] This reasoning echoes earlier Supreme Court cases dealing with photographs.[327] In the *Burrow-Giles* case, for example, the court had to decide whether a photograph of Oscar Wilde was original.[328] In concluding that it was, the court noted the creative choices made by the photographer, including pose, costume, lighting, accessories, and the set itself.[329]

The question before the US Supreme Court in *Feist* was what should be rewarded: mere work (and, perhaps, investment), or creativity? The court clearly found that creativity was required by the US Constitutional Copyright Clause, which states that Congress has jurisdiction over copyright

---

[326]   Feist (n 314) 348:

Factual compilations, on the other hand, may possess the requisite originality. The compilation author typically *chooses* which facts to include, in what order to place them, and how to arrange the collected data so that they may be used effectively by readers. These *choices* as to selection and arrangement, so long as they are made independently by the compiler and entail a minimal degree of creativity, are sufficiently original that Congress may protect such compilations through the copyright laws (emphasis added).

See also Alan L Durham, 'Speaking of the World: Fact, Opinion and the Originality Standard of Copyright' (2001) 33 *Arizona State Law Journal* 791, 794–95 drawing an accurate distinction between 'creative' choices and 'discovery' choices:

In factual works—works that describe aspects of the world in which we live— 'creation' generally includes the author's choice of language, arrangement of materials, and selection of materials to include or exclude. These are choices made at the author's discretion. They are not imposed by an order found in the world, but reflect the author's judgment as to how and what to communicate to his audience. Together, these choices produce the kind of original 'expression' traditionally protected by copyright. 'Discovery' includes any information about the world communicated through the medium of the author's expression. Sometimes that information is 'original' in the sense that it has never been communicated before, but it is not 'original' in the sense that the author *made* it. If the information is accurate, the author *found* it. Such information, according to *Feist*, belongs to the public (footnotes omitted).

[327]   *Burrow-Giles Lithographic Co v Sarony*, 111 US 53, 60 (1884); *Bleistein v Donaldson Lithographing Co*, 188 US 239, 250–51 (1903). Several lower courts adopted a similar approach. See, e.g., *Falk v Brett Lithographing Co*, 48 F 678, 679 (SDNY 1891); *Gentieu v John Muller & Co*, 712 F Supp 740, 742–44 (WD Mo 1989); see also Patricia L Baade, 'Photographer's Rights: Case for Sufficient Originality Test in Copyright Law' (1996) 30 *John Marshall Law Review* 149, 150–53.

[328]   *Burrow-Giles*, ibid., 58.

[329]   Ibid., 60. See also *In re Trade-Mark Cases*, 100 US 82, 94 (1879) finding that a work of authorship must evidence the 'creative powers of the mind'; Ysolde Gendreau, Axel Nordemann, and Rainer Oesch (eds), *Copyright and Photographs: An International Survey* (Kluwer 1999) 305–6.

(and patent) law to promote the Progress of Science and the Useful Arts by giving *Authors* exclusive rights in their writings.[330] The court brought compilations on to the same footing as other categories of copyrighted works, and clarified the distinction between copyright (and its underlying policy objectives, namely a reward for the sake of incentivizing creation[331]) and misappropriation.[332]

Is there, as a result of *Feist*, as Koestler might have asked, a *Feist* ghost in the copyright machine? Many US cases since *Feist* have tried to pinpoint the location of the creativity threshold articulated in *Feist*.[333] A good example is the decision of the Court of Appeals for the Second Circuit (New York) in *CCC Info Servs, Inc v Maclean Hunter Mkt Reports, Inc*.[334] In determining whether the Red Book[335] was protected by copyright, the court noted:

> The thrust of the Supreme Court's ruling in *Feist* was not to erect a high barrier of originality requirement. It was rather to specify, rejecting the strain of lower court rulings that sought to base protection on the 'sweat of the brow', that *some* originality is essential to protection of authorship, and that the protection afforded extends only to those original elements. Because the protection is so limited, there is no reason under the policies of the copyright law to demand a high degree of originality. To the contrary, such a requirement would be counterproductive. The policy embodied into law is to encourage authors to publish innovations for the common good—not to threaten them with loss of their livelihood if their works of authorship are found insufficiently imaginative.[336]

---

[330]  See n 318.

[331]  Jessica Litman, 'Revising Copyright Law for the Information Age' (1996) 75 *Oregon Law Review* 19, 28–9.

[332]  *Int'l News Serv v Associated Press*, 248 US 215, 243–5 (1918) affirming an injunction that prohibited INS from selling, in competition with AP, news that INS had copied from AP. Generally, under the doctrine which emerged from the INS case, a cause of action for misappropriation arises when (1) the plaintiff has *invested substantial time and money* to develop a 'property', (2) the defendant has appropriated the property at little or no cost, and (3) the plaintiff has been injured by the defendant's conduct. The *INS* case has been interpreted narrowly, and it is unclear to what extent misappropriation claims survived copyright preemption. *Bonito Boats, Inc v Thunder Craft Boats, Inc*, 489 US 141, 151, 156–7 (1989); *Nat'l Basketball Ass'n v Motorola, Inc*, 105 F3d 841, 852–3 (2d Cir 1997); Sheils and Penchina (n 319) 579. Conceptually, however, the purpose of misappropriation is to impose liability on methods of competition that undermine rather than advance the competitive process. Restatement (Third) of Unfair Competition § 38 cmt a (Am Law Inst 1995). Protecting investments to allow the market to function would seem to meet the same objective.

[333]  Feist (n 314) 346–9.

[334]  44 F3d 61 (2d Cir 1994), *cert denied* 516 US 817 (1995). See also Polivy (n 317) 805–6.

[335]  Ibid., 63 ('Automobile Red Book—Official Used Car Valuations').

[336]  Ibid., 66.

Though it requires some creativity, the originality threshold in US law is low. *Feist* did not destroy copyright protection for compilations. Indeed, a majority of post-*Feist* cases dealing with factual compilations found such compilations to be protected.[337] In addition, and more importantly, even if some factual compilations are not protected by copyright, this does not mean that copyright is a bad tool for databases (and thus somehow must be changed); it means that factual databases are bad targets for copyright.[338] Protection of informational 'data pools' that do not pass the *Feist* 'minimal creativity' threshold can be protected in a variety of other ways, including contracts and torts (especially misappropriation[339]), or *sui generis* legislation, though that experiment in Europe is widely seen as a failure.[340] Copyright is not the proper vehicle to protect these non-creative, non-original compilations. That is, if they needed legal protection at all.

---

[337] For appellate cases where a factual compilation was found to be copyright-able, see *US Payphone, Inc v Executives Unlimited of Durham, Inc*, 18 USPQ2d 2049 (4th Cir 1991); *Kregos v Associated Press*, 937 F2d 700 (2d Cir 1991); *Key Publ'ns, Inc v Chinatown Today Publ'g Enters, Inc*, 945 F2d 509 (2d Cir 1991); *CCC Info Servs, Inc v Maclean Hunter Mkt Reports*, 44 F3d 61 (2d Cir 1994); *Lipton v Nature Co*, 71 F3d 464 (2d Cir 1995); *Warren Publ'g, Inc v Microdos Data Corp*, 52 F3d 950 (11th Cir 1995), *vacated*, 67 F3d 276 (11th Cir 1995) (en banc), *remanded to*, 115 F3d 1509 (11th Cir 1997) (en banc), *cert denied*, 522 US 963 (1997); *TransWestern Publ'g Co LP v Multimedia Mktg Assocs, Inc*, 133 F3d 773 (10th Cir 1998); *Nihon Keizai Shimbun, Inc v Comline Bus Data, Inc*, 166 F3d 65 (2d Cir 1999). In *US Payphone*, however, the basis for protection still seems to be the 'sweat of the brow' of the compiler: '[t]he Guide . . . is the result of hundreds of hours of reviewing, analyzing, and interpreting [the data]'. 18 USPQ2d at 2050. For cases where protection was refused, see *Victor Lalli Enterprises, Inc v Big Red Apple, Inc*, 936 F2d 671 (2d Cir 1991); *Sem-Torq, Inc v K Mart Corp*, 936 F2d 851 (6th Cir 1991); *Bellsouth Advert & Publ'g Corp v Donnelley Info Publ'g, Inc*, 999 F2d 1436 (11th Cir 1993); *Mid America Title Co v Kirk*, 867 F Supp 673 (7th Cir 1994), *cert denied* 516 US 990 (1995). See also Sheils and Penchina (n 319) 566–8.

[338] In fact, trying to bring a database under the copyright umbrella might mean making a database less exhaustive due to increased selection, or harder to use due to non-standard arrangement of the data. Jane Ginsburg, 'No "Sweat"? Copyright and Other Protection of Works of Information After *Feist v. Rural Telephone*' (1992) 92 *Columbia Law Review* 338, 347; Polivy (n 317) 796–802; see also *Schoolhouse, Inc v Anderson*, 275 F3d 726 (8th Cir 2002) noting that the protection was very thin despite an admission by the defendant that a table was copyrightable.

[339] Feist (n 314) 353–5; Sheils and Penchina (n 319) 572–83.

[340] See n 348; Anant Narayanan, 'Standards of Protection for Databases in the European Community and the United States: *Feist* and the Myth of Creative Originality' (1993–1994) 27 *George Washington Journal of International Law and Economics* 457, 477–80. Because of the impact of a sui generis regime on existing intellectual property rights and the resulting rearrangement of the intellectual

Putting the author/creator at the centre of the copyright picture[341] by requiring evidence of a human (intellectual) creativity as the *Feist* court did not stem from an author-friendly perspective, or one meant particularly to benefit authors. In fact, the reverse may be true.[342] As one commentator put it, 'by overturning sweat of the brow, the Supreme Court reemphasized that the primary benefactor of copyright laws is the public, and benefits to the author are secondary'.[343] It seems that by requiring the mark of creativity, rather than looking at the work, time, or money invested in the creation process, the Supreme Court clarified the consideration that society expects from its copyright 'contract' with the author, and that copyright is not an investment protection scheme.[344]

### 4.1.1.2   United Kingdom

One of the first cases that comes to mind when looking at original-ity in the UK is *Walter v Lane*,[345] where the House of Lords granted copyright protection to a reporters' notes of a speech by the Earl of Rosebery because the note-taking process had required an 'industrious collection' effort. Another such decision was *University of London Press Ltd v University Tutorial Press Ltd*,[346] where the court found that, to gen-

---

property matrix (interfaces among the various rights), there should be ample empirical data showing a market failure is present before such legislation is enacted. A number of bills were introduced in the 106th Congress containing such sui generis rights, including the Collections of Information Antipiracy Act, HR 354, 106th Cong. (1999), and the Consumer and Investor Access to Information Act of 1999, HR 1858, 106th Cong. (1999).

[341]   For an interesting discussion of the relationship between the author and her work, and how the work is expressed, see Leslie A Kurtz, 'Speaking to the Ghost: Idea and Expression in Copyright' (1993) 47 *University of Miami Law Review* 1221, 1248–50.

[342]   Marci Hamilton, 'Justice O'Connor's Opinion in *Feist Publications, Inc. v. Rural Telephone Service Co.*: An Uncommon Though Characteristic Approach' (1990) 38 *Journal of the Copyright Society of the USA* 90:

> While the result is not surprising, much of the rhetoric is, which, unlike the rhetoric in *Harper & Row*, is undeniably on the side of the debate that pushes hard for public access rather than author's rights. The pervasive spirit of the opinion is strongly reminiscent of the spirit of Justice Stevens' approach in his opinion for the Court in *Sony* [v. *Universal*, 464 US 417, 442–56 (1984),] and his dissent in *Stewart v. Abend* [495 US 207, 239–43 (1990)].

[343]   Lea Meade (n 315) 268.

[344]   Feist (n 314) 357–8.

[345]   [1900] UHKL J0806-3, [1900] AC 539. See also *Morris v Ashbee* (1868) LR 7 Eq 34 and *Kelly v Morris* (1866) LR 1 Eq 697.

[346]   [1916] 2 Ch 601.

erate sufficient originality for copyright protection, 'independent creation' (defined as absence of copying) and skill and labour were sufficient.[347] This traditional UK test seems very close to the pre-*Feist* 'sweat of the brow' doctrine. It was applied in *Express Newspapers plc v News (UK) Ltd*,[348] where the court decided to follow *Walter v Lane*. This is significant because, between *Walter v Lane* and *Express Newspapers*, the UK Statute had been amended to add a standard of originality.[349]

At first glance, the picture emerging from the UK seems difficult to reconcile with *Feist*. However, the past few years may point to an evolution of the test, prompted perhaps by the progressive harmonization of British copyright law with the copyright laws of EU member-states.[350] UK litigants are also actively trying to change the test. Hence, in *Interlego AG v Tyco Industries Inc*[351] the defendant tried to convince the Privy Council that:

> [t]he word 'original' means the same for literary works as it does for artistic works. What is produced by the author need not be new in the absolute sense. There must be original creative input by the author. If in copying something is added, it is a question of degree as to whether that makes it an original artistic work or not. The skill and labour in doing the copying is irrelevant.[352]

Lord Oliver of Aylmerton, on behalf of the Council, did not accept the defendant's argument.[353] He noted that skill and labor were

---

[347]  Ibid., 608:

The word 'original' does not in this connection mean that the work must be the expression of original or inventive thought. Copyright Acts are not concerned with the originality of ideas, but with the expression of thought ... [T]he Act [requires] that the work must not be copied from another work—that it should originate from the author.

   The skill and labor element was further developed in *Ladbroke (Football) Ltd v William Hill (Football) Ltd* [1964] UHKL J0121-1, [1964] 1 All ER 465, 469. In a number of cases, the test is actually referred to as 'skill, labour and judgment', which may change the meaning somewhat, as is discussed below.

[348]  [1990] FSR 359 (Ch).

[349]  Ibid., 365: 'The word "original" in the statute does not imply inventive originality; it is enough that the work is the production of something in a new form as a result of the skill, labour and judgment of the reporter.'

[350]  Daniel J Gervais, 'Transmissions of Music on the Internet: An Analysis of the Copyright Laws of Canada, France, Germany, Japan, the United Kingdom, and the United States' (2001) 34 *Vanderbilt Journal of Transnational Law* 1363, 1403–07.

[351]  [1989] AC 217 (PC).

[352]  Ibid., 232.

[353]  Ibid., 260.

insufficient to confer originality; the work also had to 'originate from the author'.[354]

In two cases, the House of Lords (now the UK Supreme Court) insisted on the need for *original* skill and labour, and, in one case, *original artistic* skill and labour.[355] If the Supreme Court of the UK further elaborates on this test, it may get to a clear, creativity-based test because 'original skill and labour' cannot have the same meaning as 'skill and labour'.[356] I suggest, therefore, that the *Express Newspapers* case[357] may have to be reconsidered. The introduction of originality in the statute cannot be meaningless. In other words, if 'original' means something, which it must, it is more than mere skill and labour, and the additional element is likely the intellectual creativity that seems to be required by EU Directives.[358] A hint of such evolution may have been given when the court used the expression 'artistic skill and labour'.

---

[354]   Ibid., 263–4.

[355]   *Newspaper Licensing Agency Ltd v Marks & Spencer plc* [2001] UKHL 38, [2003] 1 AC 551 [19]–[20]:

> *[C]opying of certain of the ideas expressed in that [fabric] design* which, in their conjoined expression, had involved *original artistic skill and labour*, constituted the copying of a substantial part of the artistic work. . ..The notion of *reproduction . . . is sufficiently* flexible to include the *copying of ideas abstracted from a literary, dramatic, musical or artistic work*, provided that their expression in the original work has involved sufficient of the relevant *original* skill and labour to attract copyright protection (emphasis added).

See also *Designer Guild Ltd v Russell Williams (Textiles) Ltd* [2000] UKHL J1123-1, [2000] 1 WLR 2416.

[356]   To use *University of London Press* terminology, 'original' cannot be read as meaning that the work is the product of skill and labour. Interestingly, the 1988 UK Act specifically mentions that works must be original. See Copyright, Designs and Patents Act 1988, Pt,1 s. 1(1). The counter-argument is that the Act simply codified what the courts had previously defined as originality, namely skill, labour, and absence of copying.

[357]   *Express Newspapers* (n 348).

[358]   Council Directive 91/250/EEC of 14 May 1991 on the legal protection of computer programs [1991] OJ L122/42, art. 1(3): 'A computer program shall be protected if it is original in the sense that it is the *author's own intellectual creation*. No other criteria shall be applied to determine its eligibility for protection' (amended by Council Directive 93/98/EEC of 29 October 1993 harmonizing the term of protection of copyright and certain related rights [1993] OJ L290/9); see also European Parliament and Council Directive 96/9/EC of 11 March 1996 on the legal protection of databases [1996] OJ L77/20, art. 3(1). In an obiter opinion, a British court seems to agree that adding an originality requirement to the statute had the effect of overturning *Walter v Lane*: see *Roberton v Lewis* [1976] RPC 169, 174 (Ch).

The outcome of the *University of London Press* case may also have to be reconsidered in light of the EU's concept of 'intellectual creation';[359] which played a major role in cases such as *Infopaq*; *Softwarová*; *FAPL*; *Painer*; and *Football Dataco*.[360] In a number of those cases, the Court of Justice of the European Union identified the need to show that a work be an intellectual creation to justify copyright protection.[361] The opinion of the court in the *SAS* case is clear: 'It is only through the *choice, sequence and combination* of those words, figures or mathematical concepts that the author may express his creativity in an original manner and achieve a result, namely the user manual for the computer program, which is an intellectual creation.'[362]

Should Brexit proceed, which remains unclear as of this writing, then UK courts may be tempted to abandon a notion ostentsibly anchored in EU directives and return to previous precedents.

### 4.1.1.3 Canada

According to the Supreme Court of Canada, there are two 'extremes' in the extant definitions of the notion of originality in various countries.[363] The first 'extreme' was initially defined in part in the *University of London Press* case[364] of 1916 ('*ULP*'). In that case, the judge relied on the author's effort and labour, adding that the work, to be considered original, should not be copied from another work[365] (at least that is the interpretation of

---

[359] Ibid.

[360] Judgment of 16 July 2009, Case C-5/08, *Infopaq International A/S v Danske Dagblades Forening* [2009] ECR I-6569; Judgment of 4 October 2011, Joined Cases C-403/08 and C-429/08, *Football Association Premier League and others v QC Leisure and others and Karen Murphy v Media Protection Services* [2012] FSR 1; Judgment of 1 December 2011, Case C-145/10, *Eva-Maria Painer v Standard VerlagsGmbH and others*, [2011] nyr, available on curia.europa.eu; Judgment of 1 March 2012, Case C-604/10, *Football Dataco et al. v Yahoo UK! et al.*, nyr, available on curia.europa.eu. On *Infopaq*, see "Wonderful or worrisome? The impact of the ECJ ruling in *Infopaq* on UK copyright law" [2010] 32(5) EIPR 247–51. On *Softwarová, see* E Derclaye, 'L'arrêt Softwarová: une révolution en droit d'auteur ou une "erreur de jugement"? [2011] 43 Revue du Droit des Technologies de l'Information (RDTI) 57, 59–60

[361] *Infopaq*, n 360 above, at paras. 39–45; *FAPL*, at paras 97, 98, 155, 156, 159; *Painer*, at paras 87–89, 94, 99; *Football Dataco*, 37–39.

[362] Court decision of 2 May 2012, Case C-406/10, *SAS Institute Inc v World Programming Ltd*, at para. 67 (emphasis added).

[363] *CCH Canadian Ltd v Law Society of Upper Canada*, [2004] SCC 13.

[364] *ULP* (n 346).

[365] The problem of the copyist, mentioned by some authors, and even the House of Lords in *Interlego v Tyco Industries*, [1989] AC 217 (n 351), is, it seems to

*ULP* that was taken up in later rulings). In the case of a factual compilation (such as a phone book), a second 'author' who would arrive at exactly the same result as the first would not violate copyright if she redid the work of collecting the data. The author is thus, from this point of view, the blue-collar worker[366] of the content industry.

According to the Supreme Court in *CCH*, the other 'extreme' approach is the requirement of creativity that the US (perhaps surprisingly, given its utilitarian philosophy) and the human rights-inspired countries of the *droit civil* tradition share.[367] This notion, which excludes a number of insignificant (in the literal sense of the term) works from the sphere of copyright, benefits authors since it places them in the forefront. What merits or justifies protection is the creative nature of the author's contribution.

In *CCH*, the Supreme Court ostensibly opted for a third, middle path— no doubt reflecting the very Canadian tendency toward compromise. I am not so sure that this is actually the case, however. Certainly, the Supreme Court declared that it preferred not to follow American jurisprudence, including the famous *Feist* case discussed above,[368] where the US court found that a basic telephone directory did not meet the required criterion of originality despite of the amount of work spent compiling the data and arranging the names, addresses and numbers of subscribers in the usual alphabetical table format. A first, quick reading of *CCH* would lead one to believe that the 'Canadian' notion of originality starts with the 'test' of effort and labour (without 'copying'), but adds one caveat: the effort and labour must be neither mechanical[369] nor trivial.[370] At first glance therefore (see Figure 4.1 below), it seems that Canada is now situated between the two 'extreme' standards.

---

me, a red herring, since *ULP* excludes copied works. The real problem of *ULP* is not that of 'copying', but the fact that the standard of effort and labour is fundamentally erroneous, as discussed below.

[366] This is not a value judgment. I invoke the image to emphasize that *Telstra* (n 373) recognizes, taken to the limit, the *manual* work of authors rather than their intellectual contribution.

[367] Without going into detail, some European countries, including Germany, have considerably lowered the threshold for originality. This being said, two European Directives require that a work be an 'intellectual creation' by its author, which seems to codify the requirement of creativity. See Directive 91/250/EEC and Directive 96/9/EC (n 358).

[368] Feist (n 314).

[369] 'This exercise of skill and judgment will necessarily involve intellectual effort. The exercise of skill and judgment required to produce the work must not be so trivial that it could be characterized as a purely mechanical exercise'. *CCH* (n 363) [16], [25].

[370] Ibid., [88].

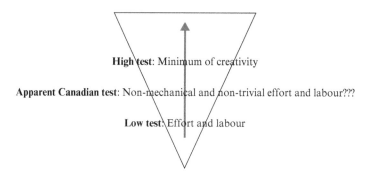

*Figure 4.1    Apparent Canadian test*

Things are not always what they seem, however. *Canada has taken on a standard essentially identical to its American neighbours and to the European systems.* This is relatively clear. The level of originality as defined by the Court is functionally almost impossible to distinguish from the 'modicum of creativity' approach in *Feist.* Consider, what makes it so that the effort and labour are neither mechanical nor trivial? The answer is precisely the presence of a modicum of creativity. In a detailed analysis of *Feist* and relevant civil law rulings, I tried to demonstrate that the notion of minimal creativity (the 'modicum of creativity' of *Feist*) is in fact a 'test' that is both easy to use and objective.[371] It consists of measuring the *creative choices* of the author, where 'creative choices' are defined as those that are not dictated by the eventual function of the work, by the technique used, nor, in cases where the work is more technical in nature, by the applicable standards or practices. A simple way of conceiving of this 'test' is as follows: would another author likely have created the same 'work' in the same context? If the answer is yes, the work is of a mechanical or manual nature and there is no originality in the sense of copyright because there is no room for creative choices. If the answer is no, i.e., it is likely that another author would have reached a substantially different result, the work is not merely functional because there was a creative 'space' to make choices, conscious or not, rational or not, that the first author would not have made, or at least would not have made in the same manner. This is what is said not only in *Feist* but also in the rulings of the French *Cour de cassation* [Supreme Court],[372] which used this test in cases in which a search for the presence of

---

[371]    Gervais (n 202), 7; Gervais (n 46).
[372]    A detailed analysis of those cases is presented in the book mentioned in the previous note.

the author's personality became illusory or impossible (the French notion of originality is discussed below). Finally, it is also the definition of originality that emerges from work related to the Berne Convention.

In short, the standard established in *Feist*—itself similar to the current one in France and elsewhere in the world with regard to more technical works—is essentially identical to the Canadian standard, in spite of the apparent effort made by the court to differentiate itself from foreign jurisprudence. This standard is based on the author's creativity, defined here as non-mechanical and non-trivial effort, skill and labour.

### 4.1.1.4   Australia

Australia produced a very interesting case also dealing with telephone directories.[373] Judge Finkelstein of the Federal Court provided a thorough analysis of British cases concerning the copyrightability of factual compilations, and then studied *Feist*[374] and *Tele-Direct*.[375] The court found there were cogent policy arguments both for and against following Feist[376] but decided against it:

> [T]he very nature of copyright requires the work to be the product of creative thought. The first copyright statute was enacted 'for the Encouragement of learned Men to compose and write useful Books'. These books were necessarily the result of the author's intellectual effort. That was also true of other works (engravings, sculptures, dramatic works and the like) that were given copyright protection by the early statutes. But a compilation is of a different character from a work of art or literature. This is especially true of a compilation of facts that are in the public domain . . . the creativity is of a different order from that involved in producing a work of art or literature.[377]

---

[373]   *Telstra Corporation Ltd v Desktop Marketing Systems Pty Ltd* [2001] FCA 612.

[374]   Ibid., [69]–[78].

[375]   Ibid., [79]–[82].

[376]   Ibid., [83]:

> [T]here are those who argue that the abandonment of the 'sweat of the brow' theory has threatened the progress of information. The argument is that the collection of factual material is essential to the economy. Databases provide a wealth of information to business people, professionals, scientists and consumers. If copyright protection is not given, the investment of the time and money that is required to produce these compilations will not be forthcoming. Perhaps it was the risk of this occurring that led to the introduction of a bill to repeal the effect of *Feist* in the United States House of Representatives (citations omitted).

Referring to the Collections of Information Antipiracy Bill (n 340) introduced in the 105th Congress).

[377]   Ibid., [84].

This reasoning is either incorrect or imprecise. The central assertion is that copyright in compilation is by its very nature different from copyright in other subject matter. There is no statutory basis for such a claim and, as we shall see later, no basis in the history of international copyright law. What the court was perhaps trying to express was that there is a single threshold of originality but that some works merely crawl over it while others are a mile beyond. But the differentiation among various creativity/originality thresholds based on the type of work concerned is unfounded.

In reversing the decision, the High Court[378] 'focused primarily on the substantiality of the defendant's taking and not on the issue of originality'.[379] However, 'dicta in the judgments strongly suggest that the proper originality touchstone is the skill and effort directed at a particular form of expression rather than just a broad inquiry into expense and labor extended'.[380]

In 2009, as Professor Ricketson noted

> the Australian position on originality appeared to shift upwards, following the decision of the High Court in *IceTV v Nine*.[381] Among other things, this suggested that the standard of originality required something more than just the expenditure of labour and investment—some element of intellectual skill and judgment on the part of the author or authors was also necessary.[382]

The debate as to the exact nature of the mental effort required to generate originality, especially in the case of computer programs, continues.[383]

---

[378]   *IceTV Pty Ltd v Nine Network Australia Pty Ltd* (2009) 239 CLR 458.
[379]   Bryce Clayton Newell, 'Discounting the Sweat of the Brow: Converging International Standards for Electronic Database Protection' (2011) 15 *Intellectual Property Law Bulletin* 111, 121.
[380]   Ibid.
[381]   *IceTV Pty Ltd v Nine Network Australia Pty Ltd* (n 382).
[382]   Sam Ricketson, 'The Need for Human Authorship – Australian developments: Telstra Corp Ltd v Phone Directories Co Pty Ltd' (2012) 34(1) *European Intellectual Property Review* 54–60, 55.
[383]   See Jani McCutcheon, The Vanishing Author in Computer-Generated Works: A Critical Analysis of Recent Australian Case Law (2013) 36 *Melbourne University Law Review* 915, 917.

### 4.1.2    Originality in Civil Law Systems

The traditional originality test in France is that the work must express or reflect the author's personality, a fairly subjective notion to be sure.[384] According to a French commentator, it was normal that such a subjective notion would emerge during the nineteenth century because:

> the modes of expression then in vogue—sculpture, painting and writings—[are] ... the expression of (inner) turmoil (*'tourmente'*) of the author, this emotional, subjective and non-rational aspect of human thought. In a way, what differentiates one work from another is its irrationality, a reflection of the author's own irrational mind.[385]

This approach, while understandable for the types of works mentioned (sculpture, writings and painting), does not mesh well with compilations and databases. Yet, the protection of several types of compilations has been recognized by French courts, including statistical studies,[386] comparative tables of television audience ratings,[387] and even specialized telephone directories[388] and calendars.[389] The French *Cour de cassation* [Civil Supreme Court] made it clear that labour itself was insufficient[390] and that courts had to look at the choice of the method used by the author of the compilation.[391] In fact, in recognizing that the classical test could not be used for newer types of works such as databases (compilations) and computer software, several French courts have tried to develop a new test or, more precisely, to elevate the classical test to a higher level of abstraction, by answering the following question: what is it that an author does to show her personality through a work? The fairly unanimous answer given by French courts is that creative choices make the difference.[392] In the *Harrap's* Case, a case involving a bilingual dictionary, the Court of Appeal of Paris found that 'the choices and intellectual operations required to create the [dictionary] tend to give the

---

[384] Andre Lucas, Henri-Jacques Lucas and Agnes Lucas-Schloetter, *Traité de la Propriete Litteraire et Artistique* (4th edn, Litec 2011) 117: 'The classic thesis is simple: Originality must be understood as the mark of the author's personality.'
[385] Jean Martin, 'Le droit d'auteur applicable au logiciel' in Isabelle de Lamberterie (ed.) *Le droit d'auteur aujourd'hui* (CNRS 1991) 111.
[386] TGI Paris, réf, 18 jan 1999, JurisData 043760.
[387] CA Paris, le ch, 22 mai 1990, Légipresse 1990 I, p 67.
[388] CA Paris, 18 dec 1924, D 1925, p 30.
[389] CA Paris, 4e ch, 14 avr 1986, D 1987 Somm 152, obs Colombet.
[390] Cass civ le, 2 mai 1989, JCP 1990 II 21392, note Lucas (Coprosa Case).
[391] Cass crim, 18 mai 1938, Gaz Pal 1938, 2 p 311; Cass civ, 27 May 1942, S Jur I, p 124.
[392] See Gervais, *La notion* (n 46) 85–6.

resulting work a certain degree of originality, even when dealing with a technical type of work'.[393] The court made it clear that merely sorting data that was difficult to generate in alphabetical order was not original. Originality can only follow from intellectually creative choices (as opposed to mechanical or functional choices).[394] A similar conclusion was reached by the same court a few years later concerning a collection of Cajun words.[395]

Another interesting case involved a compilation of short stories based on traditional folklore.[396] The stories themselves were in the public domain because the term of protection had expired, but copyright could still subsist in a (original) selection and arrangement of stories. The court found that 'by choosing the stories, by narrating them with his own style and by arranging them according to a sequence chosen by him and which was not necessary,[397] and by giving the book a specific structure, Mr. Guillois created a creative work'.[398]

In sum, when French courts tried to elevate the level of abstraction, they realized that what distinguishes one work from another are in fact creative choices. Similar, although not as completely developed doctrines, have also been accepted by courts in the civil law countries of Belgium,[399] the Netherlands,[400] and Switzerland.[401] In fact, Swiss copyright scholars Bannelet and Egloff assert that what creates originality are choices made by the author that were not dictated by custom or good practice.[402]

---

[393] CA Paris, 4e ch, 21 mar 1989, 142 RIDA 333, 338–9 (*Harrap's* Case) (author's translation).

[394] Ibid.

[395] CA Paris, 1e ch, 14 jan 1992, 152 RIDA 198.

[396] CA Paris, 4e ch, 23 sept 1992, 156 RIDA 224 (*Fayard* Case).

[397] In the sense that the sequence was not dictated by the technique used, or any norms concerning this type of compilation.

[398] *Fayard* Case (n 396) 224–5 (author's translation).

[399] Cass civ, 27 avr 1989, RW 1989–90, p. 362; Cass civ, 25 oct 1989, RW 1989–90, p. 1061; see also Alain Strowel, 'The Originality of the Work' in Association Littéraire et Artistique Internationale Congress, *Copyright and Industrial Property: Congress of the Aegean Sea II* (ALAI 1992) 392; Alain Strowel, *Droit d'Auteur et Copyright: Divergences et Convergences, Ètude de Droit Comparè* (Bruylant 1993) 420–31.

[400] *Van Dale v Romme I*, HR 4 january 1991, *IER* 1991 (8) at 177; *Van Dalle v Romme II*, HR 1 april 1993, *IER* 1993 (3) at 82. *See also* Strowel, *Droit d'Auteur* (n 399) 425–6.

[401] Gervais *La notion* (n 46) 87–8; Max Kummer, *Das Urheberrechtlich Shützbare Werk* (Stämpfli 1968) 30; Denis Bannelet and Willi Egloff, *Le Nouveau Droit d'Auteur: Commentaire de la Loi Fédérale Sur le Droit d'Auteur et les Droits Voisins* (Stämpfli 1994) 24.

[402] In French, 'règles de l'art'. *See* Bannelet and Egloff (n 401) 10–24.

### 4.1.3  Originality in International Copyright Treaties

There is no definition of the concept of 'originality' in international copyright treaties.[403] In fact, the requirement that a work be 'original' is not even mentioned. There are, however, several statements in records of diplomatic conferences and committees of experts meeting under the aegis of the World Intellectual Property Organization ('WIPO') that confirm the requirement that originality be present, and that this is the only applicable criterion (to the exclusion of, e.g., artistic merit or purpose).[404]

The expression 'work' itself is defined officially by the list of categories of works in Article 2 of the Berne Convention.[405] A WIPO Committee of

---

[403]  Actually, very few national laws contain such a definition. We studied 93 national laws and found a specific definition of originality in only three countries: Bulgaria, Burkina Faso, and Malaysia. See Gervais *La notion* (n 46) 72–6. Indirectly, a definition of 'originality' is contained in the two EU Directives that require that a work be the result of the author's 'own intellectual creation'. See n 358; *Bridgeman Art Library, Ltd v Corel Corp*, 36 F Supp 2d 191, 195 (SDNY 1999).

[404]  One additional criterion would require that the subject matter to be protected fit within one of the categories of works (literary or artistic) defined in art. 2(1) and (5) of the Berne Convention (n 313), and in national laws, such as 17 USC § 101. It is interesting to compare this with the Supreme Court dictum in *Feist*, according to which originality was the 'key to resolving the tension' among the conflicting approaches to copyright. Feist (n 314) 1287.

The first statement on originality was made during the Revision Conference of the Berne Convention held in Rome from May 7 to June 2, 1928. The Acts of this conference were originally published only in French (Actes de la Conférence réunie à Rome du 7 mai au 2 juin 1928 (Bureau de l'Union internationale pour la protection des œuvres littéraires et artistiques 1929)), but WIPO published an English translation of the records of all Berne revision conferences on the occasion of the centenary of the Berne Convention. WIPO, *1886–1986: Berne Convention Centenary* (WIPO 1986). In the General Report, rapporteur Edoardo Piola Caselli wrote:

> The protection enjoyed by other works of art should be reserved for cinematographic productions which meet the requirements of originality laid down in paragraph (2) [of Article 14]. In order to show clearly that *the only requirement concerned here is that of the originality with which every work of the mind must be endowed*. Ibid. (emphasis added).

[405]  Berne Convention (n 313) art. 2(1):

> The expression 'literary and artistic works' shall include every production in the literary, scientific and artistic domain, whatever may be the mode or form of its expression, such as books, pamphlets and other writings; lectures, addresses, sermons and other works of the same nature; dramatic or dramatico-musical works; choreographic works and entertainments in dumb show; musical compositions with or without words; cinematographic works to which are

Experts concluded that this expression was synonymous with 'intellectual creation',[406] and that such creation should contain 'an original structure of ideas or impressions'.[407] The same committee also noted that originality 'was an integral part of the definition of the concept of "work"'.[408]

In its memorandum for the meeting of the Committee of Experts, the International Bureau of WIPO explained:

> Although this is not stated explicitly in Article 2(1) of the Berne Convention, the context in which the words 'work' and 'author' are used in the Convention—closely related to each other—indicates that only those productions are considered works which are *intellectual creations* (and, consequently, only those persons are considered authors whose intellectual creative activity brings such works into existence). This is the first basic element of the notion of literary and artistic works.
>
> The records of various diplomatic conferences adopting and revising the Berne Convention reflect that the reason why Article 2(1) of the Convention does not state explicitly that works are intellectual creations is that that element of the notion of works was considered to be evident.[409]

---

assimilated works expressed by a process analogous to cinematography; works of drawing, painting, architecture, sculpture, engraving and lithography; photographic works to which are assimilated works expressed by a process analogous to photography; works of applied art; illustrations, maps, plans, sketches and three-dimensional works relative to geography, topography, architecture or science.

[406]   The concept of 'intellectual creation' has been acknowledged as a synonym of 'work' in several international meetings. See Gervais *La notion* (n 46) 45–9.

[407]   First Session of the Committee of Experts on Model provisions for Legislation in the Field of Copyright Report CE/MPC/I/3 of 3 March 1989, para. 78, also stating that:

> originality [is] part of the definition of 'work' and [. . .] a reference to it should be included in Section 2(1) . . . The idea of providing a definition of the concept of 'work' was, however, opposed by a number of participants; it was felt that that question should rather be left to national legislation and/or to the courts.

[408]   Ibid. While international meetings of this kind are not normative in nature, their findings are relevant as doctrinal input, and in certain cases may reflect an existing international custom. See, e.g., Statute of the International Court of Justice, art. 38 s. 1(b). The history of the Convention was also used extensively by a WTO dispute-settlement panel to interpret provisions of the Convention that were incorporated by reference into the TRIPS Agreement.

[409]   First Session of the Committee of Experts on Model Provisions for Legislation in the Field of Copyright Memorandum CE/MPC/I/2-III of 20 October 1988 on Draft Model Provisions for Legislation in the Field of Copyright, paras 51–52 (emphasis in original). The second element of the definition 'is determined by the adjectives "*literary*" and "*artistic*"', ibid., para. 56.

The General Report of the Berne Convention Revision Conference held in Brussels in 1948 specifically states:

> You have not considered it necessary to specify that those works constitute intellectual creations because . . . if we are speaking of literary and artistic works, we are already using a term which means that we are talking about personal creation or about an intellectual creation within the sphere of letters and the arts.[410]

The Convention itself provides two important hints as to what constitutes an original work. Article 2, when discussing the protection of collections, states that '[c]ollections of literary or artistic works such as encyclopaedias and anthologies which, *by reason of the selection and arrangement of their contents*, constitute *intellectual creations* shall be protected as such, without prejudice to the copyright in each of the works forming part of such collections'.[411] Again, as the court found in *Feist*, selection and arrangement are essentially choices that must be creative in order to generate copyright protection; and a creation may be considered 'intellectual' if it fits that description.[412]

Finally, the TRIPS Agreement only contains an *a contrario* definition, as it were.[413] For the first time in an international agreement in this field, a list of exclusions was agreed upon.[414]

## 4.2   ASSESSMENT AND SYNTHESIS

### 4.2.1   The Key Role of Originality

There were two schools of thought in the US when it came to defining originality in copyright law. The first, which I would call objectivist and

---

[410]   Berne Convention Centenary (n 404) 179.
[411]   Berne Convention (n 313) art. 2(5).
[412]   See n 326, discussing Feist (n 314).
[413]   During the negotiation of the Agreement, the Swiss delegation had proposed a definition of 'work' which would have included any literary or artistic creation of the mind, which has an original character, independently of its literary or artistic merit or commercial value. See GATT Document MTN.GNG/NG11/W/73 of 14 May 1990 on Draft Amendment to the General Agreement on Tariffs and Trade on the Protection of Trade-Related Intellectual Property Rights.
[414]   Agreement on Trade-Related Aspects of Intellectual Property Rights (1993) art. 9(2), 'Copyright protection shall extend to expressions and not to ideas, procedures, methods of operation or mathematical concepts as such'. This article mirrors § 102(b) of the US Copyright Act.

vaguely Lockean, defined it as something that resulted from skill and labour. The traditional British test was to that effect, and was applied for several decades in Australia and Canada, and in a number of federal Appellate Circuits in the US prior to *Feist*.[415] Led by France, nineteenth century civil law systems adopted an approach that searched for the mark of the author's personality in the work, requiring more than evidence of skill and labour. I would call this second approach 'subjectivist'.

*Feist* established, arguably for the first time with this level of clarity, that *creative choices* are what gives a work its originality.[416] In Britain, there is evidence of a shift towards something *more* than skill, labour and judgement in two decisions of the UK House of Lords, perhaps articulated on the basis of the third word in the trilogy, namely 'judgment' and/or using the EU notion of intellectual creation. This shift may be taking place in Australia as well, though there matters are not limpid.

In parallel, civil law systems adapted themselves to new technologies not by abandoning their traditional model based on the search for the mark of the author's personality, but rather by increasing the level of abstraction of the traditional concept, which led them to a doctrine of creative choices strikingly similar to the test articulated in *Feist*. This does not mean that the traditional approach is dead: certain works of highly creative nature might contain so many creative choices that they in fact do 'reflect the author's personality'.[417] Other works that do not, especially more technical creations, may, however, still be protected by copyright.

This test based on creative choices is a more modern approach, which not only relieved a tension amongst US federal circuits[418] but also bridges the conceptual gap between common law and civil law countries with respect to the core notion of originality. *Feist* is not just a part of this new worldview of originality, it may have been the impetus for an international trend.[419]

The 'new' test also provides a way to measure creativity by measuring the quality and quantity of creative choices.[420] Copyright statutes recognize a single originality standard, and this creativity standard clearly is not restricted to compilations. It has been applied to several other types

---

[415]  The Seventh, Eighth, and Tenth Circuits. See Lea Meade (n 315).
[416]  See n 326, discussing Feist (n 314).
[417]  Lucas (n 384) 117.
[418]  Dowd (n 317).
[419]  Sunny Handa, *Copyright Law in Canada* (Butterworths 2002) 232–3.
[420]  It may also be useful in applying the idea/expression dichotomic test. *Robinson* (n 425).

of works.[421] From a copyright standpoint, therefore, either a creation is original or it is not. If it is, then it is protected.[422] If a work contains just a minimal number of creative choices,[423] then its creativity level (from a copyright perspective) is sufficient. Then as the number increases, originality increases proportionally, which in turn may lead to a broader scope of protection.[424]

If the two major copyright systems appear to have almost melded one of the most fundamental notions, namely originality,[425] a key question remains: what exactly are 'creative choices'?

### 4.2.2 Creative Choices

The notion of creativity seems to be inexorably linked to the human mind. But what is creativity? The exercise of choice? Computers can and do 'choose' based on pre-programmed instructions, but that does not make them authors.[426] I suggest that a definition of the notion of 'creative choice' that would meet the requirements of international treaties, and mesh

---

[421] *Atari Games Corp v Oman*, 979 F2d 242 (DCC 1992) (audiovisual works); *Ets-Hokin v Skyy Spirits, Inc*, 225 F3d 1068 (9th Cir 2000) (photographs); *CMM Cable Rep, Inc v Ocean Coast Prop, In*c, 97 F3d 1504 (1st Cir 1996) (promotional materials); *Boisson v Banian, Ltd*, 273 F3d 262 (2d Cir 2001) (letter patterns on quilts); *Cty of Suffolk, NY v First Am Real Estate Sol*, 261 F3d 179 (2d Cir 2001) (maps); *Yurman Design, Inc v PAJ, Inc*, 262 F3d 101 (2d Cir 2001) (jewellery designs); *Superior Form Builders, Inc v Dan Chase Taxidermy Supply Co, Inc*, 74 F3d 488 (4th Cir 1996) (animal mannequins (sculptures)).

[422] 17 USC § 102(a), 'Copyright protection subsists, in accordance with this title, in original works of authorship'. This does not mean that the scope of protection will not vary based on the degree of 'extra' originality, i.e., originality that surpasses the threshold. See Michael J Meurer, 'Copyright Law and Price Discrimination' (2001) 23 *Cardozo Law Review* 55, 108; see also Feist (n 314) 349–51.

[423] *Key Publications, Inc v Chinatown Today Publ'g Enter, Inc*, 945 F2d 509, 513 (2d Cir 1991), 'Selection implies the exercise of judgment in choosing which facts from a given body of data to include in a compilation.' As we will see in the next section, certain creative choices might be qualitatively more important for purposes of copyright protection, and, in that case, fewer creative choices would be required.

[424] See n 422.

[425] *Sands and McDougall Pty Ltd v Robinson* (1917) 23 CLR 49, 56 (High Court of Australia): '[I]n copyright law the two expressions "author" and "original work" have always been correlative; the one connotes the other.'

[426] *Matthew Bender & Co v West Publ'g Co*, 158 F3d 693, 699 (2d Cir 1998). *See also* Evan H Farr, 'Copyrightability of Computer-Created Works' (1989) 15 *Rutgers Computer & Technology Law Journal* 63, 65.

with both *Feist* and civil law system definitions, is as follows: a creative choice[427] *is one made by the author*[428] *that is not dictated*[429] *by the function of the work,*[430] *the method*[431] *or technique used, or by applicable standards*[432] *or*

---

[427] 'Choice' is used here in the traditional sense of an act or instance of choosing from among a number of possibilities.

[428] This expands on the notion that the choice must be made 'independently' by the author. Feist (n 314) 1288; CMM Cable Rep (n 421); Urantia (n 426).

[429] This terminology was used in *CDN Inc v Kapes*, 197 F3d 1256, 1259 (9th Cir 1999), a case that interpreted *Feist* rather narrowly. It was also in the famous decision for *Computer Assocs Int'l, Inc v Altai, Inc*, 982 F2d 693, 707 (2d Cir 1992), but in a different context, namely the idea/expression dichotomy:

> Professor Nimmer suggests, and we endorse, a 'successive filtering method' for separating protectable expression from non-protectable material. This process entails examining the structural components at each level of abstraction to determine whether their particular inclusion at that level was 'idea' or was dictated by considerations of efficiency, so as to be necessarily incidental to that idea; required by factors external to the program itself; or taken from the public domain and hence is nonprotectable expression.

[430] Similar to the numbering system that served as a shorthand description of the relevant characteristics of each fastener described in *Southco, Inc v Kanebridge Corp*, 258 F3d 148, 152 (3d Cir 2001):

> Southco uses product numbers that convey specific properties of the products manufactured. The numbers are not assigned at random or in sequence; they are assigned based on the properties of the parts. The Numbering System is a complex code expressing numerous detailed features of Southco hardware products; each part number tells the story of a part's size, finish, and utility.

Under this system, each fastener was assigned a unique nine-digit number, with each digit describing a specific physical parameter of the fastener. The 'market' may, by extension, be considered as a 'functional requirement' if what is required is so clear as not to leave room for creativity. See, e.g., Warren Publ'g (n 337) 1520 n. 31: 'The mere discovery of an organizing principle which is dictated by the market is not sufficient to establish creativity'; but see *CCC Information Servs* (n 337) 67:

> The fact that an arrangement of data responds *logically* to the needs of the market for which the compilation was prepared does not negate originality. To the contrary, the use of logic to solve the problems of how best to present the information being compiled is independent creation.

[431] In the sense of the creation method. The creation of a method (e.g., to present facts) would be copyrightable. See *Eng'g Dynamics, Inc v Structural Software, Inc*, 26 F3d 1335, 1346 (5th Cir 1994), *opinion supplemented on denial of rehearing*, 46 F3d 408 (5th Cir 1995).

[432] Or 'garden-variety' variations on a theme. Feist (n 314) 1296; *see also Perma Greetings, Inc v Russ Berrie & Co, Inc*, 598 F Supp 445, 448: 'Clichéd language, phrases and expressions conveying an idea that is typically expressed in a limited

*relevant 'good practice'.*[433] Purely insignificant[434] selection is insufficient.[435] A human choice must be made although as in certain forms of art, it need not be made 'consciously'.

One element of this definition that might seem controversial is the exclusion of choices dictated by the function of the work. This in fact is very close to the test of 'practical inevitability' in *Feist*: if function dictates the course to be followed, there is no room for creativity. From a copyright standpoint, therefore, the result is indeed 'inevitable'.[436] Function is meant here in a technical sense, and is linked to the interface between copyright and industrial designs. Take, for example, a chair or table: if a leg were added at a specific location to make sure the chair would support the weight of a person, then that choice would be functional; to benefit from copyright protection, an author would have to show that *other* choices were made, such as when deciding the aesthetic shape of the leg, etc.[437] An application of this element of the suggested definition is illustrated in *Allen-Myland, Inc v IBM Corp*.[438] Allen-Myland argued that portions of computer code that were added

---

number of stereotypic fashions, [sic] are not subject to copyright protection'; *CMM Cable Rep* (n 421). This concept is similar to the notion of 'non-obvious' described in Matthew Bender & Co (n 426), or to the 'mechanical or routine' in Feist (n 314)1289, *Mid Am Title Co* (n 337) 680, and BellSouth (n 337) 1443.

[433]   Victor Lalli Enter (n 337) 673:

In Lalli's charts, as Judge Glasser correctly found, he arranges factual data according to 'purely functional grids that offer no opportunity for variation'. The format of the charts is a convention: Lalli exercises neither selectivity in what he reports nor creativity in how he reports it.

[434]   *Donald v Zack Meyer's TV Sales & Serv*, 426 F2d 1027, 1030 (5th Cir 1970), *cert denied* 91 S Ct 459 (1971). This case was blended in with *Feist* by the Fifth Circuit in *Eng'g Dynamics* (n 431) 1345:

[T]he input/output formats fail to satisfy the *Feist-Zack Meyer* originality test. In *Feist,* the Supreme Court held that an alphabetically arranged phone book lacks the creativity and originality necessary to sustain a copyright. In [the *Zack Meyer* case], this circuit held that boilerplate contractual language printed on a blank form was insufficiently original.

[435]   See, e.g., *Mitel, Inc v Iqtel, Inc*, 124 F3d 1366, 1373–74 (10th Cir 1997).
[436]   Feist (n 314) 1297.
[437]   This distinction between utility and aesthetic is fairly common. See, e.g., *Wal-Mart Stores, Inc v Samara Bros, Inc*, 529 US 205, 214 (2000). The definition does not take account of art. 2(7) of the Berne Convention (n 313), which provides countries with an option not to protect works of applied art under copyright if 'special protection' is granted.
[438]   770 F Supp 1004 (ED Pa 1991).

to an existing IBM program lacked originality because programming choices were dictated by earlier programming choices.[439] The court found that there were creative choices because IBM's programmers had to pick from several possibilities for both the structure and the data.[440]

Similarly, following applicable standards means that there is unlikely to be enough room for creative choices.[441] The same conclusion would be reached if choices were dictated by the mere application of relevant principles.[442] This also means that 'true' artistic works[443] (arguably with purer aesthetic considerations) are protected: the vast majority of the choices made by an author of a novel or painting clearly are not dictated (or 'inevitable') by function, technique or standards.[444]

Perhaps the best way to illustrate the application of the proposed definition is to look at the art of photography. Photographs involve several technical choices made by the photographer (aperture, etc.), and these choices are usually dictated by good photographic practices. It is not those choices that may give rise to copyright protection but rather the choices not so dictated to the photographer such as pose, angle, décor, lighting arrangements, etc.[445] This notion brings us to *Bridgeman Art Library, Ltd v Corel Corp*, where a court in New York had to decide whether 'technically

---

[439] Ibid., 1011.

[440] Ibid., 1012.

[441] See Mid Am Title Co (n 337) 722.

[442] Similar to the criteria used for selecting data in the *BellSouth* case (n 337) 1441:

> To be sure, [BellSouth] employed a set of strategies or techniques for discovering this data. Any useful collection of facts, however, will be structured by a number of decisions regarding the optimal manner in which to collect the pertinent data in the most efficient and accurate manner. If this were sufficient, then the protection of copyright would extend to census data . . . .

See also Reytblat (n 325) 200–202.

[443] Terminology in this area is problematic. A distinction is sometimes made between 'low authorship' and 'high authorship' works. See Ginsburg (n 338) 340–41. We find that these terms can be misleading. Originality should be seen as a continuum. Above a minimum threshold, protection under copyright arises. This is, in fact, the central message in *Feist*. Above that threshold, originality increases gradually. An essay or how-to book, for example, could be viewed as a 'medium authorship' situation. An interesting example is the case of *Suntrust Bank v Houghton Mifflin Co*, 268 F3d 1257, 1271 (11th Cir 2001), in which the court found that *Gone With the Wind* was 'undoubtedly entitled to the greatest degree of protection as an original work of fiction'.

[444] The determination of whether choices were dictated would seem to be a question of fact more than law. See Reytblat (n 325) 207–12.

[445] See n 328, discussing *Burrow-Giles* (n 327).

perfect' photographs of public domain paintings were copyrightable.[446] Because no copyright subsisted in the works of art per se, the only possible copyright was in the photographs themselves. Undoubtedly, making perfect photographic reproductions of works of art requires a high degree of skill and technique, in other words, considerable skill and labour, but whether creative choices were made is less clear.

Because the photographs were made by a British photographer, Judge Kaplan decided to analyse their copyright status from both a British law and American law perspective:

> But one need not deny the creativity inherent in the art of photography to recognize that a photograph which is no more than a copy of the work of another as exact as science and technology permit lacks originality. That is not to say such a feat is trivial, simply not original.[447]

Quoting in part from *Durham Industries, Inc v Tomy Corp*,[448] he added that '[t]here has been "no independent creation, no distinguishable variation from preexisting works, nothing recognizably the author's own contribution" that sets Bridgeman's reproductions apart from the images of the famous works it copied'.[449] The court found that the same result would be reached under UK law, because the photograph was simply copied from another work.[450]

Contrast *Corel* with *Ets-Hokin v Skyy Spirits, Inc*,[451] where the US Court of Appeal for the Ninth Circuit found that photographs of a vodka bottle used to create promotional material were original because:

> creative decisions involved in producing a photograph may render it sufficiently original to be copyrightable and [courts] 'have carefully delineated selection of subject, posture, background, lighting, and perhaps even perspective alone as protectable elements of a photographer's work'.[452]

In other words, non-dictated choices had been made.

In the case of compilations, it is even easier to apply the test. Taking a *Feist*-type compilation (telephone directory), one can see that the efforts

---

[446]   25 F Supp 2d 421, 427–8.
[447]   Ibid.
[448]   630 F2d 905, 910 (2d Cir 1980).
[449]   *Bridgeman Art Library* (n 403) 427.
[450]   Ibid., 426.
[451]   225 F3d 1068 (9th Cir 2000).
[452]   Ibid., 1077 (quoting *Los Angeles News Serv v Tullo*, 973 F2d 791, 794 (9th Cir 1992) (quoting *United States v Hamilton*, 583 F2d 488, 452 (9th Cir 1978))).

needed to amass the data are not 'creative'. Similarly, sorting the data according to a standard or 'good practice' filter (such as alphabetical order) is uncopyrightable. My proposed definition leads me to conclude that a database in which all available data on a topic is entered is not protected under copyright.[453] Creative choices that would render a compilation protectible, however, can be made through a selection or arrangement[454] that is not 'dictated'.[455] For example, the selection of poems for an anthology requires an intellectual effort that is not entirely dictated by standards and technique; otherwise all anthologies on the same topic would be almost identical.[456]

Compilations that hover just beyond the creative threshold will only have thin copyright protection.[457] But the key point is to determine whether they display and result from creative choices, even when other copyrighted works may well exceed that minimum line. Thus there seems to be a fairly broad international consensus that originality is not only copyright's single 'sieve', but also, and more importantly, that the presence of creative choices in the making of the work is the adequate test to determine whether the work is worthy of copyright protection.

Recognizing the role and place of creative choices as the proper threshold would in fact be a part of a structured reform effort. It does not require a legislative solution (though a definition of originality in a statute is possible). The purpose of this analysis is to show that originality properly defined should be factored in the analysis by courts.

## 4.3   FIXATION

Fixation is a threshold criterion to obtain copyright protection in a number of legal systems. It is a requirement expressly allowed by the Berne Convention.[458] It seems that fixation was imposed historically

---

[453]   Other forms of protection are available. See n 338, and accompanying text.

[454]   The presentation of a compilation (e.g., the book cover) is also copyrightable of course, but its protection is independent from the protection of the compilation.

[455]   See n 429, discussing the *Kapes* and *Altai* cases.

[456]   See *Eckes v Card Prices Update*, 736 F2d 859, 862–3 (2d Cir 1984) (choice of best baseball cards).

[457]   TransWestern (n 337) 776–7; Melville B Nimmer and David Nimmer, *Nimmer on Copyright* (M Bender 1997) s 13.03[A], 13–28.

[458]   International copyright instruments, to which the US is party, allow countries to require fixation. Article 2(2) of the Berne Convention, ratified by the US on November 16, 1988, provides that '[i]t shall, however, be a matter for legislation

to distinguish forms of creativity that produce copyright works from those that do not. Fixation plays a dual role. It may—though it does not always—serve both as an expression of the author's intent to create a more or less permanent work—the commercial exploitation of which might benefit from copyright protection. It also plays an evidentiary role in that it allows an objective determination of the existence of a work. Technological developments mean that intent is less and less clearly manifested. With the capture of every word (text instead of telephone conversation is perhaps the best example) as well as free[459] photography and video recording (including dissemination via social media), fixation is now almost a default situation. Privacy, and the ability to have unfixed conversations and moments, is increasingly becoming a rarity.

Fixation is thus unlikely to feature prominently in an effort to restructure copyright. A majority of countries do not require fixation, but do require evidence that a work has been 'objectified', that the author's ideas have been expressed in some form that is perceptible by others. For copyright purposes, a work does not exist if it is only in the author's mind, even in countries that do not require fixation. Philosophically, fixation runs counter to a possibility that digital technology affords. Digital technology allows the development of living creations that a creator or indeed a group or community can change. 'Fixation' in time is thus not intrinsically coherent with technological capability that allows modification and 'republication' of updated versions. Codes should be developed to identify versions (e.g., by date). Social norms and practices will continue to develop in this area and no legislative solution is required, though the library community must keep this issue on their radar.

---

in the countries of the Union to prescribe that works in general or any specified categories of works shall not be protected unless they have been fixed in some material form'. That provision of the Berne Convention (n 313) was incorporated into the TRIPS Agreement (n 414) in art. 9.1.

[459]   In the sense that no film or other more expensive carrier is required.

# 5.  Vicarious and participative creativity

## 5.1  INTRODUCTION

In old style photography, to print a picture photographic paper was immersed in a liquid known as 'developer'. The liquid slowly revealed the picture 'captured' on the negative. I use this pre-digital image here to describe the impact that a very digital phenomenon known as user-generated content (UGC) has had on copyright policy. It has indeed revealed much about the underlying structural problems with copyright law and policy and the underlying assumptions on which the copyright system is based. UGC may be defined as content that is created in whole or in part using tools specific to the online environment and generally also disseminated using such tools. The label is useful to identify the societal shifts in content creation brought about by the Internet and best epitomized perhaps by the remix[460] phenomenon. It also extends to fan fiction, mash-ups, collages and many other forms of participatory cultural productions. It is the result of the shift from a one-to-many entertainment and information infrastructure to a many-to-many infrastructure. UGC has deep consequences on many levels, from the way culture is created, apprehended, and disseminated. It has rocked the copyright boat to the tipping point.

UGC forms part of a broader human tendency to 'create by participation', that is, either in groups of Internet users (who may or may not be known to one another), often reusing material created by others. Digital technology allows Internet users to create truly new works in a variety of ways. In some cases, it allows them simply to create vicariously. UGC is used in this chapter as the flag-bearer for the creative side of the

---

[460]   See Lessig, note 173 above, 28: Lessig compares the 'Read/Write Culture' and the increasing tendency to make works available as 'Read-Only' and notes: '[Citizens] add to the culture they read by creating and re-creating the culture around them. . .Culture in this world is flat; it is shared person to person' (footnotes omitted).
   Using the Internet and other digital tools, 'users' of digital content can thus create and recreate using pre-existing content: the 'remix' culture.

'participative web' (or Web 2.0), terms which refer to an Internet-based network of content and services based on increasingly 'intelligent' web-based software that empowers Internet users to contribute to developing, rating, collaborating on and distributing content and customizing Internet applications.[461] As the Internet gets embedded in more aspects of peoples' lives, users draw on new apps to express themselves through content they upload and make available to others. Life stories are written on Facebook as they happen—often in enhanced or distorted ways compared to 'real life'. This participation is the active side of the UGC story. Some Internet users are happy to just watch others create and 'live' online. This is true of video games of course: some top players have millions of 'followers' who watch them play.[462] Millions tuned in to see Joshua Cohen write an instalment of PCKWCK, his take on Dickens '*Pickwick Papers*', as a live online event.[463] These newer forms of vicarious creativity add a significant layer to the art school experience of watching a master at work. There may undoubtedly be a desire to learn by some viewers but I strongly suspect that many are just watching to see someone else 'create'.

What does copyright law say about participative and vicarious creativity? Two right fragments in the copyright bundle (see Chapter 1), namely the right of reproduction and the right of adaptation (or the right to prepare derivative works), are most directly involved in the production of UGC. Other right fragments may be involved in its use (for example if the work is publicly performed). Defences against claims of infringement in the

---

[461]   See J Markoff, 'Entrepreneurs See a Web Guided by Common Sense', *New York Times*, 12 November 2006 (<http://www.nytimes.com/2006/11/12/business/12web.html?pagewanted=1&ei=5088&en=254d697964cedc62&ex=1320987600> accessed 17 November 2016)

> Their goal is to add a layer of meaning on top of the existing Web that would make it less of a catalog and more of a guide—and even provide the foundation for systems that can reason in a human fashion. That level of artificial intelligence, with machines doing the thinking instead of simply following commands, has eluded researchers for more than half a century. Referred to as Web 3.0, the effort is in its infancy. . . .

[462]   See Carolyn Gregoire, 'Why Are Millions Of People Spending So Much Time Watching Others Play Video Games?' *Huffington Post*, 12 September 2014 (<http://www.huffingtonpost.com/2014/09/12/twitch-video-games_n_5755568.html> accessed 17 November 2016).

[463]   Abby Ohlheiser, 'Inside PCKWCK, the Live-streamed Novel Writing Experiment that is Stressing Everybody Out', *Washington Post*, 14 October 2015 (<https://www.washingtonpost.com/news/the-intersect/wp/2015/10/14/inside-pckwck-the-live-streamed-novel-writing-experiment-that-is-stressing-everybody-out/> accessed 17 November 2016).

UGC context typically rely on one of two things.[464] One can argue, as in the US Supreme Court decision in the *'Pretty Woman'* case (*Campbell v Acuff-Rose*),[465] that the UGC work is a parody and/or what US law now calls a 'transformative fair use' of one or more pre-existing works. Alternatively, depending on the facts of the case, one may argue that only an insubstantial amount of the pre-existing work(s) was used, something akin to a quotation.[466] Other defences may be available in specific circumstances, for example that the second work was used in news reporting.[467]

Viewed in historical perspective, creating original content by reusing pre-existing content is nothing new. If one looks back at the history of copyright, many a Walt Disney production is based on a medieval fairy tale. Indeed countless screenplays are adaptations of pre-existing novels and plays. Such reuse should thus not be a fundamental problem for the theories that have traditionally undergirded copyright. But the participative Web has transformed reuse both quantitatively and qualitatively. On the former point (quantity), when hundreds of millions of Internet users are downloading, altering, mixing, uploading and/or making available audio, video and text content, the enormity of the policy task of regulating this exponentially increasing activity has hit copyright law and policy like a major hurricane. The copyright levee was designed to fight identifiable (commercial) pirates, and allow the marketplace for copyrighted content to organize itself. Will it hold? On the latter front (quality), the fact that UGC is mostly amateur content—typically unlicensed—makes a difference, at least in some cases, as will be apparent in Chapter 8 when discussing the types of authorship that restructured copyright policy should be able to accommodate.[468]

## 5.2   THE RISE OF THE NONPROFESSIONAL USER

As Chapter 1 explains, for approximately 290 of its 310-year (common law) history, copyright rights were traded among professionals, including authors, publishers, producers, broadcasters, etc. Copyright was occasionally used to enforce unauthorized uses by *professional* pirates. Only in the past 15 years or so has it also been used in a systematic way

---

[464]   I am assuming of course that the allegedly infringed work is still copyright-protected.
[465]   *Campbell v Acuff-Rose Music, Inc.*, 510 US 569, 114 S Ct 1164 (1994).
[466]   A 'right to quote' is contained in art. 10(1) of the Berne Convention.
[467]   See, e.g., *Nunez v Caribbean Int'l News Corp*, 235 F3d 18 (1st Cir 2000).
[468]   I discuss this in section 5.3, below.

against individual consumers and end-users.[469] This is, I suggest, the source of much of the tension in the copyright system. It also greatly increased the level of attention paid to copyright law and policy by the public. Put differently, while the law has not changed, its target has.[470] This was possible because formally copyright rights are formulated in fragments that reflect technical restricted acts, such as reproduction, public performance, etc. There is little if any focus in copyright legislation on the nature or category of users, except for a few targeted exceptions.[471]

Trading copyright between and among professionals or enforcing it against those same professionals (or professional pirates) assumed that users were identifiable (that is, known persons and quantities) and that normal licensing transactions were possible. The copyright marketplace functioned because copyright holders would contractually grant authorizations to (professional) users. In cases where a large number of users used a large repertory of works owned by a plurality of owners, collective systems were put in place to allow the licensing of hundreds, sometimes thousands of users.[472] Those systems are sometimes supported by compulsory licenses to avoid the costs and delays of negotiation.[473]

Typically, however, collective and compulsory licenses were and still are for *non-altering uses* and/or integral copying, such as reproduction of sound recordings (to make e.g., CDs, or more generally what US law refers to as 'phonorecords')[474] or public performance. Copyright

---

[469] Although in January 2008 the recording industry announced it would no longer be filing massive amounts of lawsuits against individual end-users. See Sarah McBride and Ethan Smith, 'Music Industry to Abandon Mass Suits', *Wall Street Journal*, 29 December 2008 (available at http://online.wsj.com/article/SB122966038836021137.html).

[470] This also explains the emergence of para-copyright norms such as anti-circumvention of technological protection measures. See, e.g., 17 USC §1201 and foll. and *WIPO Copyright Treaty*, S. Treaty Doc. No. 105-17, 2186 UNTS 152 (1997).

[471] For example 17 USC §108, which provides an exception for libraries.

[472] *See* Gervais (n 473).

[473] See, e.g., the compulsory license for making and distributing phonorecords contained in 17 U.S.C. §115.

[474] US copyright law is different from other national copyright laws in many respects. One of them is the distinction drawn in 17 USC §101 between sounds recordings and phonorecords. The former are copyrighted *works* 'that result from the fixation of a series of musical, spoken, or other sounds, but not including the sounds accompanying a motion picture or other audiovisual work, regardless of the nature of the material objects, such as disks, tapes, or other phonorecords, in which they are embodied', (ibid.) while phonorecords are the *material objects* in which sounds, other than those accompanying a motion picture or other audiovisual work, are fixed. *See* Gervais (n 350).

collective management organizations (CMOs) do not routinely license the right to prepare derivative works, for example, at least not on the basis of pre-existing 'tariffs' (akin to price lists).[475] Nor have they licensed individual end-users, other than exceptionally.[476] Now individual Internet users have become 'content providers' even though they are not professionals. Consequently, a number of major copyright holders have tried to analogize individual users to professional content providers. Meanwhile, licensing mechanisms—to the extent one believes they should apply—have largely been unable to follow. In fact, some might say that one reason why end-users were traditionally left out of the equation was the fact the system could not license/integrate them.

In sum, the inability and/or unwillingness to license end-users, the imposition of sometimes frustrating use controls and limits, and uncertainties about the scope of exceptions such as parody or fair use, are two major sources of the tension in the system. One can respond that individual end-users have always been an (unlicensed) part of the copyright equation or that they used works on the basis of an implied license. After all, the system could not ignore them: is not most content designed to be viewed/read/listened to by them? The answer is yes, of course, but this does not end the discussion, far from it.

First, the verbs themselves (view, listen, read) describe a *passive* approach to the content and fail to reflect the participative web and user empowerment that digital tools have generated. Second, major copyright holders did not much care about the copyright impact of end-users' use provided that end-users remain just that, end-users. The notion of implied license was not necessary. Most passive uses did not require a license until online uses, most of which involve a reproduction. Rights holders took notice by trying

---

[475] A tariff may be defined for these purposes as a set of licensing conditions, including a price which may be set on various bases (units produced, user revenue, etc.), that any qualified user (normally, any person to whom the tariff applies) may invoke and use a work contained in the repertory of works covered by the tariff according to the conditions contained therein. Competition (antitrust) law often prevents collectives from refusing to issue a license based on such a tariff to a qualified user.

For example, if a tariff allows a broadcaster to broadcast a repertory of musical works for a given period of time in exchange for the payment of a percentage of the broadcaster's advertising revenues, then any broadcaster (who qualifies—this may be determined under other (e.g., broadcasting) statutes would be entitled to the license. In the United States, this is 'regulated' by consent decrees negotiated between ASCAP and BMI, on the one hand, and the Department of Justice, on the other.

[476] Copyright Clearance Center, Inc. (CCC) will grant individual users reproduction licenses. See www.copyright.com. However, CMOs have not been in the business of granting micro-licenses.

to keep end-users where they could continue to ignore their copyright foot-print.[477] Third, it is true that pre-Internet end-users occasionally adapted content but never on the same scale as their passive content 'consumption'. Interactive uses were a small minority and/or those responsible for them could not produce multiple generations of perfect copies.[478] From a policy point view, this was arguably *de minimis*. Not anymore.

## 5.3   PRIVATE USE, AMATEUR USE, OR BOTH?

The Internet has radically transformed the possible. Individual users naturally want to harness the enormous capabilities of the Internet to access, use and disseminate information and content. The demand is huge and ever increasing. As Richard Stallman explained over 20 years ago, 'The Internet is relevant because it facilitates copying and sharing of writings by ordinary readers. The easier it is to copy and share, the more useful it becomes, and the more copyright as it stands now becomes a bad deal.'[479] Technology has responded to this huge pull of possibilities by providing the powerful technological means, thus increasing the pull itself.

The fact that copyright was not initially designed to be routinely applied to uses in the private sphere of users is evidenced by the fact that excep-tions and limitations to copyright allowing 'active' uses of protected material were written with the professional user in mind. This explains why in several national laws, the main exceptions can be grouped into two categories: first, private use, which governments previously regarded as 'unregulatable' as a practical and/or normative matter,[480] an area where

---

[477]   I am not making an empirical claim, merely a modest anecdotal one. The dozens of End-user Licensing Agreements (EULA) I have read tend to limit reuse by end-users and ensure that end-users remain just that, the end of the distribution chain.

[478]   An example would be music tracks copied on cassette tapes. These 'private compilations' were not authorized by rights holder, even though they may have been fair use. But few rights holders tried to prevent the copying because an analogue tape could not produce generations of good-quality copies. When (short-lived) digital audiotapes were introduced, the music industry reacted by getting Congress to mandate technological locks to prevent second generation copying and imposing a levy of blank tapes. See Audio Home Recording Act of 1992, 17 USC §§ 1001 1008 (2006).

[479]   Richard Stallman, 'Reevaluating Copyright: The Public Must Prevail' (1996) 75 *Oregon Law Review* 291, 294–5.

[480]   Professor Alain Strowel considers the defence of the private sphere as one of the three main justifications for exceptions to copyright, the other two being circulation of information, and cultural and scientific development. See Alain

copyright law abdicated its authority but where the 'passive' or consumptive nature of the use made regulation much less relevant; second, specific and often much more 'active' and transformative uses by professional intermediaries: libraries (and archives) and certain public institutions, including schools, courts and sometimes the government itself. Regarding the former, there are still today several very broad exceptions for private use.[481] End-users have traditionally enjoyed 'room to move' because of exceptions such as fair use and also due to rights stemming from their ownership of physical copies of protected works.

Entering the private sphere of individual users also means that copyright must now fight a new, formidable opponent: the right to privacy, which is anchored, inter alia, in Article 8 of the European Convention for the Protection of Human Rights and Fundamental Freedoms;[482] and in Articles 17 and 19 of International Covenant on Civil and Political Rights of 16 December 1966.[483] The right to private use is considered fundamental in several European copyright statutes and the EU Charter[484] and may have a constitutional basis in a number of legal systems.[485] This fight may be episodic or systematic and the path chosen by rights holders to distribute content will be the principal determinant. When privacy-invasive tools are used to distribute and/or monitor end-users,[486] privacy becomes an issue. Using monitoring systems that decouple usage data from individual identities early on (upstream) reduces the size of the problem. Indeed, as a

---

Strowel, 'Droit d'auteur et accès à l'information: de quelques malentendus et vrais problèmes a travers l'historie et les développements récents', (1999) 12 *Cahiers de propriété intellectuelle* 185, 198.

[481] Exceptions expressed either dirrectly as 'private use' or as a combination of chattel rights of the owner of the copy and open-ended exceptions to copyright, in particular fair dealing.

[482] As amended by the Protocol No 11, (adopted in Rome, Nov. 4, 1950) (available at http://conventions.coe.int/treaty/en/Treaties/Html/005.htm).

[483] 23 March 1976, (1976) 999 United Nations Treaty Series, 187 (available at <http://www.ohchr.org/en/professionalinterest/pages/ccpr.aspx> accessed 17 November 2016).

[484] See Lucie M C R Guibault, 'Contracts and Copyright Exemptions', in P B Hugenholtz (ed.) *Copyright and Electronic Commerce, Legal Aspects of Electronic Copyright Management* (Kluwer Law 2000), 232. See Charter of Fundamental Rights of the European Union, 2012/C 326/02, arts. 7 and 8.

[485] In the United States, see Julie E Cohen, 'A Right to Read Anonymously: A Closer Look at Copyright Management in Cyberspace' (1996) 28 *Connecticut Law Review* 981; and, by the same author, 'DRM & Privacy' (2003) 18 *Berkeley Law & Technology Journal* 575, 576–7.

[486] See Nicola Lucchi, 'Countering the Unfair Play of DRM Technologies' (2007) 16 *Texas Intellectual Property Law Journal* 91, 94–102.

matter of copyright law, most rights holders do not need to know who uses what but rather how much of what is used, notably to distribute monies collected for mass uses.[487] From this (licensing) perspective, privacy-compliant systems are possible. Uses need to be aggregated and de-linked from individual users. This becomes an argument: selling privacy-protection as part of the copyright license. This approach is possible and even desirable for privacy advocates but it may not mesh with the direct marketing needs of major Internet intermediaries who need or at least want to know exactly who is using what. Put differently, although capturing only aggregated demographic data on users for marketing purposes is a viable option, the move from micro to 'nano-marketing' targeted to individual preferences now seems irreversible. It poses privacy challenges but they are not copyright-specific.

An additional problem with the shift of the copyright policy target to individual users is that, while copyright professionals (publishers, producers, broadcasters, etc.) tend to follow copyright rules as a business decision and as a matter of basic risk assessment, individual end-users need to internalize the norm. Otherwise, huge, and sometimes futile and even counter-productive, enforcement efforts are required.[488] Owing to this perceived inadequacy of copyright licensing and normative concerns about privacy and/or ownership of copies, social norms have emerged according to which some uses or reuses of digital content are seen as acceptable. Those norms, fuelled by the fuzziness of many exceptions and limitations, have not responded well to the traditional prohibitions against reproduction, the preparation of derivative works and communication/ public performance of protected content. In fact, combined with ineffective enforcement,[489] copyright has barely made a dent in the massive reuse of protected content and that is often a good thing, namely when the reuse is allowing new forms of creativity to emerge.[490] Those social norms are arguable supported by often rather vague notions of 'fair use'[491] or *de*

---

[487]   As a concrete example, if a client monitoring which songs are transferred between users online (in an hypothetical licensed 'sharing' model), then collectives or equivalent entities administering the funds would need to know how often each song is transferred, not by whom. Demographic or geographic data would likely be captured for marketing purposes.

[488]   See above note 469.

[489]   Measured in terms of overall decrease in unauthorized use.

[490]   See Brett Lunceford, 'The Irrelevance of Copyright in the Public Mind' (2008) 7 *Northwestern Journal of Technology & Intellectual Property Law* 33; and note 496 below.

[491]   See Julie E Cohen, 'WIPO Copyright Treaty Implementation in the United States: Will Fair Use Survive?' (1999) 21 *European Intellectual Property Review*

*minimis* use, [492] and further buttressed by perceived social value in letting users create freely and, at least for some, making content 'more available'.

There is, in other words, a strong νόμος (nomos) supporting access and reuse. This nomos often forms the backdrop for any discussion about copyright reform. Nomos is powerful: '[t]he structure of the world created by human and social activity is treated not as contingent, but as self-evident provisional codes (habits or customs) of social and political behaviour'.[493] Whether social norms and practices can be imbued with legal status and have an effect on how courts apply copyright to UGC remains unclear.[494] Still, there is undeniably a 'meme', with a strong built-in feedback loop, that many forms of UGC are 'acceptable' within (mostly undefined) parameters. This may explain the model codes and similar efforts to define those parameters and 'tweak the meme'.[495]

Copyright's ineffectual match with the social norms that underpin UGC and other forms of participative creativity is multifactorial: application of a regulatory system not designed for mass reuse (but rather for mass *consumptive* use); inability and/or unwillingness to license both because of the type of use (reproduction/creation of derivatives) and because of the type of user; normative battles with the rights of end-users, including privacy and consumer protection;[496] and a marked lack of understanding, at least until very recently, of network effects by major right holders. The use of

---

236; Peter Jaszi, 'Copyright, Fair Use and Motion Pictures' (2007) 3 *Utah Law Review* 715. Who would have been able to say with any certainty that making available thumbnails pictures was fair use? See *Perfect 10, Inc v Amazon.com, Inc*, 508 F3d 1146 (9th Cir 2007).

[492] The lack of enforcement is a key consideration. In patent law, it has been argued that, while most forms of experimental use are illegal (see *Madey v Duke University*, 336 F Supp 2d 583 (MDNC, 2004; and *Madey v Duke University* (*Madey II*), 307 F3d 1351, 1362 (Fed Cir 2002)), it is nonetheless routinely practiced because the cost of enforcement is high and the damages typically low.

[493] A good summary found on the great Internet variorum, namely Wikipedia. One could discuss this in detail, but this is not the place. For one thing, it may seem an inherent contradiction of nomos (according to the sociological definition of the term) that it is seen as self-evident and non-contingent but is by definition historically and geographically specific.

[494] See Edward Lee, 'Warming Up to User Generated Content' (2008) *University of Illinois Law Review* 1459.

[495] For two different efforts on that front, see Electronic Frontier Foundation, *Fair Use Principles for User Generated Video Content* (online at http://www.eff.org/issues/ip-and-free-speech/fair-use-principles-usergen); and the Principles for User Generated Content Services made available by leading commercial copyright holders (available at http://www.ugcprinciples.com/).

[496] See Jeremy Stanley, 'Managing Digital Rights Management: Effectively Protecting Intellectual Property And Consumer Rights In The Wake Of The Sony

the Internet to create/join virtual groups of friends or people with similar interests and who, acting gregariously (and thus naturally. . .) want to 'share' the pictures, shows, books or music they like, but that in most cases they have not authored is a vibrant example of relevant network effects.[497]

This poses the question, how far does the private sphere extend? Does it 'explode' when a digital use inside the sphere is made available to others online? The social norms at play do not seem to reflect the traditional distinction between private (tolerated) and public (unauthorized) use. Those have been the norms for decades and they are reflected in the traditional views expressed by large rights holders. For example, the Recording Industry Association of America (RIAA) condoned limited copying for private use, but not the making available of copyright content online.[498] Yet, technologically it is often the *same copy* that it says is legal to make (for personal use) but whose use then becomes illegal if made available to others. On a technical level, making it available would then be an infringement under one of several possible legal theories in different legal systems. For example, in Canada, it could be considered the authorization of a communication to the public,[499] and, in the US, an inducement (or some other contribution giving rise to liability) to download or perhaps stream and, therefore, copy without authorization, and/or to publicly perform.[500] Put differently, the social norm/legal norm disconnect lies in the blurring of the private/public distinction.

We can conclude from this analysis that, traditionally, there were two distinctions made, one between private and public use and another between professional and amateur uses. The technological environment

---

CD Copy Protection Scandal' (2008) *Journal of Law & Policy for the Information Society* 157.

[497] See Gervais (n 498).

[498] See (<http://www.riaa.com/physicalpiracy.php?content_selector=piracy_online_the_law> last accessed May 11, 2015):

> . . .burning a copy of CD onto a CD-R, or transferring a copy onto your computer hard drive or your portable music player, won't usually raise concerns so long as:
>
> - The copy is made from an authorized original CD that you legitimately own
> - The copy is just for your personal use.

[499] See *Society of Composers, Authors and Music Publishers of Canada v Canadian Assn. of Internet Providers,* [2004] 2 SCR 427 (Can) and Gervais (n 297), 323–5.

[500] See *Metro-Goldwyn-Mayer Studios Inc v Grokster, Ltd*, 545 US 913, 919 (2005); and Bennett Lincoff, 'Common Sense, Accommodation And Sound Policy For The Digital Music Marketplace' (2008) 2 *Journal of International Media & Entertainment Law* 1, 8.

until approximately the turn of the century meant that those two 'Venn diagrams' were almost perfectly superposed. Amateur meant private (and vice versa) and professional meant public. The shift from a one-to-many to a many-to-many dissemination modes has destabilized this system; amateur no longer means private by any means. Normatively, the question that emerged is this: should amateur prevail over public when the two Venn diagrams are separated? Some—most famously perhaps Professor Lawrence Lessig—have argued for an amateur 'exemption' to allow remix.[501] Canada has adopted one such exception, which excludes commercial uses, however.[502] Several normative arguments have been made to support this view, and also some pragmatic ones such as the difficulty of licensing (microtransactions) amateur uses. If, however, the amateur leaves her private sphere,[503] then normatively the question is no longer a confrontation of privacy and copyright, but one of amateur intermediary/provider v professional. This is why the equation to solve has changed. Put differently, if the absence of the amateur from the copyright radar was not driven principally by normative considerations but mostly by mere practical ones, then those amateurs must now find ways to use exemptions other than private use such as fair use or specific safe harbours. A valid normative case can be made that at least 'small' everyday usage need not be in copyright's sights, and should focus only on what Paul Ohm has called 'superusers'.[504] As a practical matter, this rings true if transactional licensing (for one-off uses) is envisaged—although blanket licenses for some uses may also be used. I return to this below. To help us move this normative debate forward in more granular fashion, I now suggest a possible taxonomy of UGC.

## 5.4   A COPYRIGHT TAXONOMY OF USER-GENERATED CONTENT

There have been efforts to categorize UGC. For example, the Organization for Economic Co-operation and Development (OECD) report on

---

[501]   See above note 460.

[502]   See Daniel Gervais, 'User-Generated Content and Music File-Sharing: A Look at Some of the More Interesting Aspects of Bill C-32', in M Geist (ed.) *From "Radical Extremism" To "Balanced Copyright": Canadian Copyright And The Digital Agenda* (Toronto: Irwin Law 2010).

[503]   Deciding in which cases this happens would require a different book, and the answer is likely to be different in each legal system.

[504]   See Paul Ohm, 'The Myth of the Superuser: Fear, Risk, And Harm Online' (2008) 41 *University of California at Davis Law Review* 1327.

User-Created Content[505] (UCC[506]) distinguished UCC along two axes. First, according to the type of content (text, novel or poetry; photo/images; music and audio; video and film; citizen journalism; educational content; mobile content; virtual content); and, second, according to the distribution platform (blogs; wikis and other text-based collaboration formats; sites allowing feedback on written works; group-based aggregation; podcasting; social network sites; virtual worlds; and content or file-sharing sites).[507] This effort is certainly a useful descriptive one, and it allows us to draw certain distinctions, but it is unsatisfactory from a copyright perspective for a number of reasons. First, the distinction between type and platform is not exactly crystalline (e.g. virtual world is used in both); second, copyright has purported to be technologically neutral[508] and it has generally avoided, at least in terms of basic rights and exceptions, to draw distinctions between categories of content.[509] It is true, however, that some distinctions between types of use and users induce normative distinctions about possible exceptions. Educational users, for example, may stake a public interest claim to free, spontaneous use of classroom material.[510]

To understand the application of copyright, I suggest that one should distinguish three and only three categories of user-generated content, namely: user-authored content; user-derived content; and user-copied content. The first two may be grouped under the umbrella notion of 'user-created content'.

### 5.4.1   User-authored Content

This type of content involves neither copying nor derivation/adaptation of previous material. It may involve the taking of ideas expressed by others but copyright allows this type of taking. An author is free to copy, upload, perform and/or make available such content on any basis, including free

---

[505]   OECD. *Participative Web: User Created Content.* 12 April 2007. Document DSTI/ICCP/IE(2006)7/ FINAL [hereinafter 'OECD Report'].

[506]   An unfortunate acronym for US readers, who are more accustomed to associating it with the Uniform Commercial Code.

[507]   OECD Report, 15–16.

[508]   See, e.g., H.R. Rep. No. 105-551, pt.2, at 25 (2d Sess. 1998).

[509]   Apart from the limited performance right in sound recordings (which in any event are not copyrighted works in legal systems outside the US, but rather objects of a 'neighbouring' or related right), §106 rights apply to all categories of works.

[510]   See Agreement on Guidelines for Classroom Copying in Not-For-Profit Educational Institutions with Respect to Books and Periodicals, House Report 94-1476.

and unrestricted use, imposing conditions for free use such as those found in Creative Commons licenses, or licensing commercially.

One issue that may surface, however, is the interaction between the contracts that users of UGC-empowering sites and technologies, including social networking sites, use and that in some cases convey a license to the operator of the site.[511]

### 5.4.2   User-derived Content

This second category of UGC is by far the hardest because the exact scope of the right to make adaptations (or 'derivative works' as the term is used in the US Copyright Act) is unclear. In the last part of this chapter, I provide an analysis of the right. In most cases, however, whether or not user-derived content involves the right of adaptation, it will also trigger the possible application of the right of reproduction.

### 5.4.3   User-copied Content

The third category is not a priori complicated. Copying substantial parts of pre-existing works is prima facie infringement. Uploading a song, picture, film, created by someone else will be infringement unless it can be considered a fair use or is covered by another exception and limitation.

A few questions do emerge, however. First, the 'ratio' issue is relevant: if only a short excerpt is used—this is not limited to the online environment, then the right of quotation might apply. That said, many works uploaded or made available online are integral copies of pre-existing works. Second, the 'Google defence' might apply, a matter to which I return in a moment.[512]

The basic application of copyright to user-copied (and user-derived) content is simple: using substantial portions of pre-existing works (not in the public domain) is infringing unless a defence applies. It may be that a *specific* defence such as parody or pastiche is contained in the law of the country concerned. It may be that an *open-ended* defence is potentially applicable. (Fair use doctrine and fair dealing are explained in the Appendix and this discussion will assume that the reader is familiar with them.)

---

[511]   See, e.g., Christina J Hayes, 'Changing the Rules of the Game: How Video Game Publishers Are Embracing User-Generated Derivative Works' (2008) 21 *Harvard Journal of Law & Technology* 567. Most websites require users to agree to a set of terms and conditions in which the user agrees to grant a license to the website owner to use the material the user posts. *See* Marcelo Halpern, 'Copyright and the Internet—The Legal Evolution' (2008) 938 *PLI/Pat* 259, 275.
[512]   See below note 514 and accompanying text.

User-copied content will be considered by US courts a fair use if the user's act of providing access to it is fair use. This may be based on free expression grounds.[513] This facet of fair use has been greatly expanded by the 'Google defence'. Reversing in part a decision[514] that had declined to find that making thumbnail versions of Perfect10's 'adult' images was a fair use because it could hamper the market for such thumbnails on, for example, cell phones,[515] the US Court of Appeals for the Ninth Circuit in California found[516] that the thumbnails were a fair use. Referring to *Campbell v Acuff-Rose Music, Inc*,[517] the court noted that the first fair use factor[518] required a court to consider:

> the purpose and character of the use, including whether such use is of a com-mercial nature or is for nonprofit educational purposes' The central purpose of this inquiry is to determine whether and to what extent the new work is 'transformative.' A work is 'transformative' when the new work does not 'merely supersede the objects of the original creation' but rather 'adds something new, with a further purpose or different character, altering the first with new expres-sion, meaning, or message.'[519]

Although this analysis seems correct, it was not a straight application of *Campbell*.[520] In *Campbell*, the allegedly infringing work, a hip-hop version of Roy Orbison's *Pretty Woman*, was new created content, whereas the *Perfect10* court applied it to the dissemination of unmodified (creatively,

---

[513]  Ibid. Netanel (at 81) discusses the test enunciated in, e.g., *Turner Broad. Sys., Inc. v FCC*, 520 US 180, 185 (1997).
[514]  *Perfect10 v Google, Inc*, 416 F Supp. 2d 828, 851 (C D Cal 2006).
[515]  Which ignored the additional steps required to get the thumbnail image to a cellphone. See Britton Payne, 'Imperfect 10: Digital Advances And Market Impact In Fair Use Analysis' (2006) 17 *Fordham Intellectual Property, Media & Entertainment Law Journal* 279, 289–90.
[516]  487 F 3d 701 (9th Cir 2007), amended on rehearing by 508 F 3d 1146.
[517]  See above note 465.
[518]  17 USC § 107(1).
[519]  *Perfect10 v Google, Inc*, above note 514, at 1164.
[520]  Paul Goldstein suggested that the decision was 'a triumph of mindless sound bite over principled analysis', adding that:

> [p]arody is a fair use category; the mere transport of a work intact from one medium to another – without abridgment or other modification – is not. Is there any doubt that, faced with facts like these, Justice Story – or Justice Souter – would have placed them on the infringement side of the line? What principle has changed in the 167 years since Folsom to make a relevant difference?

Paul Goldstein, 'Fair Use in Context' (2008) 31 *Columbia Journal of Law & the Arts* 433, 442.

that is) content. In other words, the court jettisoned the traditional difference between work-centred use and dissemination-centred use. This reinforced, at least as a matter of US law, the overlap between user-derived
and user-copied content.

The court may or may not have generated this overlap deliberately. For
example, the court noted it in quoting its own *Wall Data* opinion:[521] 'A use
is considered transformative only where a defendant changes a plaintiff's
copyrighted work or uses the plaintiff's copyrighted work in a different
context such that the plaintiff's work is transformed *into a new creation.*'[522]

Transformativeness—as the notion emerged in US copyright cases—
was historically and normatively linked to new expression (and, generally,
the creation of new copyrightable works), not re-dissemination.[523] One
may nonetheless argue that there are public interest imperatives to allow
thumbnail access and, more generally, to favour broad access to material
on search engines such as Google.[524] It remains unclear, however, that
transformativeness is the optimal vehicle to carry those concerns forward.
A specific safe harbour might do a better job.

Professor Reese's analysis of relevant fair use cases since *Campbell*[525]
makes a critical point in that inquiry, namely that asking whether the use
of a work, from a teleological perspective, is transformative is not the
same as asking whether copyright (his analysis focuses on the derivative
work right) was infringed.[526] Theoretically at least, a 'transformative use'
to which a fair use defence applies may otherwise infringe the reproduction right, the right to make derivative works, or both. It follows that not
all derivative works are transformative; and that some transformative uses
do not involve the creation of a derivative work.

Be that as it may, with the addition of a clear opinion from the Court
of Appeals for the Second Circuit in New York finding that scanning,
and then making available entire books word-searchable online was a
fair use (results shown in 'snippets'), the Google defence seems rather
firmly established as a matter of US law.[527] Whether other countries

---

[521]  *Wall Data Inc v Los Angeles County Sheriff's Dept*, 447 F 3d 769 (9th Cir
2006).

[522]  *Perfect10*, at 1165.

[523]  See Pierre Leval, 'Toward a Fair Use Standard' (1990) 103 *Harvard Law
Review* 1105.

[524]  This concern was central in the Ninth Circuit's previous decision in *Kelly v
Arriba Soft Corp*, 336 F 3d 811, 816, 819 (9th Cir 2003).

[525]  R Anthony Reese, 'Transformativeness and the Derivative Work Right'
(2008) 31 *Columbia Journal of Law & the Arts* 467.

[526]  Ibid., 494.

[527]  *The Authors Guild Inc, et al v Google, Inc*, 2d Cir 16 Oct 2015.

will follow suit is an open question. As just noted, especially as the text and data mining industry continues to grow, a specific safe-harbour with proper limits and/or a licensing mechanism could be put in place instead.

## 5.5   THE DERIVATE RIGHT AND CONSTRAINTS ON CREATIVE REUSES

The right to prohibit adaptation or derivation from a pre-existing work to create a new work lies at the core of copyright theory and policy. It is a right to prevent new expression and must thus be applied with the utmost caution. Yet it is equally true that a slightly modified version of a pre-existing work might easily interfere in an unfair way with the market for an existing work.

This 'right of adaptation', which is part of the Berne Convention (see Chapter 2), is situated at the border between infringement and inspiration. Drawing its limits is thus an inevitable step of any effort to develop an understanding of what uses and reuses are allowed. The growth of a vibrant culture, one making full use of the potential of digital tools to create and disseminate new works (in particular the Internet) within a copyright-compatible framework is at stake.[528] The problem lies in defining and properly cabining this 'derivative right'.[529] This is not a debate about semantics; it is about the ability of a copyright holder to prevent others from creating by reusing nonliteral parts of her work. The doctrinal and normative challenge is two-fold: first, to define the derivative right properly; second, to develop an adequate test to implement the right thus delineated.

In French, a derivative work is known as *'une œuvre dérivée'*.[530] The verb *dériver* can mean to derive but also to drift. This double-entendre is applicable here, for when copyright drifts too far from its normative moorings, it risks going down on the shoals of free expression or at least creating obstacles to cultural and economic progress. At the risk of pushing the metaphor a bridge too far, the notion of derivative work is at dangerous cross-currents as we define the space available for Internet users to reuse, remix, modify and make available audiovisual and audio content such as mash-ups, sampling-based sound recordings, and fan sites to name just

---

[528]   Another important area of culture directly impacted by the definition of the derivative right is appropriation art. See below Part 5.5.

[529]   *See* 17 USC ¶106(2).

[530]   *Oeuvre* is a [copyrighted] 'work'.

three obvious examples.[531] This debate may well be a battle royal in the determination of the shape of tomorrow's culture.

### 5.5.1 The Emergence of the Derivative Right Internationally

Early in the twentieth century, European nations did not generally recognize a derivative right. In fact, many key countries failed to recognize even a basic right of translation. For example, as of 1903, Russia limited the translation right to 'scientific works', and that right was only valid for two years.[532] Denmark only prohibited translation in a Nordic language.[533] More importantly, in several countries the existence of the right depended on the author making a translation available within a specified timeframe—often only two to three years from the publication of the original version.[534] The underlying concerns were clear: access to foreign language works was primordial and trumped copyright.[535] Those concerns would be reflected in the 1896 text of the Berne Convention, which included a translation right, provided, however, that an authorized translation was made available within ten years.[536] This amendment to the original (1886) text of the Convention was adopted as a compromise.[537] France was one of the few countries (a major world power and exporter of books at the time) to insist on a full translation right.[538] France had been one of the first European countries to introduce a full translation right in its domestic copyright legislation.[539] This domestic example served as the

---

[531]   The issue is not exactly new, though new tools allow Internet users to create ever more creative derivatives. See Lydia Pallas Loren, 'The Changing Nature of Derivative Works in the Face of New Technologies' (2000) 4 *Journal of Small & Emerging Business Law* 57, 58–9.

[532]   See Gustave Huard, *Traité de la propriété intellectuelle* vol. 1, 74 (1903).

[533]   See ibid.

[534]   See ibid.

[535]   See ibid.

[536]   See notes 82 and 83 and accompanying text.

[537]   Huard, above note 532, 275.

[538]   Étienne Bricon, *Des Droits d'Auteur dans les Rapports Internationaux* 87 (1888).

[539]   An 1852 decree by Louis-Napoléon protected the translation right 'at the same level as the right of reproduction'. Decree-Law of March 28, 1852 on Literary and Artistic Property Rights in Foreign Published Works, reproduced in Ch. Lyon-Caen and Paul Delalain, *Lois françaises et étrangères sur la propriété littéraire et artistique* (1889), vol. 1, 35. The Decree is also mentioned by Bricon, ibid., 44.

Prince Louis-Napoléon made a statement that might rejoice Lockean theorists, in a letter written in 1844 to a Mr Jobard: 'Intellectual works are property like land and houses.' Quoted in ibid., at 48–9 (Author's translation).

basis for bilateral treaties entered into by France.[540] Interestingly, under French law infringement depended on the existence of monetary damage to the author.[541] French courts considered that differences between a new, allegedly infringing work and a pre-existing one were not relevant; they focused instead on how much and what parts of the pre-existing work had been appropriated.[542] The inquiry proceeded as follows: first, were elements that gave the primary work its 'originality' taken; second, did this appropriation cause a (financial) prejudice to the author of the primary work?[543] Under this two-prong test, abridgements, musical arrangements and translations were generally prohibited because the author would lose the benefit of being able to license such uses and those uses took the 'pith and marrow' of the primary work.[544]

Access to foreign-language works, however, was a clear concern for several other Berne countries.[545] Arguing in favour of subordinating the existence of the right of translation to the publication of an authorized

---

As it happens, Jobard was an advocate for strong authors' rights and 'lobbied' for perpetual rights, a thesis which the Berne Conferences rejected. See Édouard Romberg, *Compte-Rendu Des Travaux Du Congrès De La Propriété Littéraire et Artistique* (1859) at iii and 275. This was also the interpretation by French courts (see ibid).

[540]  Not unlike current US practice in bilateral trade treaties. See Peter K. Yu, 'Sinic Trade Agreements' (2011) 44 *University of California at Davis Law Review* 953, 955.

[541]  *See* Huard, above note 532, 175. How far we have moved from this state of affairs! Especially under the Digital Millennium Copyright Act (DMCA), Pub. L. No. 105-304, 112 Stat. 2860 (1998), which made circumvention of technical protection measures illegal even if there is no underlying infringement of the copyright in the work protected by such measure. See e.g., *Sony v Gamemasters*, 87 F Supp. 2d 976 986 (ND Cal 1999); and *MDY Indus v Blizzard Entm't, Inc*, 629 F 3d 928, 945–6 (2010), noting that traditional copyright infringement was not required but reading the statute broadly to extend protection to 'the right to prevent circumvention of access controls', *reh'g denied* (2011 WL 538748). Contra, see *Chamberlain Grp v Skylink Tech. Inc*, 381 F 3d 1178, 1197 (2004).

[542]  'No plagiarist can excuse the wrong by showing how much of his work he did not pirate', *Sheldon v Metro-Goldwyn Pictures Corp*, 81 F 2d 49, 56 (2d Cir 1936), cert. denied, 298 US 669 (1936). On French law on this point, see Huard, above note 532, 175.

[543]  *See* Huard, ibid., 175–6.

[544]  Ibid., 176–9.

[545]  The 'Acts' of Congresses of the Literary and Artistic Association (ALAI) that took place before 1884 shed additional light on the matter. The first Diplomatic Conference to negotiate the Berne Convention was held in 1884. ALAI had submitted a draft which the Swiss Government modified and submitted as a draft treaty. ALAI was a key player at several levels, having produced the initial draft of the Berne Convention. See Stephen P Ladas, *The International Protection*

translation (access, in modern parlance) within a certain period of time, the organizers of the 1859 ALAI Congress wrote:

> The starting point of the literary property right is the publication of a work. Society guarantees authors certain advantages in exchange for those he himself provides. Yet the translation privilege, when the author fails to use it, is an effect without a cause. It is not fair that society shall be forever deprived, by his negligence or omission, an enjoyment on which it could count, and that people other than the author are prepared to provide.[546]

A broader right of adaptation (beyond translation) did not get the same level of even partial support because it clashed with the practice of many Berne members. The adaptation of three-dimensional works of art in two-dimensional formats or vice versa (industrial design) was a major concern for Austria, Finland, Germany, Japan and Mexico.[547]

Matters were not wholly different in the United Kingdom. Translations were protected under the International Copyright Act.[548] However, Britain allowed other adaptations of non-British works.[549] For example, in *Wood v Chart*, the court found that the translation of the French play 'Frou-Frou' was in fact a permissible 'imitation or adaptation' to the

---

*of Literary and Artistic Property* vol. 1 at 56–76 (1938); and 6 *Revue Internationale du droit d'auteur* 144, 144–5 (1955).

ALAI continued to take part (as what in modern parlance would be called a non-governmental organization) in the discussions, however. ALAI was founded in 1878 by French playwright and public intellectual Victor Hugo, its first President. ALAI Congresses were held (during the relevant period) in 1879 (London); 1880 (Lisbon); 1881 (Vienna); 1882 (Rome); 1883 (Amsterdam) and 1884 (Brussels). See Actes du Congrès de Dresde (1895), 11. ALAI had argued in favour of a full reproduction right and an adaptation right (at least the production of a dramatic version of a nondramatic work, starting in starting in 1887 (Madrid) and essentially at every ALAI Congress after that. See ibid., at 7–8.

[546] Édouard Romberg, *Compte-Rendu Des Travaux Du Congrès De La Propriété Littéraire Et Artistique* (1859) at 11. (Author's translation—I retained the gendered references in the original text.)

[547] See Huard, above note 532, 74.

[548] See International Copyright Act (1852), Primary Sources on Copyright (1450–1900), eds. L Bently and M Kretschmer (available at <http://www.copyrighthistory.org/cam/tools/request/showRecord.php?id=record_uk_1852accessed> 17 November 2106).

[549] Ibid. A number of European playwrights chose not to publish their plays and only allow their public performance to avoid have their plays adapted without their authorization in the US. See Bricon, above note 538, 34–6.

This concern about access is still reflected today in the Appendix to the Convention, which allows developing countries to grant compulsory translation licenses for works not made available in a national language.

English stage and not a translation, quoting the language of the statute at the time.[550] The apparent distinction was that a translation would afford 'the English people [. . .] the opportunity of knowing the French work as accurately as possible'.[551] By contrast, the defendant's *version* transferred some scenes from France to England, made the characters English and introduced English manners which, the court was prompt to note, 'differ from French manners'.[552] The nature of the adaptor's work was emphasized by commentators to support the freedom to adapt foreign works.[553] They referred to the 'great talents, ingenuity, and judgment' of authors of notes or additions to existing works not just permissible but worthy of their own copyright.[554] This is part of the key distinction I see between copying and derivation.

The notion of derivative work changed in the 1948 text of the Berne Convention, to include *non-copying 'alterations'*, that is, infringement by derivations not involving (only) a reproduction.[555] Here we see that, at the international level, the right against unauthorized derivatives was conceptually distinct from the right of reproduction. The cradle of the early notion of derivation was the suggestion that what constitutes an infringing *appropriation*[556] is the *taking of those elements which gave the infringed*

---

[550]   See Walter Arthur Copinger, *The Law of Copyright in Works of Literature and Art* (1893) 232–3. The case itself is at 22 LT (NS) 432; 39 LJ (NS) Ch 641.

[551]   Ibid.

[552]   Ibid. Interestingly, in the index to the book, under the entry Adaptation, it says 'see Imitations'. Ibid., cxix.

[553]   Richard Godson, *A Practical Treatise on the Law of Patents for Inventions and on Copyright* (1832) 242. Godson, a member of the British Parliament, cites a case (*Tonson v Walker*) where a new edition of Milton's *Paradise Lost* (which was in the public domain) could not be reprinted without authorization because it contained additional notes still protected by copyright. See ibid., 244.

[554]   See ibid.

[555]   See WIPO, *Berne Convention Centenary: 1886–1986*, 231 (1986).

[556]   I hesitate to use 'misappropriation' because of the term has its own significance, although the overlap between the illicit appropriation in the Berne *travaux* and the common law notion of misappropriation is significant. For a discussion on the issue in the US, where it tends to revolve around federal preemption, see Lauren M Gregory, Note, 'Hot Off The Presses: How Traditional Newspaper Journalism Can Help Reinvent the 'Hot News' Misappropriation Tort in the Internet Age' (2011) 13 *Vanderbilt Journal of Entertainment & Technology Law* 577, 596: discussing *NBA v Motorola, Inc*, 105 F.3d 841, 850 (2d Cir. 1997, the author notes that

the 'extra element' [from *NBA*] test it produced is useful in defining the boundaries of hot news misappropriation [. . .] The court was trying to demonstrate that misappropriation is distinct enough from copyright infringement to stand on its own legal footing. In other words, misappropriation—stealing from a *work its originality*, elements which were then transformed or recast.[557] The approach was consistent: a work was protected under that proposal if it was original and it was infringed if what was taken by the defendant was what made it original in the first place. In more modern parlance, this analysis aligns the test to grant protection (originality) and the infringement analysis (how much or what originality-generating elements of the plaintiff's work were taken). This is also precisely what courts tend to do, for example when they apply the principle of filtering out of unprotectible elements in their infringement analyses.[558] The approach also allows one to make appropriate distinctions about the copyright value of what was taken, on the one hand, and of what was produced by the reuser, on the other.

The current text (1971) of the Berne Convention contains a number of provisions that are relevant to this analysis. The first worth mentioning is Article 2(3), which reads as follows: '*Translations, adaptations, arrangements of music and other alterations* of a literary or artistic work shall be protected as original works without prejudice to the copyright in the original work.'[559] The original *WIPO Guide to the Berne Convention* noted in connection with this provision that '[t]his paragraph deals with *what are often called derivative works, i.e.*, those based on another, pre-existing, work'.[560] The Guide explained that there are four types of derivative works. First, *translations*, which 'express another's thoughts in a different language'.[561] Second, *adaptations*, which are generally works in their own right and consist of adapting a work in a different format, for example a novel finding its way onto a stage or screen. An adaptation may, of course, also be a translation.[562] Third, musical arrangements; and fourth, 'generally all other alterations of literary and artistic works'.[563] The first

---

competitor to get ahead in business—is distinct from the generalized bad-faith taking that copyright law prohibits, and is not, therefore, preempted by copyright law.

The approach chosen here is reminiscent of the improper appropriation test applied in *Arnstein v Porter*, 154 F 2d 464, 468 (2d Cir 1946).

[557] And similar to the approach taken by a number of US courts, as we will see below.

[558] See e.g., *Computer Assocs. Int'l, Inc v Altai, Inc*, 982 F 2d 693, 707 (2d Cir 1992). See also Melville B. Nimmer and David Nimmer, *Nimmer on Copyright* Vol. 4, § 13.03 [A] (2006).

[559] Berne Convention (1971), art. 2(3) (emphasis added).

[560] Claude Masouyé, *Guide to the Berne Convention*, 19 (WIPO, 1978) [hereinafter 'Guide'].

[561] Ibid.

[562] Ibid.

[563] Ibid.

three are named derivatives. The last covers what I would call penumbral derivatives. While no express criteria are provided in the Convention to determine where the line should be drawn between the creation of a derivative work and simple 'inspiration' that does not require an authorization, commentators have argued that the normative footing for the entire category is identical because the 'skills necessary for adaptation and arrangement could be compared to those necessary for translation'.[564]

Other substantive provisions (compilations, translations, and adaptations) are structured along the same lines.[565] The Convention contains, first, a right of translation and a number of rights related thereto.[566] Second, the Convention provides for a right of adaptation defined as the right of authorizing 'adaptations, arrangements and other alterations of [authors'] works'.[567] This suggests that the notion of derivative works in the Berne Convention is an *umbrella notion* that encompasses translations, adaptations (including changes of 'format'), musical arrangements and other alterations but also that is distinct from reproduction.[568]

The new *WIPO Guide to the Berne Convention,* published in 2003, explains that the right of adaptation 'may find *its origin* in the right of reproduction' because an adaptation means 'the combination of the pre-existing elements of the works concerned – the use of which in the adaptation etc., may well be regarded as reproduction of those elements – with some new ones, as a result of which normally a new work emerges'.[569] The *New Guide* suggests, however, that Article 12 (the main provision on the right of adaptation in the Convention) added in 1948 was meant to limit confusion 'in respect of those cases where adaptations, etc., amounted to the creation of new derivative works'.[570]

---

[564]   See Sam Ricketson and Jane C. Ginsburg, *International Copyright and Neighbouring Rights*, vol. 1 (2d edn, OUP 2006) 476.

[565]   Berne Convention arts 2(3), 2(5), 8 and 12.

[566]   Ibid., arts 8, 11*bis*(2) and 11*ter*(2). The former provides that authors of dramatic and dramatico-musical works enjoy 'the same rights with respect to translations thereof'. As the Guide (above note 560) explains, art. 8 applies if a libretto is translated, but if that translated libretto is publicly performed, then art. 11*bis*(2) applies (ibid., 65). Article 11*ter*(2) provides for a right to 'recite' translations of literary works. Public recitation would be considered a public performance under US law.

[567]   Ibid., art. 12.

[568]   *See* Mihály Ficsor, *Guide to the Copyright and Related Rights Treaties Administered by WIPO and Glossary of Copyright and Related Rights Terms* (2003) 81 [hereinafter the '*New Guide*'].

[569]   Ibid.

[570]   Ibid., 81–2.

From this analysis, we can draw a number of insights. First, there is a difference between derivation as defined in Berne and reproduction. While both rights are normatively motivated by a desire to protect legitimate market expectations, derivation is not a subset or de minimis adjunct of reproduction, unlike, say, trademark dilution, which some see as an adjunct to the right to prevent a likelihood of confusion.[571] Derivation has its own domain, which will become clearer as we consider French and German doctrines, two countries that played a major role in the evolution of the Convention.

In France, Henri Desbois suggested that authors of original works who borrow 'borrowed elements' from pre-existing works were entitled to copyright protection, though not if they infringe a primary work, a solution not surprising to US readers.[572] He then suggested a list of named derivative works, based on the French statute in existence at the time (namely the 1957 Copyright Act): translations and literary adaptations; transformations (which typically imply a transposition from one genre to another, e.g., painting to sculpture); and musical arrangements including variations.[573] In trying to define derivative works, Desbois suggested that their originality stemmed *from their composition, their literal expression or both.* Derivation by adaptation usually has some of both, because even if the adaptor was following someone else, he followed his imagination in adding elements of his own.[574] By contrast, a translator is enslaved to the primary work and is not expected to add compositional elements. The originality is then strictly based in the expression of the translator, not the composition.[575] However, the translator also makes creative choices in adapting the work to her own language and in selecting 'more or less adequate wording'.[576] Desbois saw the existence of originality in the fact that two translators usually come up with very different results if asked to translate the same text (unless perhaps it is very short or highly technical).[577] According to Desbois and the authors he relied on, includ-

---

[571] In *Ty Inc v Perryman*, 306 F 3d 509, 512 (7th Cir 2002), Judge Posner seems to consider free-riding as a form of dilution. Free-riding is also one of the asserted foundations of the right: see Greg Lastowka, 'Trademark's Daemons' (2011) 48 *Houston Law Review* 779, 813–14. I see it more as a normative driver than a tool to define the scope of the right.

[572] Henri Desbois, Le droit d'auteur en France 9 (1978).

[573] See ibid.

[574] See ibid., 33.

[575] See ibid.

[576] See ibid.

[577] See ibid. Surprisingly, Desbois was willing to give a copyright to someone copying a work of art because of the skill involved, by comparing the copyist effort

ing Professors de Sanctis and Saporta, a visual artist who 'disfigured' a character described in a pre-existing novel could be liable for a moral right violation, but not for infringing the derivative right because he did not see that right as crossing from the figurative arts to the literary ones.[578] The explanation given is interesting. Desbois quoted Saporta, among others, who justified his view by stating that the exploitation of one genre had no impact on the economic exploitation of other genres.[579] Desbois agreed, but only partially, noting that a painting made from a novel might be analogized to a movie made from the same novel. Since the latter was a recognized form of adaptation, there was no good normative reason to consider the former any differently.[580] The lesson from this is in the normative intuition, more than in crossing the genre barrier.

Professor André Lucas, a co-author of a leading treatise on French copyright law, has suggested that what makes a work a derivative of another is the fact that *it borrows the elements that generated copyright protection in the primary work*, which typically would be by copying parts of it or its 'general composition'.[581] Lucas discusses Desbois' approach, which he calls a 'composition test'.[582] The test teaches that to decide whether an appropriation crosses the derivative right line, one must remember that copyright does not protect the ideas or main incidents, but rather *the particular way in which the idea is developed* by the author.[583] He compares this test with Jozef Kohler's distinction between the internal and external

---

to a translation, although the two types of work seem wholly different. He seems to imply that choosing to copy is a manifestation of personality. See ibid., 75–6. This might inform an analysis of some appropriation or forms of similar contemporary art, a matter to which we return below.

[578] See Desbois, above note 572, 106.

[579] See ibid., and Marcel Saporta, 'A Few Notes on the Creation of "Personnages"' (1956) 11 *Revue Internationale du droit d'auteur* 63. Saporta was the author of a book on the limits of copyright protection entitled *Les Frontières du Droit d'Auteur* (1951) in which he suggests that impact on economic exploitation should guide the policy maker in deciding whether an exclusive economic right applies.

[580] See Desbois, above note 572, 107.

[581] See Lucas et al, above note 384, 227.

[582] See ibid., 228.

[583] Lucas is careful about separating plagiarism from copyright infringement, the former being a more general deontological analysis, the latter based on copyright principles. See ibid., 303. Copyright law focuses on the taking of what makes a work original, while plagiarism focuses on unattributed takings, whether or not, for example, the work taken from is still protected by copyright. See Walter A Effross, 'Owning Enlightenment: Proprietary Spirituality in the 'New Age' Marketplace' (2003) 51 *Buffalo Law Review* 483, 551.

form of a work. The latter seems more properly as forming part of the realm of reproduction and the former is better viewed as a form of derivation, especially if the purpose of copying the internal form was to add to or transform it. This approach has theoretical appeal but is easier to apply in the case of, e.g., a compilation, than to several forms of artistic creation.[584] I come back to the German approach in the next section.

Germany's authors' rights doctrine is rich and very helpful in understanding the derivative right. One of its most famous copyright scholars, Josef Kohler, explained that a work is produced by expressing what is taken from a common font, which he named *Weltschöpfungsidee*, from which an abstract representation was derived (*imaginäres Bild*) by the author.[585] From this representation the author would give a work its skeleton or 'inner form' (*innere Form*) and then its outer form (*äussere Form*), which adds layers of detail to the copyright work.[586] The question becomes whether only pre-existing ideas were appropriated, or also protected expression, as in the latter case this might trigger the derivative right. This idea that authors create by progressively increasing the precision of their creation from a general (and unprotected) idea to a protected expression is also found in Desbois' writings as in a number of others.[587] While one could object to the subjectivity of Kohler's test (peering into an author's mind) because the process may imply that a protected expression exists before its full, objectively perceptible expression is available, the difficulty may be avoided by considering only the objectified form (in most cases, its first fixation) as protected and, consequently, appropriable.[588]

---

[584]  See ibid., 245. For a fuller discussion of Kohler's thesis, see Philippe Gaudrat, Réflexions sur la forme des œuvres de l'esprit in Mélanges en l'honneur de André Françon (1995) 195, 201–3. This distinction may have been intended to make the work of courts easier. *See* Brad Sherman, 'What Is A Copyright Work' (2011) 12 *Theoretical Inquiries in Law* 99, 114.

[585]  See Ivan Cherpillod, *L'Objet du Droit d'Auteur* (1985), 26–7.

[586]  See ibid.

[587]  See ibid., 32. Andrzej Kopff speaks of building a work in 'layers' or 'strata' (*Schichtenaufbau des Werkes*). See ibid., 38. De Boor, building on insights from Goethe, adds that another 'layer' is added when the work is perceived because the reader/viewer/listener adds her own layer. See ibid., 42–3. A communication theorist might add that the work is only 'complete', therefore, once perceived because that is when the form of the work actually communicates its content, but then each perception is different so that there would be as many works as there are readers/viewers/listeners. See also Tyler Ochoa, 'Dr. Seuss, the Juice, and Fair Use: How the Grinch Silenced a Parody' (1998) 45 *Journal of the Copyright Society of the USA* 546, n. 54.

[588]  See Cherpillod above note 585, 35–41. Italian doctrine and in particular the work of Mario Are, suggests a distinction not between idea and protected

Like France, Germany requires that the derivative work be original, in the sense that it must be a *personal intellectual creation* and, specifically in the case of musical works, the result of more than insubstantial work.[589] Germany also has an interesting doctrine of 'free utilization' (*freie Benutzung*) aimed at accentuating the distinction between derivation and inspiration.[590] The test is one of 'significant dependence'.[591] German law distinguishes adaptations or 'reworking' (*Bearbeitungen*) from transformations that modify the inner structure of a work (*Umgestaltungen*).[592] This is key to establishing the proper scope of the derivative right, because changes to the form or structure (*Gestalt*) of the primary work is perhaps the key distinction between reproduction and derivation.[593] A derivation changes the form or structure, but not the fundamental character of the primary work. Like France, a doctrinal difference is drawn between copying expression and derivation, seen as taking 'something else' that cannot be appropriated without infringing.[594] This avoids the overreach of the right or reproduction and is more likely to allow reuses that truly transform the primary work as being beyond the reach of the derivative right. Put differently, the 'free utilization' doctrine is used by courts essentially to limit infringement of copyright to an appropriate array of cases of reuse.[595]

This analysis can be taken to a finer-grained level, one that goes beyond the *de minimis* limit applied to (mere) reproductions. It considers what and how much was taken, and how much was added and/or the level of transformation. Professor Ivan Cherpillod, who is well acquainted with both French and German doctrine, explained that, when the originality of what was taken from the primary work is dubious (*discutable*), infringement is less likely.[596] When the primary work's message is fundamentally altered

---

expression, but between the form and content of a work. The form is protected. But so are some parts of the content (not ideas, theories or knowledge but any content produced by the author's 'imaginary'. See ibid., 46–9. A difficulty at least of an evidentiary nature may be posed by the fact that fixation is not required under German law for copyright to subsist.

[589] See Adolf Dietz, 'Germany', in P Geller (ed.) *International Copyright Law and Practice* vol. II (loose-leaf, 2011) GER-33.
[590] See ibid.
[591] See ibid.
[592] *See* Dietz above note 589, GER-108.
[593] See Cherpillod, above note 585, 145–6. The free utilization doctrine also applies under Swiss law. See ibid.
[594] See ibid.
[595] See Paul E Geller, 'Hiroshige vs. van Gogh: Resolving the Dilemma of Copyright Scope in Remedying Infringement' (1998) *Journal of the Copyright Society of the USA* 39, 45.
[596] Ibid., 46.

and much is added, a similar case can be made because in both cases the proximity between the two works is less apparent. Cherpillod cites a court opinion to explain this view. The court noted that the elements common to the plaintiff's and the defendant's works, two well-known novelists, were 'purely exterior and without originality'.[597] The appropriation was lawful because the elements taken from the plaintiff's work were of 'uncertain originality' and used mostly as background for the new work.[598] The approach is complex because it is infused with normative considerations, such as the need to allow certain transformations such as parody, not as a fair use (defence) but as being outside the scope of the derivative right.[599] Cherpillod also suggests that the impact of the derivative work on the market for the original work is only an indicia, and not the definition of the scope of the derivative right proper, because it must draw distinctions between types of derivative works, such as a parody and, say, two scientific articles on the same subject.[600]

Finally, under British law, it is an infringement of the copyright to reproduce any substantial part of a literary work.[601] However, as explained in the well-known treatise by Copinger and Skone James, the inquiry focuses on whether the originality was appropriated by the derivative user:

> As already stated, the overriding question is whether, in creating the defendant's work, substantial use has been made of *the skill and labour which went into the creation of the claimant's work and thus those features which made it an original work* [. . .] The issue thus depends therefore not just on the physical amount taken but on its substantial significance or importance to the copyright work.[602]

Copinger and Skone James also explain that the question may depend on whether what has been taken is novel or striking, or is merely a commonplace arrangement of words or well-known material, an application of a limiting doctrine not unlike *scènes à faire* in US law.[603] They also note that:

---

[597] See ibid. The case, opposing Jean Hougron and Francoise Sagan, may be found at 111 *Revue Internationale du droit d'auteur* 188 (1982) (Court App. Paris).

[598] See Cherpillod, above note 585, at 147.

[599] See ibid., 147–9: a court 'may authorize the appropriation of protected elements if the reproduction is justified by a particular interest' [Author's translation], German courts also limit the derivative right 'when constitutional considerations come into play'. See Dietz, above note 589, GER-103.

[600] See Cherpillod, above note 585, 151.

[601] See ss 16(3) and 17(2) of the 1988 Act.

[602] *Copinger and Skone James on Copyright* (15th edn, Sweet & Maxwell 2005, §7–27 (emphasis added).

[603] A US copyright doctrine that prevents the application of copyright to

[a]s a corollary of the last point, the more simple or lacking in substantial originality the copyright work, the greater the degree of taking will be needed before
the substantial part test is satisfied. In the case of works of little originality,
almost exact copying will normally be required to amount to infringement.[604]

Those insights, based mainly on two cases,[605] target the normative distinction that delineates the domain of the derivative right: it is the taking
of the originality of the primary work that generates an infringement but
that a line is drawn at a level of abstraction where the idea/expression
line is crossed. Explaining the applicable distinction, Lord Hoffmann, in
*Designers Guild Ltd*,[606] noted the following:

[C]opyright subsists not in ideas but in the form in which the ideas are
expressed. The distinction between expression and ideas finds a place in the
Agreement on Trade-Related Aspects of Intellectual Property Rights (TRIPS)
[. . .], to which the United Kingdom is a party. [. . .] What does it mean? [. . .] It
represents [the author's] *choice* to paint stripes rather than polka dots, flowers
rather than tadpoles, use one colour and brush technique rather than another,
and so on. The expression of these ideas is protected, both as a cumulative
whole and also to the extent to which they form a 'substantial part' of the
work. Although the term 'substantial part' might suggest a quantitative test,
or at least the ability to identify some discrete part which, on quantitative or
qualitative grounds, can be regarded as substantial, it is clear upon the authorities that neither is the correct test. [. . .] [T]here are numerous authorities
which show that the 'part' which is regarded as substantial can be a feature or
combination of features of the work, abstracted from it rather than forming
a discrete part. That is what the judge found to have been copied in this case.
Or to take another example, the original elements in the plot of a play or novel
may be a substantial part, so that copyright may be infringed by a work which
does not reproduce a single sentence of the original. If one asks what is being
protected in such a case, it is difficult to give any answer except that it is an idea
expressed in the copyright work.

European jurisprudence explicates the distinction between reproduction
and derivation. That difference lies in the transfer *of elements of original
expression from the primary work to the derivative one for the purpose of
adding or transforming it, but not to the point of a fundamental transformation or the primary work.* Here again we see this idea that market impacts

---

standard elements typical to a genre. The justification for the doctrine is to avoid
hindering the creation of other expressive works.
 [604]   Copinger and Skone James, above note 602, §7.27.
 [605]   *Designers Guild Ltd v Russell Williams (Textiles) Ltd* [2001] 1 WLR 2416
(UKHL); and *Ladbroke (Football) Ltd v William Hill (Football) Ltd* [1964] 1
WLR 273.
 [606]   *Designers Guild Ltd*, ibid., 2422.

of the derivative are an indicia used in appropriate cases to determine whether the derivative right is infringed; they do not delineate the right.

Whether or not one considers derivation as a subset of a broader right of reproduction, the analysis of European jurisdictions suggests that, teleologically, normatively and doctrinally, real distinctions exist between the two rights: a reproduction *copies the expression* of the primary work, while a derivation *transfers elements that make the primary work original* with the purpose of adding to, or transforming, those elements.[607] The two inquiries are thus distinct because the reproduction inquiry focuses primarily on the form of what was taken while the derivation inquiry looks at a deeper level at what was taken in the creative choices that made the primary work worthy of copyright protection, and then at the nature of what was added to it or transformed.[608] *It is in the nature of derivation that something is added or transformed.*[609]

Hence, while the rights of reproduction and derivation are joined at the hip, they differ normatively. In many cases, this is true operationally as well because some cases of derivation also amount to copying; but not all of them do. Conversely, most cases of reproduction do not trigger the derivative right. For example, a quote (that goes beyond fair use) infringes reproduction but not derivation. The work that quotes generates a message that does not transform the primary work. Instead, it uses the primary work as support or illustration. By contrast, mounting or gluing a picture on a wall tile may infringe the derivative right (the hard question here is whether the recontextualization is still proximate enough to constitute derivation)

---

[607] As the US statute makes clear, a derivative need not add to the primary work. 'Abridgement' and 'condensation' are examples that show that an infringing derivative work may take the form of deletion and abbreviation.

[608] As Professors Lucas and Kamina note in the discussion of modern French law, but in a remark that can be generalized, '[d]ifficulties arise when courts have to determine at what point sufficient originality in changing the underlying work warrants protection of any resulting derivative work'. Andre Lucas, Pascal Kamina and Robert Plaisant, 'France', in *International Copyright Law & Practice*, above note 589, vol. 1, FRA-29. Again, I leave aside for now the question whether the derivative work's originality must stem entirely from the author of the derivative work.

[609] The limit of the right may be reached when the message of the primary work is fundamentally transformed, but then the (I return to this in the following Part). Indeed, Professor Cherpillod uses the verb 'to fade' when describing this situation in which 'the individuality of the copied features (*traits*) fades before the originality of the second work.' See Cherpillod, above note 585, at 147. As a matter of US law, in harder cases that fit within the latter situation the limit of the derivative right is likely to meet its fair use limits. That does not mean that the doctrinal work on the nature and scope of the derivative right can simply be ignored.

but not the reproduction right if no copy is made (that is, if an authorized copy of or the original image is used). Situating the distinction normatively seems essential to understand the role it should play, if any, in drawing lines for acceptable mass reuse of online content. Operationally, it is much easier to draw those boundaries if the purpose of the right is better understood.

US courts have not done well when trying to apply derivation as a distinct right, but I see room for that distinction to do more work as new cases emerge. One could start with *Arnstein v Porter*, in which the court identified two separate elements essential to a plaintiff's suit for infringement, namely copying and unlawful appropriation.[610] Then we might consider the outlier case *Sid & Marty Krofft Television Products, Inc v McDonald's Corp* and its intrinsic/extrinsic test, which separates substantial similarity in ideas (extrinsic) and substantial similarity in expressions (intrinsic).[611] From *Krofft,* one might then move to *Cavalier v Random House, Inc*, which proposes a different two-part analysis, namely an extrinsic test (objective comparison of specific expressive elements) and an intrinsic test (subjective comparison that focuses on 'whether the ordinary, reasonable audience' would find the works substantially similar in the 'total concept and feel of the works').[612] Finally, one might go back to the Second Circuit in *Boisson v Banian, Ltd,* which employs an ordinary observer test to determine copying but a 'more refined' version of the test when the work alleged to have been infringed incorporates public domain elements.[613] The tests were often used to decide whether expert testimony was admissible or probative in deciding infringement.[614] It seems fair to suggest that a number of US courts have increasingly tried to separate reproduction from derivation *qua* derivation (that is, whether or not a reproduction may also be occurring) but without fully getting there.

It may be time to consider a more nuanced approach. I believe that even a quick *tour d'horizon* such as the one contained in the previous pages suffices to illustrate the role that drawing proper distinction between the reproduction right and the derivative right might play. I suggest a two-step approach. The first step under the derivation inquiry boils down to

---

[610]   154 F 2d 464, 468–69 (2d Cir 1946), cert denied, 330 US 851, 67 S Ct 1096 (1947).

[611]   562 F 2d 1157, 1163–64 (9th Cir 1977).

[612]   297 F 3d 815, 822 (9th Cir 2002).

[613]   273 F 3d 262, 272–73 (2d Cir 2001).

[614]   For a discussion of the slightly different tests (or versions) applied by the various Circuits and the role of expert testimony, see Michael D Murray, 'Copyright, Originality, and the End of the Scènes à Faire and Merger Doctrines for Visual Works' (20006) 58 *Baylor Law Review* 779.

asking *whether what makes the primary work original was taken without fundamental alteration.* Market impacts may be a guide in appropriate cases, as, for example, market success is a guide that an invention is non-obvious (or inventive) for purposes of patent law.[615] The second step is considering the nature of what was added or transformed, including by recontextualization. Various limiting doctrines, in particular fair use and the idea/expression dichotomy, limit the reach of the right but that is a separate inquiry. This approach strikes me as not only normatively preferable, but also as more consistent with statutory and historical developments (in the US, in France, in Germany, and internationally) that have put the spotlight on derivation *qua* derivation—in named forms or as penumbral right—instead of market impacts per se.[616] The protection of markets allows a clearer analytical separation of fair use and derivation.

Visually, this could be shown as in Figure 5.1:

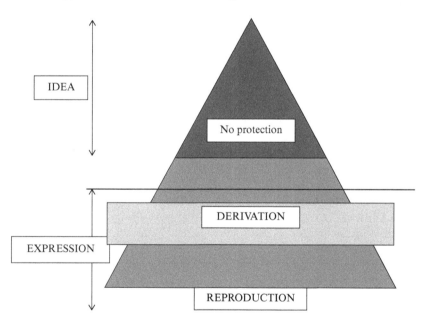

*Figure 5.1    The idea/expression dichotomy in reproduction and derivation*

---

[615]    Commercial success is one of the secondary considerations used to determine non-obviousness under *Graham v John Deere Co*, 383 US 1, 17 (1966). It is only that, however, not a hard test. See *Tokai Corp v Easton Enterprises, Inc* 632 F 3d 1358 (Fed. Cir. 2011).
[616]    See Ricketson and Ginsburg, note 564, 479.

This shows that some cases of derivation are also reproductions, but at least some are not. Additionally, it shows that derivations often appropriate elements higher in the idea-expression abstraction continuum. Obviously, to be protected the appropriation must be below the level of unprotected ideas.[617] Even if one sees derivation as form of reproduction in many cases, or as somehow subsumed under reproduction in a categorical taxonomy of copyright right, derivation stands on its own normative footing and must be considered (at least as a first step) as a fully distinct right. Then and only then can the analyses (derivation and reproduction) be combined (in a specific case).

To determine whether a derivation *qua* derivation has taken place, it may be useful to recall that one must ask whether it is originality—rooted in *creative choices* made by the author of a primary work—that is appropriated (and thus presumably worth taking) by a derivative user/author *for the purpose of reworking originality-generating elements* often to create a new work.[618] It is originality (resulting from creative choices) that a court should aim to protect, absent an applicable defence/exception.[619] This should not depend on a showing of the existence of a real or expected market nor on copying of the form of the expression, which is the realm of the reproduction right proper.[620] In sum, *derivation is best seen as taking what makes a pre-existing work (or more than one) original for the purpose of transforming it,* but not to the point of a fundamental alteration of the message. Market impact is only a secondary consideration. A translation or sequel is a perfect example or a derivative that would typically infringe absent a valid defence. By contrast, a reuse that alters the fundamental message of the primary work typically does not appropriate the protected elements of that work.[621]

Admittedly, the distinction, while theoretically interesting in a few cases, will not matter in most infringement analyses. Indeed the Berne

---

[617] The space below the idea/expression line but above the derivation 'box' is for reproductions at a higher level of abstraction (from the expression of the first work).

[618] See Chapter 10.

[619] We see this in a number of cases. For example in *Export Ventures, Inc v Einstein Moomjy, Inc*, 338 F 3d 127, 133 (2d Cir 2003), the court noted, first, that '[j]urists have long been vexed by the task of precisely identifying that which separates inexact copies that infringe from those that do not'.

[620] Other considerations, such as whether the author of the second work had sought a license (for the work at issue or previously) may also impact a finding of fair use. However, trying to identify a lost licensing transaction may be inappropriate. *See Campbell*, 510 US, 592.

[621] See Nimmer and Nimmer, above note 558, vol. 4, § 13.03 [A].

Convention (art. 12) speaks of authorizing adaptations, and the US statute (s. 106(2)) of preparing derivative works. It is not the case that someone making copies of a derivative or adapted version of a work would infringe the derivative right if that person did not also make the adaptation or derivative work. In such cases, it is other right fragments (reproduction, distribution etc.) that would most likely apply.

I end this analysis of the derivative right with a note of caution concerning art that copies art, a major form of which is known as 'appropriation art'. This will require courts to consider the derivative right with utmost caution. It is also an area where understanding the derivative right will become increasingly important.[622]

Appropriation art, a major strand of postmodern art, has already generated a significant amount of litigation involving not just the 'appropriators', but also museums debating their acquisition policies.[623] It is the poster child for hard derivation cases under copyright law. Works by artists such as Andy Warhol, Robert Rauschenberg, and Jeff Koons have been the subject of intellectual property disputes.[624] In a movement that was already well known by the Dadaists, appropriation art is the latest form of decontextualization.[625] But art copying art is not new. Would we consider Delacroix or Cezanne 'copying' Rubens' *The Landing of Marie*

---

[622]   See Daniel Gervais (n 173), 842–3; and Steven Hetcher, 'The Kids Are Alright: Applying A Fault Liability Standard To Amateur Digital Remix' (2010) 62 *Florida Law Review* 1275, 1326–7.

[623]   See John Henry Merryman, 'Museum Ethics', A.L.I.-A.B.A. Course Of Study: Legal Issues In Museum Admin 3, 9 (2006).

[624]   See e.g., Dauman v. Andy Warhol Foundation for the Visual Arts, 43 USPQ 2D (BNA) 21, in which the defendant's motion to dismiss claim of misappropriation of a copyright image by the late Andy Warhol, which formed the basis for his work 'Sixteen Jackies' was denied. Similarly, the publicity photo of Marilyn Monroe taken by Gene Korman used by Andy Warhol for his 'Marilyn' series was the subject of a private settlement with the Warhol Foundation. Molly A Torsen, Beyond Oil on Canvas: New Media and Presentation Formats Challenge International Copyright Law's Ability to Protect the Interests of the Contemporary Artist; (2006) *SCRIPTed*, § 3.1.2, suggesting Warhol's work was original enough to preclude liability (<available at http://www.copyrighthistory.org/cam/tools/request/showRecord.php?id=record_uk_1852> accessed 17 November 2016). See also *Robert Rauschenberg and Pete Turner*, Copyright Website, LLC: Rauschenberg was sued by Turner for using Turner's photograph, which appeared in an issue of *Time* magazine, in his work (http://www.benedict.com/Visual/Rauschenberg/Rauschenberg.aspx). See *Rogers v Koons*, 960 F 2d 301, 305-06, 314 (2d Cir 1992); holding that Koons' work, which incorporated Rogers' photograph, infringed Rogers' copyright in his photograph.

[625]   Jean-Pierre Cuzin, Au Louvre, D'après les Maîtres, in *Réunion des Musées Nationaux, Copier, C'est Créer : De Turner A Picasso*, 26, 28 (1993).

*de Médicis at Marseilles* as infringers?[626] Certainly they were adding their
own personality, copying themselves as much as Rubens in the words of
Catherine Kintzler.[627] What of Dali 'copying' Raphael?[628] A derivative use
may be amply original, but its originality does not save it from also being
an infringement. I do, however, suggest, as noted above, that it is an equation that reflects the amount of originality of the primary work; the quality
and quantity of the originality transferred from the primary work to the
derivative work; and the amount of originality and purpose added by the
author of the derivative work.

Modern artists, such as Sherri Levine, David Salle, Susan Pitt, Richard
Prince, and, in the 2008 US presidential campaign, Shepard Fairey, have
made the incorporation of previous works into their own works (without
permission) a central element of their artistic statement.[629] In the realm
of copying as art, as noted above, there is an argument that copying and/
or deriving is itself creative and, more broadly, that art is different.[630] Art
is art if it transforms (or even destroys). Art incorporates and sometimes
becomes a meme. It is copied as an element in a broader cultural construct, a vehicle for communal expression. Art may imitate, for example
as homage when Man Ray created his *Violon d'Ingres*.[631] Often, artists
begin by copying, as any art school instructor could attest.[632] Copying is
learning, homage and a necessary step for art to grow. It is the method by
which artists appropriate the past, an often indispensable step to their own
contribution.

This is a hard issue: what if the reuser seems to be exploiting the primary

---

[626]   Assuming here that there is no expiration of the term of protection for the
sake of discussion. (A copy of Rubens' masterpiece may be seen at http://www.
wga.hu/html_m/r/rubens/40histor/01medici.html).
[627]   Catherine Kintzler, La Copie et l'Original, *Démeter* 1, 6 (December 2003).
[628]   See ibid. For an example, see http://vunex.blogspot.com/2006/10/dali-on-
raphael.html.
[629]   I wish to thank Walt Lehman for providing much useful background and
insights on this point.
[630]   *See* Daniel J Gifford, 'Innovation and Creativity in the Fine Arts: The
Relevance and Irrelevance of Copyright' (2000) 18(3) *Cardozo Arts & Entertainment
Law Journal* 569, 578–9.
[631]   See Cuzin (n. 625)., 29.
[632]   See Johnson Okpaluba, 'Appropriation Art: Fair Use or Foul?' in Daniel
McClean and Karsten Schubert (eds), *Dear Images: Art, Copyright and Culture*
(Ridinghouse 2002), at 198–9. As a matter of 'art policy,' does it matter much
whether the artist uses an actual article clipped from the *New York Times* or
'copies' it with her brush? As a matter of copyright policy, the difference is, of
course, crucial, because the first use does not include a reproduction. It may,
however, involve a transformation and, hence, application of the derivative right.

work and affecting its market? How does one fairly distinguish that 'step' from a new contribution that should be allowed? That is precisely the question that properly scoping the derivative right (with its reproduction cousin in many cases) poses. It also shows that market impacts are likely a poor normative guide to deciding what art should be allowed.

By copying a master's work, the 'pupil' might get into or at least get a glimpse of the great author's mind, which would seem a normatively desirable process.[633] '*L'art naît d'un regard sur l'art*,' as the French would say: art is born from a view on existing art.[634] As such, one may see it as categorically excluded from the notion of derivation. In some cases, because of the equation just mentioned, the choices made by the reuser are such that this may be the right outcome. In harder cases, especially if there is commercial exploitation of the derivative, a court might decide that the amateur (or not) nature of the use is best considered a protected deriva-tion, based on the principle of proximity. That, I suggest, is the proper approach. That principle is subject to the test suggested previously in the form of a policy equation (page 154). As a subsequent step, a fair use or similar analysis may be used to limit the reach of the right.

UGC writ large is subject to a similar note of caution. Many forms of UGC are non-commercial but also non-private. An excellent example is doujinshi, comic-like magazines combining *anime*, *manga* and video games.[635] Major social events attended by thousands of fans are organized to share doujinsjhi.[636] Online fan sites also come to mind.[637] These sites and forms of UGC cannot all be comfortably pigeonholed as non-com-mercial.[638] This clashes with traditional accounts, which tend to present UGC as non-commercial or 'amateur'.[639] While this view may have been

---

[633]  See ibid., 30–31.

[634]  Cuzin, above note 625, 35.

[635]  *Anime* a form of animation and *manga* a form of Japanese comics. See Nathaniel Noda, 'Copyrights Retold: How Interpretive Rights Foster Creativity and Justify Fan-Based Activities' (2010) 20 *Seton Hall Journal of Sports & Entertainment Law* 131, 132; and Salil Mehra, 'Copyright and Comics in Japan: Does Law Explain Why All the Cartoons My Kid Watches are Japanese Imports?'(2010) 55 *Rutgers Law Review* 155, 164.

[636]  See ibid. This includes a three-day market in Tokyo known as 'Comiket' (see <http://www.comiket.co.jp/index_e.html> last visited Jan. 4, 2012)

[637]  See Aaron Schwabach, *Fan Fiction and Copyright* (Ashgate Publishing 2011) 18.

[638]  From *Campbell v Acuff-Rose Music, Inc.*, 510 US 569, 584–5 (1994), we know that commerciality is not a bar to a finding of fair use but it is a (major) strike against the defendant under the fourth factor.

[639]  See e.g., Lessig, *Remix*, note 460 above, 254.

fully justified in the early days of UGC, a number of ways to monetize at least some forms of UGC are emerging, and litigation tends to follow as soon as a significant commercial line is crossed.[640] Courts should make room for some forms of commercial (or at least non-amateur) UGC to balance the promotion of new forms of creativity and the need to maintain valid ex-ante incentives/ex-post rewards for creators of primary works used, even if the new forms strike the court as being of poor quality.[641]

It is also important to note the possible absence of strong correlations between decisions to create fresh material instead of borrowing. Recent empirical research suggests that authors are not (in aggregate) particularly good at maximizing welfare and efficiency, and that the ability to reuse (whether because it is licensed, fair use, etc.) pre-existing content is not very closely tied to copyright constraints but rather to a host of other factors.[642]

The normative implications are clear: should one stop generations of younger creators who were 'born digital' and see no good reason not to use those tools to create, even if it includes some measure of appropriation? When does that appropriation cross the line? [643] When there is sufficient proximity between the works, especially where much of the primary work's creative choices have been appropriated and little added? The analysis should be informed by the fact that copyright has always tried to avoid judgment on the quality or artistic merit of new forms of creation, and the fact that the appropriation of the past is a necessary ingredient of an intergenerational dialogue, which might take several new and possibly irreverent forms.[644] At the very least, judges should be aware of any

---

[640]   See Casey Fiesler, 'Everything I Need To Know I Learned from Fandom: How Existing Social Norms Can Help Shape the Next Generation of User-Generated Content' (2008) 10 *Vanderbilt Journal of Entertainment & Technology Law* 729, 752.

[641]   This 'trap' of judging the quality of a primary or allegedly infringing work is common, and may well be justified as a cultural matter, but not as a factor under copyright law (no judging of artistic merit). For a discussion of the former (cultural) aspects, see Andrew Keen, *The Cult of the Amateur: How Today's Internet is Killing Our Culture* (Doubleday 2007) 3–4. On the latter (copyright) aspect, see James Grimmelman, 'The Ethical Visions of Copyright Law' (2009) 77 *Fordham Law Review* 2005, 2006.

[642]   See Stefan Bechtold, Christopher Buccafusco and Christopher Jon Sprigman, 'Innovation Heuristics: Experiments on Sequential Creativity in Intellectual Property' (2016) 91 *Indiana Law Journal* 1251.

[643]   On that distinction, see Gervais, (n 173) 850–55.

[644]   The exclusion of artistic merit in copyright policy is well established at least theoretically in most legal systems. In the US, Justice Holmes's made the point famously in *Bleistein v Donaldson Lithographing Co*, 188 US 239, 251 (1903). Yet

underlying 'bias'.[645] Originality is what is added by the artist, both as a contribution to the work's inherent structure (what one might call aesthetic originality), but often also, especially for new art forms, as a posture of the artist vis-à-vis her creative milieu.[646]

If we mean it when we say that we want to foster the emergence of new expression, this form of evolution of art, whether seen as positive or not, should be encouraged.[647]

---

even courts that try often fail; see Amy B Cohen, 'Copyright Law and the Myth of Objectivity: The Idea-Expression Dichotomy and the Inevitability of Artistic Value Judgments' (1990) 66 *Indiana Law Journal* 175, 231.

[645] See Christine Haight Farley, 'Judging Art' (2005) 79 *Tulane Law Review* 805, 845–6.

[646] Kintzler, above note 627, 8.

[647] See ibid. In some cases, transgression might, in an ironic twist, become the norm.

# 6.   A place for authors

## 6.1   AUTHORS AND THE GREAT LIBRARY IN THE SKY

The Internet provides access to an incredible array and variety of cultural products from around the world.[648] It is the Great Virtual Library, available at your local café and everywhere else.[649] It makes cultural products not only easier to access but also, as is explained in the previous chapter, to modify and then to re-disseminate. Because the Internet allows access and easy reuse, the Internet is a global meme factory: it makes possible a great cycle of: (a) access to existing works; (b) copying them; (c) modifying them; and (d) disseminating them, which repeats endlessly in various directions.[650] The Internet offers major advantages for authors (though there is a downside, to which I turn a little later), for users and for online intermediaries.

Beneficiaries of older intermediation models based on the distribution of physical copies see things somewhat differently. Traditional professional distributors such as book publishers, record companies and others whose job it is (or was) to find, *filter* and provide access to copies of cultural productions after identifying the most commercially promising ones, are unable to contain the flood of unfiltered online 'content' streaming down Internet pipes all around the world: books are self-published, songs and sound recordings can be produced using basic software, and YouTube can be used to provide access to homemade and even semi-professional

---

[648]   The expression 'cultural products' is meant to capture productions that may or may not be or consist of copyrighted material that have cultural import but does not imply physicality.

[649]   Actually, this statement seems *literally* correct. See Lea Bishop Shaver, 'Defining and Measuring A2K: A Blueprint for an Index of Access to Knowledge' (2008) 4(3) *I/S: A Journal of Law and Policy for the Information Society* 235, 247: 'Where access to the ancient Great Library of Alexandria was physically out of reach for most of the world's denizens, the digital collections of the modern Bibliotheca Alexandrina can be accessed instantly from anywhere.'

[650]   This expression was used and discussed in Daniel Gervais and Daniel J Hyndman, 'Cloud Control: Copyright, Global Memes and Privacy' (2012) 10 *Journal on Telecommunications and High Technology Law* 53, 64.

videos.[651] The filters still exist but now they tend to take different forms: either famous publisher trademarks (such as *Nature, Science* or major trade imprints) or the various forms of feedback provided by individuals and aggregated in the form of stars, ratings, reviews, etc.[652]

Traditional content distributors emerged in a non-digital environment where cultural products were generally distributed in the form of the physical copies (books, DVDs, CDs) and/or through a limited number of professional distributors such as the cinemas, television networks or other broadcasters. Often, those distributors acquired the copyright from the author and thus became 'right holders'.[653] This also allowed right holders to control release dates in what has been referred to as the chronology of media.[654] It is hardly possible today even for a Hollywood studio to try to maintain any kind of chronology, as users expect new releases to be available online almost on the same day as the theatrical release.[655]

New intermediation models, by contrast, are typically implemented by entities *not* operating as right holders. Those new entities—for example search engines—are in the business of connecting individuals with whatever form of information or 'content' they are looking for. Content is not their core business; it is merely a tool to generate more use, which in turn generates advertising revenue.[656] Traditional intermediaries—whose business model depend on *selling* content (copies and/or access) they own or have licensed—must thus now compete with free (advertising-based) distributors of unfiltered content often produced by amateurs, semi-amateurs and what I will call 'unaffiliated' professionals.[657] Whether the content

---

[651] See Maureen A O'Rourke, 'A Brief History of Author–Publisher (Fn2) Relations and the Outlook for the 21st Century' (2003) 50 *Journal of the Copyright Society of the USA* 425, 462: describing the emergence of self-publishing starting in the 1990s.

[652] See Gabe Bloch, 'Transformation in Publishing: Modeling the Effect of New Media' (2005) 20 *Berkeley Technology Law Journal* 647, 669.

[653] See Sarah C Anderson, 'Decontextualization of Musical Works: Should the Doctrine of Moral Rights Be Extended?' (2006) 16 *Fordham Intellectual Property, Media and Entertainment Law Journal* 869, 881–2.

[654] See Séverine Dusollier and Caroline Colin, 'Peer-to-Peer File Sharing and Copyright: What Could Be the Role of Collective Management?' (2011) 34 *Columbia Journal of Law & the Arts* 809, 834.

[655] See ibid.

[656] See Urs Gasser, 'Regulating Search Engines: Taking Stock and Looking Ahead' (2006) 8 *Yale Journal of Law & Technology* 201.

[657] 'Unaffiliated' professionals are a category 'above' semi-amateurs. Unlike amateurs who may generate occasional income from cultural products they create, unaffiliated professionals consider that they are full-time authors or at least they generate revenue on their own, and creation is typically their main occupation, but

is legal or not does not matter much to the new intermediaries' business model. While access to maximum amounts of content becomes the new normal, when combined with the intermediaries' understandable wish to maximize revenue and minimize expenses, the push not to pay for content whenever possible becomes inevitable. This leads to what I see as a fundamental cognitive dissonance: namely the belief that authors will find the time to create content even with little or very limited income. Some will, and do, by the millions each day. But is there a societal cost to pay? Before turning to the answer to that question, let us look at the ethos of many of the new intermediaries as encapsulated by a *New York Times* columnist, who notes how it differs from traditional content distribution:

> The first principle is to be a middleman — or in tech lingo, a platform — connecting the people who post on YouTube with those who watch their videos, or the people who need a ride with people who will drive them. As platforms, the thinking goes, they are just connectors, with no responsibility for what happens there. For websites, this is codified in law — they are not legally responsible for what their users publish, according to the Communications Decency Act, perhaps the most influential law in the development of the web. 'These folks grew up in a world where platforms are not responsible, and then when they go do stuff in the real world, they expect that to be the case,' said Ryan Calo, an assistant professor at the University of Washington law school who studies cyber law. [. . .] Regulators are little more than roadblocks standing in the way of innovation.[658]

An approach in which advertising (unrelated to a licensing transaction concerning use of the content) is the core business affects the very nature of intermediation. It dictates choices offered to the user—or at least the order in which search results will appear.[659] This matters.[660] My intuition is that users often tend to follow previous users and to limit themselves to top search results. They decide what to listen to or watch or read by

---

they are not affiliated with the traditional right holders (major industrial distributors such as publishers, etc.).

[658] Claire Cain Miller, 'When Uber and Airbnb Meet the Real World' *New York Times* (NY 17 October 2014) (<nyti.ms/1wrf624> accessed 1st October 2015). Not all tech companies fit this description of course, as several of them have tried to respect third-party rights in developing new business models.

[659] Rolfe Winkler, 'Google Pushes Its Own Content— As More Users Move to Smartphones, the Search Game Is Changing in Novel Ways', *Wall Street Journal* (NY 19 August 2014) B1.

[660] It has been said to even influence election results. See Craig Timberg, 'Research in India Suggests Google Search Results can Influence an Election' *The Washington Post* (Washington, D.C. 12 May 2014) (<wapo.st/1t9cmqn> accessed 29 September 2015).

considering feedback left by such previous users among the top choices offered by the search tool they used.

In this new environment, there is clearly no physical scarcity (of copies). Scarcity of copies is an obsolete notion, and the economics of intellectual property writ large must be reconsidered as a result.[661] But one should not overlook another type of scarcity, this one of connections. Physical scarcity has been replaced by what I would call '*like* scarcity'.[662] Time that people spend online is necessarily limited. Hence being able to limit or orient their choices is hugely powerful and is likely to affect present and future preferences. This has become the key to creating connection, and, hence, value. User time and preferences are now the main value creation tools for cultural content on the Internet.[663] Too often, this value is now zero.[664]

It is to be expected that changes in technology and the possibility that it offers to access, use, and manipulate content will change our constructs about intellectual property in that they affect patterns of behaviour, related social norms and constructs about notions such as propriety that often inform courts in hard cases. For example, in the famous 1918 case of *International News Service v Associated Press*, for example, the majority used tort law to prevent the appropriation of 'hot news'[665] Justice Pitney, writing for the majority, saw a form of property arising from the investment in news generation and transmission:

> In order to sustain the jurisdiction of equity over the controversy, we need not affirm any general and absolute property in the news as such. The rule that a court of equity concerns itself only in the protection of property rights treats any civil right of a pecuniary nature as a property right [. . .]; and the right to acquire property by honest labor or the conduct of a lawful business is as much entitled to protection as the right to guard property already acquired. [. . .] It

---

[661]  Mark A Lemley, 'IP in a World without Scarcity' (2015) 90 *New York University Law Review* 460.

[662]  I use the word to 'like' here to refer to the Facebook and other devices that allow individuals to indicate that they enjoyed a particular comment, video, song, etc.

[663]  I discussed this idea in greater detail in Daniel Gervais, 'Individual and Collective Management of Rights Online', in J Axhamn (ed.), *Copyright in a Borderless Online Environment* (Kluwe Law International 2012) 89, 98l; and in 'The Price of Social Norms' (n 498), 56.

[664]  See Elizabeth Renzetti, 'When Iggy Pop Can't Live off His Art, What Chance Do the Rest Have?' *The Globe and Mail* (Toronto 18 October 2015) A2, quoting Tim Kreider as saying 'money is also how our culture defines value, and being told what you do is of no ($0.00) value to the society you live in is, frankly, demoralizing'.

[665]  248 US 215 (1918).

is this right that furnishes the basis of the jurisdiction in the ordinary case of unfair competition.[666]

This is nothing new. As the famous American economist and sociologist Thorstein Veblen noted in a book published barely a year after *INS*, a system of 'natural rights', including property, 'has served as the unquestioned and immutable ground for public morals and expediency, on which the advocates of enlightened and liberal policies have always been content to rest their case'.[667]

Justice Holmes, one of the dissenters in *INS,* thought, like the author of the other dissenting opinion, Justice Louis Brandeis, that the law should not prevent the use of 'the thoughts or facts that the words express' because '[p]roperty, a creation of law, does not arise from value'.[668] But Holmes also thought it was improper for INS to reuse AP's hot news without proper attribution. As he noted '[i]t is a question of how strong an infusion of fraud is necessary to turn a flavor into a poison'.[669] This construct about proper attribution, which is one of the pillars of the author's moral right in international copyright law (see Chapter 2), was shaken by the technological ease of reuse of digital material. As a result law must evolve, but, like Veblen, I believe that this development can and should be guided and not left to a battle of vested interests trying to maintain the status quo ante or destroy it for purely financial reasons.[670]

The tension and resulting malaise in the copyright system is part of a broader socio-economic shift. André Gorz, a leading French philosopher of the late twentieth century and early part of the twenty-first, explored whether what he termed immaterial or 'cognitive' capitalism could function like traditional capitalism.[671] Cognitive capitalism, which dominates the online environment, affects financial flows in a way that has taken a heavy financial toll on many creators trying to earn a living. One should also readily admit, as I have noted previously (see pages 91 and 198), that no business model has any right to survive and, therefore, it should not be the focus of innovation-based policy to prevent Schumpeterian crea-

---

[666]  Ibid., 236.
[667]  Thorstein Veblen, *The Vested Interests and the Common Man* (New York: Huebsch 1919) 35.
[668]  *INS v AP*, 246.
[669]  Ibid., 247.
[670]  This is a theme discussed by Veblen in several publications. A good analysis of vested interests' role in policy development is contained in the book cited at note 667.
[671]  André Gorz, *The Immaterial* (University of Chicago Press 2010) 65.

tive destruction.[672] But when regulation is structured in an inefficient and obsolete way to make it nearly impossible for authors to receive a fair share, then there is a structural problem that can and should be addressed.

Commenting on Gorz's critique, Slovenian Marxist philosopher Slavoj Žižek wrote that there might be witnessing an application of the 'contradiction between productive forces and relations of production' that may undermine capitalism itself.[673] This is neither the time nor the place to fully address this point but I am very far from convinced. Authors create value, which generates what economists call 'surplus'. It has always been difficult for authors to retain the surplus they generate. Before the advent of the Internet, however, many creative industries functioned in a way that allowed several categories of professional authors to make a decent living, and often better. Now the surplus is split among intermediaries and a fast-shrinking portion goes to authors. Žižek goes a step further, arguing that the:

> very nature of the World Wide Web seems to be Communist, tending towards the free flow of data—CDs and DVDs are gradually disappearing, millions of people are simply downloading music and videos, mostly for free. This is why the business establishment is engaged in a desperate struggle to impose the form of private property on this flow by enforcing intellectual property laws.[674]

He then refers to Jaron Lanier's critique of possible threats posed by this 'openness'; what is:

> celebrated as 'the digital space's] greatest social achievement, the free circulation of data and ideas . . . gave birth to non-creative providers (Google, Facebook) who exert an almost monopoly power to regulate the flow of data, while individuals who create the content are lost in the anonymity of the network'.[675]

I see a fundamental divide here. New intermediaries see very little value in owning content, and have little interest in rewarding those who create it. They *monetize relationships*, connections with their users and between users and 'content'. The new intermediaries see content as a commons they can exploit by using it to weave connections through the fabric of constantly emerging and fluctuating flows of content. Capitalism has traditionally seen unowned content not as a commons but rather as a *res nullius*—property 'waiting to be owned' as it were. This explains why

---

[672]   Daniel Gervais, Uber Copyright Reform in Daniel Gervais and Susy Frankel eds. *Intellectual Property and Regulation of the Internet: The Nexus with Human and Economic Development* (Wellington: Victoria University Press 2017).

[673]   Slavoj Žižek, *Trouble in Paradise* (Melville House 2014) 31.

[674]   Ibid., 61.

[675]   Ibid,. See Jaron Lanier, *Who Owns the Future* (Simon & Schuster 2014).

traditional intermediaries are so tied to ownership narratives that reverberate as increasingly quaint echoes of models past. The very nature of ownership is called into question, and with it, some might say, the infrastructure of capitalism.

Those issues are real, to be sure, but the idea that cyberspace and the global companies that more or less own it—or in any event have become unavoidable doorways to access it—and the business models they use are entirely unregulatable strikes me as naïve.[676] Indeed, regulation is at the very core of the issue. To take two simple examples of dysfunctional regulation, services such as YouTube pay next to nothing for the music its users stream tens of millions of times each day. YouTube is exempt from copyright liability as an intermediary in several jurisdictions because it provides a takedown service when notified by copyright holder.[677] Suggestions that YouTube's parent Google/Alphabet could disgorge even an infinitesimal part of its annual profits (approximately US$25 billion[678]) to pay authors—perhaps because the bulk of which comes from advertising which in turn is highly dependent on making 'content' available to Internet users—are often met with scorn, especially in academia. It is also regulation that dictates that Spotify and Pandora must pay almost all the royalties they pay in the US to the owners of copyright in the sound recording, and next to nothing to the songwriter and lyricist.[679] Regulation could easily contain less leonine terms.

The question that this chapter aims to answer is this: what is the way forward for authors? How can authors appropriately monetize not file transfers from point A to point B but the connections between creative works and fans of those works? The current law's structural focus on technical operations done on protected digital content (such as reproduction, distribution and various file-transfer rights such as the right contained in section 106(6) of the US Copyright Act on 'digital transmissions' of sound

---

[676] Google, just like film and record companies, spend billions lobbying politicians and funding elections. If it were unconcerned by regulation, it might have better use for its money. See Simon Marks and Harry Davies, 'Revealed: How Google Enlisted Members of US Congress it Bankrolled to Fight $6bn EU Antitrust Case' *The Guardian*, December 17, 2015 (available at bit.ly/2eNEE9y> accessed 17 November 2016 >).

[677] See Daniel Gervais, 'The Landscape of Collective Management' (2011) 24(4) *Columbia Journal of Law & the Arts* 423.

[678] See 'Alphabet Announces Third Quarter 2015 Results of Google' (available at <https://investor.google.com/earnings/2015/Q3_google_earnings.html> accessed December 12, 2015).

[679] Eddie Schwartz, 'Coda: Fair Trade Music: Letting the Light Shine in', in Daniel Gervais and Susy Frankel (eds) *Evolution and Equilibrium* (CUP, 2014).

recordings) seems increasingly antiquated and indeed often obsolete. This is the structural problem that needs to be addressed. The dominant ethos is to translate the fact that new creations can easily and freely be made available online into a normative conclusion that it should all be without compensation to those who have created the 'content'.

A 'law' of the online/mobile environment is that the value of an information object on the Internet is not derived from its scarcity but rather from the fact that those who value it most will find it. The preference-dictating algorithms mentioned above are based on a user's search and use history.[680] Those algorithms thus assume that a user will value what she valued in the past and keep her in her 'value zone'. In a world where almost everything is in the Cloud, the inescapable truth is that the value of a particular cultural artefact is an amalgam created by the number of users connected with the content that they themselves value individually and share with others. This sharing creates network effects that in turn create more value.[681] The point here is that it is the new intermediaries, including social media, who provide the tools for but also goad users into finding, connecting to and 'liking' new cultural products. To get back to the question alluded to in the foreword, is this change in intermediation models a form of *progress*? As this author once wrote '[c]hange is simply predictable, inevitable and ceaseless as the basic social fact. In the words of the old song, "[w]e don't know where we're going, but we're on our way"'.[682]

An *assumption* that changes in the way cultural products are created and disseminated will necessarily be translated into human progress arguably drives our copyright regime.[683] And indeed progress there has been. The Internet has shown that it can pierce the shield of censorship.[684] Distance education is providing a low-cost way to send the latest information to far reaches of the planet. Sight-impaired users have access to more books than ever before. Information-sharing tools have made revolutions and large manifestations easier to organize. True, one can find most anything

---

[680]   See Lisa Larrimore Ouellette, 'The Google Shortcut to Trademark Law' (2014) 102 *California Law Review* 351, 401. It may well be that even non signed-in users will see customization based on history and preferences.

[681]   Gervais and Hyndman 69–70 (note 650).

[682]   Ibid.

[683]   See Marci A Hamilton, 'The Historical and Philosophical Underpinnings of the Copyright Clause' (1999) 13 Benjamin N Cardozo School of Law, Occasional Papers in Intellectual Property Working Paper 5.

[684]   See Paul R Williams and Colleen (Betsy) Popken, 'U.S. Foreign Policy and the Arab Spring: Ten Short-Term Lessons Learned' (2012) 41 *Denver Journal of International Law & Policy* 47, 59.

online. Whether that greater access is necessarily a form of *progress* requires making two significant logical jumps, however namely, first, that users can find and, second, that then will want to access, a wide array of diverse information and cultural products. As mentioned above, online culture is being reshaped by ad-based intermediation models that drive user choices.[685] The Internet is driving informational and cultural choices to a user's familiar territory. For many, it is a world of more of the same. Users access a lot but they access what is recommended or pushed by ad-based intermediaries and/or by peers. This may lead to a significant narrowing of real choices and certainly is not a guarantee of quality.

To paraphrase American philosopher and educational reformer John Dewey, Democracy's sister is Education.[686] Why did Dewey think that education was so important in a democracy? Because to realize the democracy ideal, new humans must acquire the best from the past and have the opportunity to keep building on it.[687] As he put it:

> [S]ocial efficiency as an educational purpose should mean cultivation of power to join freely and fully in shared or common activities. *This is impossible without culture*, [. . .] and there is perhaps no better definition of culture than that it is the capacity for constantly expanding the range and accuracy of one's perception of meanings.[688]

Culture implies that one has access to (quality) books, films, music and art, works that carry within them, and expand the meanings of, the past and present, and open horizons about the future. Culture thus grows

---

[685] Up to a point, which depends on how general the search parameters are. If an online search is very precise, there is less 'wiggle room' for a search engine to influence outcomes. For example if one searches for Anne Tyler's bibliography, one will find a list of her books, including Accidental Tourist (1985) but also my personal favorite, Breathing Lessons (1988). However, if I search for best movies based on books, *Accidental Tourist* is not on the list of the top 100 (See John Campea, 'Top 100 Movies Based On Books' (*The Movie Blog*, 21 November 2008) (<themovieblog.com/2008/the-movie-blogs-top-100-movies-based-on-books/> accessed 2 October 2015)), a dubious selection given that the novel was a finalist for the Pulitzer Prize, won the National Book Critics Circle Award for Fiction in 1985 and the Ambassador Book Award for Fiction in 1986 and was adapted into a 1988 award-winning film starring William Hurt, Kathleen Turner, and Geena Davis (for which Davis won an Academy Award).
[686] John Dewey, *Democracy and Education: An Introduction to the Philosophy of Education* (University of Chicago Press, 1916), discussing the aims and methods of education and how they can help or hamper the adequate realization of the democratic ideal.
[687] See ibid., 2.
[688] Dewey (n 686) 144–5.

richer when one has access to—one might say is confronted with—new forms of high-quality creation.[689] Great works and other cultural products form part of one's intellectual toolset. This toolset provides ways to *understand, analyse* and *criticize* information. It seems fair to ask whether the Internet, as it is now driven by hyper-targeted ads and user-preference shaping tools, will prove to be as beneficial for cultural production simply because it is such a great mode of access to and source of information.

The changing role of filters means that informational and cultural flows are immense and much too big for any human mind.[690] This means that users *must* resort to some type of filter, portal, search agent or bot. The issue here is that those tools are clearly not neutral. They are operated by companies who derive almost all of their income from advertisement and have become among the largest companies in the world. Those paying for ads and placement can influence the filters. The fact that the companies operating those filters sometimes add real value (think of book scanning and searching—again as an effort to generate more and more 'content' online) does not change that in any way. In an attempt to make content more 'relevant' to users, by which one probably means more familiar, filters give people what they want based on what they already know but often twisted to reflect the priorities of advertisers. Filters, often in the form of search engines or ad-driven social media, govern. Filters may prevent us from seeing other cultures, being exposed to 'unwanted' content and viewpoints (or they will be distorted and made fun of). The Internet, like may technological tools, is thus a double-edged sword: it greatly increases access to and availability of information and cultural productions, and makes available simple, inexpensive tools to promote culture, cooperation, joint action and consensus building. By the same token, the overabundance of information and culture can easily produce a tunnel vision effect.

## 6.2   MAKING IT WORK FOR AUTHORS

How can we make this new environment work for authors? To begin with, a policy error that is too often made, deliberately or not, in suggesting any type of copyright reform is to stick to the premise of a 'one-size-fits-all' copyright regime. I see this as a fundamental error because, while reform

---

[689] Quality is defined here as accomplishing the goals just identified.

[690] The professional filters of course made mistakes, for example in refusing to publish people who would become great authors. Yet they somehow kept the volume of new material a bit more manageable.

proposals based on the perceived needs of one category of authors can certainly be validly advanced, they should not drive the entire copyright policy effort.[691] There is, in other words, an epistemological error at the very root of analyses concerning the operation of the copyright system when they identify and then focus on the need of a single category of authors. As Professor Carroll noted at an ATRIP Congress, '[o]ne-size-fits-all patents and copyrights necessarily are inefficient because the magnitude of appropriability problems that these rights are designed to remedy varies considerably across and even within industries, and private ordering often fails to match these rights with those who would make use of them'.[692] True, those who propose a different structure must bear the burden of showing that 'tailoring' will generate benefits that outweigh the costs of uniformity.

Bearing this in mind, and acknowledging that several different taxonomies of the various categories of authors are certainly possible, I offer a fairly simple categorization of four different types of authors, for the purposes of identifying flaws in, and possible improvements to, the copyright system. This brief descriptive account is a prelude to Chapter 8 in Part II of this book, in which I propose a formal quadrantal structure of authorship.

The first category of authors resemble scholars but have some different characteristics. These are authors who are *'just sharing'* and who have no serious possibility of making significant income from the sale of their work. This might be because of the size of the potential market (epigraphs, poetry), or because it concerns works whose purpose is only to disseminate ideas or views (blog posts). Unlike scholars, however, few authors in this category are likely to support financial flows to publishing houses or other commercial intermediaries.

Which takes us to our second category, *scholars*. Scholars are typically employed by universities or research institutes. They are generally paid both to teach and add to the body of the knowledge in their field.

---

[691] We see this for example in the spat between the Authors Alliance which supports authors 'who write to be read' and who 'who want to harness this potential to share their creations more broadly in order to serve the public good' ('About us' (*Authors Alliance*) (available at <http://www.authorsalliance.org/about/> accessed 29 September 2015) and the Authors Guild. On the Guild's site, T J Stiles—who also delivered a keynote address reproduced in 38 Colum JL & Arts—noted: 'If any of you earn a living as a writer, or hope to, I strongly urge you not to join the Authors Alliance.') Note from T J Stiles to the San Francisco Writers Grotto (15 May 2014) (available at <http://www.authorsguild.org/general/what-is-the-authors-alliance> accessed 29 September 2015).

[692] M W Carroll, 'A Framework for Tailoring Intellectual Property Rights', in A Kur and V Mizaras (eds) *The Structure of Intellectual Property law: Can One Size Fit All?* (Edward Elgar Publishing 2011) 25.

They rarely make any substantial income from the sale of copies of their works and are often happy just 'to be read'.[693] In other words, their income is mostly independent from the commercial potential, if any, of their research and publications.[694] For them producing and publishing copyrighted works is more about visibility, the sharing of ideas, and access (access to one's works and gaining access to the work of other scholars in the field). Some scholars may have an indirect interest in having healthy financial flows to publishers who can provide peer review and continue publishing at least the more well-known titles, because scholars may want the recognition of being published by those publishers.

The third category is for creators who believe that they can 'make it' but have not (yet) obtained support from a professional distributor. They are in a phase that I would call visibility-seeking creators in their *'promotional' phase*. The prime behavioural driver of authors at this stage might logically be that to maximize the number of potential users of their work, that is people who will find them in an ocean of new cultural productions and, hopefully, 'like' them.

Fourth, and last, there are *professional or 'career' authors* whose income depends on users paying for their work (that is, for a copy or access to a performance of the work). These authors work within different industrial constraints depending on the type of professional distributor with which they are working. These range from professional novelists to songwriters to film directors and scriptwriters. They also include artists who sell artwork through galleries, etc. Their common denominator is that they need an enforceable basis to exert some degree of control over commercially significant forms of exploitation or adequate monetization of their work.

If one were to consider the differences among these four categories of authors, I suggest that whether an author (still) sees her work has her 'child' once it is 'out there in the world' might the drive some of the analysis: is the author a good and willing parent?[695] The point here is that if authors have parental responsibility, they must also have the necessary rights to exercise that responsibility.

The new environment undoubtedly leads to a major paradigm shift in the notion of authorship. As Marshall McLuhan wrote, 'to treat [new

---

[693] See ibid.

[694] I explored the distinction between the motivations of scientists and technologists in an essay based on several conversations with university researchers in physics, chemistry and engineering. I would suggested that a similar analysis would be justified and determining the type of ip-based incentive that the scholars need. See Daniel Gervais, 'The Patent Target' (2013) 23(2) Fed Cir Bar J 305.

[695] After all, when a work is without a parent we do say that it is 'orphaned'.

media] as humble servants of our established conventions would be as fatal as to use an x-ray unit as a space heater'.[696] We (authors, users and distributors) must undoubtedly adapt. Opinions differ widely as to how. Some advance anti-authorialist arguments rooted in post-modernism, the inevitable death of the author and the emergence of post-human creation.[697] I am unable to predict whether human authors will or will not survive as a significant source of cultural production in the medium to long run. In the short run, however, a fair question to ask is whether copyright policy should try to keep a place for human authors and whether career (human) authors should exist and, therefore, get paid (I mean with money not just by recognition in the form of likes or otherwise or 'attribution').

Other than the possibility of replacing them entirely with automated creation software, which does not necessarily strike me as a highly desirable outcome, there are two major strands of argument used to support claims that human authors should *not* get paid for their work (by the grant of a copyright and ability to license or sell their rights). First, one can claim in what amounts to a logical fallacy that many, if not even most authors do not expect monetary reward, and, therefore, authors do not need copyright—or at least the economic component of copyright.[698] What can one respond? That some authors use copyright to obtain payment from users for access to and/or use of copyrighted material and that others are free not to use or exercise their rights.[699] Authors can give their work away without payment, using Creative Commons for example.[700] Authors of audiovisual or musical content can upload it to several sites (e.g., YouTube) where it can be accessed for free. Academic authors (especially those in the US legal academy who publish mostly with student-edited, and not large commercial, journals) can make material available for free, as the success of the Social Science Research Network has demonstrated.[701] Scientists who

---

[696] Adalaide Morris and Thomas Swiss (eds), *New Media Poetics* (MIT Press 2006) v, citing Marshall McLuhan, *Electronic Revolution in North America* (International Literary Annual 1, 1959) pages 165–9.

[697] See Jane C Ginsburg, 'The Concept of Authorship in Comparative Copyright Law' (2003) 52 *DePaul Law Review* 1063, 1064–5; and Adalaide Morris, 'New Media Poetics: As We May Think/How to Write' in Morris and Swiss, ibid., 1, 4.

[698] See *above* note 691 and accompanying text.

[699] Basically, because making a copy or a public performance requires permission unless an exception, such as fair use, applies. 17 USC §§106–121 (2015).

[700] See *Creative Commons* (available at <creativecommons.org> accessed 29 September 2015).

[701] See, e.g., <papers.ssrn.comwhe> thousands of academic articles are available for free (*Social Science Research Network* accessed 2 October 2015).

do not want to be published in *Nature* or *Science* can just upload papers to 'free' sites as well. That said, I suggest that we also need a basis that works for professional authors to create viable financial flows. Only then will copyright truly accommodate the needs of all. In my estimation, forced return to patronage is *not* progress. I suggest that autonomous human creation is desirable in science and art. This means financial flows for authors who so wish—understanding that a more 'bourgeois' or corporatist mode of creation will be seen as desirable by some authors.

For now, let us observe that of the four categories of authors identified above, using copyright rights to get paid is arguably only true for one of them (professionals). For authors in the third category, namely those using the Internet basically to disseminate their work for free but as a form of promotion, there is a temporal factor at play. If those authors do eventually succeed in becoming known and are then able to use this fame to seek payment for their work, they may well switch to the fourth category, namely professional or career authors and 'use' copyright to get paid.

It is undoubtedly true, in my mind at least, that most professional or career authors are not thinking intensely about possible financial incentives *as they are writing* or otherwise creating, that is, when they are in the creative 'moment'. They too, therefore, are subject to this temporal critique. However, the response is precisely that professional authors need a revenue stream to have the time to be 'in the moment'.[702] They need to have the time to invest to create new, hopefully high-quality works.[703] This is supported by recent empirical research that disproved the fallacious rhetoric that financial incentives are irrelevant because authors do not have their chequebook in hand while writing or creating.[704] Financial

---

[702] See Renzetti (n 664): 'Someone has to produce this content—this art—and sadly, the shoemaker's elves are all busy elsewhere. [. . .] It comes down to a question of value: Do we value artists' effort?'

[703] To go back to Anne Tyler mentioned in note 685 above:

Tyler works in this room Monday through Friday from early in the morning until about two in the afternoon, unless she breaks earlier to have lunch with a friend. While she is writing, Tyler doesn't like to think about her audience. She doesn't read reviews about her work because she says that would remind her that she has readers. But she does care about the connection she makes with her audience.

Patricia Rowe, '*Watching through Windows: A Perspective on Anne Tyler*' (1992) summer VQR (available at <http://www.vqronline.org/essay/watching-through-windows-perspective-anne-tyler> accessed 3 October 2015).

[704] See Jiariu Liu, 'Copyright for Blockheads: An Empirical Study of Market Incentive and Intrinsic Motivation' (2015) 38 *Columbia Journal of Law & the Arts* 467.

incentives allow authors to buy better equipment, to collaborate with others (travel, etc.), to compromise less on artistic freedom. It also helps 'justify a career that requires enormous effort' in a 'society where wealth is the standard measurement of personal success and social status'.[705] True, Bourdieu advocated *l'art pour l'art*. While copyright admittedly does not work as an economic incentive for certain forms of art, it works for many, from pop music to Jeff Koons to Steven Spielberg. They need time and resources to do what they do.

A second strand of argument against copyright is that a lot of new creations are now based on the reuse of pre-existing content such as fan fiction, appropriation art, etc as discussed in the previous chapter.[706] The appropriate response to this argument is not to eliminate copyright rights or incentives but rather to both clearly delineate the derivate right and to espouse a proper and adequate fair use doctrine or a similar type of exception and limitation.[707]

There is an understandable tendency on social media and in the Academy to defend those who want to provide unfettered access to 'content' created by writers, songwriters, and other authors. Greater access obviously enhances welfare. It pierces through the shield of censorship, making it much less likely that authors will need courts to support their right to be heard. Disabling the gate-keeping function does enhance welfare when it provides access to material not otherwise available. Whether it be Henry Miller's plays, *Lady Chatterley's Lover* or *Ulysses*, they can all be 'released' online and are then very unlikely to be completely 'taken off the Internet'. The power of the Internet and its social media tools in the case of movements like the 2011 Arab Spring is undeniable. Yet there are less obvious, societally risky and more pernicious welfare losses that many commentators ignore or refuse to acknowledge. The filtering function of professionals does imply new limits to the quantity of published material factually available to most users. They also have an impact on quality. If this is true, the fact that no payment of any kind is made to creators of material—or a very modest stream of income, insufficient to create any kind of incentive—is perilous for the progress of science and useful arts.[708] Biographies of hundreds of the greatest writers show that they worked closely with editors and their

---

[705]   Ibid., 507.

[706]   If those who claim authors should work for free gave up their salary and/or tenure, they may have more credibility in my eyes.

[707]   See Michael W Carroll, 'Fixing Fair Use' (2007) 85 *North Carolina Law Review* 1087.

[708]   While those providing the mediation function amass fortunes based on ads watched by those who access the 'content'. *That*, we are told, is progress.

publishers and that the great books they penned would be of lesser quality or would not exist if they had not been able to work with them. Think of Carver, Ginsberg, and Nabokov, just to name a few. The relationship between professional authors—often in the genius category—and people who can help them either structure better or adequately complete a project is based on the availability of incentives both for that author to have the time to create and for the publisher, etc. to have the resources to help. We are much too quick to applaud the destruction of those incentives. Songwriters need time to produce the songs that will live through the ages— songs one might call 'anthems', not the short-lived fads that make it to the top and are then quickly erased from popular cultural memory. Music publishers and producers need resources to invest in discovering talent, making it possible to pay them to invest. Hundreds of names could be cited but the biographies of Aretha Franklin, Billy Holiday, Bob Dylan, Lady Gaga and Amy Winehouse to name just a few across different genres and time periods, would, I submit, support this claim. They are examples of artists who were given resources to develop before they made anything on the world stage.[709]

Having responded to those two strands of argument, how should we proceed to make copyright work (better) for authors? I would posit as the starting point of any prescriptive vision of a better copyright regime that we need to find a system that can accommodate all kinds of authors (at least as far as the four categories above).[710] Showing an ability to modulate copyright rules and their enforcement (remedies appropriate to the type of infringement) to accommodate various types of authorship is likely to make copyright more understandable and accepted. This in turn is likely to narrow the gap between the legal norm and online social norms. In the words of the former Chief Justice of Australia, '[a] comprehensible normative basis for an intellectual property right is necessary to its moral clarity'.[711]

In determining whether copyright policy can accommodate all categories of authors, at least three issues come to mind. First, there is a major unfairness in certain areas of digital distribution.[712] Music seems by far the

---

[709] Admittedly, as I discuss below, the three large record companies are apparently now more in the business of hoarding than helping develop talent. But with adequate financial flows, my hope is that other entities will take over as those who have decided to turn themselves into dinosaurs slowly fade in the distance.

[710] Then it must also work for others, including users, but without somehow forgetting about all categories of authors.

[711] Robert French, 'A Public Law Perspective on Intellectual Property' (2014) 17 *Journal of World Intellectual Property* 61, 65.

[712] Eddie Schwartz, 'Coda', in Daniel Gervais and Susy Frankel, *Evolution and Equilibrium* (CUP, 2014).

biggest culprit here. In the US this is due to a major regulatory capture issue. While the two main Performing Rights Organizations (PROs) that represent songwriters and publishers are subject to antitrust consent decrees that tie their hands, record companies have full exclusive rights in respect of interactive digital transmissions of sound recordings.[713] This has allowed record companies to shift financial flows for digital music so that the current ratio of payments to record companies to songwriters is untenable.[714]

The second issue is the massive reuse of existing works as a new creation paradigm. If to create is to transform, then fair use and other flexibilities must be carefully recalibrated accordingly. Because reuse (using digital tools) often entails cutting and pasting and other forms of copying, reuse has become a major source of tension for a regulatory system (copyright) which has allowed the reuse of ideas but has been the historically much more stingy in allowing unauthorized the reuse of someone else's expression.[715] This means that doctrines allowing 'transformative uses' such as fair use should stretch but can do so only up to a point and determining where that point is calls for more policy forethought than allowing courts to make law case-by-case.[716] This was discussed in greater detail in the previous chapter.

There is a third, related issue, namely the need to examine carefully the evolution of the case law, especially US cases on access-based (non-creative) fair use. In a few cases, as discussed in the previous chapter, courts have found that the simple act of providing digital access to works—even if those works were already available in digital format and already on the Internet—was 'transformative' because the intermediary was making it easier to find (and, consequently, reuse) works.[717] Whether or how this interferes with normal exploitation (see Chapter 3) is an open question.

---

[713] See Daniel Gervais, 'The Landscape of Collective Management' (2011) 24 *Columbia Journal of Law & the Arts* 423, 435–6.

[714] This is based on the study mentioned by Schwartz (see n 679) showing approximately 97 cents of every royalty dollar being paid to the labels (some of it shared with artist if the label so decides) and less than 3 cents to the songwriter.

[715] After all, as, 'Judge Hough said in *Frankel v Irwin* DC 34 F2d 142, 143, "Infringement of copyright is a tort, the burden of proving which is on the plaintiff, and it can be committed in only one way: By copying some substantial part of that which is lawfully copyrighte".' (Cited in *Oxford Book Co v Coll Entrance Book Co* 98 F2d 688, 692 (2d Cir 1938).

[716] See R Anthony Reese, 'Transformativeness and the Derivative Work Right' 31 (2008) *Columbia Journal of Law & the Arts* 467, 468.

[717] For example, *Perfect 10 Inc v Amazon.com Inc*, 508 F3d 1146 (9th Cir 2007).

The fate of professional creators is a major cultural issue. While specific copyright rules are obviously contingent and should be adapted to the new realities of online distribution and easy reuse, I believe that professional authorship is still necessary. I also believe that to be a professional author, creators need *time* and that, in turn, requires some form of payment. We need healthy financial flows to allow professional authors to make a decent, market-based living. This requires a move away from 'one-size-fits-all' copyright and the resulting 'tug of norms' that requires a shift of the entire policy package to the benefit of one category of authors and/or users to the detriment of all others.

If we are to have 'progress of science and useful arts',[718] as the US Constitution directs, we need to do better. To quote a professional author who spent hours most days writing, Ernest Hemingway wrote: '[f]or him it was a dark passage which led to nowhere, then to nowhere, then again to nowhere, once again to nowhere, always and forever to nowhere',[719] I hope he was not talking about the future of authorship.

---

[718]   US Const art. 1§ 8, cl 8.
[719]   Ernest Hemingway, *For Whom the Bell Tolls* (Charles Scribner 1940) Ch. 13.

# 7.   A place for users

## 7.1   INTRODUCTION

Exceptions and limitations (E&Ls) are not an afterthought, a response
after the fact to a perceived excessive reach of exclusive rights. E&Ls are
a central element of copyright policy. Indeed, whether considered from a
loosely Lockean perspective (leaving 'as much and as good' for others);
from an economic perspective (efficient protection and focus on maximum
net welfare gains for all); or indeed even on the simple basis that authors
'stand on the shoulder of giants' and thus regularly reuse pre-existing
material, copyright policy cannot be reduced to a [rights + $x$ = optimal
policy] equation, where $x$ is just space left for any number of countervailing policy levers including E&Ls, but also limits on remedies, etc.

Normatively, the equation to solve looks like this. Copyright should,
as the previous chapter argues, allow authors who so wish to generate
income from and, in fewer cases, maintain some degree of 'control' over,
the use of their works. The 'monopoly rent' that intellectual property
can create allows authors to add to the marginal cost (which is often
zero online, at least if one does not consider ads placed by intermediaries
for their own profit), but it can also raise a barrier to access.[720] Access
for certain purposes, (and, as the last chapter of this book argues, even
more so in developing countries), must be as free from restrictions as
possible.[721] Users must be allowed to access and reuse content in fair
ways without the need to license pre-existing work and use. This is the
equilibrium that must be achieved and properly structured E&Ls are an
indispensable part of it.

As explained in the first two chapters, almost all the right fragments of
the copyright bundle evolved in the pre-Internet era. More or less each
time a new right was added to the bundle, a discussion on its limits took

---

[720]   Moreover the rent itself is too often unfairly captured by people up and
down the distribution chain and not by the authors.
[721]   See Rebecca Giblin, 'Is It Copyright's Role to Fill Houses with Books?'
in Susy Frankel and Daniel Gervais, *Intellectual Property and Regulation of the
Internet: The Nexus with Human and Economic Development* (Wellington: Victoria
Univ. Press, 2017 Forthcoming).

place. Sometimes, though rarely, the limits were inherent in the right itself. For example, a performance must be 'in public' to require an authorization; a communication must be 'to a public'; and, in common law jurisdictions, a reproduction must be 'of a substantial part' of the work.[722] In other cases, limitations and exceptions[723] were deemed necessary to either exclude (in whole or in part) certain *classes of users* or certain *classes of uses* from the reach of the copyright holders. An example of the former might be a non-profit library, museum or archive, which might enjoy special copying privileges; an example of the latter would be exceptions for research or criticism, which anyone can benefit from.

Unfortunately, E&Ls have too often been seen in this pallid light, sometimes accompanied by a view that the $x$ in the above equation will somehow 'work itself out' in practice and/or that $x$ must be as circumscribed as possible because more rights produce better outcomes.[724] While the latter view is often advocated by interest groups that are trying to convince lawmakers to enact higher levels of copyright protection, some pro-user groups have been guilty of oversimplification as well. The use of harsh rhetoric to make points is understandable, but rhetorical salvos should not pass for accurate or well-crafted policy statements. For the same reason, it is a sad day when in copyright policy circles everyone is a 'stakeholder' pigeonholed as copy*right* (more rights) or copy*left* (more exceptions). Let me naïvely assert that being in favour of copyright should mean finding a system that actually works. And lest I misguide the reader, let me also state that my point is *not* to lament how copyright policy is made in legislative bodies, but rather to suggest that there can and should be as much effort in shaping E&Ls and other limits to copyright rights than there are on adding new rights or new subject matter.

The US Copyright Principles Project report noted that copyright law should:

---

[722] Which allows brief quotations, which one could define as reproductions of an insubstantial part.

[723] A limitation is a restriction on the exclusive nature of the right concerned, such as a compulsory license. It usually involves compensation to the rights holder. An exception removes the act covered by the exception from the scope of application of the right and thus typically does not involve the payment of compensation.

[724] On Locke, see, e.g., Justin Hughes, 'The Philosophy of Intellectual Property' (1988) 77 *Georgetown Law Journal* 287, 297–310. On the economic approach, see, generally, William M Landes and Richard A Posner, *The Economic Structure of Intellectual Property Law* (Harvard University Press 2003). On the 'shoulder of giants' aphorism, see Robert K Merton, *On The Shoulders of GIANTS: The Post-Italianate Edition* (University of Chicago Press 1993).

promote the creation and dissemination of new works . . . by encouraging the provision of capital and organization needed for the creation and dissemination of creative works; by promising creators opportunities to convey their works to their intended audiences; and by limiting control over uses of creative works, as appropriate, to aid education, cultural participation, the creation of new works, and the development of new forms of creative output.[725]

This report further suggested that copyright law 'should limit control over uses of creative works by setting boundaries on the rights of copyright holders and on remedies for infringement'; and that 'deciding whether a particular type of use should be within the scope of copyright's exclusive rights requires balancing the sometimes-competing interests of creators, distributors, consumers, and the public'.[726]

Similarly, the proposed European Copyright Code[727] drafted by a number of prominent European copyright experts noted in its preambular provisions that:

copyright protection in the European Union finds its justification and its limits in the need to protect the moral and economic interests of creators, while serving the public interest by promoting the production and dissemination of works in the field of literature, art and science by granting to creators limited exclusive rights for limited times in their works,

and further that 'copyright legislation should achieve an optimal balance between protecting the interests of authors and right holders in their works and securing the freedom to access, build upon and use these works'.

This debate is not about whether courts or legislators are better equipped to make copyright policy—a fascinating but different issue. It may be of course that (often absent) empirical data will teach us that formulating standards that leave courts broader discretion in determining appropriate E&Ls or limits on remedies—such as whether an injunction should necessarily be issued because a use is infringing or whether statutory damages are adequate for any infringement—is a better option when outcomes are evaluated critically to see if desired results were obtained. That does not detract from what I see as an obligation to develop analytical tools to tailor E&Ls and other limits on the realm of copyright holders—many,

---

[725] Principle 2. See Pamela Samuelson et al., 'The Copyright Principles Project' (2010) 25(3) *Berkeley Technology Law Journal* 1175–246.

[726] Ibid., principles 5 and 6.2.

[727] See Copyrightcode.eu. For an analysis see Daniel Gervais, 'Fair Use, Fair Dealing, Fair Principles: Efforts to Conceptualize Exceptions and Limitations to Copyright' (2010) 57(3) *Journal of the Copyright Society of the USA* 499.

perhaps most of whom are also copyright users—as an indispensable part of the policy equation.

The importance of carefully balanced E&Ls was also noted in a speech by the former US Register of Copyright.[728] She was in good company. Victor Hugo, the French author and polemist mentioned in Chapter 2 who chaired the predecessor of the International Literary and Artistic Association (ALAI), the organization that prepared the initial draft of the Berne Convention, stated at the opening ceremony of the 1878 Literary and Artistic Convention—the event that unofficially launched the Berne Convention negotiations—that: (a) a book belongs to its author but the ideas belong to humankind; (b) if either the right of the writer or the right of the 'human spirit' must be forfeited ('sacrificed'), it is assuredly the right of the writer that must be, because public interest is the sole preoccupation and must come before everything else; and finally that (c) one must recognize literary property, but at the same time establish ('found') the public domain.[729]

Normatively, copyright has traditionally *sought* to reflect a balance between protection and what is now known as 'access' in myriad forms, as Victor Hugo himself recognized.[730] An effort to design specific E&Ls to the right of reproduction in the Berne context was ultimately replaced by the three-step test, which does not offer normative guidance for specific E&Ls (see Chapter 3).[731] Instead, it restricts the ability of individual legislators to create the E&Ls used to maintain balance.[732] The three-step test is now the single sieve for E&Ls applicable to any copyright right in the TRIPS

---

[728] At a speech also given on Intellectual Property Day (26 April 2010), the Hon Marybeth Peters reportedly said that:

since the advent of the internet, 'the focus has been on exceptions to copyright law,' and that such exceptions to the exclusive rights afforded to authors under copyright law are important because 'if we lived in a world where rights were totally exclusive, we couldn't tolerate it.' She posited that if stakeholders can come to an agreement on how to deal with some of those exceptions [. . .] 'we will have a good outcome in the United States, and the rest of the developing world will eventually create intellectual property rights.'

See Nathan Pollard, 'Copyright Law "Out of Date", Must Rethink The Internet, World IP Day Panelists Say' (2010) 79 PTCJ 818.

[729] Victor Hugo, Discours d'ouverture du Congrès littéraire international de 1878 (Paris, 17 July 1878) 5–6 (<http://www.inlibroveritas.net/lire/oeuvre1923.html> accessed 3 October 2015) (author's translation) see p. 34.

[730] See ibid.

[731] On the Berne Convention, see Ch. 2. On the three-step test, see Ch. 3.

[732] UN-WIPO, 'Berne Convention for the Protection of Literary and Artistic Works' (1886) 1161 United Nations Treaty Series 3 (last revised at Paris on 24 July 1971 and last amended 28 September 1979 (available at <http://www.wipo.

Agreement. As a result, beyond the Marrakech Treaty, E&Ls are now largely *unregulated policy space* at the international level. This explains why efforts to define E&Ls are mostly present at the national or regional level, even though the World Intellectual Property Organization (WIPO) successfully led an effort to craft a specific E&L regime to improve access to copyrighted material by visually-impaired users.[733]

The complexity of the exercise of structuring copyright 'whole' has arguably increased in recent years because copyright is sparring with rights outside its own sphere, such as the right to privacy, human rights principles of free expression and cultural diversity and cultural development, the right to information, the right to education, and the nascent right to development, each of which implies striking a balance in intellectual property protection.[734] One could leave it to courts or international tribunals to determine appropriate interfaces and boundaries among the different rights, but this option should not allow policy makers to shirk their obligation to think E&Ls through, bearing in mind that some of them may be there precisely as a recognition of concerns stemming from other normative spheres, including relevant human rights.[735] Put differently, a principled approach to the determination of limitations and exceptions must factor in the need for balance against the backdrop of the principles and values that inform the intrinsic public interest balance of copyright, its utilitarian/economic function, and the recognition of the extrinsic factors that affect the realm of copyright.

Once the role of E&Ls has been properly situated at the core of copyright policy, the next question is what structure of E&Ls works better. Open-ended forms of permitted use, such as fair use and fair dealing, work well in providing courts with the necessary flexibility (a feature of common law systems) to devise or shape E&Ls to new fact patterns and technological developments. In countries with a civil law tradition or those who prefer not to give their courts this degree of latitude, a finite list of exceptions might work better though it likely requires constant review by

---

int/treaties/en/ip/berne/trtdocs_wo001.html> accessed 3 October 2015) [Berne Convention].

[733] UN-WIPO, 'Marrakesh Treaty to Facilitate Access to Published Works for Persons Who Are Blind, Visually Impaired, or Otherwise Print Disabled (MVT)' (27 June 2013) <http://www.wipo.int/wipolex/en/details.jsp?id=13169> accessed 3 October 2015.

[734] See Daniel Gervais, 'Intellectual Property and Human Rights: Learning to Live Together', in Paul Torremans (ed.), *Intellectual Property and Human Rights* (Wolters Kluwer 2008) (<http://works.bepress.com/daniel_gervais/13/> accessed 3 October 2015).

[735] See ibid.

the legislator, and perhaps monitoring by an appropriate administrative entity. While there is no universal answer, Part II of the book contains a proposed approach to structuring E&Ls that can be applied in any legal system. In the pages that follow we consider two reports—one published in the US, the other in Europe—that propose different approaches yet reflect a high degree of normative overlap.

## 7.2   THE EUROPEAN COPYRIGHT CODE PROJECT

The Wittem Group's proposed European Copyright Code (ECC) adds interesting stones to the E&L policy edifice. The Code fundamentally does two things: it formulates exceptions in their own right, based on groupings that reflect proper normative concerns for each one; and it acknowledges the centrality of the three-step test. Let us consider each one sequentially.

The ECC contains four groupings of E&Ls, namely 'uses with minimal economic significance', 'uses for the purpose of freedom of expression and information', 'uses permitted to promote social, political and cultural objectives', and 'uses for the purpose of enhancing competition'.[736] The first group seems part of the intrinsic balance of copyright, one that eschews simplistic rhetoric about 'property' and 'piracy' and focuses instead on commercial significance, which one might be tempted to describe as the flipside of the commercial harm coin.[737] If copyright is a vehicle to maximize revenue for copyright holders, then uses which have no significant bearing on that element but are supported by a valid public interest justification should be outside the boundaries of exclusive rights.[738] If the purpose of copyright is, to use the words of the United States

---

[736]   European Copyright Code 2010, arts 5.1–5.4.
[737]   See Daniel Gervais, 'A Canadian Copyright Narrative' (2009) 21 *Intellectual Property Journal* 269, 303.
[738]   Several ancillary questions remain, in particular burden of proof. A loose normative parallel could be drawn here with the enforcement of patent rights on pharmaceutical products in countries where there is no substantial market, usually because patients are simply unable to afford the drugs. As the pending amendment (art. 31bis) to the TRIPS Agreement implementing the so-called 'paragraph 6 system' adopted by the WTO demonstrates, the issue here for patent holders was not market preservation (for the immediate future at least) but rather making sure that generic or lower-priced bioequivalents made available in those countries were not diverted to richer countries. See Amir H Khour 'The "Public Health" of the Conventional International Patent Régime and the Ethics of "Ethicals": Access to Patented Medicines' (2008) 26 *Cardozo Arts & Entertainment Law Journal* 25, 39–40.

Constitution, to 'Promote the Progress of Science and Useful Arts', or, as the CPP principle 2 notes, to 'promote the creation and dissemination of new works', then the scope of rights and E&Ls must ideally be coextensive with that objective. Enforcement of rights in cases where there is no or a very limited market impact does not seem correlated to such objective.[739] It is also I suggest the normative core of Judge Story's test in *Folsom v Marsh*, often seen as the first fair use case even though its does not use that term.[740]

The three other groups of E&Ls in the ECC text interface with rights outside the sphere of copyright, namely freedom of expression and information, the promotion of social, political and cultural objectives, and uses for the purpose of enhancing competition. The first (freedom of expression and information) is perhaps the oldest cousin of copyright. Copyright, it was famously said, is the engine of free speech.[741] A private press and publishing industry, not controlled by government in terms of ownership and/or censorship is one of the best guarantees of free speech.[742] However, the equation is more complex because copyright can also stand in the way of free speech at times.[743]

Copyright's sparring with free speech is not new.[744] Nor is the well-established need to limit copyright when the public's 'right to information' is involved, as the *Berne Convention* recognizes in a number of ways. But copyright must now face other rights. Copyright enforcement vis-à-vis end-users (for example, to obtain a subscriber's identity from an Internet Service Provider) requires a normative battle with the right to privacy.[745] Technological Protection Measures (TPMs) limiting use and enjoyment of consumer goods may involve violation of consumer protection legislation (for example, if the restriction is insufficiently explained at the time of sale).

---

[739] See Melville B Nimmer and David Nimmer, *Nimmer on Copyright* (2d edn, Bender 1978) vol 1, § 1.10 [D], 1–87. See also Britton Payne, 'Imperfect 10: Digital Advances and Market Impact in Fair Use Analysis' (2006) 17 *Fordham Intellectual Property, Media & Entertainment Law Journal* 279.

[740] 9 F Cas 342, 345 (CC Mass 1841) (US). See Chapter 3. It has been described several times as the most important of the four factors in 17 USC § 107 (2015). See, e.g., *Harper & Row Publishers v Nation Enters* 471 US 539, 566 (1985).

[741] Harper & Row ibid., 613.

[742] See Neil Netanel, *Copyright's Paradox* (OUP 2008) 81–4.

[743] See ibid., 169–76; and Michael Birnhack, 'Global Copyright, Local Speech' (2006) 24 *Cardozo Arts & Entertainment Law Journal* 491, 539–45.

[744] See Netanel (n 742).

[745] See Pamela Samuelson, 'Privacy as Intellectual Property?' (2000) 52, 5 *Stanford Law Review* 1125–73, 1128 (<http://people.ischool.berkeley.edu/~pam/papers/privasip_draft.pdf > accessed 3 October 2015).

In designing an appropriate interface, the ECC distinguishes uses that should be free (that is without authorization or payment) from those that, while they do not require an authorization which might be used to stifle free speech or freedom of the press, should be accompanied by compensation for the copyright holder. This idea of separating free (unpaid) uses from uses that do not require permission but may require payment is present in all the groupings suggested in the ECC. The compensated approach would allow European countries to impose a compulsory license for certain uses.[746]

In the first (uncompensated) subgroup (freedom of the press), the ECC includes the reporting of contemporary events; use of published articles on current economic, political or religious topics or of similar works broadcast by the media; use of works of architecture or sculpture, made to be located permanently in public places; use by way of quotation of lawfully disclosed works; and use for the purpose of caricature, parody or pastiche.[747] In the second (compensated) subgroup, the draft Code includes the use of single articles for purposes of internal reporting within an organization; and uses for purposes of scientific research.[748]

The next group interfaces with the newer right to participate in social and cultural life. Again, this is not new but does bear emphasis. Article 27 of the Universal Declaration on Human Rights (UDHR), which saw the light of day 238 years after the Statute of Anne, protects *both* the authors' right to the protection of their moral and material interests resulting from scientific, literary or artistic production *and* users' rights freely to participate in the cultural life of the community, to enjoy the arts and to share in scientific advancement and its benefits.[749] The objective of protection embraces, at least indirectly, the moral desert theory (protection of interests resulting from scientific, literary or artistic production), while the objective of access is expressed teleologically as a tool to allow everyone to enjoy the arts and to share in scientific advancement and its benefits. Article 15 of the International Covenant on Economic, Social and Cultural Rights is also directly relevant.[750] It enshrines the right to participate in

---

[746] It is worth noting that a *voluntary* license is available in the US for many of the uses encompassed by the first element on this second subgroup.

[747] ECC (n 736), art 5.2(1).

[748] Ibid., art. 5.2(2).

[749] UN, 'Universal Declaration of Human Rights' (1948) art. 27 (<http://www.un.org/Overview/rights.html> accessed 4 October 2015).

[750] UN, 'International Covenant on Economic, Social, and Cultural Rights' (1966) art 15 (<http://www.ohchr.org/EN/ProfessionalInterest/Pages/CESCR.aspx> accessed 4 October 2015).

cultural life, defined as 'a benefit to which every member of the community is entitled. Culture here is not to be viewed as an esoteric activity of a superior social elite'.[751] Arguably, those instruments justify exceptions that demonstrably augment access, where such access (enjoyment) is not commercially reasonable or possible, and thus enhance the right to reuse and thereby participate in the cultural life of the community.

A key element of this grouping is the promotion of education, and it is framed in the ECC as an E&L with compensation. It is obvious that in a knowledge- and innovation-based global economy, education is a key determinant of success.[752] Countries that are not globally competitive as knowledge and innovation producers might see the gap between them and the most advanced economies increase if educational tools—often made for and controlled by entities in countries that currently dominate the global innovation game—are not readily accessible in poorer nations.[753] However, even in more industrialized nations, not every use of material used in education can or should reasonably be transactionally licensed.[754]

Beyond education, the second grouping mentions use for the benefit of persons with disabilities; use to ensure the proper performance of administrative, parliamentary or judicial proceedings or public security; use for the purpose of non-commercial archiving by libraries, educational establishments or museums, and archives should be allowed without authorization or payment. As in the previous grouping, the ECC adds E&Ls for which compensation should be made available, namely reproduction for private use.

Josef Kohler had argued for the preservation of a private sphere for users.[755] This affected several European national systems. In the words of Professor Hugenholtz:

---

[751]  Yoram Dinstein, 'Cultural Rights' (1979) 9 *Israel Yearbook on Human Rights* 58–81, 76.

[752]  See Gervais (n 175), 2362–3.

[753]  See ibid.

[754]  Especially spontaneous uses. This was reflected in the US Classroom Guidelines, formally the Agreement on Guidelines for Classroom Copying in Not-For-Profit Educational Institutions with Respect to Books and Periodicals. It is reproduced in US Copyright Office, Circular 21: Reproduction of Copyrighted Works by Educators and Librarians (<www.ivir.nl/publications/download/PBH-DIPPER> pdf accessed 17 November 2016).

[755]  Josef Kohler, *Das Autorrecht: eine zivilistische Abhandlung; Zugleich ein Beitrag zur Lehre vom Eigenthum, vom Miteigenthum, vom Rechtsgeschäft und vom IndivIbidualrecht* (Gustav Fischer, 1880) 230 [Josef Kohler, *Author's Right: A Civil Law Treatise. Which is also a contribution to the theory of property, joint property, legal transactions and individual rights* (Gustav Fischer, 1880) 230 (<http://dlib-pr.

[C]opyright protects against acts of unauthorized communication, not consumptive usage [. . .]. [T]he mere reception or consumption of information by end-users has traditionally remained outside the scope of the copyright monopoly. Arguably, the right of privacy and the freedom of reception guaranteed in Articles 8 and 10 of the European Convention on Human Rights would be unduly restricted if the economic right encompassed mere acts of information reception or end use.[756]

The final grouping of E&Ls in the ECC focuses on the cohabitation of antitrust law and intellectual property. Europe has had many difficult cases involving copyright rights, including an attempt to use copyright to restrict access to television listings; and the rather famous case against Microsoft.[757] The ECC attempts to recognize that the possibility that a copyright holder will use her rights to block a 'chain of events', that is prevent the creation of derivative works even where those have no demonstrable negative bearing on her ability to generate revenue, may be conducive to negative welfare outcomes. The ECC thus proposes two subgroups of competition-related E&Ls. First, uses for the purpose of advertising public exhibitions or sales of artistic works or goods which have been lawfully put on the market and use for the purpose of reverse engineering in order to obtain access to information by a person entitled to use the work should be allowed without remuneration.[758] The second subgroup suggests uses that should be allowed but against the payment of a negotiated remuneration: where use is indispensable to compete on a derivative market and where a license the use on reasonable terms is unavailable, leading to the elimination of competition in the relevant market, provided the use does not unreasonably prejudice the legitimate interests of the owner of the copyright in the work.[759]

Again, this set of proposals ostensibly stems from the group's perception that in the above cases, providing exclusive rights is unlikely to promote optimal welfare outcomes in the form of the creation and dissemination of new works. The ECC group is aware that imposing a negotiated license

---

mpier.mpg.de/m/kleioc/0010/exec/books/%22160676%22> accessed 4 October 2015)].

[756] P Bernt Hugenholtz, 'Caching and Copyright: The Right of Temporary Copying' (2000) 22 10 *European Intellectual Property Review* 482, 485–6. (Early version available at <http://www.ivir.nl/publications/hugenholtz/PBH-DIPPER. doc> accessed 17 November 2016). See also J H Spoor, *Scripta manent* (Amsterdam, 1976) 137–8.

[757] See Francois Leveque and Howard Shelanski (eds), *Antitrust, Patents and Copyright – EU and US Perspectives* (Edward Elgar Publishing 2005).

[758] ECC (n 82) art 5.4(1).

[759] Ibid., art 5.4(2).

(as opposed to the compulsory regimes advocated for the previous groups of E&Ls) is a potential stumbling block.

## 7.3   THE COPYRIGHT PRINCIPLES PROJECT

The CPP group formulated its own prescriptions somewhat differently. Instead of articulating groups of E&Ls around their normative core, it stated principles and derived specific reform proposals. Those proposals are as follows:

(a)   the language of the US Copyright Act's subject matter exclusion is too narrow and should be expanded to facts, data, know-how, or knowledge; stock elements; laws, regulations, or rules, etc.;

(b)   fair use should be expanded, certainly beyond the purposes stated in the US Act, and encompass many reuse cases, such as when a second author transformatively recasts a work in the course of making a new work; when a second author productively uses some or all of an earlier work in the course of news reporting, teaching, scholarship, artistic expression, or the like; when a second author makes incidental copies that enhance access to information, such as by reverse engineering computer programs; when a competitor uses part of the author's work to engage in comparative advertising or otherwise to promote fair competition; when a person makes private non-commercial uses that do not compete with or otherwise undermine the author's market; when market failures prevent the development of a viable market for clearing rights; when administrative, legal, or other governmental uses of the work is necessary to achieve legitimate government purposes; or when courts are faced with a use not contemplated by Congress and where the fair use balancing process will result in an interpretation of the law consistent with copyright purposes;

(c)   a number of personal uses should be protected; and

(d)   copyright exceptions for library, archives, and museums should be updated to better enable preservation and other legitimate uses.

Unlike the ECC text, the CPP proposals are explained in great detail in the CPP report and I need not belabour them here and now. I hasten to note, however, that the degree of overlap between the two sets of proposals is striking. Structurally, the ECC is more thorough because its authors were crafting a draft code, while the CPP group identified, based on a set of congruent principles, areas in dire need of reform. It is also clear that the

CPP group expects more of the fair use doctrine as opposed to suggesting a group of discrete E&Ls. This reflects the current structure of US copyright law, where fair use is the dominant E&L structure, and lets courts do more in terms of setting policy, something that a positivist European scholar might find less appealing. Yet, both sets of proposals overlap in their normative *infra*structure, in terms of excluding control where such control is unlikely to produce positive outcomes in terms of enhancing the creation and dissemination of new works.

## 7.4 OPTIONS

In updating exceptions contained in any national copyright law, several options may be considered. The first would be simply to adopt the (seemingly) more open-ended US 'fair use' provision, which does not limit the purposes for which a user can claim use was fair. A second option would be to open up the list of purposes for which fair dealing is allowed. Both options would enable courts to determine the scope of the exceptions. A third option would be to revise some of the existing exceptions and improve them where a need for change has been demonstrated, for example, to allow parody and some forms of 'remix' and to allow broader non-commercial educational use of material, especially spontaneous use of limited amounts of published works. Regardless of the course of action taken, the interface between *any* new exception and the three-step test must be carefully considered see Chapter 3.

# PART II

# Proposed structural reforms

# 8.   The quadrants of authorship

## 8.1   INTRODUCTION

Hit me with your best shot! That may be read as an invitation to critique the proposals contained in this book. It is also the title of a well-known hit from the early 1980s, performed by Pat Benatar among others. The author of that worldwide hit is Eddie Schwartz. Mr Schwartz wrote the song around 1980, at a time when the music industry was transitioning from vinyl to CDs and selling millions of physical copies of products in record stores. He did well in the days when a gold record meant approximately $50,000 for the songwriter.[760] Today, a similar number of streams would generate $35 for the writer (2015 number).[761]

The success of any structural reform of copyright should be judged in part on whether sustainable financial flows to authors are restored. Structured copyright reform must differentiate, where appropriate, the interests of those who commercially exploit assets (distributors and access providers, whether as owners of copyright or not as will be discussed later) from those of authors.[762] For authors, the situation is more nuanced. The word 'author' often creates a policy pareidolia, in that law treats all forms of 'authorship' on the same footing, which may then lead to the 'dominant authors' (however this is defined) perspective becoming the rule for all authors. Yet this is a distorted and inaccurate perception. There are authors who want attribution and those who do not. There are authors who want to get paid if they can, and those for whom this is unimportant, including those who are paid in other ways. Then, one must also acknowledge that the interests of authors and users are interwoven in

---

[760]   In the era of physical media, a gold record meant 500,000 copies. At 9.1 cents per copy (per song) in the US (under the mechanical compulsory license contained in 17 USC §115), $50,000 was eminently achievable for a successful song.

[761]   See note 780 below.

[762]   Debates about copyright's inadequacies and the need for fundamental reform are many. This footnote can only provide an example of this urgent need, namely the proposal made by the US Register of Copyrights for a 'next great' Copyright Act. See Maria A Pallante, 'The Next Great Copyright Act' (2013) 36 *Columbia Journal of Law & the Arts* 315.

a tight cultural and normative knit—simply put, authors are (also) 'users'. Twenty-first century authors often reuse material created by others, which is much easier when it is available in digital form, and individual licensing transaction may simply not be reasonably possible. This feeds into a postmodernist vision that jettisons the link between the work and her author. It pushes authorship to the brink of irrelevance. As Professor Jane Ginburg noted, '[r]eaders give meaning to the texts they peruse; reading itself becomes a creative act. . .Reception becomes regeneration, and you can see how the distinction between consumptive and transformative use can be blurred'.[763] Clearly, digital technology has made the border between the two sides of the copyright scale increasingly porous. Authors' increasingly frequent reuse of existing material challenges the distinction between (mis)appropriation and inspiration; between the reuse of protected expression and unprotected ideas.[764]

Copyright policy must reflect twenty-first century authorship by allowing a fair culture of literary borrowing, allusion, and incorporation to flourish. This would more fully reflect the entirety of modern literary history since at least the Renaissance and through modernism itself, contemporary authors and scholars reveal current copyright law's one size-fits-all approach and rigid focus on commercial exploitation to be an aberration that endangers the interests of the very authors it pretends to protect.

## 8.2   PROPOSED STRUCTURE

Copyright is often depicted or even justified as a right to control the making and distribution of units (copies of works). In reality, in several cases it is but an *entitlement to a share of a revenue pie*. From the point of view of a corporate 'right holder' to whom rights in a work are transferred or licensed (or made for hire), a work is first and foremost a financial asset.[765] By contrast, for the twenty-first century author priorities are

---

See Jane C Ginsburg, 'Authors and Users in Copyright' (1997) 45 *Journal of the Copyright Society of the USA* 1, 8.
[764] See Chapter 5.
[765] See Jessica Sibley, *The Eureka Myth: Creators, Innovators and Everyday Intellectual Property* (Stanford UP 2014) 110. This book presents the results of interviews with 50 different creators and innovators. Professor Sibley notes that 'for [. . .] business strategists and lawyers, the presence of IP assets signals a strong competitive position because of its ostensible ability to exclude others from the same or overlapping commercial interests'.

| **QI**: Parent does not 'care' to maintain relationship and dedicates work to the public domain | **QIII**: Parent cares about attribution and income but has no real control (or desires none) over dissemination after initial publication |
|---|---|
| **QII**: Parent cares only or mostly about attribution. These parents are often otherwise compensated for their work | **QIV**: Commercial custodian trying to optimize commercial exploitation (exert control over dissemination) |

*Figure 8.1   The quadrants*

attribution and, for some of them, compensation. Although often framed rhetorically as a matter of natural law, that compensation is often a means to end, namely the ability to spend the time to write/create.[766] Authors often also want the ability to share and collaborate.[767] For authors trying to make a living from their creative work, there is an overlap of interests with commercial intermediaries on the issue of compensation, but there may be significantly diverging views on other objectives of copyright and in particular on the need or desirability to control uses as a means to achieve the objective, and specifically on the appropriateness of harsh enforcement measures against end-users. Against this backdrop, the way forward in any effort to improve copyright structurally is to recognize that *copyright means different things to different categories of authors, and to commercial owners of copyright.*

An author may be described as the *parent* of a work.[768] By contrast, the person from whom an authorization to use the work (in a way which would require it) may be sought and specifically empowered to manage the economic exploitation of the work is best described as a *custodian*. This terminology will be useful in structuring the policy discussion. With this in mind, I suggest that a structured effort should adopt the quadrantal structure shown in Figure 8.1 (above).

It is important to note two things at the outset. First, an author can be situated in the quadrantal structure for each of her work along a cline of authorial activity. Some authors will live squarely in Q1, while another may move from, say, Q4 (a novelist) to Q2 (a blog-post). An author need not, therefore be pigeonholed in an exiguous normative category. Second,

---

[766]   Ibid., 61.

[767]   Ibid., 75.

[768]   A person may be the parent of different works, and have a different 'relationship' with different types of work.

the structure embodies a taxonomy. It is qualitative, as it were. Each quadrant does *not* represent an equivalent number of authors or owners of protected works.[769] In other words, the proposed structure is not contingent on attributing a similar weight to each quadrant. Both observations will be taken into account as proposals to operationalize the structure are made later on.

Quadrant I represents parents of copyrighted material who have waived copyright protection (for example by offering an unlimited, royalty-free license to anyone), abandoned their copyright by dedicating their work to the public domain or who did not consider the issue but would be happy to waive or abandon any right the statute may give them. Whether a dedication to the public domain may be 'taken back', what happens to prior users if and when that happens, and whether appropriate mechanisms exist for authors who wish to dedicate their work in this fashion are all important matters to address.[770] A properly structured effort that reflects the needs of QI parents should establish a clear and simple procedure for irrevocable dedication (such as a notice)—or at the very least statutorily defining the rights that may re-emerge if dedication is taken back—and limit remedies against bona fide users.[771] If one considers the tens of millions of blog-posts, emails, pictures, mash-ups, etc. produced by millions of online authors, it would seem that a vast amount of material protected by copyright not destined for commercial exploitation may surpass material created with any desire for commercial exploitation (and the possibility of generating income for professional creators) in mind. What differentiates QI and QII is the author's desire to be recognized as parent, or absence thereof.

The QII parent/author is a 'responsible parent' but she is not interested in commercial exploitation.[772] Quadrant II's prototypical author operates

---

[769] The author does not know how one could reliably evaluate or generate credible empirical data to perform this task.

[770] Proposals to allow authors to effect such a choice are discussed in the literature. See L P Loren, 'Building a Reliable Semicommons of Creative Works: Enforcement of Creative Commons Licenses and Limited Abandonment of Copyright' (2007) 14 *George Mason Law Review* 271, 278; Laura N Gasaway, 'A Defense of the Public Domain: A Scholarly Article' (2009) 121 *Law Library Journal* 451, 462–3; and M W Carroll, 'Creative Commons as Conversational Copyright' in P K Yu (ed.) *Intellectual Property and Information Wealth: Issues and Practices in the Digital Age* (Praeger Publishers 2007) 421, 445–8.

[771] There would naturally have to be additional details to consider, including erroneous notices with penalties for false notices and remedy modulation for users relying on the notice.

[772] Jeanne C Fromer, 'Expressive Incentives in Intellectual Property' (2012) 98 *Virginia Law Review* 1745, 1777.

under a Creative Commons or similar license. QII authors include all those who publish because they 'must' (for example scientists writing articles to have their works peer reviewed and recognized; academic authors who publish as part of their normal duties). That does not mean QII authors do not care about copyright, or something like it. Statistics show that among CC licensors, almost 97 per cent of authors opted to require attribution when it was optional.[773] While QII authors are not initially interested in trying to commercially exploit their works and/or do not believe they have a reasonable 'market opportunity', they often do care about prohibiting unauthorized *commercial* exploitation by others and often want to share if their work turns out to be commercially valuable.[774] They often insist on attribution even in cases of non-commercial use. This is understandable: a historical or deontological analysis shows that a right of attribution pre-dates economic copyright. It is found in many ancient cultures.[775] Many QII works should be essentially copyright-free other than an obligation to mention source or at the very least not remove or alter it when using the work. This could include publications of various types in several areas, for example those generated by publicly funded research.

The next quadrant, QIII, is a very significant part of the core of copyright policy.[776] QIII authors are poets, and also those who write the music we love, paint, sculpt, or create choreographies. They usually care about attribution but in most cases are also trying to break into the marketplace, often using intermediaries. They hope to make a living. They

---

[773] According to (not too recent) statistics released by Creative Commons for 2006, 96.63 per cent of licensors opted for attribution when this was an option. See M Linksvayer, 'Midyear license adoption estimates' (*Creative Commons*, June 13, 2006) (available at <https://creativecommons.org/weblog/entry/5936> accessed 29 October 2014); The current license selector page seems to *impose* attribution. See 'Choose a License' (*Creative Commons*) (available at <http://creativecommons.org/choose/> accessed 31 October 2014).

[774] According to Creative Commons, while 96.63 per cent of authors require attribution, 70.54 per cent picked noncommercial and/or no-'derivative'. See ibid.

[775] Cheryl Swack, 'Safeguarding Artistic Creation and the Cultural Heritage: A Comparison of Droit Moral Between France and the United States' (1998) 22 *Columbia-VLA Journal of Law & the Arts* 361, 366–7; David Nimmer, 'Of Jewish Kings and Copyright' (1998) 71 *Southern California Law Review* 219, 231–2; Amir Khoury, 'Ancient and Islamic Sources of Intellectual Property Protection in The Middle East: A Focus On Trademarks' (2003) 43 *IDEA: The Intellectual Property Law Review* 151, 153–4.

[776] Jessica Litman, *Digital Copyright* (2nd edn, Prometheus Books 2006) 35–70; and Leslie A Kurtz, 'Speaking to the Ghost: Idea and Expression in Copyright' (1993) 47 *University of Miami Law Review* 1221, 1223.

understand that copyright is not a 'salary', and that the 'primary objective of copyright is not to reward the labor of authors'.[777] Yet they have a legitimate expectation to a share of the revenues generated by their work if it should be successful in the marketplace. It is often because that income that will give them the time to be professional creators; there are, as this book argues in Chapter 6, societal benefits in having a professional group of creators who can take the time to hone their creative skills and improve their craft.[778]

QIII authors typically do not much care about *control* of commercial distribution channels, other than in the rare cases where they might find a particular use (say, a song or image used in a commercial for a cause the author does not support) objectionable.[779] They typically much prefer maximum exposure to any form of actual control, especially online.[780] They also are rightly upset when new services that exploit their works do not offer them a fair shake, such as many of the new music services.[781] This is an argument about fair remuneration, not control, however.

The last quadrant, QIV, is the policy home of a number of professional authors but also, and mostly, of custodians (including the copyright industries), who are actively exploiting, or intend to exploit, a work commercially. Those who live here often care about enforcement and trying to stop unauthorized online usage. They manage notice-and-take-down systems under the US Digital Millennium Copyright Act (DMCA) and other similar legislative measures in other jurisdictions.[782] A QIII author,

---

[777] *Feist Publications Inc v Rural Telephone Service Co*, 499 US 340, 349 (1991).

[778] See Chapter 6.

[779] This type of scenario would normally be actionable though the moral right contained in most national laws and in art. 6*bis* of the Berne Convention. Art. 6*bis* provides that:

> even after the transfer of the said rights, the author shall have the right to claim authorship of the work and to object to any distortion, mutilation or other modification of, or other derogatory action in relation to, the said work, which would be prejudicial to his honor or reputation.

While the US adhered to this Convention in 1989, it has not provided moral rights other than the limited right contained in 17 USC §106A for certain works of visual art.

[780] Schwartz (n 679) 316: 'Music creator support and encourage new ways for people to enjoy our music.'

[781] See ibid., 314; See Peter S Menell, 'This American Copyright Life: Reflections on Re-Equilibrating Copyright for the Internet Age' (2014) 61 *Journal of the Copyright Society of the USA* 235, 294–5.

[782] Digital Millennium Copyright Act, 17 USCA § 512. See Andrew Johnson, 'Down with the DMCA' (2012) 15 *SMU Science & Technology Law Review* 525,

by contrast, would not be happy about unauthorized online use but may much more happily put up with some unauthorized leakage in hopes of: (a) not alienating current and potential users ('fans'); and (b) more softly monetizing the usage than harsh enforcement measures signal.[783]

Journalists deserve a special mention. The paper press model has obviously suffered from the shift to online platforms. From over 1,800 in the 1980s, the number of newspapers in the US has dropped to just over 1,300.[784] There is an increasing interplay between social media and 'news'. Anyone can be 'a journalist' reporting breaking news by posting a picture or video. Professional journalists have codes and practices that social media platforms do not share, and the debates about fake news and the post-truth world may be in part a reflection of this. Professionals check information and sources, or at least they should. They can contextualize. Is the online 'news' environment forcing us to jettison those codes and practices? The issue is that, as with more 'creative' authorship, checking, investigating and thinking take time and resources.

The University of Indiana conducted a major survey of professional journalists in the US in 2014. Among its major findings were these:

> U.S. journalists today are less satisfied with their work, less likely to say they have complete autonomy to select stories, much more likely to say that journalism is headed in the wrong direction than in the right one, and much more likely to say that *their news staffs have shrunk in the past year* rather than remained the same or grown. Other findings indicate that U.S. journalists are less likely to consider reaching the widest possible audiences and getting information to the public quickly as very important roles, and more likely to emphasize the importance of investigating government claims and analyzing complex problems. [. . .] *Findings indicate that U.S. journalists rely heavily on social media in their daily work.* Most use social media to check for breaking news and to monitor what other news organizations are doing, and fewest use these interactive media for

---

539.
[783] The desirability of suing fans is debatable. See Matthew Rimmer, *Digital Copyright and the Consumer Revolution: Hands off my iPod* (Edward Elgar Publishing 2007) 207–8. By the same token, unauthorized uses may also 'empower artists in new ways and connect communities of fans'. See Siva Vaidhyanathan, *The Anarchist in the Library: How the Clash Between Freedom and Control Is Hacking the Real World and Crashing the System* (Basic Books 2004) 104. The problem for QIII authors is to find a way to monetize use by the fan base without letting all the surplus be appropriated by commercial intermediaries (Internet-based entities that need any kind of attractive 'content' to sell ads, etc.).

[784] See Statista, 'Number of daily newspapers in the United States from 1985 to 2014', (online: <http://www.statista.com/statistics/183408/number-of-us-daily-newspapers-since-1975/> accessed 21 December 2015). I am of course unable to verify the accuracy of these numbers.

verifying information and interviewing sources. *Most agree that social media promote them and their work, keep them more engaged with their audiences, and lead to faster reporting. Far fewer say* that social media have decreased their workload, improved their productivity, allowed them to cover more news or enhanced their credibility.[785]

Although it is undeniably true that no business model has a 'right' to survive, it is equally true that quality information is crucial to a well-functioning polity. Without proper models to remunerate professional journalists, there are fewer of them. Fewer press organizations are able to pay for journalists to spend time investigating overreaching government, corrupt business organizations or dictators. That is, I submit, not progress. University experts can continue to research and opine because their institutions can pay them to do so and do not typically depend on profitable publications. Those authors can live in QIII—with possible impacts on peer review and other functions performed by commercial publishers, however. Public intellectuals may be able to tap a variety of financial flows (university salary, speaking fees etc.), but who will pay for investigative news? The diminution in the number of news outlets is troubling. It may be that viable models at this reduced level can survive, with a mix of premium access subscriptions and advertising. Yet relying on Facebook posts or a Twitter feed to find out what is happening as an alternative to professional journalism strikes me as a deeply flawed model. I do not doubt, as mentioned above, that they have a useful role in piercing the veil of censorship and help popular movements get organized. But that is not the kind of function that replaces journalism. Progress would be *adding* this function to journalism, not cannibalizing it. In the field of journalism, the monetization challenge takes on another key societal hue. Can the fifth column meet the fifth estate?

As the borders between professional and amateur become increasingly blurred—to the extent that they exist at all—so it goes with journalism. Yet journalism is also a mechanism that structures information. It partakes in the epistemological alchemy that transforms information into knowledge. As one strolls through Facebook posts—from a link to a 'long read' on the Syrian crisis to learning about a friend's delayed flight or watching the 'cutest cat video ever'—information is dispersed across genres and knowledge is less structured. The principal risk here, as I see

---

[785]   Lars Willnat and David H Weaver, *The American Journalist in the Digital Age: Key Findings* (Bloomington, IN: School of Journalism, Indiana University, 2014). (Online: <http://news.indiana.edu/releases/iu/2014/05/2013-american-journalist-key-findings.pdf> accessed 31 December 2015) [emphasis added].

it, is that knowledge must structure information before it can be distilled into wisdom, and wisdom is what may prevent us from repeating past mistakes and lead to progress. Naturally, copyright policy cannot solve all of these issues, but properly structured copyright policy should pull in the direction of progress. This implies proper monetization of professional authors. *Pecunia nervus belli est.*[786]

## 8.3 THE EXCESSIVE ROLE OF COMMERCIAL INTERMEDIARIES

Quadrant IV has been driving copyright policy for at least two decades. Since the adoption of the DMCA in 1998 and at several points since, including the failed SOPA/PIPA bills in Congress, the comatose Anti-Counterfeiting Trade Agreement (ACTA) and the Comprehensives and Progressive Transpacific Partnership (CPTPP), the core of copyright policy, which this chapter views largely as the authors of QII and III, has been abandoned to provide QIV custodians with tools to (try to) maximize commercial control.[787] This myopic focus on control of online uses should not be used to put copyright policy at odds with the interests of many QII and QIII authors who do not need or indeed desire harsh enforcement against individual users. A related risk is that it can also reduce the system's legitimacy.[788] Simply put, the trajectory of copyright policy since the mid-1990s of *distancing copyright from authors* is a poor policy choice, and

---

[786] This Latin proverb, translated as 'money is the sinew of war' and often attributed to Cicero, was cited, inter alia, by Rabelais (*Gargantua and Pantagurel*, at end of Chapter 1.XLVI).

[787] Stop Online Piracy Act (SOPA), HR 3261, 112th Cong § 103(a)(1)(B) (1st Sess 2011); Preventing Real Online Threats to Economic Creativity and Theft of Intellectual Property Act of 2011 (PROTECT IP), S 968, 112th Cong § 3(a)(1)(B) (1st Sess 2011); Anti-Counterfeiting Trade Agreement (ACTA), Oct 1, 2011, 50 ILM 239, 243 (2011); Trans-Pacific Partnership, Chapter 18: Intellectual Property (<https://ustr.gov/trade-agreements/free-trade-agreements/trans-pacific-partnership/tpp-full-text> accessed 17 November 2016); for a brief discussion and comparison, see Michael A Carrier, 'SOPA, PIPA, ACTA, TPP: An Alphabet Soup of Innovation–Stifling Copyright Legislation and Agreements' (2013) 11 *Northwestern Journal of Technology & Intellectual Property Law* 21.

[788] A professionally performed market survey in Canada showed that users desire to pay for online music was largely dependent on knowing where their money went and in particular whether the songwriter and performer got paid fairly. See Schwartz (n 679) 313; see also Songwriters Association of Canada, 'Canadian Music Consumption Behaviours Research Preliminary Report' (March 2011) 71 <www.songwriters.ca/sacsurvey2011.aspx> accessed 17 November 2016).

explains many of the woes suffered by the copyright industries since then. To quote Nicolas Suzor:

> The failure of copyright industries to take fairness norms into account has been undermining the normative moral legitimacy of copyright law. The increasingly punitive nature of copyright enforcement, the disconnect between copyright law and morality, and the perceived unfairness with which copyright industries treat both artists and consumers is likely to substantially weaken the motivation of individuals to pay for digital goods. The focus of copyright industries on strengthening copyright, then, is misguided. In order to encourage users not to free-ride, copyright industries should instead set about ensuring that copyright law and practice is fair.[789]

Copyright has undeniably suffered much in recent years. The entry in the copyright sphere of software produced by faceless pools of programmers in large corporate settings has weakened the link between copyright and author. Copyright has become, in a way, an industrial substratum allowing the value of an intangible asset called 'content' to be set or increased. In such a world, though it is more and more difficult for the author to carve out or maintain a normative position, the struggle to keep authorial creativity as a fundamental underpinning of copyright policy must continue. Basing copyright on the simple fact that time or money has been invested in a facially literary or artistic production, without a trace of creativity, distorts copyright and empties it of its substance. The mission of copyright is to encourage the emergence of creativity and not to palliate insufficiencies, real or not, of the law of unfair competition.

While copyright had not been totally knocked out by these industrial and commercial upheavals, clearly they have dealt it several blows and then the Internet increased that impact exponentially. Because anyone can appropriate material distributed in digital form, new methods and forms of creation have been invented, as have new modes of distribution. Many people have taken advantage of the opportunity to 'share' works with others, friends or strangers—the latter manifestation having led to the phenomenon of peer-to-peer networks.

These developments have highlighted the inadequacy of the law, resulting in part from its fractioning. If *contractual* fragmentation (of the economic portion of copyright) has traditionally been a prerequisite to optimization of certain forms of commercial exploitation of copyrighted works, fragmentation of the rights themselves seems rather to be the

---

[789] Nicolas Suzor, 'Free-riding, Cooperation, and "Peaceful Revolutions" in Copyright' (2014) 28:1 *Harvard Journal of Law & Technology* 137, 192.

result of a somewhat incoherent historical evolution. As was explained in Chapter 1, fragments were added to the bundle to grant an exclusive right regarding new types of works (e.g., movies and software) or new forms of exploitation (radio and television broadcasting, cable, satellite, etc.). This fragmentation worked relatively well when one use (considered a single economic operation) corresponded to one fragment. If it did not, the tendency was to sweep it under the policy rug, often by making an exception, as was the case for ephemeral recordings. Today, the legal nature of uses is plural: reproduction, communication, adaptation, and so on.

In addition, one must deal with the change of target also discussed in the opening chapter. Copyright never had much of an interest in end-users/ consumers, as illustrated, for example, by the doctrine of exhaustion of rights after the first sale of a copy or the exception allowing copying for private use. Because users have become a very relevant element in the commercial equation, due notably to the possibilities for distribution on the Internet, QIV custodians have tried to rewrite the rules. The stated reason to bring end-users into the fray was that they abused their leeway and/or that certain private uses or reuses had a negative impact on the market.[790] Nonprofessional users quickly became aware of a right that they had rarely noticed up to then and saw all the 'trust' that had been placed in them via rules and exceptions concerning private use evaporate before their eyes. Their role changed from that of consumer to that of budding pirate.[791]

The attempt to control them was not limited to national statutes and international treaties. Contracts and other forms of private ordering were also used. As a partial admission that copyright has become 'insufficient' (or worse), technical protection measures were used to restrict either access to works (e.g., by password) or use of them (e.g., a PDF file that cannot be saved or printed). Users who do not have 'hacking' tools cannot choose whether or not to respect such measures. Nor will these measures cease to apply once the content falls into the public domain or to allow free and fair uses.[792]

---

[790] This bears some resemblance to the second part of the three-part test in art. 9(2) of the Berne Convention and art. 13 of the TRIPS Agreement. See Chapter 3.

[791] Ironically, this could change their attitude about being 'good citizens' and induce them to engage in marginal behaviour. Eric Posner has shown that the rate of tax evasion grows in proportion to efforts to control it. A citizen who is treated like a (potential) thief thus will have more of a tendency to behave as the government 'expects' him or her to. See Eric A Posner, 'Law and Social Norms: The Case of Tax Compliance' (2000) 86 *Virginia Law Review* 1781.

[792] Which, we must not forget, takes place at least 20 years earlier in Canada than in the US or Europe.

On top of that technical layer of protection is a legal layer, which prohibits circumvention of technical measures. This protection flows from implementation of the 1996 WIPO Treaties[793] and, in the US, the DMCA of 1998. Technical measures operate even if users benefit either from an authorization or from an exception.[794] This technical layer is distinct from economic rights. It is typically managed by QIV entities, not by authors and often referred to as 'para-copyright'. All of this has moved the centre of gravity of copyright policy toward these industries and, as a consequence, away from authors.

The industry's battle has not been very successful. By closing down Napster, the industry created a Hydra of peer-to-peer networks and is now forced to take individual users to court[795]—which, beyond the costs, has had a huge negative impact on the image of the industry, not to mention the potential rebound effect of such an approach. This being said, users are not naïve. They know that the law forbids them to upload files and make them available on a peer-to-peer network. Yet the absence of legal solutions and the temptation of the Internet, with its enormous power to transform, or even transcend, a model of distribution deemed obsolete by many users, is too strong. By increasing repression, the industry (along with authors) is losing (considerable[796]) revenues, while users are increasingly frustrated.

All of this has also had the undesirable effect of taking responsibility away from users and, in many cases, eliminating their *marge de manœuvre*.

---

[793]   WIPO Copyright Treaty, 20 December 1996, 36 ILM 65 (1997); WIPO Performances and Phonograms Treaty, 20 December 1996, 36 ILM 76 (1997).

[794]   Article 11 of the WIPO Copyright Treaty (which corresponds to art. 18 of the WIPO Performances and Phonograms Treaty) provides:

Contracting Parties shall provide adequate legal protection and effective legal remedies against the circumvention of effective technological measures that are used by authors in connection with the exercise of their rights under this Treaty or the Berne Convention and that restrict *acts, in respect of their works, which are not authorized by the authors concerned or permitted by law*. (emphasis added)

[795]   See Recording Industry Association of America (RIAA), 'Recording Industry to Begin Collecting Evidence and Preparing Lawsuits against File "Sharers" Who Illegally Offer Music Online' (25 June 2013) (<bit.ly/2gqCcXr> accessed 17 November 2016).

[796]   Napster at its apogee had about 60 million users, or, at the time, almost 70 per cent of American Web surfers. If about half of those users had agreed to pay $5 per month, Napster would have generated about $2 billion per year, or 30 per cent of the total revenue of the industry in the US. Extrapolating from the increase in numbers of Web surfers since Napster closed, it is reasonable to think that Napster today would have had 300 million users throughout the world, generating (using the same figures) $12 billion per year.

Users had some leeway in their dealings with physical carriers such as books or CDs, essentially because 'private' uses had little effect on the market.[797] Much of this leeway is gone. Recourse to technical measures has also strengthened the position of marketing and distribution entities in relation to classic copyright holders, particularly authors. It has indeed been a major policy failure to see control of use as an end in itself. It was but a means to an end in the bricks-and-mortar world. The end is and has always been the generation of incentives in appropriate cases by using levers provided by the market and user demand.

The myopic focus on the perceived needs of fourth quadrant custodians is both misguided and anachronistic. The twenty-first century author is often a reuser of pre-existing material, which would seem to require less protection against reproduction (to avoid infringement while creating a 'new' work).[798] Nowadays, authors often have a preference for attribution. QIII authors also have a reasonable expectation of income when their work succeeds in the marketplace. This need not be a straitjacket. For example, the Creative Commons licenses 'have a flexible attribution requirement, so there is not necessarily one correct way to provide attribution. The proper method for giving credit will depend on the medium and means you are using, and may be implemented in any reasonable manner'.[799] While QIV custodians try to occupy centre stage and perhaps the entire stage in discussions of reform proposals, the objective should be to ensure the availability of options that meet the need of parents in the other quadrants as well, especially those whom the system was designed to create incentives for (namely attribution and, in QIII, financial compensation). Intermediation is necessarily contingent; authorship is not.

The difference between QIII and QIV is thus clear. The QIII author typically supports open subscription models, with fair distribution of revenue. Many professional authors who target mass audiences would accept this view, I suspect. By contrast, QIV custodians want to try to control dissemination, often by maintaining ownership interests in the disseminators. They fight Internet-based businesses they do not control—such as search engines—because those businesses maximize the availability of content to maximize page views and ad revenue but often have no relationship with or legal duty to compensate either the creators of the 'content' or the

---

[797] One can wonder about photocopies. What is the cumulative effect of hundreds of millions of copies made around the world?

[798] Gervais (n 768).

[799] Creative Commons, 'Frequently-Asked Questions' (available at <http://wiki.creativecommons.org/Frequently_Asked_Questions> accessed 30 March 2015).

custodians. QIII authors would support systems that provide fair compensation but allow Internet entities to operate while QIV authors are instead playing a zero-sum game with them.

## 8.4    OPERATIONALIZING THE PROPOSED STRUCTURE

To operationalize the proposed quadrantal structure, the first step is to acknowledge that copyright law cannot be all things to all people in everything—that is, a single set of rights, exceptions and term.

Operationalizing Quadrant I would require a recognized system to dedicate works to the public domain.[800] If that system were not irrevocable, rights of users would have to be protected if a work was moved out of the public domain.[801] Quadrant II can be seen as a variation on the public domain but it is fundamentally different. The work is a legally emancipated child, but the author-parent wishes to retain attribution. This can easily be done using a licensing system such as Creative Commons and specifically a license incorporating 'BY' or attribution.[802] While many, and perhaps most twenty-first century authors want attribution, especially if their work is reused, all do not expect major monetary rewards, if any, or enhanced financial remedies. Many QII authors are already compensated to write independently of any commercial distribution of their work, if any. Most professional authors do not fall into this category, however. They expect compensation, that is, a fair share of the surplus that their work has generated.

Authors other than those in QI should have access to 'minimum' rights as provided under the Berne Convention. For those in QII, the license terms they choose may prevent them from claiming damages, at least for uses covered by the license.[803] However, the *default should be QIII*, with remedies amounting to an injunction and actual damages or limited

---

[800]    A legislative solution to modulate remedies would be desirable, but a possible private ordering solution already exists: the CC0 Creative Commons license. See Creative Commons, 'About CC0 — 'No Rights Reserved' (<http://creativecommons.org/about/cc0> accessed 17 November 2016) (The issue is possible termination if the mechanism used is the license.)

[801]    *Eldred v Ashcroft* 537 US 186 (2013): The Supreme Court indicated that this movement out of the public domain was possible if so intended by Congress.

[802]    Creative Commons, 'About the Licenses' (available at <http://creativecommons.org/licenses/> accessed March 30 2015).

[803]    Subject of course to the application of appropriate exceptions and limitations, including fair use/fair dealing.

(proportionate) statutory damages in lieu of actual damages. Injunctions would not be automatic. Courts should factor in the public interest, including manifestations of authorial intent, as reasonably communicated to the user/defendant under equitable doctrines.[804] Authorship is a relevant element of context.[805] Remedies not subject to formalities could still be subject in most cases to inclusion by the author of her name on the work 'in the usual manner (anonymous and pseudonymous works may be considered an exception)'.[806] In the US, Quadrant III implements the Constitutional direction that copyright should promote the progress of science and useful arts, by providing a better balance between access, the possibility of reusing, attribution and financial rewards. Financial rewards for successful authors who wish to enter the avenues of commerce should remain fully available, subject to intentionality.

A feature of the proposal is the recognition that QII and QIII authors form part of the core of copyright policy.[807] For those who expect attribution but whose production does not depend on and who do not expect financial retribution when their works are used in commerce, QII should be their home. Many academics and scientists in particular would fit into this picture. For others who expect both attribution and financial gain if their work is successful in the marketplace, QIII should be the target. This also means that works in Quadrant IV, which would benefit from enhanced remedies, should be limited and *not* the default quadrant. Nor should policy decisions be primarily (and a fortiori exclusively) driven by QIV. Membership in the fourth quadrant should provide 'benefits' such as adequate statutory damages and attorneys' fees but that membership should be earned by the use of declaratory measures, in particular recordation of transfers.[808]

Internationally, each country should assess the vitality of each quadrant. A country with a very small QIV but a great need for information access (e.g., for educational purposes) and a significant but largely undeveloped potential for individual certainty would be well-advised to focus

---

[804]  Under US law, *eBay Inc v MercExchange, LLC*, 547 US 388 (2006).
[805]  Mark P Gergen, John M Golden and Henry E Smith, 'The Supreme Court's Accidental Revolution? The Test For Permanent Injunctions' (2012) 112 *Columbia Law Review* 203, 242–9; Dan B Dobbs, *Dobbs Law of Remedies: Damages-Equity-Restitution* (2d edn, West Publishing 1993) § 2.4(1) 91–2.
[806]  This would be subject to the need for the author to indicate her name on the work 'in the usual manner', which is consistent with both the Berne Convention and the attribution desire shown by most authors.
[807]  See Kurtz (n 776).
[808]  For a fuller explanation of the role that formalities could play within international rules and US law, see Ch. 12.

on QI–III in setting policy goals. That said, it is likely that trade pressure may be exerted to affect the outcome and tilt it towards the perceived interests of QIV.[809] By contrast, a country with a large QIV contingent should not undermine the industries in that space but should do so in a balanced way, including proper limitations and exceptions as explicated below and as discussed in Chapter 7.

Finally, a word about orphan works. These are copyrighted works still under copyright protection (or presumed to be) but whose parent or custodian is not known or easily identifiable.[810] Such works are the main target of proposals concerning the establishment of an orphan works regime.[811] A very large percentage of works, especially older ones, fall into this category. This should not be confused with anonymous or pseudonymous works, however, which are not non-attributed but rather best seen as a different form of attribution.[812]

The next task is to structure the rights, exceptions and limitations. Let us look to this in the next two chapters.

---

[809]    As in the TPP; see Peter K Yu, 'TPP and Trans-Pacific Perplexities' (2014) 37 *Fordham International Law Journal* 1129. The word 'perceived' is used here to signal that some demands made on legislators in the context of those discussions may ultimately not actually serve the interests of the demanders.

[810]    Justice Breyer's dissent in *Eldred v Ashcroft* makes an interesting point in that regard:

> [T]o some extent [permission] costs of this kind accompany any copyright law, regardless of the length of the copyright term. But to extend that term, preventing works from the 1920s and 1930s from falling into the public domain, will dramatically increase the size of the costs just as—perversely—the likely benefits from protection diminish. [. . .] The older the work, the less likely it retains commercial value, and the harder it will likely prove to find the current copyright holder. The older the work, the more likely it will prove useful to the historian, artist, or teacher.

*Eldred* (n 801) 251.

[811]    For an evaluation of the scope of the problem, see Robert Kirk Walker, 'Negotiating The Unknown: A Compulsory Licensing Solution To The Orphan Works Problem' (2014) 35 *Cardozo Law Review* 983, 989–90.

[812]    17 USC §101 ('anonymous work' and 'pseudonymous work').

# 9. Structuring the right(s)

Is copyright dead?[813] The first death announcement was probably John Perry Barlow's. In his seminal 1993 essay, 'The Economy of Ideas',[814] he argued that dematerialization has made copyright, which was designed to protect the bottle and not the wine, irrelevant, for in the digital era the bottle has disappeared. He then handed down his verdict:

> Intellectual property law cannot be patched, retrofitted, or expanded to contain the gasses of digitized expression any more than real estate law might be revised to cover the allocation of broadcasting spectrum. (Which, in fact, rather resembles what is being attempted here.) We will need to develop an entirely new set of methods as befits this entirely new set of circumstances.[815]

In the slipstream of this former rancher and spokesperson for the *Grateful Dead,* academics in the United States and then in other countries began to explain why copyright had become obsolete in the Internet era.[816] However, the funeral was a bit premature. Copyright is still with us, and few can prove that a (capitalist) society without copyright would ensure as well, or better, the creation and distribution of new works.[817] While Barlow's prognosis was overly negative, the diagnosis was in large part

---

[813] Eben Moglen uses a 'Star Wars' analogy to make the point: 'the obsolescence of the IP droid is neither unforeseeable nor tragic. Indeed it may find itself clanking off into the desert, still lucidly explaining to an imaginary room the profitably complicated rules for a world that no longer exists.' 'Anarchism Triumphant: Free Software and the Death of Copyright' in N Elkin-Koren and N W Netanel (eds), *The Commodification of Information* (Kluwer, 2002) 107, 131.

[814] John Perry Barlow, 'The Economy of Ideas: Selling Wine without Bottles on the Global Net' (1994) 2.03 *Wired* (available at <https://www.wired.com/1994/03/economy-ideas/> accessed 17 November 2016).

[815] Ibid.

[816] The reader will find a good example in the article by Glynn S Lunney Jr, 'The Death of Copyright: Digital Technology, Private Copying, and the Digital Millennium Copyright Act' (2001) 87 *Virginia Law Review* 813; See also Robert C Denicola, 'Mostly Dead? Copyright Law in the New Millennium' (2000) 47 *Journal of the Copyright Society of the USA* 193.

[817] Of course, some advocate replacing copyright with something else, but they nevertheless recognize the necessity of the function.

correct, however. As Chapter 1 illustrated, there have been fundamental changes and shifts that copyright policy has struggled to reflect.

The rights were poorly architected from the beginning. Their focus was on the organization of a marketplace for physical goods such as books or records, or the dissemination of their contents by professional distributors like cinemas, broadcasters theatres, etc. Exclusivity made sense. A movie could be released first in cinemas, then on the market (rental or pay per view) and then on 'free' television broadcasts (paid for by watching advertisements). As the previous chapter shows, not all authors want any form of exclusivity or control in the dissemination of their creative work. Many parts of the 'copyright industries' do. This is often misplaced, and does not mesh with the reality of access on multiple platforms, devices and at a time and place chosen by the user, not the distributor (unlike, say, commercial radio or television). Nor does it reflect the difficulty of trying to keep material offline. The best defence is to make it available, and monetize the use. Chapters 6 and 8 explicate why this monetization must be fair to authors. The reality is that control is the exception, not the rule and that appropriate monetization should be the objective. Efforts to control are often futile; fuel the drive to use unauthorized access sources, and they often deprive authors and others of income. Whether one likes it or not, the online realm often amounts to a *de facto* 'compulsory' license in the sense that attempts to prevent or control or license every use is so skewed by transaction costs that, in line with Coase's theorem, either the value or allocation of rights is negatively affected for both right holder and user, or the non-copyright costs (such as privacy diminution) to the user outweigh the perceived value of acquiring the license, or both.

The copyright industries that live in QIV (see the previous chapter) have not been dazzling in their rush to adapt to the Internet in part because they failed to understand the nature of the changes induced by an almost complete transition to online platforms and tools. These industries have essentially fought the Internet. Arguably, the music and movie industries are still fighting.[818] I was among those who suggested as far back as 1998 that a 'business model' approach should be used instead, including

---

[818] We might remember the fight against the photocopier. In a 1961 report of the Register of Copyrights in the US, a similar alarm was being sounded: 'Copying has now taken on new dimensions with the development of photocopying devices by which any quantity of material can be reproduced readily and in multiple copies . . .' H Comm on the Judiciary, 87th Cong, Report of the Register of Copyrights on the General Revision of the U.S. Copyright Law (Comm Print 1961) 102–3.

massive but rational licensing efforts.[819] The text industry and scientific journals reacted better. Many publishers put their material years ago, and some have considerably broadened the choices offered to their readers, whether by making available lab data files (too voluminous to print) or three-dimensional models of molecules, or simply by accelerating distribution.[820] While this will not satisfy those who say it should all be free (e.g., because research is often publicly funded) or non-right holder intermediaries who want to provide 'free' access in exchange of ad-viewing, those were manifestly steps in the right direction.

Where are we now? After some setbacks concerning standardization issues and many sensational trials aiming to impede exchanges of files between Web surfers on a central site such as Napster[821] or a peer-to-peer network, the recording industry has authorized both the downloading and streaming of music files, though it is not yet an open competition area.[822] The movie and television industry has more or less allowed streaming for payment of almost all content, via services such as Netflix or Hulu. The main concern of most industries seems to be to avoid any reuse of the downloaded content and reducing the possibility of ad skipping by users. And this is precisely where the problem of adaptability of copyright to the digital world is most obvious.

The structure of copyright rights *should not pick and choose* among business models. From a pragmatic point of view, it would seem much more efficient to structure copyright so that it corresponds to its primary objective, leaving it up to authors, other rights holders, distributors, and users to define the authorized uses rather than trying to make each use artificially correspond to one or several legal fragments. Put differently, is it efficient or useful to ask an author who wants to authorize distribution of his or her work on television if this will require one or several reproductions, one or several communications to the public, and so on?

Let us consider the case of cameras making an 'image' of a three-dimensional object itself protected by copyright (say, a Mickey Mouse

---

[819] Daniel Gervais, 'Electronic Rights Management and Digital Identifier Systems' (1999) 4 *Journal of Electronic Publishing* (at <http://bit.ly/2fbEwza> accessed 17 November 2016). This was a report presented to WIPO (Geneva) in December 1998.

[820] Daniel Gervais, 'Copyright and eCommerce' in Melvin Simensky, Lanning Bryer, and Neil J Wilkof (eds), *Intellectual Property in the Global Marketplace. 2001 Supplement* (Wiley, 2002).

[821] Including the famous suit against Napster.

[822] By which I mean that record companies often hold a veto right over interactive streaming services, thus limiting competition, in part, some say, because they own a stake in one of the major providers in this space (Spotify).

toy). The file can then be used to generate a three-dimensional object using a 3D printer. A traditional hermeneutics of copyright rights would consider whether the computer file created by the camera (basically computer code) 'describing' the object and allowing a copy to be generated is itself a copy (reproduction); whether limiting doctrines like merger apply;[823] under which circumstances (if any) transmitting that file from one computer to another can be a public performance, whether a public display occurs at some point etc., bearing in mind that each right fragment in the copyright bundle may be owned by a different party. Asking whether there should be an exclusive right of commercial use of the files containing the printing instructions—and then whether there is a reasonable, normatively-grounded way to monetize that value—are better questions to ask. A copyright industry knee-jerk answer to 3D printing might look like the lawsuit that shuttered Napster; a better one should be more like Spotify (in terms of open access via a subscription model and leaving aside the extremely skewed financial flows generated by Spotify). Why? Because otherwise the likely result will be years of litigation, frustrated users, possible impeded development of 3D printing technology and less revenue for copyright owners. A lose-lose all around—once again.

In spite of the restructuring that this approach implies, normatively this is nothing new. As discussed in the first chapter, most of the issues resulting from fragmentation could be remedied by private ordering in the pre-digital realm mostly because a limited number of professional entities were involved. Yet copyright policy has traditionally been refractory to an accumulation of rights fragments on a single use. Beyond private ordering, solutions to obviate difficulties stemming from fragmentation are sometimes contained in legislation, such as defaulting to a 'dominant' fragment. For example, because broadcasting can be viewed as a single economic operation,[824] the 'dominant fragment', namely public performance/communication to the public, can be used as the main vector to set tariffs, effectuate licensing arrangements. This explains why several national laws contain an exception (for so-called 'ephemeral' recordings though they are far from ephemeral and may often be retained for months)[825] for use of the reproduction fragment in the broadcasting context—indispensable but of secondary importance. Having to provide for such exceptions is but one

---

[823]   Deven R Desai and Gerard N Magliocca, 'Patents, Meet Napster: 3d Printing and the Digitization of Things' (2014) 102 *Georgetown Law Journal* 1691, 1709.

[824]   Rebroadcast on cable, etc., can of course be seen separately.

[825]   Berne Convention, art. 11*bis*(3).

sign of lack of alignment between the structure of copyright fragments and the objective of the copyright system.

Copyright rights need to be realigned at what I might call the molecular level. I suggest two mobilizing principles to do so. First, some fragmentation is useful to tailor authorizations to use protected works in certain markets, etc., but any such fragmentation should be done by contract. The underlying economic right should thus be a single right divisible by contract. This will allow the right to respond to any technological change. Second, copyright must be a right to authorize or prohibit *uses that restrict the market or the possibilities for exploiting the product*, not technical operations performed on the work or a copy thereof. The suggested approach is to emphasize the *effect* of the use, rather than its *technical nature*.[826] It is not unauthorized 'reproduction' (even the making of 10,000 copies) of a book that harms the author or publisher, but the distribution to the public of these copies. Hence, reproduction *for the purpose of distribution* is the relevant operation.[827] A *teleological approach* to define a 'use' right has the advantage of being technologically neutral.

Other scholars have proposed that copyright be reformulated using an approach-based effect. Professor Jessica Litman suggested a right of commercial exploitation,[828] while Professor Andrew Christie proposed that the legislation as a whole be simplified, one ground being, notably, that users-consumers are increasingly obliged to apply, and thus to understand, it.[829] Christie proposed that economic rights be grouped in two categories: reproduction and dissemination,[830] an approach critiqued by his colleague

---

[826] Shira Perlmutter, 'Convergence and the Future of Copyright' (2001) 24 *Columbia-VLA Journal of Law & Arts* 163, 172–3.

[827] Two American authors have in fact proposed that copyright be replaced by a right of distribution to the public. Their analysis of the problem is interesting, but it must be noted that distribution is not the only way to enter a market. E Miller and J Feigenbaum, 'Taking the Copy Out of Copyright' (2001) *Digital Rights Management Workshop* 233–44 (<http://www.cs.yale.edu/homes/jf/MF.pdf> accessed 17 November 2016).

[828] Jessica Litman, *Digital Copyright* (2nd edn, Prometheus Books 2001) 180; and J Ginsburg, 'Can Copyright Become User-Friendly? Review: Jessica Litman, Digital Copyright (2001)' (2002) 25 *Columbia-VLA Journal of Law & the Arts* 71, 83. I leave aside for now evidentiary issues. If one were caught with boxes containing 10,000 unauthorized copies of a DVD, I am not suggesting that evidence of actual distribution would necessarily be required. It could well be inferred.

[829] Andrew Christie, 'A Proposal for Simplifying United Kingdom Copyright Law' [2001] EIPR 26.

[830] Ibid., 37–8.

Sam Ricketson.[831] A simplification along those lines, which reduces the number of fragments but *maintains rights based on the technical nature of the use*, strikes me as suboptimal.

There have been other efforts to reformulate copyright, but generally along the lines of 'technical form of use' fragments. For example, the creation in the United States of a right of 'Internet transmission' in sound recordings,[832] which might solve certain problems specific to the Internet, resolves neither the conceptual nor the pragmatic questions examined here.[833] Its application has been disastrous for US authors, but in their case not just because of copyright's poor structure but rather because authors and publishers who belong to a performing rights organization (PRO such as, in the US, ASCAP, BMI and SESAC) must grant a license due to the application of an antitrust consent decree,[834] and thus have little if any negotiating power, while sound recording right holders (mostly the three major labels) have a full exclusive right in the case of interactive services (basically those where the user selects the song they want to listen to). In the case of non-interactive services, a second layer of problem is caused in the US by the split of the rate-setting process for authors (whose association within one of three PROs is treated as anticompetitive and was used to strip authors of their exclusive rights under antitrust laws) and the three 'labels' that control most of the market for sound recordings (which perhaps strangely, is not seen as an antitrust issue by the United States Government) and that is subject to much more 'generous' rate-setting system, namely the Copyright Royalty Board. This has led to a split of total income generated from digital services approaching 98:2, that is 98 cents of every dollar goes to labels (with some sharing, subject in some cases to 'creative accounting', with performers) and 2 cents to publishers and songwriters.[835] Adding a right fragment to an already poor policy is not better policy. Its interrelation with pre-existing fragments is unlikely to produce desired outcomes. I do not think that the US Congress actually *intended* to expropriate songwriters when it added the digital transmission right but empirically this is exactly what has happened.

How does one move forward? Definitely *not* by following the US approach for music rights. The approach suggested by Litman is *a priori*

---

[831]    Sam Ricketson, 'Simplifying Copyright Law: Proposals from Down Under' [1999] EIPR 537.

[832]    Mark A Lemley, 'Dealing With Overlapping Copyrights on the Internet' (2002) 22 *University of Dayton Law Review* 547, 582–3.

[833]    17 USC §106(6).

[834]    See Chapter 11.

[835]    Schwartz, note 679 above, 316.

the most interesting, but as Jane Ginsburg noted,[836] the conceptualiza-
tion must be pushed much farther. This is my attempt to do so. One
must also take into account international treaties, particularly the TRIPS
Agreement. Then there are examples of simplification in certain national
laws. These attempts are interesting, though I have not found one that
truly adopts an effects-based paradigm. A good example is perhaps the
Swiss Copyright Act,[837] which provides, in Article 10: 'The author has
the exclusive right to decide when and how his work will be used.' It is an
overbroad right tempered by several exceptions and limitations.

As noted in the Introduction, the approach I advocate for in this book
is to *incorporate proper limits in the scope of the right itself* by aligning the
right with its purpose. [838] To do so, I use some of the flexibility afforded
by the three-step test discussed in Chapter 3. The test allows national
legislators to rescope copyright with an inherent teleological limit, which
also serves as a normative anchor for the right. This, I suggest, would be
a considerable improvement over the current fragmented right based on
technical uses of copies of works. The idea of injecting limits in the scope
of a right is obviously something that is already well known. For example,
a performance or communication must be in or to a public for those right
fragments to apply.

It seems reasonable to suggest that copyright holders would be content
with a strong economic right that applies in cases where use is prejudicial
to their (commercial) interests and, specifically, using the language of the
test, when such use conflicts with normal commercial exploitation. Other
uses, such as private use or use for research would presumably in most
cases fall outside the scope of the new use-based right. If the new norm
encompassed notions of normalcy and reasonableness, it would be flexible, dynamic and allow the right to evolve through a common law process
with the invention of new technological uses. Normalcy is not set in stone:
what constituted normal commercial exploitation 15 years ago has been
dramatically and irreversibly altered and more Schumpeterian changes
will no doubt happen.

My proposal, therefore, is that the economic component of copyright
should be a *right to prohibit uses that demonstrably interfere with actual or
predictable commercial exploitation*. This would of course be subject to limitations and exceptions, but in keeping with the dual principle articulated

---

[836]    Ginsburg, note 828 above, 83.
[837]    Loi fédérale sur le droit d'auteur et les droits voisins, 9 October 1992 (Swiss
Federal Copyright Act).
[838]    Suzor, note 789 above, 192.

above, the objective is to *build intrinsic limits in the scope of the right itself* and make it *independent of the technical nature of the use* made. In order to comply with international norms, the right should be interpreted by defining 'use' to encompass current technical uses (reproduction, performance, communication), as does the Swiss statute, but using the three-step test to factor in commercial exploitation.[839] As also noted in the Introduction, an implementation of the proposed reform in the Berne Convention context is contained in the Epilogue. The introduction by courts or the legislator of market-based presumptions in favour of copyright holders in certain situations to reverse the burden of proof would seem to be logical if an effects-based approach was chosen.

Is this TRIPS-compatible? The idea is to rescope the right not just by complying with but actually *using* the three-step test.

Nothing in the text of Berne or TRIPS requires that limitations on the right *be a separate step* from the definition of the right itself. If a copyright exception or limitation is viewed as an area *not* protected by copyright, conversely the three-step test *can be said to preserve the area* covered by copyright. It thus provides the contours of 'unfair' use[840] (if unauthorized). My approach is to craft a new, single international copyright norm that effectively defragments economic rights and creates the necessary distance between the right and the technology used to exploit the value of or otherwise use the work. Because it is market- and effect-based, not a reflection of technical operations performed on copies of works, it is technologically neutral. *I suggest that copyright be structured teleologically rather than technologically.*

Structuring the right this way would imply in many cases a temporal component. Initially, the proposed approach would provide *strong exclusive rights used during preparations for and actual commercial exploitation* for uses that impact commercial exploitation and are not covered by a specific exception or limitation.[841] The right would weaken after this to allow certain uses, subject in appropriate cases to a right to remuneration (for the remainder of the term). This strikes me as not fundamentally different in terms of effects from the 'permitted but paid' category suggested by Professor Ginsburg.[842] This can be justified normatively (because it is seen as a desirable outcome) and pragmatically (because efforts to

---

[839]    Art. 10:2, Swiss Federal Copyright Act.
[840]    Okediji, note 208 above, 79.
[841]    'Specific' in this context does not refer to how the exception or limitation is formulated. Fair use would be included, for example, even though it is not 'specific.' Its specificity comes in its case-by-case application by courts.
[842]    Jane C. Ginsburg, 'Fair Use for Free or Permitted-But-Paid' (2014) 29 *Berkeley Technology Law Journal* 1383.

stop or control Internet uses have not been particularly successful either technically or commercially). The proposed approach realigns copyright structurally with the reality on online uses.

This brings us to moral rights. As noted in previous chapters, attribution is a well-established principle. It serves not just authors but users as well to know who has written or created a work, unless of course the author has deliberately chosen an anonymous/pseudonymous publication. Hence, a *right to prevent first publication* should be provided, with adequate public interest limits.[843] It has long existed at common law even in the absence of a 'European-style' moral right. In keeping with Article 6*bis* of the Berne Convention, a right of attribution (post publication) should also be provided.

A right of integrity should be recognized but in very limited fashion to reflect the nature of possibilities offered by digital technology to transform and reuse works, in keeping with freedom of expression concerns. The suggestion is to rescope the right to limit it to cases *when the prejudice to honour and reputation is both significant and demonstrably present.* This should involve a very small number of cases. Use of a work by an author who strongly believes in choice in an anti-abortion campaign comes to mind.

The proposed structural reforms would include reform of the *remedies.* Remedies affect the scope of the right. While the proposed approach is not to eliminate statutory or pre-established damages (because it is true that actual damages are often hard to prove), the range of damages assessed in cases other than of commercial piracy should be in line with the nature of the use by individuals, that is, in most cases in the range of a few hundred dollars per use (not necessarily by work). The amount could be increased at the court's discretion in cases of bad faith by the user.

A final fix that seems essential is to impose unwaivable rights reversion, that is, the ability of an author who contractually transferred her rights to claim them back, subject to the accomplishment of certain formalities. This is part of US law (17 USC §203(a)(4) (2000)) and should become an international norm. The current reversion time-frame in the United States is 35 years after the transfer. An international norm should likely be between 25 and 35 years after the transfer and not, as is the case in, e.g., Canada, a certain number of years after the author's death, which seems highly illogical as it is completely disconnected to the time of the transfer.

---

[843] In some cases publication will be in violation of a contract (for example an obligation not to publish a document and/or keep it secret). Copyright law should not be viewed in such cases as a mere adjunct to contract law.

# 10. Structuring exceptions and limitations

Exceptions and Limitations (E&Ls) matter; they allow the copyright system to adapt to change. Structured appropriately, they can create predictability and provide a policy backup in case of a licensing market failure. How should they be structured? First, one must conceptualize their object and purpose. Second, one must recognize that E&Ls are contextual.[844]

## 10.1  CONCEPTUALIZING LIMITATIONS AND EXCEPTIONS

Trade in intangibles (services and goods whose value is mostly derived from intellectual property (IP)) represents a major area of world trade and forms part of an economy in which competitiveness is predicated on innovation.[845] Industrialized nations that have negative trade balances in the manufacturing sector often have positive balances in trade in intangibles.[846] Beyond that economic debate and its political ramifications, there is a fundamental normative argument, namely that each person, in any country, should have a right to develop him or herself as fully as possible. When translated into collective terms, welfare is maximized when each individual leads as productive a life as possible. The ultimate aim of policy making in the field of IP (and other related areas) should thus be to accomplish that very goal, namely ensuring that law and its various accoutrements *maximize the development of human creativity and innovation.*

How does this translate into policy making concerning copyright

---

[844]  See Y Gendreau, 'Towards a contextual copyright', in L Bently, U Suthersanen and P Torremans (eds), *Global Copyright: Three Hundred Years since the Statute of Anne, from 1709 to Cyberspace* (Edward Elgar Publishing 2010).

[845]  See Zvi Griliches, *R&D, Education, and Productivity -A Retrospective* (Harvard University Press 2000).

[846]  See Robert E Lipsey, 'Measuring International Trade in Services' in Marshall Reinsdorf and Matthew J Slaughter (eds), *International Trade in Services and Intangibles in the Era of Globalization* (University of Chicago Press 2009).

limitations and exceptions? Efforts by the World Intellectual Property Organization (WIPO) to produce economic studies of IP impacts have helped significantly in developing adequate policy options in this regard, as previous efforts by the World Bank and others had done in the past.[847] The variegated picture that emerges from these studies paints IP as part of a broader landscape of *innovation policies.* Seeing copyright in this light helps to calibrate national policies in countries that strive to join the club of world-class creators and innovators. It also allows all of us better to comprehend the social costs of certain forms of IP and allow mitigation where necessary.[848] Clearly, therefore, limitations and exceptions should not be seen as an afterthought. They form part of the core of copyright policy because they perform multiple essential functions.[849] They can be expressed in a variety of ways, however, which makes comparative analysis more challenging.

Historically, each time a new right fragment was added to the copyright 'bundle' as explained in the first two chapters, a discussion on its limits took place. Sometimes, some limits were inherent in the right itself. For example, a performance must be 'in public' to require an authorization; a communication must be 'to a public'; and, in common law jurisdictions, a reproduction must be 'of a substantial part' of the work.[850] In other cases,

---

[847] For example the Global Innovation Index 2012. See Soumitra Dutta, *The Global Innovation Index 2012-Stronger Innovation Linkages For Global Growth* (INSEAD-WIPO 2012) (available at <http://www.wipo.int/freepublications/en/economics/gii/gii_2012.pdf> accessed 24 October 2015).

[848] Let us remember that, not long ago, even while TRIPS was being negotiated in the late 1980s and early 1990s, innovation narratives were essentially absent beyond the lip-service paid to technology transfer. This is not altogether surprising: studies on the specific impacts of IP were hard to find in the industrialized world and virtually nonexistent for the developing world. Negotiators put the policy cart before the empirical horse.

[849] Okediji and Hugenholtz, (<http://www.ivir.nl/publicaties/download/limitations_exceptions_copyright.pdf> accessed 17 November 2016) suggest five purposes for E&L: (a) elimination of barriers to trade, particularly in regard to activities of information service providers; (b) facilitation of access to tangible information products; (c) promotion of innovation and competition; (d) support of mechanisms to promote/reinforce fundamental freedoms; and (e) provision of consistency and stability in the international copyright framework by the explicit promotion of the normative balance necessary to support knowledge diffusion, 42.
They then devise a matrix of mandatory and optional E&Ls based, as their report notes on a presentation by Prof. Pam Samuelson during a workshop sponsored by the OSI and held at the Cardozo School of Law in New York on 16–18 December 2007 (ibid 43–4). I do not disagree but I would structure it somewhat differently, as this Section and the next explicate.

[850] Which allows brief quotations, which one could define as reproductions of an insubstantial part.

limitations and exceptions[851] were necessary to either exclude (in whole or in part) certain *classes of users* or certain *classes of uses* from the reach of the copyright holders. An example of the former might be a non-profit library, museum or archive, which might enjoy special copying privileges; an example of the latter would be exceptions for research or criticism, which anyone can benefit from.

The Internet has radically altered this 300-year-old evolution. First, individual end-users, who, up to 1995 or so rarely encountered copyright law (no one needed to sign a licence when buying a copy of a book at a bookstore or a CD at a record store), suddenly had to confront rules about what they could or could not legally do with pictures, music, etc. Indeed, many users felt, and continue to feel, that restrictions on uses of copyright material on the Internet are at odds with established practices of non-commercial 'sharing' and reusing of content to create something new—a phenomenon sometimes referred to as the 'remix culture'.[852] Educators, who draw considerable benefits from the great global, hyperlinked and interactive library that is the Internet, pointed to the lack of clarity and/ or the obsolescence of limitations and exceptions, several of which are bounded in the national legislation of several countries by a reference to the physicality or location of the use (which e.g., must be 'on the premises' of the educational establishment).

In updating exceptions contained in any national copyright law, several options should be considered. The backdrop for this evolution is the *three-step test* of course, and it was discussed in detail in Chapter 3. The first option is to adopt a more open-ended model which could look like US 'fair use' but could also be another open model of permitted uses. A second option is to open up the list of purposes for which fair dealing or some version thereof is allowed in countries where there is a finite list of purposes in the national copyright statute. Both those options enable courts to determine the scope of the exceptions on a case-by-case basis. The issue that this may pose in terms of predictability and slow evolution in jurisdictions with a low number of cases are well documented. They may be outweighed by the flexibility that an open-ended exceptions and limitations regime provides. A third option is to revise some of the existing exceptions and improve them where a need for change has been

---

[851]  A limitation is a restriction on the exclusive nature of the right concerned, such as a compulsory license. It usually involves compensation to the rights holder. An exception removes the act covered by the exception from the scope of application of the right and thus typically does not involve the payment of compensation.
[852]  'User generated content' is also commonly used, though arguably a misnomer. 'Users' are often authors in their own right. See Chapter 5.

demonstrated; for example, to allow parody and some forms of 'remix' and to allow broader non-commercial educational use of material, especially spontaneous use of limited amounts of published works. Regardless of the course of action taken, the interface between *any* new exception and the three-step test must be carefully considered. In other words, whichever legislative technique is used, the legislator should ensure that the purposes for which exceptions and limitations are established (a list of which is provided below) are in fact appropriately enabled.

Having recognized the importance of the role of exceptions and limitations, it is now time to try to structure them. In theory, they can be organized according to the following categorization: whether they apply to some categories of users;[853] whether they apply to some categories of use; whether they apply to some categories of countries; whether they apply to some categories of authors; and finally whether they apply to some categories of works. A tabular illustration (Table 10.1) illuminates the suggested taxonomy more clearly:

Four categories of authors were identified in the quadrantal structure presented in Chapter 8. Five categories of users are identified here: limited ability users; consumers; governments; institutions; and a broad category that cuts across all categories of users, and includes authors. Table 10.1 shows balancing approaches by type of use, type of work, and suggests that developing countries may have special needs, as is reflected in the Appendix to the Berne Convention.[854]

Table 10.1 presents a series of categorizations that I consider useful. A categorization *not* found in the table below is *by type of right*. Such a categorization would be suboptimal. It would reflect the problems posed by fragmentation, as discussed in the first chapter. Downstream, such as categorization, would be of little use because: (a) many uses do not involve a single right fragment, (for example uploading material to the Internet may involve the right of reproduction, the right of public performance/ communication, the right of display (where applicable) and the right of adaptation); and (b) now that copyright is applied to end-users, it has become even more illusory to expect that individual consumers can parse which right or sub-right fragment they may need. Upstream it also offers little. Why should an exception depend on the technical nature of the use? Put differently, as a matter of principle the legislator should not grant a limitation or exception because it is the right of reproduction that

---

[853] This category may be a proxy for restrictions to an exception that would otherwise be difficult to capture. What should matter is the function.

[854] See Ch. 2 and the Appendix.

*Table 10.1 Proposed conceptualizations of limitations and exceptions*

| Categorization | Categories | Internal balance | External norms |
|---|---|---|---|
| By type of user | Limited ability users | Braille copies | Non-discrimination |
| | Consumers | Private sphere/ difficult enforcement | Privacy, consumer protection |
| | Government | Public interest uses | Education, culture, information (national security) |
| | Institutional* | Public interest uses | Education, culture, information, archiving and preservation |
| | All | Access and reuse (quotation, parody, transformation) | Information, free expression |
| By type of use | Consumptive | Private sphere/ difficult enforcement | Privacy, consumer protection, education, information, culture |
| | Creative/ transfor- mative | Limit right to prohibit when beyond commercial impact + public interest balance | Free expression, culture, information |
| | Informational | Public interest balance | Information, free expression |
| By type of country | Developing country | | Right to development; education |
| By type of work | Computer software | Public interest function does not require prohibition of reverse engineering** | Competition |
| | Printed publications | Access does not interfere with copyright's function | Education, information |

*Notes*:
\* Libraries, museums, archives and educational institutions.
\*\* See Pamela Samuelson and Suzanne Scotchmer, 'The Law & Economics of Reverse Engineering' (2002) 111 Yale LJ 1575.

is involved rather than the right of adaptation or public performance. The focus should be on the underlying justification, both as a matter of internal copyright balance and to reflect external normative forces and the search for new equilibria. The non-inclusion of *rights* in Table 10.1 is thus justified because most limitations and exceptions should be expressed in terms that are *independent of the technical nature of the use* (reproduction, communication, performance, etc.) unless reference to the nature of the use is contextually *required*. For instance, if normatively a use that is truly in the private sphere (whether expressed as private performance, private copying or teleologically as, say, private study) should not be subject to exclusive copyright rights, this policy direction should not be technology-dependent.[855] For example, if I have the right to make use of a song for teaching in class, the fairness of the use should not depend on whether I stream or download it. This approach is further supported by the three-step test, the filter through which limitations and exceptions must pass to be or remain TRIPS-compatible (see Chapter 3).

## 10.2 PRINCIPLED EXCEPTIONS AND LIMITATIONS

Although it is not possible to provide a complete set of all conceivable exceptions and limitations that a national law might contain, a structured approach is possible. Within the parameters of the suggested approach, each country must decide not just which exceptions and limitations to put in its copyright statute but also how much work should be left to courts e.g., in applying a more open test such as the four fair use factors rather than an exception with a high degree of specificity. This will depend in part on its legal system and traditions. International rules allow a variety of approaches.[856] Bearing this in mind, I believe that it is possible to derive from the table's categorizations of the purpose and role of exceptions and limitations mobilizing principles to guide national legislators. They are as follows:

1. copyright rights should not prohibit use in the private sphere of users;[857]

---

[855]  I realize that this may be illusory, now that social media require and/ or make possible the release of personal information and that highly-targeted marketing has become a basic business model, particularly on social media.

[856]  See Chs 2 and 3.

[857]  If a need for enforcement arises, it will be because the user has stepped out of her private sphere and her actions have reached a level where a commercial impact is perceptible. From an effects-based perspective, it should not matter which type of

2.  copyright rights should not prohibit access in countries or to groups of users who have otherwise no reasonable means of access to copyright material;[858]
3.  copyright rights should not prevent educational uses that cannot be reasonably licensed;
4.  copyright rights should not prohibit access and adequate uses by institutions whose purpose is to document and preserve cultural assets;
5.  copyright rights should not prevent uses and reuses that serve the public interest in free expression, including the creation and dissemination of culture and information. This includes much of what one can loosely refer to as 'transformative' uses.[859] More specifically, it includes research, criticism and review (subject to (8) below). In addition, reuses that do not interfere with commercial exploitation of the original work should be allowed. Reuses that may interfere with commercial exploitation should also be allowed if a licensing transaction would be unreasonable[860] or against the public interest, including quotation, parody, caricature and pastiche;
6.  courts should have the latitude not to apply exclusive rights when they interfere unreasonably with the right of information or the rights of a free press;[861]
7.  copyright rights should not prevent governmental access to and use in the public interest (though generally with compensation of copy-

---

content is used or whether the issue is space, time or format-shifting if there is no significant market in selling additional copies ('selling' is used here generically and not to refer to copying, performing, etc.) when compared to the burden on the consumer.

[858]   This includes educators in less economically developed areas and access by disabled users.

[859]   Transformative use could be defined by using the terminology used in the initial versions of the Berne Convention, namely works that *'present the character of a new original work'*. The right to authorize translations, adaptations, arrangements of music and other alterations (referred to in the Berne Convention under the heading 'derivative works') aims to protect derivative markets that the author of the work from which the derivative is made may reasonably wish to exploit herself, and this (the 'market harm' criterion) should thus form part of the equation. Transformative should probably be measured using a more complex test of societal value and impact of the commercial exploitation of the work derived from.

[860]   If the public interest justifies the exception but will cause a significant loss of income, a compensation mechanism should be in place.

[861]   This right, perhaps the most foundational of democratic systems and the most potentially transformative in fledgling democracies, should be of paramount importance—though the commercial nature of the media should not be completely ignored. This equilibrium is reflected by the use of the term 'reasonably' and the inherent content of the right of information.

right material). Internal or corporate uses by the government should, however, remain subject to exclusive rights;

8. copyright rights should not prevent access and at least non-commercial use of governmental publications of a general nature. Relatedly, edicts of law should not be protected by copyright.

Logically, uses covered by an exception should not be entirely 'circumvented' by a TPM. This may require a governmental mechanism (courts or a specialized agency or tribunal[862]) to order that a TPM be removed in whole or in part in cases where the use permitted by the exception or limitation is not possible. The competent authority should, however, be allowed to refuse this remedy (and perhaps offer compensation instead) in cases where unlocking the TPM is liable to cause substantial harm to the right holder in a way that outweighs the user interest in unlocking a particular work for a given purpose.

## 10.3 PROPOSED STRUCTURE

Professors Okediji and Hugenholtz proposed a categorization that distinguishes mandatory from permissive exceptions and limitations.[863] However, as they noted in their report, historically most countries have sought to keep exceptions and limitations open to meet domestic needs while net exporters of copyrighted goods tried to limit the use of exceptions and limitations domestically and in other jurisdictions.[864] This was visible in the IP chapter of the defunct Trans-Pacific Partnership (TPP) for example.[865] For the first time a treaty was signed in 2013 to impose copyright exceptions and limitations, for access by users with a

---

[862]  For example, the Autorité de régulation des mesures techniques established under art L 331–17 of the French Intellectual Property Code, as amended by the Loi n° 2006-961 du 1er août 2006 relative au droit d'auteur et aux droits voisins dans la société de l'information known as HADOPI, (JO n° 178 du 3 août 2006 p 11529).

[863]  Okediji and Hugenholtz (n 849).

[864]  See Peter K Yu, 'TPP and Trans-Pacific Perplexities' (2014) 37 Fordham Int'l LJ 1129, 1172: '[T]he entertainment industry's push for controversial domestic copyright legislation, such as the PROTECT IP Act (PIPA) and the Stop Online Piracy Act (SOPA).'

[865]  See Susan K Sell, 'TRIPS Was Never Enough: Vertical Forum Shifting, FTAs, ACTA, and TPP' (2011) 18 J Intell Prop L 447, 465. The TPP has been replaced by the Comprehensive and Progressive TPP (CPTPP).

print-disability, including blind users.[866] The exceptions and limitations contained in the treaty are mandatory but only once a state has ratified it of course.[867] The treaty is an unmistakable sign that some exceptions and limitations have become 'normatively unavoidable' as it were.

A related legal structural issue is whether to impose compensation for some exceptions and limitations. In the proposed Copyright Code for the EU (see Chapter 7), a prominent group of copyright experts and scholars proposed a list of E&Ls, some of which would be subject to fair and adequate remuneration.[868] This is in part to reflect the strictures of the three-step test.[869] It seems difficult to agree in advance on a vast number of broad categories of uses that would *never* require compensation.[870] For some uses, however, the choice not to impose remuneration does seem clear and reflects an international rule or established practice. Examples include copies for backup purposes, parody, uses related to administrative, parliamentary or judicial proceedings or public security and reverse engineering.[871]

To be clear, the proposed solution is not a licence to freely copy anything or to upload it to any social site, far from it.[872] It is a limited right to reuse parts of existing works or, in cases where a licensing transaction is not reasonable and there is no demonstrable impact on the market for existing works.

## 10.4  APPLICATION OF PROPOSED SOLUTION TO EDUCATION

One of the key areas of difficulty in structuring copyright correctly is education. The encouragement of learning and creativity strike me as important normative considerations. Learning requires access to, and the ability

---

[866]   WIPO, 'Marrakesh Treaty to Facilitate Access to Published Works for Persons Who Are Blind, Visually Impaired, or Otherwise Print Disabled (MVT)' (27 June 2013) <http://www.wipo.int/wipolex/en/details.jsp?id=13169> accessed 25 October 2015. (Marrakech Treaty).

[867]   Marrakech Treaty.

[868]   European Copyright Code 2010, arts 5.1–5.4 and 5.7 (available at <copyright code.eu> accessed 15 October 2015). For a discussion, see Gervais, 'Fair Use' (n 727).

[869]   For a discussion of the test's parameters, see Okediji and Hugenholtz, (n 849) 19–25.

[870]   See Ch. 3.

[871]   Those examples are all contained in the proposed European Copyright Code (n 868).

[872]   In any event, the three-step test would not allow this type of exception. It would seem to fail on all three steps.

to copy from, the existing font of human scientific and cultural history in the form of literary and artistic works. Masters are copied by pupils, and students learn by copying, adapting and 'playing' with existing works, many of which are still copyright-protected. How much leeway should schools and educators have? Complete freedom from copyright might damage the market for textbooks and online content created for educational purposes, possibly necessitating massive public investment in lieu of market-based revenue generated by the sale of copyright textbooks. There may be other options.

The arguments concerning use of copyright material in schools are well known:

- people want their children to get the best education available, to prepare them to be engaged citizens and have successful careers in the information society and a knowledge-based economy;
- to achieve this fundamental goal, schools must have access to the funds they need to hire good teachers, provide adequate sports and educational facilities and library resources, and first-rate books, manuals and online materials;
- people want their children to learn from domestically produced textbooks and materials, which means that authors and publishers must be able to recoup the investment in time, creativity and money necessary to create and publish those textbooks and produce those resources;
- schools pay their teachers, electric bills, desks, blackboards and light bulbs, the computers they use and the people who manage schools and school boards. There is no reason that access to books, manuals or educational resources made available online should be free. Shortfalls in education budgets should not be compensated by transferring funds from authors and publishers to schools;
- educators must have the ability to make available paper or online resources on an occasional basis for school projects, research, or to discuss current events, etc.;
- we all 'stand on the shoulders of giants', and students and educators, as well as authors of textbooks, may want to reuse pre-existing material to incorporate into their own work.

Copyright policy is a key parameter in the policy equation that governments must solve to achieve the above set of partly contradictory objectives.

Let us start with easy fixes. Some existing educational exceptions are (still) linked to the physical location of the user (e.g., on the premises of the educational establishment). This reflects neither the approach of the three-step test, which focuses on commercial impact, nor the needs of modern education and its increasing reliance on online material. Domestic statutes should remove physical limitations, but do so in a way that does not overstep the boundaries set by TRIPS. This can be done by eliminating any 'on the premises' or similar clauses.

A second fairly obvious fix is to allow a general spontaneous use exception or use of material for which there is no educational market and reasonable transaction potential (financially and administratively). To do so, one could simply introduce an exception for occasional, spontaneous use by way of illustration for teaching; or one could opt for specific quantitative restrictions, as was done for example in Australia, where the Copyright Amendment Act 2006 tried to make limits precise to enhance the public's understanding of such limits, although perhaps with limited success. The Australian provision reads as follows:

> (3) Despite subsection (2), a reproduction, for the purpose of research or study, of all or part of a literary, dramatic or musical work, or of an adaptation of such a work, contained in an article in a periodical publication is taken to be a fair dealing with the work or adaptation for the purpose of research or study.
>
> (4) Subsection (3) does not apply if another article in the publication is also reproduced for the purpose of different research or a different course of study.
>
> (5) Despite subsection (2), a reproduction, for the purpose of research or study, of not more than a reasonable portion of a work or adaptation that is described in an item of the table and is not contained in an article in a periodical publication is taken to be a fair dealing with the work or adaptation for the purpose of research or study. For this purpose, ***reasonable portion*** means the amount described in the item.

| Works, adaptations and reasonable portions | | |
| --- | --- | --- |
| Item | Work or adaptation | Amount that is reasonable portion |
| 1 | A literary, dramatic or musical work (except a computer program), or an adaptation of such a work, that is contained in a published edition of at least 10 pages | (a) 10% of the number of pages in the edition; or (b) if the work or adaptation is divided into chapters—a single chapter |
| 2 | A published literary work in electronic form (except a computer program or an electronic compilation, such as a database), a published dramatic work in electronic form or an adaptation published in electronic form of such a literary or dramatic work | (a) 10% of the number of words in the work or adaptation; or (b) if the work or adaptation is divided into chapters—a single chapter |

(6) Subsection (5) applies to a reproduction of a work or adaptation described in both items of the table in that subsection even if the amount of the work or

adaptation reproduced is not more than a reasonable portion (as defined in that subsection) on the basis of only one of those items.

(7) If:

(a) a person makes a reproduction of a part of a published literary or dramatic work or published adaptation of a literary or dramatic work; and

(b) the reproduction is of not more than a reasonable portion (as defined in subsection (5)) of the work or adaptation;

subsection (5) does not apply in relation to any subsequent reproduction made by the person of any other part of the same work or adaptation.[873]

Quantitative restrictions provide the benefit of clarity at the expense of flexibility. On balance, it may better to leave the provision more flexible, however, and if need be incorporate the last two steps of the tree-step test in the statutory text to ensure TRIPS compliance. One must indeed tread carefully in this area as explained in Chapter 3.

Imposing a broad, uncompensated exception for all educational uses would *not* achieve all the objectives enumerated above. Authors and publishers would lose the incentive to produce educational books or materials if those could then be freely copied. Schools could have to resort to copies of older or foreign textbooks, leading to a quick deterioration of educational resources, absent massive public investment to compensate for the failure of market-based incentives. Conversely, in order not to stifle educators, they must not be prevented from spontaneously using of copies of copyright material (whether in print or online).

Using the same logic, there could be an exception for education distinguishing educational and general resources. I use the term 'general resources' to describe generally available resources for which the primary and secondary school market is not substantial, and which may occasionally be used in schools. With the three-step test as backdrop, an educational exception could certainly exempt occasional, spontaneous use of general resources. If use of a particular resource, such as generally available web pages taken individually, was indeed occasional, there should be no demonstrable significant interference with commercial exploitation.

In light of the above discussion, a map of three copyright layers may be drawn (Table 10.2):

Layer A is 'regulated by' the market now and additional government intervention seems necessary at this juncture. The main difference between layers B and C are: (a) the three-step test; and (b) the fact that preventing

---

[873]    New subss 40(3)–(7), replacing subss 40(3) and (4). Copyright Amendment Act 2006 (Australia), Law 158, 2006. It should be noted that this provision applies to copies for research and private study, not education, which was covered by a more general provision, namely s. 200AB.

*Table 10.2   Layers of material used in education*

| A |
|---|
| Material created for education (as primary or substantial market) and sold or licensed (to a school, school board etc.) by rights holders |

| B |
|---|
| Material for which education is a significant market, occasionally used by schools and not sold or licensed to a school by right holders |

| C |
|---|
| Material for which education is not a significant market and/or made available under general license (subject to contract breach) |

payment for use of material in layer B will harm authors and publishers of material created for education as a main or significant market. A significant part of publicly-available online resources would fall in Layer C. It is also important to note that there is a grey area between layers B and C. Introducing a connection test (how substantial is the connection between the material and the educational market) would likely pass the three-step test if narrowly formulated, but may lead to transaction costs, such as lengthy trials and case-by-case determinations. Use of material in Layer B (i.e., the use of which was not authorized by the rights holder for education) would probably constitute copyright infringement except (arguably at least) in cases of small-scale, spontaneous use. A practical, voluntary solution would be to agree on a broad per student license to cover **layers B** and **C**, *with a recognition that a significant portion of uses may already be licensed (including to the extent it can be established by an implied license) or do not require a license.* This would be negotiated as part of the tariff determined by the appropriate authorities (e.g., a copyright tribunal or board, possibly by arbitration).

To ensure that such a license would provide the 'peace of mind' and room to move required by educators to do their job, an extended repertoire approach (or the somewhat less palatable limitation of remedies available to non-participating rights holders) could be used.[874]

---

[874] See Daniel Gervais, 'Application of an Extended Collective Licensing Regime in Canada: Principles and Issues Related to Implementation' (2003) Canadian Heritage, available at <http://works.bepress.com/daniel_gervais/29/> accessed 25 October 2015).

Alternatively, remedial modulation such as limits on damages for works used under the scheme determined in the license could be imposed. If specific educational resources were increasingly licensed by rights holders directly, the license/tariff could be adjusted to reflect this. Conversely, rights holders might decide that collective licensing offers advantages and decide to rely on that mechanism (see Chapter 11). Many, perhaps most rights holders in the publishing industry would likely see the latter possibility as unlikely, but examples in other industries show that it is simply too early to tell, because the online educational resources market is still in the organizational phase.

An annual license is available to US colleges and universities for example from Copyright Clearance Center, Inc., the US reprographic rights collective (RRO). The license allows the reuse of text-based copyrighted content within higher education institutions. Educational uses include:

● coursepacks—paper and electronic
● class handouts
● library reserves—traditional and e-reserves
● electronic course content.

Excluded from this license are:

● inter-library loan (ILL)
● advertising or marketing
● creation of a database or a repository of works if it replaces the need for a subscription or is available for the use of multiple people outside the context of a class
● cover-to-cover copying of whole works.

Interestingly, the agreement does not 'license any uses by an institution that constitute fair use under the Copyright Act— a license is not required for those uses because they are permitted by law (under the fair use provisions of Section 107)'.

The third exclusion is a reflection of the fourth US fair use criteria ('the effect of the use upon the potential market for or value of the copyrighted work') and the second step of the three-step test. It should inform any decision to support unlicensed use of copyright material in education. Creating a web site for a class is an increasingly popular teaching tool. It should be encouraged, but with reasonable access and use restrictions if substantial parts of copyright material is used, especially material destined for that market.

Finally, any reconsideration of exceptions should include an assessment of the applicability of enforcement. Harsh remedies for infringements that

are barely over the line of what an exception allows are often counterpro-
ductive.[875] A huge gap between social norms and the legal norm is undesirable. It limits the degree of internalization and leads to more enforcement,
which in turn may further decrease respect for the law.[876] It may thus be
appropriate, as in the Israeli Copyright Act,[877] expressly to limit injunctive relief and statutory damages[878] for uses with limited commercial
impact that would still be captured by the restructured right proposed in
the previous chapter, and/or where public interest considerations, such
as compliance with consumer protection or protection of privacy must
be reconciled with copyright protection. This would catch most uses by
individuals and many of the other cases where potential litigation is used
to justify demands for new exceptions. Fortunately, courts typically have
the discretion to reduce damages and to refuse equitable remedies such as
injunctions.

---

[875]   See John Tehranian, 'Infringement Nation: Copyright Reform and the
Law/Norm Gap' (2007) 27 Utah L Rev 537 (available at <http://papers.ssrn.com/
sol3/papers.cfm?abstract_id=1029151> accessed 25 October 2015).
[876]   See Gervais (n 498).
[877]   2007 Law Statutes of Israel 34, adopted on November 25, 2007. According
to s 77, the Act enters into force on May 25, 2008.
[878]   In section 38.1.

# 11. Collective and extended licensing

## 11.1 INTRODUCTION

The three previous chapters propose a rewriting of the core copyright right and of exceptions and limitations to this right to match the role that copyright should play. Yet, even a restructured right and set of limitations and exceptions must be used and applied to 'real world' transactions, including licensing. Many licensing transactions are effected by organizations that specialize in the area of copyright licensing. They can make the system work better, though they have not always done so. This chapter explores the specific role that collective management organizations (CMOs) can fulfil in making the copyright system work better. The chapter also provides background information on the role and function of CMOs, which might be helpful for readers less familiar with this topic.

As discussed in Chapter 1, the copyright 'bundle of rights' (reproduction, public performance, etc.) can be shared by co-authors or their successors in title and it can be divided contractually by territory, language, type of media, etc. This means that, for a single use of a copyright work, a user may need several authorizations. A broadcasting example has already been mentioned (in Chapter 1): a radio station (broadcaster) wishing to copy music on its computers and then use that copy to broadcast the music over the airwaves and/or online will need to clear two rights: the right to copy (reproduction) and the right to communicate the work to the public.[879] The radio station will need both rights in respect to three different objects: (1) the musical work; (2) the sound recording; and (3) the musical performance of the musical work incorporated in the sound recording.[880] Our hypothetical broadcaster will need, at least occasionally but probably very frequently, to use works, sound recordings or

---

[879] Referred to in the US as part of the right of public performance and in some jurisdictions as part of the right of representation.

[880] Some countries grant only some of those rights. As of this writing (2016), the US is one of the very few World Trade Organization (WTO) Members that does not grant performers a statutory right in public performances. Many other countries do grant such a right but only as a right to 'remuneration' (payment)— i.e., not as a full exclusive right.

performances, the rights in which are owned in whole or in part by foreign nationals and entities.[881] The broadcaster probably uses hundreds of songs from around the world each week. However, a typical broadcaster does not know far enough in advance which songs it will play to seek individual licenses. Or the broadcaster may have a last-minute change of mind. For example, after the death of a famous artist or songwriter, several radio stations may decide to play that artist's music much more than usual. As Chapter 1 explains, a broadcaster may need several licenses if some of the rights that have been transferred are split among various right holders. A clearance process will be required for each song, performance and recording used by the station. The process may be performed for each work, performance or recording but the search and transaction costs would then likely be astronomical. New micro-transaction technology (for example using blockchain) may change this landscape but replacing the current CMO network did not seem imminent as of late 2018. A better option (at least for now) is for the broadcaster to have access to (ideally) any song, performance or recording and then be subject to a single payment and appropriate reporting requirements.

Why would a broadcaster not go online and find out who owns every piece of the work the broadcaster wants to use and obtain rights that way? There are at least three reasons. First, because, as discussed in Chapter 2, under Article 5(2) of the Berne Convention—incorporated by reference into the TRIPS Agreement—mandatory, copyright-specific formalities such as registration with a governmental entity cannot be imposed as a condition for the normal exercise or enjoyment of copyright. Put differently, a country party to the Berne Convention and/or member of the World Trade Organization (WTO) cannot impose a mandatory registration system for copyright, at least not if the sanction is a reduction in copyright rights below the minimum thresholds established under the Berne Convention (and the TRIPS Agreement).[882] Formalities can still play a role in reforming copyright, however.[883] Second, where registration systems exist (e.g., the US), not only are right holders, especially foreign ones, not required to use them, but once a work is registered, total or partial transfers of rights are often not registered, at least not in a timely fashion. This means that a radio station, even if it wanted to, could not

---

[881]  In fact, the broadcaster may not know whether the work, performance or recording is in fact from this or that country, and it may be from several. The composer might be American, the lyricist Canadian, the performer Nigerian and the producer German.

[882]  See Chapter 2.

[883]  See Chapter 12.

find some or all of the right holders it needs. Third, it is also rather obvious that the transaction costs would be astronomical and make it probably impossible to run the business.

What is needed to make the copyright system work for our hypothetical broadcaster is thus a license to use *all the right fragments* (reproduction, communication, etc.) for the copyright work(s) (music and lyrics) and the objects of related rights (performance and sound recording). In the first chapter of Part II, I suggested a way to restructure the copyright bundle to eliminate unnecessary fragmentation (leaving it up to contracts to fragment uses and assignments to reflect market realities[884]). This means that those who currently see their business as licensing rights fragments should in fact be licensing uses. This was proposed specifically for music in the US by the Copyright Office in a 2015 report.[885]

For many commercial users, the ideal license would be for all or as close to all existing works, performances and recordings that it might use (say the radio station used as an example above), which in practice means a license covering practically all music worldwide. This is what CMOs can do. In practice, they perform those licensing functions not just for radio stations (whether Hertzian or Internet-based), but also for small and large music users (hotels, cinemas, television stations, discotheques, restaurants, public event venues, etc.) and in areas other than music as well (including the reproduction of printed and online material for business and education, reproduction of images and photographs and use of plays in theatres).

## 11.2 COLLECTIVE LICENSING IN HISTORICAL PERSPECTIVE

Understanding the role of collective management may be easier with a bit of historical context. The story of the rise of collective management has become a quaint and famous tale. It begins in France with the French playwright Pierre-Augustin Caron de Beaumarchais in the

---

[884] Indeed this could be done without allowing any assignment other than by death, leaving the root copyright always with the author, as is the case in monist systems (e.g., Germany). Exclusive licensees (for all or only certain uses) should still be registered.

[885] United States Copyright Office, *Copyright and the Music Marketplace* (Washington, DC, 2015) (<copyright.gov/policy/musiclicensingstudy/copyright-and-the-music-marketplace.pdf> accessed 25 October 2015).

late 1700s.[886] Theatrical companies at the time were enthusiastic in their encouragement of promoting plays and artists, but were less generous when it came time to share in the revenues. The term 'starving artist' was more literal than figurative.[887] Beaumarchais was the first to express the idea of collective management of copyright. In 1777, he created the General Statutes of Drama in Paris. What began as a meeting of 22 famous writers of the *Comédie française* over some financial matters turned into a debate about collective protection of rights. 'They appointed agents, conducted the now famous pen strike and laid a foundation for the French Society of Drama Authors (*Société des auteurs dramatiques*).'[888] In 1838, Honoré de Balzac and Victor Hugo established the Society of French Writers,[889] which was mandated with the collection of royalties from print publishers.

A net of authors' societies, shaped by the cultural environment of each country, slowly spread throughout the world. As CMOs flourished in their own national states, the need for cooperation and harmonization at international level became apparent. In 1926 the International Confederation of Societies of Authors (CISAC) was established.[890] The founding members identified the need to establish both uniform principles and methods in each country for the collection of royalties and the protection of works and to ensure that literary and artistic property[891] were recognized and protected throughout the world.[892] Today, CISAC has 230 member societies in 120 countries,[893] a majority of which license either the public performance and communication of musical works or the reproduction of those works. Other CISAC members license reprography

---

[886]   A more detailed history is contained in the chapter on France.

[887]   Although this may be an exaggeration on the authors' part, this cliché remains, nonetheless, a somewhat accurate portrait of financially struggling artists both then and now.

[888]   See Consumer Project on Technology, 'Cptech's Page On Collective Management Of Copyrights' (2015) (available at <http://www.cptech.org/cm/copyrights.html> accessed 24 October 2015).

[889]   See Société des gens de lettres, 'Histoire' (2015) (available at <http://www.sgdl.org/> accessed 24 October 2015).

[890]   See International Confederation of Societies of Authors and Composers, 'Who We Are' (2015) (<http://www.cisac.org> accessed 24 October 2015).

[891]   The French law on authors' rights (the civil law version of copyright) is actually known as the Code of Literary and Artistic Property, Law No. 92–597 of 1 Jul 1992, last amended 5 August 2015.

[892]   By 'world', I am referring only to the Western World. This is inclusive of the Anglo-Saxon and *droit d'auteur* traditions of copyright.

[893]   As of October 2015. See International Confederation of Societies of Authors and Composers, 'Our Members' (2015) (<http://www.cisac.org/Our-Members> accessed 24 October 2015).

and reproduction of works of the fine arts and performance in theatres (the so-called 'grand rights'). Many countries have fostered the growth of CMOs through legislative initiatives in the belief that CMOs offer a viable solution to the problem of individually licensing, collecting and enforcing copyright.

Although the formation of CMOs may have once been considered revolutionary, the pivotal role that they continue to play as facilitators in the copyright system is more properly characterized as evolutionary. CMOs facilitate the establishment of unified methods for collecting and dispersing royalties and negotiate licensing arrangements for works. Yet, licensing and royalty collection and payment, while still important, are not the only preoccupations of CMOs. Over time the role of CMOs has evolved to oversee copyright compliance, fight piracy and perform various social and cultural functions.[894] Collective management has also allowed authors to use the power of collective bargaining to obtain more for the use of their work and negotiate on a less unbalanced basis with large multinational user groups.[895] Another feature of most collective schemes is that they value all works in their repertory on the same economic footing, which may be unfair to those who create works that may have a higher value in the eyes of users.

Although CMOs were initially promoted as an efficient way to collect and disburse monies to compensate right holders for use of their copyright works, increasingly the structure of CMOs, on both a national and an international level, has raised questions about their efficiency.[896] In addition to those significant structural issues, the market conditions and business trends of copyright holders are changing, and CMOs must adapt.[897]

---

[894] See Mihály Ficsor, *Collective Management of Copyright and Related Rights* (WIPO 2002) 99–106; and David Sinacore-Guinn, *Collective Administration of Copyright and Neighboring Rights* (Little, Brown & Co, 1993) 38–40.

[895] For instance, imagine if corporations such as music video television (e.g., MTV) negotiated the use and fee for each song/video it broadcast with individual artists. Although artists such as U2 or Madonna would be in a position to negotiate on a balanced power basis, the same would not be said for new groups struggling to find airtime.

[896] For example, often rights are governed by multiple CMOs within a particular nation. Coordination is therefore required not only among national CMOs, but also on an international basis. There is a significant lack of standards among many CMOs. Identification alone of an underlying right and right holder can be a convoluted process.

[897] As one author notes, 'efficiency will be what, in the end, members and music users most want and will most easily recognize, however it is measured'. See J Hutchinson, 'Collection and Distribution of Performing and Mechanical Royalties: A View from the UK' (1998) 84 *Copyright World* 30, 32.

Just as the role of CMOs is evolutionary, so is their underlying stated efficiency.[898] Although the current milieu of CMOs may have served both creators and users reasonably well in the past, the system must adapt to remain both efficient and relevant.[899]

## 11.3   HOW COLLECTIVE MANAGEMENT ORGANIZATIONS OPERATE

CMOs in various countries, and even sometimes within the same country, operate and are regulated differently. The principal comparators that one could use to categorize CMOs are:

- legal structure
- mode of rights acquisition
- mode of price-setting
- mode of licensing
- mode of distribution

The first comparator is heavily dependent on the legal regime and practices within each jurisdiction. As such it is both difficult to use it to make relevant distinctions and highly variable. Possible structures include for-profit or not-for-profit corporation; parastatal entity; state agency; cooperative; and various types of associations. Some jurisdictions require an authorization to set up a collective; others do not. In some cases, there may be value in requiring such authorizations, especially in less mature collective management markets, but that is not always so. By contrast, the four other comparators, which can be combined in myriad ways for different rights and types of uses, are fairly linear, when it comes to the modus operandi of CMOs. I now consider each one in turn.

---

[898]   As Peter Drucker notes, 'efficiency is doing better what is already being done'. See P Drucker, *Innovation & Entrepreneurship: Practices and Principles* (Harper & Row 1985) 277. Drucker discusses the nexus between technology, innovation and efficiency.

[899]   Licensing, collecting and enforcing copyright may now be done on an individual basis through the aid of technologies such as digital rights management systems. While most authors do not adopt the view that collectives will no longer have a role to play in the digital environment, the point is that new technologies alleviate some of the concerns relating to the inefficiency of individual licensing, collecting and enforcement of copyright.

### 11.3.1 Obtaining the Authority to License

Once established—sometimes, as just noted, with the support of a governmental authority—CMOs, most of which are private entities, obtain from a group of right holders (e.g., music composers, music publishers, book publishers, music performers) the ability to license on behalf of those right holders. This can be done by a full transfer of copyright (assignment) or by an agency agreement (license) allowing the CMO to represent the author or other right holder, whether on an exclusive or non-exclusive basis.

Most CMOs operate alone in their field in their territory, which means they are a de facto (and sometimes de jure) monopoly and as such subject to competition law scrutiny or to another, more specific form of governmental supervision. The 'one CMO per territory' model is not uniform worldwide, however. In the US, for example, there are several organizations licensing the same right to publicly perform music (and to perform publicly). In Europe, CMOs operating in the field of music may 'compete' within the territory of the European Union (EU) under the 2014 Directive.[900]

There is no uniformity in the type of government supervision either. In some jurisdictions (e.g., the US), the matter is dealt with under normal competition law—and enforced by the Department of Justice's antitrust division. In many European countries, a specific governmental body or commission was established for that purpose, sometimes operating in conjunction with the competition law enforcement agency.

Once a CMO has acquired the right to license on behalf of a plurality of right holders, it can enter into 'reciprocal representation agreements' with similar CMOs in other territories. Those agreements allow the parties to license each other's pool of rights, known as their repertoire (sometimes called repertory) in the other party's territory. For example, GEMA (the German music CMO) has such an agreement with the Society of Composers, Authors and Music Publishers of Canada (SOCAN), its counterpart in Canada. As a result, SOCAN can license GEMA's repertoire in Canada and GEMA can license SOCAN's repertoire in Germany.

---

[900] Directive 2014/26/EU of the European Parliament and of the Council of 26 February 2014 on collective management of copyright and related rights and multi-territorial licensing of rights in musical works for online use in the internal market [2014] OJ L84/72, recitals 26 and 27 [Collective Management Directive].

### 11.3.2   Setting Licensing Terms and Tariffs

Having acquired rights to as much of the world repertoire as possible, a CMO then turns to users. Often, the users and the CMO will disagree on the terms of a proposed license. Each jurisdiction basically decides which type of state intervention is warranted in that context. To take just a few examples, in the US, a federal judge is empowered (for the music performing rights organizations American Society of Composer, Authors and Publishers (ASCAP) and Broadcast Music, Inc. (BMI)) by the agreement entered into between those CMOs and the Department of Justice to decide the appropriate rate for the licenses. In Australia, Canada and the UK, a specialized copyright tribunal or board was established for that purpose. The power of the tribunal varies from one jurisdiction to another. In other cases, the matter is left entirely to civil courts, and in yet other jurisdictions, the terms of the license, or some of them, are set by government regulation or decree.

There is also a layer of regulation decided by the CMOs themselves, particularly in their reciprocal representation agreements. Most CMOs belong to CISAC, which has, over the years, developed a model for reciprocal representation agreements among its members. One of its features, for example, is to limit the percentage (10 per cent) of a CMO's total collections that can be used for social or cultural purposes. However, for private copying income, the percentages of funds collected used for such purposes may be much higher and that percentage is often prescribed by statute.

This takes us to the next step. Once a license has been signed by a user —often after a price-setting intervention by a court, specialized body or other third party, as just explained the CMO will receive payments from that user. In some cases, the payment is received not as consideration for the license but as a form of regulatory compensation for a form of use that is otherwise considered not licensable (as a practical and/or normative matter). A major example of this is the 'private copying' levies on blank media and on recording, copying, computer and other equipment. The monies are typically paid to a CMO according to applicable legislation or sometimes a decision by an administrative or quasi-judicial body (tribunal or board).

### 11.3.3   Usage Data Collection and Distribution

The CMO's task then is to distribute the funds. To do so, it will need data. From an operational standpoint, CMOs are essentially data collecting and processing entities.

CMOs need and process two types of information: identification and ownership. The former is used to identify works, performances and recordings in the CMO's repertoire. The latter is used to know whom to pay for the use of a particular work, recording or performance. The rights to a musical work composed by *x* may well have been sold to *y* and then to *z*. That work may have been performed by several artists and find itself on several recordings. Usage data reported by a user may use the name of the performer, song, recording, composer or any combination of the above. That identification data will not necessarily match current ownership data, and the CMO needs both. Worldwide databases of identification data have been created by CISAC and the International Federation of Reproduction Rights Organisations (IFRRO) for reprographic rights.[901] This allows their members to identify foreign works, performances and recordings licensed to them under reciprocal representation agreements. Each CMO tends to keep some or all of the ownership data (contact information, etc.) confidential.

Identification data is used to match usage data reported by users or generated by the CMO to specific works, recordings or performances. License contracts with users typically require usage reporting for all or part of the works, performances or recordings used. A radio station may use automatically generated computer logs, for example, to report 100 per cent of the music used. For other types of users (e.g., hotels, bars, restaurants), it is difficult to require 100 per cent reporting even if automatic song recognition software is used (especially for live performances). Sometimes surveys are used. For example, some (hopefully a representative number) of users may be surveyed for a specific period, and the data thus gathered will then be extrapolated to the class of users concerned using statistical regressions and other similar models.

Despite some work by CISAC in this area, there is little uniformity and each CMO decides for itself the extent of the surveys and the type and accuracy of data capture tools it wants to use and/or request its users to use. Typically, a larger pool of data will produce more accurate results and present a more fine-grained picture of works, performances and recordings actually used and the frequency of such use by each user of class of users, but it will increase the data processing costs, thereby diminishing the amount available for distribution. A CMO will normally distribute all of its collections after deduction of its administrative expenses, a small reserve and possible deductions for other purposes (e.g., social and

---

[901] See Ifrro.org, 'IFRRO' (2015) (available at <http://www.ifrro.org/> accessed 24 October 2015).

cultural purposes, including promotion of members, pension funds, award ceremonies, training programmes, etc.). A CMO's revenue includes not just the actual license fees or levies paid to it but interest earned on the 'float', that is, the period of time between the day a payment is received from a user and the day on which it will be paid (distributed) to a right holder or a foreign CMO.

Having matched usage data to identification data and knowing which works, performances or recordings have been used, the CMO then matches that dataset against ownership data to apportion the funds to each right holder and to foreign CMOs. Funds owed to right holders represented by CMO A through a reciprocal representation agreement with CMO B are typically not paid to the right holder directly. They are sent to CMO B together with appropriate usage data. CMO B will add this (foreign) income to its own income and distribute it to the right holders it represents. In some (fairly rare) cases, two CMOs will agree to let the other party to a reciprocal representation agreement license their respective repertoire but not exchange data or money. In other words, under this arrangement (known as a 'B' agreement in CISAC terminology), CMOs keep funds generated by the use of foreign works, performances or recordings in the other CMO's repertoire as part of their own revenue. This type of arrangement is less expensive to administer and may be helpful to fledgling CMOs or in situations in which strict currency exchange controls hamper cross-border financial flows. Yet, it is much less fair to right holders whose works, performances or recordings were used. For that reason, it is generally considered a temporary arrangement.

To increase fairness and accuracy, several CMOs keep discrete data pools. For example, a music performing right CMO may separate data from radio stations, television stations, cinemas, background music users (e.g., large stores), etc. It can then separate those revenue streams and use separate datasets for distribution. CMOs also sometimes use keys or factors that are applied to usage data before distribution. One model of distribution is known as 'follow the dollar' (or euro or yen, etc.). It means simply that each right holder will receive the exact share of the CMO's distribution pool that usage data has determined. Under other models, a further processing of the data occurs.[902] For example, some CMOs will give greater 'weight' to a work performed for the first time on their territory. Because first worldwide use typically occurs in the country where the composer or creator of the work resided, this tends to favour domestic

---

[902]    Even 'follow the dollar' distribution systems are sometimes tweaked to reflect other concerns.

right holders. Some CMOs actually evaluate the 'quality' of works and may give greater weight to a performance of contemporary music than to the latest pop single.

### 11.3.4  Transparency Issues

As this brief *tour d'horizon* has shown, collective management of copyright is complex. In several areas (e.g., rights ownership, financial data), CMOs tend to maintain secrecy (even from other CMOs) as a matter of policy. In other areas, the data (survey methods, distribution keys, etc.) is not released for a variety of reasons and often leads to claims of opaqueness. There is undoubtedly room for greater transparency, although many CMOs do provide annual reports and try to provide some insight into their operations.[903] What is arguably lacking is a uniform standard or a code of conduct in that respect.

## 11.4  CMOs AS CULTURAL AGENTS

Many CMOs see themselves as champions of the rights of their members (or represented right holders if not a membership organization) and recognize the value of administering rights that can be justified as human rights or natural rights. They have a cultural function but they also operate as 'businesses', handling large sums of money. The 2014 EU Directive on collective management certainly says as much. On the one hand, it provides that: '[I]nvestments made and held by the collective management organisation should be managed in accordance with criteria which would oblige the organisation to act prudently, while allowing it to decide on the most secure and efficient investment policy.'[904]

But on the other hand, it also says this:

> Collective management organisations play, and should continue to play, an important role as promoters of the diversity of cultural expression, both by enabling the smallest and less popular repertoires to access the market and by providing social, cultural and educational services for the benefit of their right holders and the public.[905]

---

[903]   CISAC also releases an annual survey of collections. See International Confederation of Societies of Authors and Composers, 'Governance' (2015) (available at <http://www.cisac.org/What-We-Do/Governance> accessed 24 October 2015).

[904]   Collective Management Directive, recitals 26 and 27.

[905]   Ibid., recital 3. Interestingly, the word 'efficient' or variants thereof appears nine times in the text of the Directive and the word 'cultural' 21 times.

CMOs perform *non-distributional* functions, that is, use of funds not meant to pay (distribute to) represented parties. Some CMOs perform *direct cultural functions*, including:

- grants, scholarship and award programs and related ceremonies;
- classes and workshops for represented parties (e.g., musical composition);
- promotion of works by represented parties, including festivals or other special events.

CMOs also perform *indirect cultural functions*, one might include:

- informational and educational function (about copyright, licensing etc.), including publications, social media presence, conferences, etc.,[906] and
- lobbying.

These activities are non-distribution related but they are different in nature. The *indirect* category is an easier case and not necessarily related to any particular cultural approach. It seems eminently defensible for an organization administering rights and licensing schemes to provide information. There are useful examples of CMOs providing this service.[907] In an era where legislative changes affecting CMOs and their represented parties are frequent and driven in significant part by lobbying, it is not only understandable that CMOs would spend some of their resources on lobbying. Indeed, it would seem negligent for them *not* to do so, especially in the face of efforts by record companies and Internet giants who use similar tools to seek their demise. The key here is to ensure proper administrative approvals by governing bodies within the CMOs and, more importantly, to focus such efforts so as to avoid unproductive overlaps with trade associations representing, for example, a subgroup of represented parties within the CMO.

The harder question is the funding of *direct* cultural activities. A CMO may easily justify small amounts of spending on, for example, annual awards, without raising too many eyebrows. Taking 10 per cent 'off the top' is, however, another matter, at least quantitatively. There is also a qualitative difference. The indirect activities described above form part

---

[906] This may include 'anti-piracy' campaigns, a matter to which the chapter returns below.

[907] Copyright Clearance Center, Inc (CCC). Naturally, one would want such information to be accurate, etc.

of a CMO's institutional function. They directly relate to its core mission. Direct cultural activities may be performed by others, in particular state or state-funded entities, including the government itself.

It may be helpful to split *direct* cultural activities performed by CMOs split into two categories, namely those that are mere good citizenship (awards) and are private to the CMO, and those that may seem to be of a more general or public nature, including funding of public events in cooperation with or instead of government. The latter can overlap with other non-distributional activities, such as the creation of a pension fund (as in Germany's GEMA's case), which does seem to be a function traditionally exercised or at least regulated by the state.

This does not mean that the category of 'public' direct cultural activities must necessarily be excluded. Such activities should, however, be subject to a higher degree of scrutiny. A CMO might argue that there is a public perception benefit in funding a public event, which may in turn make licensing easier. Many for-profit corporations perform 'public' functions of this nature to improve their image. Being associated with government in co-funding an event might provide similar benefits, at least in some contexts.[908] Finally, assisting a cash-strapped governmental authority in funding an event may generate goodwill for the CMO and thus become a form of useful 'lobbying', in addition to helping the creation of public goods.

CISAC provides in its model reciprocal representation agreement (RRA) that up to 10 per cent of funds collected including those that correspond to uses of foreign works or other material may be used for collective (including cultural) purposes. This provides CMOs with the dual pillars of legal authority they need to fund and perform such functions: direct contracts with domestic represented parties and RRAs for foreign parties.[909] One should add that law may mandate or at least create expectations that a CMO will fulfil cultural or other non-distributional purposes.[910] This legal authority does not provide the full picture, however.

---

[908] It may be seen as creating confusion as to the legal status of the CMO.

[909] See Sinacore-Guinn, n 894, 490–91.

[910] This was mentioned by the European Commission when proposing to regulate collective management in the EU, which happened in 2014, when the Collective Management Directive was adopted (see n 900). For a discussion, of the 'economic, cultural and social functions' of CMOs in the Union, see Péter Gyertyánfy, 'Why Is a European Directive on Collective Management Necessary? A Perspective from a New Member State of the EU' (2006) 53 *Journal of the Copyright Society of the USA* 71, 73.

In some cases, funds are collected not for licensing but as a form of levy 'administered' by a CMO as mandated by law. In such cases, the link between collected funds and specific represented parties is looser. This may be used to argue against such schemes, but is also provides more (some might say too much) flexibility in the use of such funds.[911] As Professor Jane Ginsburg noted, this may raise Berne-compliance issues.[912]

Whatever the source of funds, actual use of the funds should be decided fairly and democratically. If a Board makes all such decisions, then the Board's very credibility in managing the CMO will be engaged. If all members are called upon to make the decision, or at least voice an opinion, then that process should be managed transparently, but, as a matter of balance, without sacrificing the need for efficiency. There is, for example, a significant difference in that regard between a decision to set up a new, major annual award programme and making a time-sensitive executive decision to lobby for or against legislation introduced with little advance notice. In countries with less robust cultural industries, where the need to set up new systems and educational programs to implement copyright in a fair way is essential, the CMO can play an active role.

Finally, cultural activities may increase visibility and legitimacy and be a genuinely useful source of support from within a creative community, perhaps even more acutely in newer 'markets'.[913] Cultural activities also burden a CMOs' budget and resources, however. It is, in other words, a carefully crafted balance that each CMO must seek in its domestic cultural, political and economic context.

## 11.5   CMOs AND THE INTERNET

As discussed in Part I, from the seventeenth century until the 1990s copyright was aimed at, and used by, professional entities, either legitimate ones such as broadcasters, cable companies or distributors, or illegitimate ones, such as makers and distributors of pirated cassettes and later CDs

---

[911]   See Paul Edward Geller, 'Reprography and Other Processes of Mass Use' (1990) 38 *Journal of the Copyright Society of the USA* 21.

[912]   Jane C Ginsburg, 'Reproduction of Protected Works for University Research or Teaching' (1992) 39 *Journal of the Copyright Society of the USA* 181, 220.

[913]   Paul Kuruk, 'Protecting Folklore Under Modern Intellectual Property Regimes: A Reappraisal of the Tensions Between Individual and Communal Rights in Africa and the United States' (1999) 48(4) *American University Law Review* 769, 800–801 (footnotes omitted).

and DVDs. In many cases, these professionals were intermediaries with no particular interest in the content itself. Especially since the advent of the Internet, copyright has also been used to try to prevent *mass individual uses* (e.g., music and video file-sharing), in many cases without providing an equivalent market (e.g., legal downloads; monetized file-sharing). In addition, to enforce copyright, many right holders have tried to obtain usage information concerning individual users, thus confronting the right of privacy, a duel between rights not seen before because copyright was used by (or against) and transacted between professionals of the copyright industries, such as authors, publishers, producers, distributors and professional pirates, not by or against individual end-users.

Peer-to-peer (P2P) software, also known as 'file-sharing', radically altered the copyright landscape even more strikingly. P2P started as a centralized system (e.g., Napster),[914] the demise of which was made possible, in large part, by its easily locatable and controllable nature (small number of identifiable physical servers). The film and recording industry tried without much success to stop file-sharing (which uses a decentralized infrastructure, but with much less success). In addition to lawsuits, distributors use technological locks to make it harder to 'rip' music from compact discs and used spoofing (sending corrupted files into peer-to-peer networks). In response to those mostly failed attempts to control end-users, the focus shifted to a number of so-called 'graduated responses', namely schemes under which users believed to be infringing are sent gradually harsher notices possibly leading to disconnection of their Internet service.[915] Yet, exchanges of music and other files have apparently continued to grow, and events since seem to beg the question whether the music and film industry underestimated the strength of the demand for, and the societal role of, file-sharing and 'free content'. Distributed file-sharing technologies such as torrents are extremely hard to pin down, and users in jurisdictions where graduated response is in place are turning to anonymizing software and secure USENET access to continue to 'share' content undetected.[916] Even

---

[914] Napster was shut down after injunctions were issued by various courts in the US. See *A&M Records, Inc v Napster, Inc,* 284 F3d 1091 (9th Cir 2002).

[915] See Annemarie Bridy, 'Graduated Response and the Turn to Private Ordering in Online Copyright Enforcement' (2010) 89 *Oregon Law Review* 81; and P H Lim and L Longdin, 'P2P online file sharing: transnational convergence and divergence in balancing stakeholder interests' (2011) 33 *European Intellectual Property Review* 690–98.

[916] See Annemarie Bridy, 'Is Online Copyright Enforcement Scalable?' (2011) 13 *Vanderbilt Journal of Entertainment & Technology Law* 695, 705; and Lior Strahilevitz, 'Charismatic Code, Social Norms, and the Emergence of Cooperation on the File-Swapping Networks' (2003) 89 *Virginia Law Review* 505.

if the authors of the software and/or some operators of sites promoting the technology can be fined, as in the PirateBay case, trying to stop file-sharing may reduce Internet traffic and commerce and raise privacy concerns. This hardly seems an optimal solution. More importantly, the focus of the approach is a limited, property-based view of music designed to minimize unauthorized use. No one can demonstrate conclusively that the industry will in fact make more revenue because it is able to shut down Internet accounts of film or music users. As stores selling physical media disappear or morph into retail outlets for other types of products (e.g., DVDs, games and consoles) and the resentment of users whose Internet accounts were suspended (even if they were prepared to pay for a download) grows, the likelihood of a steep upward curve in the revenue stream of the film and music industry as a result of the crackdown remains low. Historically, copyright industries have done well, one could argue, *when their primary focus was not to minimize unauthorized uses but rather to maximize authorized use.*

In reality, the Internet-based picture is far more complex than the 'piracy' label implies.[917] File-sharing software is used in ways that mirror social media. People use the Internet to share music and music preferences. This is widely acknowledged as a form of free advertising, though one that does not necessarily compensate for lost sales. Yet, it seems clear that a significant, though admittedly hard to quantify, portion of film and music that is file-shared would never be purchased. It may remain on a user's computer because of today's computers' huge storage capacity, but it will be seldom if ever watched or listened to. If recipients of the file like the music, for example, they might become new fans and buy some music (data analyses show that many people get some of their music for free and pay for some—perhaps a form of self-appraisal of what music is worth to them in aggregate).

If this analysis is correct, even in part, online mass and P2P uses are best viewed as *a market* that needs to be organized. Part of that organization could be a broad license to use the music—and perhaps other types of content as well, and CMOs would be well placed to be partners in such an endeavour. In fact, it is difficult to see how such a system could operate without them.

Some observers argue that, with the aid of technology such as Digital Rights Management (DRM), the individual exercise of rights will become not only feasible but a more efficient solution, at least in certain

---

[917] For a discussion of the use of the term 'piracy', see William Patry, *Moral Panics and the Copyright Wars* (OUP 2009). Whereas the term is now used for its apparent rhetorical appeal, it has been in use for centuries as a fairly technical term of the art to refer, inter alia, to an unauthorized printing of a book, etc.

cases.[918] Perhaps a layer of individually or collectively managed transactional uses can coexist with a free or uncontrolled space that would be covered by a general license, perhaps one that would be paid as part of a monthly Internet, mobile or other subscription.

The role that CMOs will play in managing transactional uses and/ or general online use licenses (which one could then compare to a compensation regime) is unclear. It depends in large part on the degree to which they can facilitate and develop new business models. It may be the case that the advancement of new technologies will minimize the role of CMOs, but it could also lead to a significant expansion of their role. Whatever view is taken, the rationalization of the collective management of copyright remains an important task. In fact, if CMOs are to play the role of intermediary fully and efficiently, these organizations must acquire the rights they need to license digital uses of protected material and build (or improve current) information systems to deal with ever more complex rights management and licensing tasks.

The ability of CMOs to meet the needs of both authors and users is contingent on the evolution of both their internal practices, and the framework in which CMOs work to alleviate the many concerns of fragmentation within the current system explained in the first two chapters. Countries and CMOs throughout the world must adapt their laws and infrastructure to meet the challenges of digital technology irrespective of the philosophical underpinnings of each nation's copyright system—that is, whether it is rooted in economic rights, natural/human rights, utilitarian rights or any combination of these.

CMOs also will face possible competition from new players. Commercial entities that offer music and audiovisual content on the Internet, whether on a subscription basis or individual downloads, could combine their service with rights management in order to circumvent CMOs altogether. This is unlikely to work for individual authors, given the sheer number of authors, composers and lyricists concerned, but could apply to other right holders, especially publishers and producers, in light of the high concentration of the market among major labels and producers and, in the case of music, the decreasing daylight between music publishers and producers.

In countries where collective management is not mandatory or non-exclusive (e.g., the US), one already sees new entities offering their

---

[918] Martin Kretschmer, 'The Failure of Property Rules in Collective Administration: Rethinking Copyright Societies as Regulatory Instruments' (2002) 24 *European Intellectual Property Review* 126 133. Under this theory, right holders will use digital rights management systems to control and disseminate the use of their works.

services to authors and other copyright holders. New 'de facto CMOs' of that sort could operate on a trans-national basis, which raises the spectre of cross-territoriality.

After this analysis of the problems that copyright faces, illuminated by the spotlight of history and public policy and of the chaotic nature of copyright and related rights, it is time to turn to the role that CMOs are playing or may be called upon to assume in finding a way out of this rights maze.

## 11.6   DEFRAGMENTING DIGITAL USES COLLECTIVELY

Rights clearance systems are often based on the rights fragments discussed in Part I, and each tends to come with its 'practices' and other idiosyncrasies. This means that even if each such 'sub-system' (for a clearance process requiring several clearance transactions performed through different intermediaries (including several CMOs)) is efficient, the efficiency of the process as a whole is in jeopardy.

Clearly, collective management is not a neutral service. Given the fragility of Internet-based business models for delivery of copyright content on the Internet, economically efficient clearance 'should ensure that copyright administration favours no one delivery method over another'.[919] In fact, regardless of whether digital technology is involved, the standardization of practices among CMOs would lead to greater efficiencies and would alleviate some of the fragmentation under the current system. To play that role fully and efficiently, however, as noted above, these organizations must acquire the rights they need to license digital uses of protected material and build (or improve current) information systems to deal with ever more complex rights management and licensing tasks. Additionally, CMOs need to cooperate more fully on both a national and international scale to fully achieve their role as facilitators of rights clearance. The following suggestions are offered as potential means of achieving this goal.

Technology and, in particular, copyright management systems (CMS), are a useful tool in copyright clearance because they assist with proper identification of the works, performances, recordings and right holders involved and the rights that will need to be cleared. CMS are basically databases that contain information about content—works, discrete manifestations of works and related products and, in most cases, the author

---

[919]   M Einhorn and L Kurlantzick, 'Traffic Jam on the Music Highway' (2002) 8 *Journal of the Copyright Society of the USA* 417, 420.

and other right holders.[920] They may be used by individual right holders or by third parties who manage rights on behalf of others. A rights holder might use the system to track a repertory of works or products embodying such works (or substantial parts thereof), or an organization representing a group of right holders might use a CMS to track each right holder's rights and works. Such an organization might be a literary agent representing multiple writers or, more commonly, a CMO.

Some CMS allow right holders or CMOs to automatically grant transactional licenses to users without transactional human intervention, which has the benefit of keeping transaction costs low and making licensing an efficient, Internet-speed process: licenses to use a specific work can be granted online, 24 hours per day, to individual users. Ideally, such licenses will be tailored to a user's needs.[921] For example, a company may want to post a flattering newspaper article on its website or send it via email to its customer base; an individual author may decide to purchase the right to use an image, video clip or song to use in her or his own creative process; a publishing house might purchase the right to reuse previously published material.[922] CMS may also be used to deliver content in cases in which the user does not have access to such content in the required format or to create licensing sites or offer licensing options at the point at which the content is made available.

To be optimally efficient and able to deal with digital usage information, online members and work registration, user requests and online transactional licensing (where such licensing on reasonably standard terms

---

[920] See J Cunard, 'Technological Protection of Copyrighted works and Copyrighted Management Systems: A Brief Survey of the Landscape' (ALAI Congress, NY, 13–17 June 2001); and Daniel Gervais, 'Electronic Rights Management and Digital Identifier Systems' (1999) 4 *Journal of Electronic Publishing* (available at <http://quod.lib.umich.edu/cgi/t/text/text-idx?c=jep;view=text;rgn=main;idno=3336451.0004.303> accessed 25 October 2015).

[921] Many licenses to use a work are granted where the user obtains permission for several different uses of a work. It may be the case that the user requires the work for only a specific purpose. Why should the user pay to acquire rights to use a work in a manner for which the user has no intention of using it?

[922] CCC (n 907) licenses reproduction of printed material for inclusion in 'digital course packs', reuse of material on websites, intranets, CD-ROMs and other digital media. CCC also offers a repertory-based license for internal digital reuse of material by corporate users. Interestingly, in the latter programme, users can only scan material not made available by the publisher in digital form. CCC's ability to license digital uses is entirely based on voluntary and non-exclusive rights transfers from right holders. See Copyright Clearance Center, 'Rights Licensing Expert-Copyright Clearance Center' (2015) (available at <http://www.copyright.com> accessed 24 October 2015).

is possible), CMOs need CMS with both an efficient 'back-end' system and a user-friendly online interface ('front-end'). However, building an all-encompassing online multimedia licensing system operated jointly by all CMOs in a country is hard to justify under current licensing practices or indeed in light of prevailing market conditions.[923]

The sheer number of CMOs that may be involved in the licensing of a single economic use of a protected work (or works and possibly combined with one or several related rights) poses another problem. To implement an efficient system, CMOs should cooperate within appropriate groupings (i.e., CMOs having a sufficient degree of commonality) to limit the number of systems to be developed, and they should develop compatible systems and standards to ensure that the exchange of data will be possible.[924]

A repertoire license (i.e., one that allows the user to use any work or object contained in the repertory of works licensed by a CMO) presents an attractive alternative in the online environment. The two most relevant uses of such licenses are where there are inherent difficulties in advance clearance of rights and where consolidation is more practical from a user's (and sometimes creator's) perspective. From a functional point of view, CMOs are a practical and usually Berne-compatible substitute for a compulsory license because of the multitude of uses and the difficulty of advance clearance. This solution has the advantage of being fairer to users and potentially achieves administrative efficiencies for both creators and users. Such a system would be fairer to users in that there would no longer be a discrepancy in fees to be paid for similar uses of a work.[925] In essence, a single tariff could be established for different types or uses of works. A user would pay an 'admission fee' at the entrance.

---

[923] These systems often perform several functions. The first, if so required, is to break down the rights in a work (more the case with multimedia works). The second function is to identify the right holder(s) of the work. The third function is then to clear these rights, followed by establishing license terms, and payment of fees for the use of a work. Such technologies facilitate the expediency and efficiency of licensing content online. See T Koskinen-Olsson, 'Secure IPR-Content on the Internet' (ALAI Congress, NY, 13–17 June 2001).

[924] These would seem to follow the best practices emerging from ongoing efforts in countries other than the US. This will be explored in greater detail when addressing centralized licensing regimes or one-stop-shop services.

[925] As it stands, collectives sometimes negotiate different licensing terms and fees with users regardless of whether the actual 'use' of the work is similar in nature.

## 11.7  EXTENDED LICENSING

A system that is worth a serious look to make the licensing of mass online uses more efficient and workable is the extended repertoire system (ERS—also known as 'extended collective licensing'), used, for now, mostly in all Nordic countries[926] though it is under consideration, or being implemented, in other parts of the world, including the US and in Africa, Central and Eastern Europe, and Canada.[927] ERS is a voluntary assignment or transfer of rights from right holders to a CMO followed by a *legal extension of the CMO's repertoire* to encompass non-member right holders. In simple terms, the licensing system, once it crosses a certain threshold, becomes an opt-out regime for right holders instead of an opt-in. It greatly simplifies the acquisition of rights by the CMO. In fact, it has been called a 'backup legal license', but this expression is confusing because the right holder can opt out of the system. This, of course, is not possible under a compulsory or legal license.[928]

Usually the legal extension applies after a determination that a 'substantial' number of right holders in a given category have agreed to join a CMO.[929] Then the repertoire of the CMO is automatically extended (for the licensing scheme concerned) to other domestic right holders in the same category and to all foreign right holders. The license also extends to deceased right holders, particularly in cases in which estates have yet to be properly organized. Thus, ERS is a powerful solution to the orphan works issue.

The extended repertoire is an interesting model for countries where, on the one hand, right holders are reasonably well organized and informed, and, on the other hand, a great part of the material that is the object of licenses comes from foreign countries. It is often more difficult and time consuming to obtain an authorization for the use of foreign material. The extended repertoire provides a legal solution to this situation, because the agreements struck between users and right holders will include all non-

---

[926] See Tarja Koskinen-Olsson and Vigdis Sigurdardottir, 'Collective Management in the Nordic Countries' in Daniel Gervais (ed.) *Collective Management of Copyrights and Related Rights* (3nd edn, Kluwer, 2015).

[927] See Gervais (n 881).

[928] Internationally, very few countries have adopted compulsory licensing of digital uses. Such a system exists in the Danish legislation but has yet to be applied in practice. It would be an extension of the license existing under ss 13 and 14 of the Danish Copyright Act, 14 Jun 1995, No 395.

[929] Substantiality is contextual. A new collective organizing right holders in a given area for the first time should have a much lower substantiality threshold to pass than a well-established collective trying to obtain an extension of repertoire for a new licensing scheme.

excluded domestic and foreign right holders. Finally, by accelerating the acquisition of rights, the extended repertoire also increases the efficiency and promptness of royalties' collection. The monies redistributed to right holders are thereby increased.

An argument raised against the ERS is its alleged incompatibility with Article 5(2) of Berne, which prohibits formalities concerning the existence and exercise of the rights granted by virtue of the Convention. This argument must fail for the reasons explained in Chapter 2 if the opt-out system is efficient, transparent and preferably offered at no cost to the right holder.

Extended licensing can be achieved in a variety of ways. One may limit remedies available to right holders who do not opt out of a licensing regime for example, to what would otherwise have been available under the collective regime. It is a very useful way to deal with unknown or inactive right holders and thus provides a tempting solution to the orphan works issue. As noted in a report by the US Copyright Office:

> [T]he Copyright Office has proposed in this Report a statutory framework known as extended collective licensing(ECL), which can be used to authorize projects on terms set forth by the parties under government supervision. Under this model, licenses are issued and administered by collective management organizations (CMOs) representing copyright owners in particular categories of works. CMOs would be authorized by the Copyright Office to issue licenses for mass digitization projects and to collect royalties on behalf of both members and non-members of the organizations, based on transparent formulas and accounting practices. All rightsholders would have the right to opt out, and procedures for doing so would be clear and unencumbered. The framework thus would seek to eliminate the practical impediments to mass digitization by creating a centralized, market-based mechanism for the clearance of rights and the compensation of copyright owners. It also recognizes that no licensing entity has or will ever have the full portfolio of rights that are implicated by mass digitization projects.[930]

There may thus be a greater role for CMOs in the area of mass online uses. If copyright's excludability does not easily reach individual end-users, neither does it reach, without difficulty, users who have no direct (one-on-one) transactional contact with the right holders concerned. To maximize efficiency, it seems that copyright's power to exclude should be limited to cases in which an exclusive distributorship (or other form of

---

[930]   United States Copyright Office, *Orphan Works and Mass Digitization* (June 2015) (available online: <http://copyright.gov/orphan/reports/orphan-works2015. pdf> accessed 16 November 2016). The report contains a detailed description of the features of the extended licensing regime.

dissemination) is negotiated by the first owner of copyright or someone else who acquired rights from that first owner and in cases of commercial piracy. Copyright is not intended to be used to stop uses by end-users completely. Historically, it has been used to *organize* markets for those uses. Additionally, copyright works best, as an exclusion tool, when its rules are internalized by users. If one abandons attempts to *stop* end-users, copyright remains as a market organization tool, namely as an entitlement to remuneration for mass uses at least when such uses reach the level of interference with normal commercial exploitation under the Berne Convention and the three-step test.[931]

## 11.8 IS A LOCAL CMO PREFERABLE?

Why would a local CMO be preferable to a global one? As with the dilemma presented in the introductory paragraphs, one could present a case of simple business efficiency. A local CMO would normally find it easier to communicate in the local language(s), including in providing information on its website and in reports sent to represented parties; it might know and understand the local licensing markets and practices better than a foreign counterpart. It may find it easier to 'sell' licenses and talk to policy makers as a local player. Some of these advantages can be 'bought' by a foreign CMO, which could for example hire local staff and have a local presence.

Riis and Schovsbo have argued, for example, that extended collective licensing is easier to apply and use in the cultural context of the Nordic countries.[932] By contrast, US CMOs tend to do very little in terms of direct cultural functions, in part because the largest CMOs, the two principal performing rights organizations (ASCAP and BMI), are operating under constant antitrust scrutiny as reflected in their 'consent decrees'. While European CMOs are often seen as part of the cultural fabric in their territory, US CMOs operate much more as business entities, tolerated as 'monopolies' and often described as 'necessary evils'.[933] This prompted a well-known expert on US collectives to note that to 'the non-US observer, the institutions and methods by which music performing rights are defined

---

[931]   See Chapter 3.
[932]   Thomas Riis and Jens Schovsbo, 'Extended Collective Licenses and the Nordic Experience: It's A Hybrid but Is It A Volvo or A Lemon?' (2010) 33 *Columbia Journal of Law & the Arts* 471, 497–8.
[933]   Glynn S Lunney, 'Copyright Collectives and Collecting Societies: The United States Experience' in Gervais (n 473) 339, 340.

and licensed and by which the license fees are collected in the United States of America may seem very strange'.[934]

In the end, this is perhaps where the normative distinction lies. For a represented party, using a CMO implies if not collectivization at least some degree of centralization.[935] Represented parties agree to work on the same terms to license their works. In the case of ASCAP, for example, every 'member (writer or publisher) signs the identical membership agreement, which, in conjunction with the Articles of Association defines his relationship with ASCAP'.[936] This is quite typical. The underlying cultural context may dictate or at least point to a higher degree of collectivization, which in turn might lead to a greater propensity to spend some of the funds for collective purposes. In a less collectivist system, using funds to promote, say, up-and-coming authors, might be frowned upon as a form of income redistribution. A CMO licensing across borders will have to face the fact that different cultures bring different challenges. But then again, even the French eat lunch at McDonald's some of the time.

Not all represented parties, even domestics ones, will see eye-to-eye. Major music publishers might see the collectivization equation differently than smaller publishers and individual songwriters and composers. Major publishers might ponder the fact that using the services of a CMO implies transparency. They might prefer to control information flows to the songwriters they work with. They might prefer to license uses directly, which they can do under US consent decrees within certain limits. The efficiency for them in doing direct deals is considerably more noticeable than for many other represented parties. However, by taking low-hanging fruit away from CMOs, they cause an increase in the CMOs' fees to collect harder-to-reach users and license fees, which then negatively impacts all represented parties. A major publisher adding gains from direct licensing easy uses and subtracting additional fees (which are imposed on all represented parties) on other uses may still come out ahead because the losses are shared with others, not the gains. Attempts by international publishers to direct license services such as Pandora may have backfired, however, partly because of the need to be either 'in or out' not halfway in at the expense of

---

[934] John M Kernochan, 'Music Performing Rights Organizations in the United States of America: Special Characteristics; Restraints; and Public Attitudes' (1985) 10 *Columbia Journal of Law & the Arts* 333.

[935] See Sinacore Guinn (n 894), 17–23.

[936] Bernard Korman and I Fred Koenigsberg, 'Performance Rights in Music and Performing Rights Societies' (1986) 33 *Journal of the Copyright Society of the USA* 332, 353.

other represented parties.[937] Then again, major publishers, most of whom are now basically small subsidiaries of major record labels,[938] would probably not regard the resulting systemic weakening of the CMO as a negative. In the same vein, they, and financial markets, may resist letting CMOs spend any of 'their' money on collective purposes and thus negatively affect their bottom-line. For them the dilemma does not really exist.

Individual and smaller represented parties are in different situations. Those who collect the most (CMOs anecdotally report that a few members usually collect the lion's share of distributed income) may be more or less prone to a collective approach. Solidarity with represented parties with much lower payments in the form of cultural functions, both direct and indirect, may not appeal equally to all and again be a reflection of the broader cultural backdrop.

Normatively, one could posit that a local CMO would be better at understanding and defending the interests of local represented parties, including for distributional purposes. The flip coin of course is that foreign represented parties might feel differently. For example, while American and British pop music dominates that market in many and perhaps most countries, the interests of American and British songwriters and publishers are rarely represented on the boards of local CMOs. This facet of the discussion cuts both ways, therefore. It can be dealt with: a foreign CMO can hire experts in local music etc. in the same way that it can hire experts in local licensing practices. A local CMO representing mostly (in terms of material actually used by licensees) foreign parties can gain their trust by being both.

The next question is whether striving for efficiency and transparency is compatible with the performance of cultural functions. Here, as with licensing and represented parties, even a foreign CMO might be able to gauge the best way to promote 'culture' in the local scene. This requires

---

[937] See Todd Brabec, 'The Performance Right—A World in Transition' (2015) *Winter Entertainment & Sports Lawyer* 1, 38: '[I]n September 2013, Judge Cote, the ASCAP judge, ruled that a selective withdrawal of new media rights by publisher members could not be implemented without violating the consent decree.'

[938] A good example is in the blatant unfairness of financial flows. In 2013, Pandora paid $290 million to record companies and artists, with all three PROs collecting a total of less than $25 million for songwriters and publishers. Assuming songwriters and publishers shared 50/50, the songwriters got $12.5 million, and the corporate right holders pocketed $302.5 million minus an unknown *net* amount (that is, not repaid to the company) paid to and retained by artists. See ibid., 39. For interactive streaming services (such as Spotify, which is partly owned by the record companies) the splits in the US are much worse still, approaching 98:2. See Schwartz, 'Coda' (n 679).

a willingness to do so (both devoting funding and hiring the right 'talent' to find appropriate targets to spend it on). The legitimacy of the spending may, however, be questioned.

As a business matter, a case may be made that having larger CMOs perhaps working in multiple territories (subject to the caveats in the previous paragraphs) could lead to efficiency gains in systems development for example. A single 'back-office' to process data, maintain websites etc. may be less expensive. It is also possible for several distinct CMOs to cooperate to share this service. In other words, the efficiency argument can be used to justify cooperation and competition among CMOs.

# 12. Formalities

## 12.1 INTRODUCTION

Formalities, properly structured, can serve a useful role in a restructuring of copyright. The early days of US copyright law provide several examples of both good and bad impacts that formalities can have. By excluding from copyright works of foreign authors, the early US system served the interests of publishers—who felt their industry relied upon being able to reproduce foreign works without being required to pay for that privilege—and the general intellectual and entertainment interests of the early republic in having potentially faster (because it was local) and less expensive access to foreign books.[939] By requiring that copyright works display a notice indicating the identity and residence of the author, and the date of publication, consumers could ascertain whether copyright protection had been 'claimed'.[940] Requiring registration generated publicly available information on 'claimed' works that users could consult in order to obtain metadata.[941] Requiring that instruments of transfer be recorded enabled license-seekers to ascertain the identity of the present owner of a work.[942] Requiring that authors deposit copies of their works with a clerk's office enabled the cultivation of a national repository of works.[943] These formalities also served to limit the number of works receiving copyright protection, such that many works immediately entered the public domain upon publication.[944] Finally, the renewal formality, requiring that

---

[939] William Briggs, *The Law of International Copyright* (Sweet & Maxwell 1906) 637.

[940] The requirement that published copies of a work feature information about the identity of the author, date of publication, and the author's state of residence became added to the scheme of formalities in 1802. Act of Apr. 29, 1802, ch. 36, 2 Stat. 171 (1802).

[941] Act of May 31, 1790, ch. 15, 1 Stat. 124 § 3 (1790) [hereinafter 1790 Act].

[942] Act of June 30, 1834, ch. 157, 4 Stat. 728 (1834).

[943] 1790 Act, § 4.

[944] *See* Christopher Sprigman, 'Reform(aliz)ing Copyright' (2004) 57 *Stanford Law Review* 485, 503: proposing that at least 80–90 per cent of works published during the decade under the 1790 Act immediately entered the public domain for lack of registration.

creators record and publish a second time should they desire a second term of protection, likewise served a filtering function.[945]

Though beneficial in many respects, these formalities were also severely criticized. American creators complained that it was impossible to compete against royalty-free English works in the market for publication, thus limiting their own potential development and retarding the development of American literary and scholarly publishing industries.[946] A number of formalities were difficult to comply with and, as a result, many works were accidentally un-registered or registered incorrectly.[947] Moreover, the expense of complying with these formalities was not negligible. Supporting evidence may be found in the bills that authors and publishers (most of whom favoured protection of foreign works) were able to get introduced in Congress almost every year from 1837 until 1890.[948]

Protection for the works of foreign authors remained unavailable, however, until 1891.[949] Passed by Congress that year, the Chace Act provided that a work was protected if: (a) it had been printed from type set within the United States; and (b) two copies of the American imprint were deposited in the Copyright Office on or before the date of first publication anywhere else.[950] The Act was based on the principle of reciprocity.[951] The

---

[945]　See ibid., 519: noting that 85 per cent of works were never renewed under the original system.

[946]　See Briggs (n 939) 637–8. Other US authors used a backdoor to get protection. Mark Twain—who had been published without consent or payment in Canada—moved to Montreal to establish residency there and protect his copyrights in Canada and other Berne Union member states. See 'Restoring The Balance: Panel on Contracting and Bargaining' (2005) 28 *Columbia Journal of Law & the Arts* 419, 423: comment by Nick Taylor, President, Author's Guild; see also 'Oversight on International Copyrights: Hearing Before the Subcomm on Patents, Copyrights and Trademarks of the Comm of the Judiciary', 98th Cong. 42 (1984) (report of the US Copyright Office).

[947]　*See* Catherine Seville, *The Internationalisation Of Copyright Law: Books, Buccaneers And The Black Flag In The Nineteenth Century* (CUP 2006) 248.

[948]　*See* Robert Spoo, 'Ezra Pound's Copyright Statute: Perpetual Rights And The Problem Of Heirs' (2009) 56 *UCLA Law Review* 1775, 1785; and Seville, ibid., 160–61, 170, 217.

[949]　Chace International Copyright Act of Mar. 3, 1891, ch. 565, 26 Stat. 1106, 1107 (1891) [hereinafter Chace Act]; *see also* Richard R. Bowker, *Copyright: Its History And Its Law* (Houghton Miffin 1914) 314, 346–70; *see also* Spoo, ibid., at 1785–7.

[950]　Chace Act, 26 Stat 1107.

[951]　The Chace Act 'shall only apply to a citizen or subject of a foreign state when such foreign state or nation permits to citizens of the United States of America the benefit of copyright on substantially the same basis as its own citizens'. Chace Act, 26 Stat. 1110.

first requirement (known as the 'manufacturing clause') was only phased out in the 1980s.[952] The second (deposit) requirement is still in place but, as we shall see, no longer linked to copyright protection. Still, in spite of the various critiques, the American copyright system saw few changes to its formality requirements over the course of nearly two centuries.

The rest of the world—or at least Europe and its empires—was moving in a different direction. Beginning with the signing of the first Berne Convention in 1886, the seed of an international harmonization of copyright was planted and, significantly, from the very beginning it limited the impact of mandatory formalities.[953] Almost all of the participants in this endeavour, unlike the US, followed a *droit d'auteur* approach, a component of which is the recognition of the moral rights of authors in their works.[954] They espoused a 'natural rights' justification for copyright protection that fundamentally conflicted with the imposition of mandatory formalities.[955] Indeed, rights inuring as natural consequence of the act of creation should not require compliance with state-prescribed formalities. Seen as a simple Lockean proposition, it would seem inequitable to require that the labourer register his bushel of apples before being permitted to claim ownership of them. Seen in a more Hegelian hue, the question is slightly different but the answer remains the same: If the work one has created is an extension of person and identity, the government cannot or should not condition the right on compliance with administrative formalities.[956] The

---

Presidential proclamations allowed citizens of various countries access to the formalities leading to protection of their works in the US, subject to the manufacturing clause: 1891 Presidential Proclamation No. 3, 27 Stat. 981–82 (Belgium, France, Great Britain, Switzerland); 1892 Pres. Proc. No. 24, 27 Stat. 1021–22 (Germany). *See also* Briggs (n 939) 645. Further proclamations issues extended the same privileges to citizens of many other nations. *See also* Stephen Ladas, *The International Protection of Literary and Artistic Property* vol. I (MacMillan 1938) 837–8; and Binyamin Kaplan, 'Determining Ownership of Foreign Copyright: A Three-Tier Proposal' (2000) 21 *Cardozo Law Review* 2045, 2051.

[952] See Paul Goldstein, *Copyright's Highway: From Gutenberg to the Celestial Jukebox* (Stanford University Press 2003) 152.

[953] See Chapter 2.

[954] The major exception was the UK, which was party to the discussion and signed the Convention. See Berne Convention Centenary, ibid., 87, 108 and 130.

[955] See Ginsburg (n 323) 994: 'If copyright is born with the work, then no further state action should be necessary to confer the right; the sole relevant act is the work's creation.'

[956] The principle of formality-free protection can also be considered to be reflected in the 1948 United Nations Declaration on Human Rights, which mentions the 'protection of the moral and material interests resulting from any

*droit d'auteur* approach was thus enshrined in the Berne Convention (see Chapter 2).[957]

The perceived burden of complying with formalities and the strict application of the US manufacturing clause may have been in the minds of the Berne negotiators in Berlin in 1908, which resulted in the adoption of the broad ban on formalities.[958] The Berne Union members went a step further in their condemnation of 'piracy' in the US by adopting a Protocol to the Berne Convention in 1914.[959] Proposed by the UK, it was designed as retaliation for the manufacturing clause and permitted Berne members to deny protection to US works, even if first published in their territory.[960]

Meanwhile, although the US refused to join Berne (until 1989), it still desired protection for the works of American authors abroad. To that end, it entered into a series of bilateral copyright treaties.[961] It also headed

---

scientific, literary or artistic production of which he is the author': UNDHR, art. 27(2).

[957]  As measured by the number of signatories (168 as of 23 December 2015) and giving consideration to the fact that Berne has been incorporated into TRIPS Agreement.

An updated list of Berne members is available at <wipo.int/treaties/en/ShowResults.jsp?lang=en&treaty_id=15>.

[958]  The Acts of the 1908 Berlin Conference do not mention formalities in the US (or in any other country by name for that matter) but most of the examples mentioned during the debates point to the US. For example, the Records state: 'it is recalled that there was a time not so long ago when, to guarantee a work protection in a foreign country . . .. [I]t was necessary to register and often even to deposit that work in the foreign country within a certain time limit'. Berne Convention Centenary, note 82, 148.

[959]  See ibid., 20.

[960]  Additional Protocol to the International Copyright Convention on Nov. 13, 1908, signed at Berne, 1914, 1 LNTS 243 [hereinafter 1908 Protocol]. The Protocol entered into force on 20 April 1915. See Paul Goldstein, *International Copyright: Principles, Law, And Practice* (OUP 2001) 22; and William Belanger, 'U.S. Compliance with the Berne Convention' (1995) 3 *George Mason Independent Law Review* 373, n. 3. The Protocol allowed Berne members to restrict the protection given to works of authors who are nationals of a non-Union country, which 'fails to protect in an adequate manner the works of authors who are nationals of one of the countries of the Union': 1908 Protocol § 1.

[961]  Reciprocal copyright arrangement with Italy entered into force October 28, 1892: 9 Bevans 104. Presidential Proclamation No. 3, 27 Stat. 981–82 (Belgium, France, Great Britain, Switzerland); 1892 Pres. Proc. No. 24, 27 Stat. 1021–22 (Germany); See E. Gabriel Perle, 'Copyright Law And the Copyright Society of the U.S.A. 1950–2000' (2000) 47 *Journal of the Copyright Society of the USA* 397, 410:

For most of its history, the United States was insular in its regard for international, multilateral protection of the works of U.S. authors in foreign

the effort to develop an alternative to the Berne Convention, namely the Universal Copyright Convention (UCC).[962] Additionally, the US participated in the Buenos Aires Convention, which provided for mutual recognition of member nations' copyrighted works subject to those works bearing a copyright notice.[963] However, many US copyright holders found that the UCC and other instruments negotiated by the US provided insufficient protection for their works, as they contained few specific requirements aside from national treatment.[964] The fact that a number of American authors, including famously Mark Twain, would simultaneously publish their works in Berne member countries when first publishing domestically in order to avail themselves of the widest possible protection for their works bears testimony to this perception.[965]

When the US finally acceded to Berne in 1989, judging that benefits to US copyright exporters outweighed the negatives,[966] it abandoned some of its formality requirements. A number of scholars have complained that Berne's prohibition of formalities imposes deadweight costs on society and limits the public domain.[967] A number of reform proposals advocate introducing a new system of formalities that embraces modern technology

---

countries and protection of the work of foreign authors in the United States. The U.S., rigidly wedded to the pre-requisite formalities of copyright notice and registration, both anathema to most of the rest of the world, found it difficult or impossible to be part of the international copyright world except through a rather haphazard collection of unilateral copyright treaties. During the period from 1950 to 2000, however, the United States sought valiantly, and in large measure successfully, to join the rest of the world in a copyright context.

See also *Treaties and Other International Agreements of the United States of America 1776–1949* (Charles I. Bevans (ed.), 1974).

[962] The US participated in the Universal Copyright Convention (UCC), a treaty established by the United Nations mandating mutual recognition of copyright protection subject to a notice requirement. The Universal Copyright Convention, July 24, 1971, 25 UST 1341, 943 UNTS 178, arts 2, 3 (available at <portal.unesco.org/en/ev.php-URL_ID=15381&URL_DO=DO_TOPIC&URL_SECTION=201.html> last accessed April 24, 2013). The UCC has been superseded because: (a) the TRIPS Agreement incorporates Berne, not the UCC (TRIPS Agreement, art. 9.1); and (b) the Appendix declaration relating to Article XVII of the UCC provides in part that 'The Universal Copyright Convention shall not be applicable to the relationships among countries of the Berne Union.'

[963] Buenos Aires Copyright Convention, 11 August 1910, art. 3, 38 Stat. 1788.

[964] See David M Spector, 'Implications of United States adherence to the Berne Convention' (1989) 11(5) *European Intellectual Property Review* 162, 163.

[965] Ibid., 168.

[966] Berne Convention Implementation Act of 1988, Pub. L. No. 100-568, 102 Stat. 285 [hereinafter BCIA].

[967] See, e.g., Sprigman (n 944) 524; William M Landes and Richard A Posner,

while honouring the US Constitutional direction of 'progress of Science and the Useful Arts'. Evaluation of these proposals requires: dissecting the motivations for desiring a return to formalities; discussing the domestic and international constraints on such proposals; and comparing the various proposals' impact on the future of copyright jurisprudence.

To identify the proper role, if any, of formalities, I review arguments championing the imposition of new formalities and the obstacles they face and offer a set of recommendations.

A number of prominent copyright scholars have identified undesirable consequences attending the prohibition of formalities.[968] One of the most common critiques is that it leaves insufficient publicly available information about the ownership and protection status of works, making rights clearance much more difficult, at least for nonprofessional users. A more substantive critique is that formality-free copyright subjects all works to protection, creating a situation where routine activity may lead to the creation of copyrighted works (e.g., common business email) and to copyright infringement (copying of that email) and where copyright may even be exploited as a tool of censorship (e.g., enjoin the posting of the email). The critique often focuses on the interests of users but also mentions authors. Because they must opt out of their exclusive rights rather than opt in, many third-party uses that an author would be happy to authorize are prevented under the current regime.[969] It has been argued that, in some cases, these issues may also constrain the ability to create and freedom of speech.[970]

Formalities were a filter, and that filter is essentially gone. Compliance had a cost (in time and fees) and an author or other rights holder would often comply if such costs were perceived to be lower than expected

---

'Indefinitely Renewable Copyright' (2003) 70 *University of Chicago Law Review* 471, 479–81.

[968] Lawrence Lessig, *The Future of Ideas: The Fate of the Commons in a Connected World*, (Random House 2001) 251–2; by the same author, *Free Culture: How Big Media Uses Technology and the Law to Lock Down Culture and Control Creativity* (Penguin Press 2004) 287–90; and *Remix* (n 173) 260–65. *See also* Cecil C Kuhne, III, 'The Steadily Shrinking Public Domain: Inefficiencies of existing Copyright Law in the Modern Technology Age' (2004) 50 *Loyola Law Review* 549; James Gibson, 'Once and Future Copyright' (2005) 81 *Notre Dame Law Review* 167; Pamela Samuelson, 'Preliminary Thoughts on Copyright Reform' (2007) 3 *Utah Law Review* 551; and, by the same author, together with members of the CPP, 'The Copyright Principles Project: Directions for Reform' (2010) 25 *Berkeley Technology Law Journal* 1175.

[969] That is, use of copyrighted work of any category is unlawful unless authorized by the copyright holder or by law. *See* Gibson, *ibid.*, 215–16.

[970] See Chapters 7 and 10.

benefits. The current incentives for compliance, namely the availability of additional remedies, may not be strong enough for 'rights holders who do not expect their works to produce significant revenue. For these rights holders, any disadvantage that noncompliance may create in infringement litigation is irrelevant'.[971]

## 12.2 PROPOSALS TO MODIFY CURRENT FORMALITIES

A number of scholars have suggested modifications to the existing registration system. The proposals vary significantly as to the scope of the proposed reforms and their implementation methods.

At what may be considered one end of the spectrum is the proposal by Professor William Landes and Judge Richard Posner to switch to a system of indefinite copyright but with a continuous renewal requirement and a notice requirement. This facially violates Berne, by requiring the formality of renewal.[972] Be that as it may, the proposal is a good basis for a normative discussion on the role of formalities constitutive of copyright and linked to the term of protection. It might justify conditioning the Berne-Plus term of protection (currently the last 20 years of the 'life+70' term) on mandatory registration.[973]

Just shy of this end of the spectrum is the proposal by Cecil C Kuhne III, which seems more in line with the above-mentioned Constitutional Clause, but perhaps less so with the Berne Convention. Kuhne proposes the reintroduction of mandatory registration and renewal requirements, but advocates limiting the term of total copyright protection to 100 years.[974] Although constitutionally sound, this proposal violates Berne's prohibition of formalities and its provision that copyright duration be tied to the life of the author.[975]

Next along the spectrum is the major proposal of Professor Chris

---

[971] Sprigman, n 944., 495.
[972] Berne Convention, art. 5; Landes and Posner (n 967) 473.
[973] Under 17 USC §302(a), duration of copyright under US copyright law is life plus 70 years. For anonymous works, pseudonymous works, and works made for hire, the term is 95 years from the year of its first publication, or 120 years from the year of its creation, whichever expires first, 17 USC §302(c) (2000).
[974] Kuhne suggests that '[c]opyright extensions should only apply to commercially viable works', advancing the assumption that the authors' of works that are no longer commercially valuable would elect not to renew, thus allowing their works to enter the public domain. See Kuhne (n 968) 562.
[975] Berne Convention, arts 5 and 7(1).

Sprigman, joined by Professor Gibson. They see a formalities scheme that would return our copyright jurisprudence to its incentive-based system roots. Although they acknowledge that Berne presents an obstacle to such a reformalization, they believe that it may be overcome mostly by recognizing the existence of copyright rights without formalities, but conditioning remedies (including injunctions) on registration. Because there is no purpose in offering copyright claimants anything more than the opportunity to capture the commercial value of their works, protection should endure only so long as required to fulfil this aim, and it should extend only to works intended for commercial publication.

Professor Sprigman first proposed that the prohibition of formalities should be removed from Berne and replaced with a reciprocity principle as existed in the 1886 draft. Alternatively, he suggested that new-style formalities may be reconciled with a favourable reading of Berne Article 5(2), or permitted as an exception under a favourable application of the Article 9(2)'s 'three-step test'.[976] Specifically, he argued that a rights holder's 'enjoyment and exercise' of the rights protected under Berne would be preserved even if the rights holder's property interest were converted to a liability interest upon failure to comply with formalities. Under this system, instead of having authority to enjoin infringing activity, the rights holder would be entitled only to a default license amount approximating the amount that the rights holder would have had to pay to comply with formalities.[977] The justification for this proposal is that a rights holder who fails to comply with formalities 'places a minimal value on the right, a value no greater than the cost of compliance'.[978] Professor Sprigman would further require copyright holders to re-file for a second term of protection. Like Kuhne, and Landes and Posner, Professor Sprigman expects that many registered works (those with exhausted or never-realized commercial value) would enter the public domain after their first term,

---

[976]  Sprigman (n 944) 568.

[977]  The royalty payable under the default license would be low. Ideally, the royalty to license a work that a rightsholder has failed to register, notice, reregister in the case of a transfer (i.e., record), or renew should be set to approximate the cost of complying with these formalities (i.e., the total cost of informing oneself about the details of compliance and then satisfying them). That way a rightsholder who expects his work to produce revenue e xceeding the cost of complying with the relevant formality will prefer to comply with the formality, whereas a rightsholder who expects his work to produce revenue amounting to less than the cost of compliance will prefer to expose his work to the default license.

Ibid., 555.
[978]  Ibid., 556

producing a benefit to society by freeing up the works for others' use.[979] He would also require notice and the recordation of transfers.[980] Under a default license system, creators would lose the authority to control their works if they failed to comply with formalities.[981]

Professor Gibson has expressed general agreement with Sprigman about the desirability of returning to formalities and the nature those formalities should take.[982] Significantly, Gibson takes issue with the fact that rights holders must presently opt out of the copyright system if they desire to let others freely exploit their works.[983] He suggests that this presents an obstacle to 'digital democratization', and that, given the ease of compliance with formalities in the digital age, there is no justification for not putting the onus of opting in to copyright protection on those seeking protection.[984]

Whereas Professor Sprigman specifically wants to use formalities to filter out works that are not the aim of our incentive-based model, Professor Lawrence Lessig suggested that 'formalities today need not be a burden'.[985] He wants to realize the benefits of a registry, encourage willing creators to dedicate their works to the public domain before the copyright in those works has expired. An easy 'opt out' would remedy the situation described above of works protected against use despite the willingness to authorize their use.[986] Lessig proposes the reintroduction of notice, registration, and renewal, but advocates that registration be managed by private services in the way that domain name registries presently operate, expecting that this would lower the cost and complexity of compliance.[987] Furthermore, he proposes that the notice requirement be sensibly applied: instead of losing copyright for failure to provide notice, one would simply

---

[979]  Ibid., 555

[980]  Ibid., 564.

[981]  'Penalty defaults are purposefully designed to impose what the parties would not want[.]' ibid., 556.

[982]  Gibson, (n 968) 211, 223–9.

[983]  Ibid., 215–16.

[984]  Ibid., 229.

[985]  Lessig, *Free Culture*, (n 968) 288.

[986]  This is arguably what Creative Commons allows. Naturally one is free to declare publicly that one will not exercise rights, or simply not to enforce them, to maximize use and access. The point is that many creators do not wish to control uses but want to find a way to get paid for at least commercially relevant uses of their work. See e.g., musiccreatorsalliance.com (last accessed April 24, 2013).

[987]  Lessig, *Free Culture* (n 968) 289. In his subsequent book *Remix*, (n 171) 264, Lessig advocates giving copyright holders 14 years before being required to register their works to retain rights. Failure to do so would result in others being able to use the work 'either freely or with a minimal royalty payment'.

lose the right to prevent others' use of the work until demonstrating ownership of the work and notifying the infringer that permission is not granted. Upon notification, the infringer would be obligated not to make any new uses of the work, but would not incur a penalty for existing uses. Although moving registration from the public to the private sector would not necessarily circumvent a conflict with Berne, a relaxed notice requirement might conceivably be reconciled with Berne if it can be characterized as something other than a formality. This possibility is discussed in detail below.

Professor Pamela Samuelson, writing on behalf of the Copyright Principles Project (CPP), presents a proposal to reintroduce formalities specifically intended to comply with the dictates of Berne and TRIPS.[988] The CPP proposes that copyright registration could be made a more attractive option 'by restricting the availability of certain rights and remedies depending on the rights holders' registration of the work with a registry service'.[989] Advances in information technology make complying with a registration requirement substantially easier than it had been before the Internet. A registry system akin to the domain name registration system could be implemented for copyright.[990] By aiming only to reduce the consequences of infringement for unregistered works, and not conditioning copyright protection on registration, this proposal could be reconciled with Berne, provided that the creators of unregistered works are not deprived the 'enjoyment and exercise' of their rights. Provisions allowing some redress for the infringement of unregistered works under qualifying circumstances may satisfy this standard.[991]

The Copyright Principles Project additionally proposes that owners of rights should also be obliged to inform the registry about updated information, such as assignments of copyright or the death of the author and the identity of the author's successor in interest, so that the registry has current information. Failure to provide this sort of updated information could result in a loss of registration benefits.[992]

This is a point with which I agree. Another of the Principles Project's proposals is that 'Congress should limit remedies as to those who reuse in-copyright works whose rights holders cannot be found after a reasonably diligent search.'[993]

---

[988] See also Gervais, 'Fair Use' (n 727).
[989] Samuelson (n 968) 1199.
[990] See ibid.
[991] Ibid., 1200.
[992] Ibid.
[993] Ibid., 1234.

## 12.3 BERNE CONVENTION'S GUIDANCE

Recognition of natural and moral rights is an inherent feature of the Berne Convention.[994] Recognizing natural and moral rights to some degree is not irreconcilable with an incentive-based system.[995] That is precisely what many common law jurisdictions do. They recognize copyright law without mandatory formalities.[996] Those rights represent the desires and expectations of many creators.[997] Realizing those expectations as a reward for creation can be made to agree with an incentive-based system. The real question is how, and to what extent, those rights should be balanced with the rights and interests of users. For example, the power to exclude serves motivations that the opportunity to capture profit cannot. If a creator is inspired by emotion or beliefs, the creator may have no interest in realizing a profit from her work, yet may have a strong interest in seeing that the work not be commercially exploited or that it be properly attributed.

While this book proceeds from the assumption that compliance with Berne and TRIPS is desirable, there are other issues of international relevance that are worth mentioning. First, countries supporting the protection of traditional knowledge are likely to oppose modifying the international scheme to require formalities. Second, even though the Internet allows for easier compliance (automated translation programs may also help a creator deal with administrative formalities in languages other than her own[998]), both small and developing countries may have priorities for their use of—often severely limited—resources that do not include copyright formalities' administration.[999] With that said, reversion

---

[994]    See Chapter 2 for additional information on the Convention.

[995]    See Ginsburg (n 323) 995; and Jeanne C Fromer, 'Expressive Incentives in Intellectual Property' (2012) 98(8) *Virginia Law Review* 1745, 1823: '[W]hat most scholars have seen as a conflict between theories of utilitarianism and moral rights in intellectual property can in fact frequently come together in a useful harmony'.

[996]    For example, in Australia, Canada, New Zealand, South Africa and the UK copyright protection is available in some jurisdictions (e.g., Canada) with a form of registration, but unlike the US system, without any examination of the subject matter.

[997]    Fromer (n 1002) 1823.

[998]    Can it be presumed that a creator should be able to register in English? Even if he or she might want to sell into the US market, hundreds of small non-English language markets may exist here (not to mention Spanish as a major second language). Then a work might be pirated here (say an unauthorized translation). Should the author lose all rights to prevent that translation from being sold in the US because she did not register her work in the US?

[999]    See Susy Frankel, *Test-tubes for Global Intellectual Property Issues: Small Market Economies* (Edward Elgar Publishing 2015).

to a principle of reciprocity would impose much less of a burden on creators who hail from a no-formality country (that would be a vast majority of the world); they would enjoy formality-free protection in any country imposing formalities on its own creators.[1000]

This requires an explanation about the commercialization of copyright works and the requirement that transfers be in written form or recorded.

If it is merely a condition for a third party's assumption of those rights, that is, a condition to become what the Convention refers to as a successor in title, then it can be analogized to another (Berne-permissible) condition, namely that a transfer be in writing.[1001] As noted by Professor Nimmer:

> [N]othing in the Convention expressly forbids national legislation from requiring that agreements to transfer copyright or rights thereunder must be in writing. ...It would seem to be arguable that it is no more a 'formality' to require recordation than it is to require writing.[1002]

Normatively, as it may be presumed that the purchasers and licensees of creative works attribute a material value on being able to exploit the works exclusively, requiring that *commercial intermediaries* comply with formalities may be properly considered a cost of doing business. For users, it seems that the works for which rights holder identification will matter most—and which may present the greatest obstacle for rights clearance purposes—are those that are most likely to have exchanged hands at some point; likely passing from creator to publisher or other rights holder. If it is easier for prospective creators (both license-seekers and fair users) to identify and contact the person or entity whose permission is required in order to make use of a work, this may significantly reduce transaction costs,[1003] and may provide conscientious fair users a well-deserved argument in their defence if they earnestly go about seeking a copyright holder's permission unavailingly.

By contrast, it simply unfair to require that authors register internationally, especially in the absence of an international registration system. Essentially individual authors would have to register in every country where their work might be exploited. This is unfair to most authors, and more poignantly those in the developing world who do not have access to the financial resources necessary to perform this function. It is patently

---

[1000]  *See* Sprigman (n 944) 490.
[1001]  Under 17 USC 204(a); Berne Convention, art. 2(6).
[1002]  Melville B. Nimmer and David Nimmer, *Nimmer on Copyright*, (revised edn, Matthew Bender 2012) 101.
[1003]  See Sprigman (n 944) 497.

unfair to submit for example the right of first publication to a registration requirement. Authors would have to register to prevent publication of private journals, etc.

The Berne Convention offers useful guidance here again. First, Article 15(1) provides in part that: 'In order that the author of a literary or artistic work . . . shall . . . be regarded as such, and consequently be entitled to institute infringement proceedings . . . it shall be sufficient for his name to appear on the work in the usual manner.'[1004]

This does *not* mean that a negative inference can necessarily be made when the name does not appear.[1005] In addition, there are some works and some contexts when the author's name would simply not appear 'in the usual manner' as this term is used in the Convention.[1006] However, Article 15 does imply that it is acceptable and perhaps desirable (under the Convention) to consider the author differently than subsequent transferees of her rights.

Then Article 44.1 of the TRIPS Agreement provides that:

> [J]udicial authorities shall have the authority to order a party to desist from an infringement . . . .. Members are not obliged to accord such authority in respect of protected subject matter acquired or ordered by a person prior to knowing or having reasonable grounds to know that dealing in such subject matter would entail the infringement of an intellectual property right.[1007]

While this requires an injunctive remedy to be *available* in all cases (in the sense that the court must always have the authority to impose it), it does not disallow the application of equitable considerations in particular cases. Injunctive relief could be limited as a matter of equity in cases where a rights holder has failed to communicate to the public that her work is protected when circumstances do not adequately explain or excuse the omission. I will refer to this below as 'diligent recordation'.[1008] Whether an author has decided to put her name on a work ('in the usual manner') or not is another relevant contextual element.

The Convention offers guidance in Article 15 on the notion of 'usual manner'. First, commercial films are exploited not by the authors in a

---

[1004]   Berne Convention, art. 15(1).
[1005]   *See* WIPO Guide (n 184) 92: '[i]f only those creators were recognized as authors whose names appear on a copy of the works—it would be a formality as a condition of copyright protection, the application of which is forbidden under Article 5(2) of the Convention.'
[1006]   See note 1009 below and accompanying text.
[1007]   TRIPS, art. 44(1).
[1008]   See the text accompanying note 1030 below.

*droit d'auteur* sense (creators, including the screenwriter and director) but by what the Convention refers to as the 'maker'.[1009] Under Article 15(2), the maker/producer of a movie benefits from the same rights as an initial author.[1010] Then with respect to (rare) anonymous and pseudonymous works, the publisher (if any) whose name is on the work benefits from the same initial set of rights.[1011]

## 12.4   COMMERCIALITY

Some of those championing a return to formalities argue that protecting works not intended for commercial publication is not a purpose of the copyright system, and that the right to exclude is only justified under the expectation that the work will be made publicly available.[1012] In response, others says that the right to exclude might be said to motivate creators in the aggregate (more than the power to capture value), in that very few works ever stand to realize a commercial profit, but all should come into existence with promises to the author that their expressions will not be appropriated from them. The lack of protection afforded to unpublished works is thus a particular concern with any return to formalities. If issues regarding the infringement of unpublished material were consigned to privacy law,[1013] the result could be a dearth of protection that would render creators fearful that anything they create could potentially be exploited by a third party without permission.

It is true of course that, even if a creator is motivated by non-commercial incentives, and even if her interest is only in protecting her right to exclude (as opposed to a focus on capturing the work's commercial value), that creator may be willing to participate in a conditional copyright system by registering like everyone else. For creators in that situation, however, the cost of compliance is not an incidental cost of doing business, as she does not stand to recoup these costs upon profiting from the work.[1014] Moreover, she may lack the requisite information and resources to afford

---

[1009]   Berne Convention, art. 15(1).

[1010]   Ibid., art. 15(2).

[1011]   Ibid. This would presumably have little impact on major publishers (who already register).

[1012]   Gibson (n 968) 217.

[1013]   See ibid.

[1014]   Kuhne explicitly intends that a registration and renewal requirement would prevent the owners of non-commercial works from seeking and preserving protection. Kuhne (n 968) 550.

compliance, even if she places a very high value on having her rights secured.

Valuable creativity is not the exclusive province of creative professionals of course. Because the current system affords unconditional copyright to all fixed works of original expression, the message it sends the public is simply: 'Go forth and create. You will have control of your work and will be entitled to realize (at least some of) the value it may have.' This message fosters a culture of respect for all creative endeavours, and encourages society to appreciate meritorious creation wherever it may be found.[1015] Under a strict formality-based system, the message to the public is qualified, signalling instead: 'We desire you to create valuable works. If you manage to do so, and have complied with formalities, you will be entitled to realize the value of the work.'[1016] This message serves to encourage those who explicitly intend to create commercially, and who have the information and resources required for compliance with formalities. Such creators play an important role in our creative industries, but they are not alone responsible for the progress of science.[1017]

## 12.5  FORMALITIES AND INCENTIVES

The great success of present-day creative culture is that it encourages creation unqualifiedly. Whether you are professional author or a complete neophyte, if you create something good, the rights in its proceeds will inure to you if a commercial vehicle is found and the marketplace responds favourably. Moreover, whether your aim is to be commercial or not, copyright will help honour your interests, if any, in exercising partial control over whether and how the work is copied, distributed, sold, employed in the creation of a derivative work, or (in some cases) mutilated, displayed, or performed.

There is indubitable value for a creator attempting to market her work in being able to show that she is the registered creator of the work.[1018]

---

[1015]  Like the music instructor who notices that her four-year-old granddaughter has a prodigal talent, and who nurtures that talent to great effect. (See <www.youtube.com/watch?v=vUx4t4W4eVY>)

[1016]  See above note 981.

[1017]  If 'progress' has become understood to have more to do with the creation of works than the dissemination of them, then the creation of even private works should be found to further this aim (keeping in mind that some private works end up as public works; e.g., *The Diary of Anne Frank*).

[1018]  See, e.g., 17 USC § 410(c): A certificate of registration 'shall constitute prima facie evidence of the validity of the copyright and of the facts stated in the certificate'.

Likewise, there is value in having information being made available to the public (whether in the form of a registry, notice, or both) that enables users of works to seek the permission of the works' rights holders.[1019] However, knowing the identity of the creator and rights holder does not necessarily resolve the critical inquiry of ascertaining the date of the creator's death, upon which the duration of copyright is premised. Still, registration serves some useful functions in that: it signals that a work is being claimed; it helps license-seekers identify and contact rights holders; it provides information from which a work's term of protection can be ascertained in most circumstances; it can be a useful source for national statistics on creativity and culture; and, when requiring deposit, it serves to build a repository of works.[1020]

## 12.6   MISIDENTIFYING THE OBJECTIVE(S)

The discussion in the previous sections should have demonstrated that clarity and/or uniformity of views on the objectives of a re-emphasis on formalities might be lacking. There seem to be at least two distinct goals underpinning the various reformalization proposals. The first set of goals is to limit copyright to commercial works. The second is to make the system work better, not by putting works in the public domain, but by allowing the licensing market to function more efficiently (including addressing the orphan works problem) and tailoring remedies to reflect the fact that a transfer of copyright by a creator to a commercial entity should impact the infringement analysis. Mandatory registration and the limitation or elimination of exclusive rights upon failure to register a new work would achieve some of that.

If the primary aim of formalities is to limit the number of works under copyright protection, then it may be difficult to reconcile the proposal contained here with that aim. Conversely, if the animus for reform is the desire to ameliorate the difficulties of rights clearance attributable to the prohibition of formalities, the approach suggested here may be a positive path forward. What should be the consequences of a failure to make ownership information available, including for works that were available commercially but are no longer exploited, particularly in light of the excessive term of copyright protection? One can argue for greater fair use when

---

[1019]   Sprigman (n 944) 500; Samuelson, *Preliminary Thoughts* (n 968) 563.
[1020]   See   www.wipo.int/copyright/en/activities/copyright_registration/index. html (accessed 23 December 2015).

a license is unavailable, or even a new exception, as a number of proposals to deal with orphan works have done.[1021] A greater role for appropriate formalities could be transformative in this context.

The proposals outlined below reflect a belief that denying or limiting protection from the moment of creation due to an absence of registration is not just a violation of Berne (for foreign works at least), it is misguided in part because: (a) authors may not want to exploit their works commercially, but may want attribution; and (b) the opt-out regime for dedicating works to the public domain or allowing non-commercial uses (via Creative Commons) is not more complicated than registration (and it is available internationally in many languages).[1022] The Berne Convention's requirement that authors be granted rights without formalities is consonant with the prescription that the person whose name is indicated on the work (if any) be deemed to be the author.[1023]

## 12.7   A WAY FORWARD

The Copyright Principles Project reports that, a model copyright law or principles project will be faced with other challenges besides what substantive rules to propose and what kinds of institutional and process reforms might help maintain the integrity of the law or principles. One such challenge is to what extent the drafters should feel constrained in their thinking by international treaty obligations. My sense is that international obligations should be considered as a constraint, but not so much of a constraint that the drafters cannot deliberate about what the right rule might be and then consider how the right rule can be reconciled (or not) with international obligations. There may be more flexibility in international norms than some perceive.[1024]

A real property analogy might help illuminate this chapter's proposal. If one were to buy a car, the fact of the car's existence is not one that most

---

[1021]   Samuelson, *Directions for Reform* (n 968) 1200, 1234–5.
[1022]   Creative Commons has affiliates in over 70 jurisdictions worldwide. See (<wiki.creativecommons.org/CC_Affiliate_Network> accessed 18 December 2015).
[1023]   Perhaps ironically, if an author complies with the 'formality' of putting her name on a work, then law recognizes her authorship of that work. If 'formality' is defined as in art. 5(2) of Berne, this would not be because it is not a condition on the existence or exercise of copyright. See above note 1005 and accompanying text.
[1024]   Samuelson, *Preliminary Thoughts* (n 968) 570.

people other perhaps than metaphysicists would doubt if the car was in front of them.[1025] Buying the car requires a determination by the buyer that the person selling the car actually has the title to the vehicle, however. The current copyright system prods work 'manufacturers' to register new vehicles, but recordation of title is often forgotten probably because the consequences of a failure to register the work (e.g., loss of a claim for statutory damages and attorneys' fees) or, conversely, the advantages of registering a new work are greater than those linked to recordation.

### 12.7.1 A Proposal

My proposal contains two principles and seven modalities.

#### 12.7.1.1 Principles

**Principle (1)** *Authors should not be required to register new works as a pre-condition to obtain copyright protection.* Those who put their name on a work (or have a valid reason for not doing so, including because it cannot be done 'in the usual manner'[1026]) should have full rights to prevent use of that work absent fair use or another exception.[1027] This includes at least a right of first publication and a right of attribution.

**Principle (2)** *Some remedies should be tied to a subsequent copyright holder's recordation of her transfer.* Where available, reasonable statutory damages and attorneys' fees should be conditioned on timely recordation.

#### 12.7.1.2 Modalities

**Modality (1)** Recordation of an *initial transfer* (from the author) would require work/metadata registration if the work concerned was unregistered. By the same logic, if registering a subsequent transfer as

---

[1025]   Registration may confirm not the existence of a work but useful metadata (for the car: model; place of manufacture etc.). For some categories, like photographs, group (or bulk) registration may make search more difficult but the evidentiary value of the registration is still useful in infringement proceedings, 17 USC § 205(c). On group registration, *see* US Copyright Office, *Copyright Registration for Works of the Visual Arts*, 4 (available at www.copyright.gov/circs/circ40.pdf.

[1026]   See notes 1004 and 1011 above and accompanying text.

[1027]   In many cases, a collective licensing regime will be in place to allow use for payment—the practical equivalent of a compulsory license. See the previous chapter.

first recorded transfer, not just registration metadata but also the chain of title information (if there had been previous unrecorded transfers) would have to be provided. Provisions for confidentiality of material filed to support the transfer (perhaps as with computer software registration now), and/or requiring an affidavit in lieu of confidential documents would likely have to be made.[1028]

**Modality (2)** Before issuing an *injunction* to prevent use of copyright material, a court should take recordation into account. In the United States this can be done under the public-interest prong of the *eBay* test.[1029] To avoid making this a Berne-impermissible *requirement*, however, the absence of recordation should only be a factor that a Berne successor in title should be allowed to explain away. Using the language of the diligent search proponents (in the orphan works context), I suggest that *diligent recordation* may be a significant part of the solution.[1030]

**Modality (3)** *Foreign works*: the system should not apply to works not exploited or lawfully available in a territory (thus eschewing the issue of formalities imposed on right holders in foreign works exploited without authorization in the territory concerned).

**Modality (4)** The *time period* for recordation should be regulated by providing an incentive to proceed quickly. The question of the time period and consequences of a failure to record a transfer are both important, but they are not normatively essential facets of the proposal. Options include either making the requirement necessary for the transfer to be valid at all (as with the 'in writing' requirement in the United States contained in 17 USC § 204(a)) or making the recordation only valid *inter partes* until timely recordation. I endorse the latter option. However, foreign transferees should have a much longer period to record transfers, perhaps limited from the time they become aware of unauthorized exploitation of the work in question in another territory.[1031]

---

[1028] Recordation benefits can in most cases be secured by providing publicly available metadata about the transaction.

[1029] Injunctions should, however, remain 'available' in all cases.

[1030] On diligent search, *see* US Copyright Office, *Legal Issues in Mass Digitization:*
*A Preliminary Analysis and Discussion Document* 26 (Oct. 2011) (available at <www.copyright.gov/docs/massdigitization/USCOMassDigitization_October2011. pdf> accessed 17 November 2016).

[1031] The question of right of action after the transfer has been executed but not (yet) recorded is similarly interesting. Does the author have a right of action after granting an exclusive license (which in theory transfers any licensing of use by third parties to the licensee)?

**Modality (5)** Transferees should have an obligation—as they do for domain names, for example—to keep their *contact information up-to-date*.[1032] The question of consequences would have to be examined. Failure to update records could be linked to remedies as with recordation itself, but with appropriate safeguards to reflect industry practices. This modality is designed to address orphan works. If a rights holder failed to record a transfer for a significant period of time, and/or to update contact information, a major limitation of available remedies would seem warranted.

**Modality (6)** While, in accordance with Principle 1, the author as initial rights holder would not have to register or record her initial interest, if she regained title to her work then the author would have to record that transfer 'back'.[1033] This would happen if the author bought back her copyright; if the rights reverted to her, as they do in the United States after the 35-year period provided by statute, although this already includes an obligation to notify the Copyright Office[1034]); or if, for example, she regained her rights because of an out-of-print clause in a publishing agreement. The logic here accords with the principles and Berne guidance discussed above. The initial presumption that the author whose name appears 'on' the work (in the usual manner) is arguably broken by the author when she transfers her rights, so that it is not illogical to require that she comply with a formality.

**Modality (7)** Incentives for voluntary registration (including by authors) should remain.[1035] While this suggests that authors who have put their names on a work 'in the usual manner' should have a reasonably full panoply of rights—including statutory damages capped at, say, $1,000 absent exceptional circumstances—that number could be doubled or trebled if the work was registered and/or a claim for attorney's fees made available.

It is worth noting that these proposals mesh, but are not coextensive with, proposals that would limit copyright protection to commercially exploited

---

[1032]  For domain names, see the *Who is Data Reminder Policy* (available at https://www.icann.org/resources/pages/registrars/consensus-policies/wdrp-en (accessed 17 November 2016).

[1033]  One could hope that, like for small entities under the Patent Rules, the Copyright Office fees for recordation in such a case (by the author) would be lower.

[1034]  17 USC §203(a)(4) (2000).

[1035]  Consideration should be given to introducing a new notice requirement linked to registration number, such as 'CR' followed by the number, as for patents.

works. The major difference is that it does not limit the rights of the original author whose name is 'on' the work 'in the usual manner' nor do the authors want to strip authors of unpublished works of their rights under federal copyright law. Few authors commercially exploit themselves, but some do (e.g., self-published eBooks). The proposal maintains incentives for voluntary registration. It may well be that the vehicle used to disseminate the author's work (such an eBook service provider) could provide registration services. The idea of linking various databases to make metadata searchable may well compensate incomplete official records.[1036] That being said, rights to many, and probably by far the most commercially exploited, works are often transferred to copyright holders (such as publishers), however. Those works would be subject to the proposed recordation regime.

## 12.8    OTHER FIXES

There are two additional fixes that need attention in parallel to the focus on appropriate recordation obligations.

First, a (parallel) reform of statutory damages may be required in some countries, especially the US. It may not be essential to amend the statute, however, as a proper application of courts' discretion may get us there. I suggest allowing an author to claim statutory damages without mandatory formalities because in many cases actual damages are very difficult to establish. The proposal above suggests capping them at, say, $1,000 per work absent exceptional circumstances.[1037]

Second, there is no conclusively recognized mechanism under current law to irreversibly dedicate a work to the public domain. A registry could be established by law, with clearer provisions concerning rights acquired by users after dedication.

---

[1036]   The idea of using 'public-private' solutions to improve use of technology in this context is discussed in the report of the Copyright Principles Project. *See* Pamela Samuelson et al. 'The Copyright Principles Project: Directions for Revision' (2010) 25 *Berkeley Technology Law Journal* 1, 26.

[1037]   The minimum is set by 17 USC § 504(c)(1). As mentioned in the last modality above, this number could be increased and/or attorney's fees could be claimed if the author voluntarily registered. Even for works on which transfers were recorded, other than egregious cases of large-scale commercial infringement (the same type of cases that might warrant criminal penalties), a proper range could be attained by multiplying the minimum by relevant factors (willfulness/knowledge of the infringement; repeated infringement; number of infringements per work; commercial nature; possibly the availability of a license) so that the proper range in most cases would oscillate between $750 and $3,750 per work.

## 12.9  CONCLUSION

Formalities are in the zeitgeist for a number of reasons. The abundance of tools to capture and process data in myriad forms makes the absence of data harder to understand for many. Copyright-related formalities—which may have seemed to some like passport applications—could be much easier and more efficient, and data could be made more readily available. International rules, especially those contained in the Berne Convention and the TRIPS Agreement, are necessarily part of a complete discussion on formalities. The Convention's no-formality rule, which is mostly derived from a natural rights approach, is not incompatible with copyright policy. It provides useful guidance that distinguishes authors from successors in title. While advocating a reduced role for work registration, I suggest that a greater role for recordation of transfers (including transfers back to the original author) are Berne-permissible and normatively desirable, provided rules recognize the needs of foreign rights holders and do not amount to the imposition or the adoption of similar formalities by other countries.

# 13. Copyright and development

## 13.1 INTRODUCTION

This chapter could appear in Part I because it provides a doctrinal assessment of the role that copyright policy may play in development. However, I decided to include it here because in many cases the tool that developing countries invoke to calibrate copyright in specific cases is a compulsory license, which is an administrative act that could be part of a structured reform of copyright. Let us consider what may make the case of developing economies somewhat different in formulating copyright reform proposals. International trade in 'intangibles'—services and goods whose value is mostly derived from intellectual property (IP)—represents a major area of world trade and forms part of an economy in which competitiveness is predicated on innovation.[1038] A number of industrialized nations that have negative trade balances in the manufacturing sector have positive balances in trade in intangibles.[1039] They push to keep that positive balance as high as possible in several ways, including by imposing higher intellectual property norms on developing nations.

Behind that economic debate and its political ramifications, there is a fundamental normative argument, namely that each person, in any country, should have a right to develop himself or herself as fully as possible. This argument can be translated into economic terms to interface with the trade world. One could say that, in aggregate, welfare is maximized when each individual leads as productive a life as possible. Shouldn't the ultimate aim of policy making in the field of copyright (and other areas of intellectual property) be to accomplish that very goal, namely ensuring that law in its various accoutrements *maximizes the development of human creativity and innovation*. This is normatively justified as a matter of human development and economically justified as welfare enhancing.

---

[1038] See Zvi Griliches, *R&D, Education, and Productivity—A Retrospective* (Harvard UP 2000).
[1039] See Robert E Lipsey, 'Measuring International Trade in Services in International Trade' in Marshall Reinsdorf and Matthew J Slaughter (eds), *Services and Intangibles in the Era of Globalization* (University of Chicago Press 2009).

How can this be translated into a structured copyright reform effort? Efforts by the World Intellectual Property Organization (WIPO) to produce economic studies of intellectual property impacts have helped significantly in developing adequate policy options in this regard, as previous efforts by the World Bank and others had done in the past.[1040] The variegated picture that emerges from these studies paints copyright (and IP generally) as part of a broader landscape of *innovation policies.* Seeing copyright in this light helps calibrate national policies in countries that strive to join the club of world-class creators and innovators. It also allows all of us better to comprehend the social costs of certain forms of IP and allow mitigation where necessary.[1041]

The impact of high copyright protection on the developing world is often presented in broad negative terms: preventing reasonable access to knowledge, publications, educational materials, etc. Yet I also believe that a society will grow optimally if its creative minds can spend time creating and inventing as discussed in the foreword and introduction. Policy makers should seek an optimal balance to foster creativity while optimizing access. As I have discussed in greater detail in my work on the need for each country and region to 'calibrate' its IP regime as part of an innovation and access strategy,[1042] developing countries must address access issue without making it difficult for creators to thrive. This indicates both protection of new creations and reuse privilege. Creators should be actively encouraged.

This is nothing new. When a large group of recently independent developing countries joined the community of nations to discuss IP before and at the Stockholm Diplomatic Conference of 1967, which revised the Berne Convention, developmental issues emerged. They were addressed in part by the addition, four years later at a subsequent conference held in Paris, of an Appendix to the Berne Convention allowing developing countries, subject to strict timelines and administrative obligations, to issue compulsory (also known as non-voluntary) licenses to translate

---

[1040]   See, e.g., Cornell University, INSEAD, and WIPO: The Global Innovation Index 2014: The Human Factor in Innovation (Geneva 2014) (available at <www.globalinnovationindex.org/userfiles/file/reportpdf/GII-2014-v5.pdf > accessed 12 May 2015).

[1041]   Let us remember that, not long ago, even while TRIPS was being negotiated in the late 1980s and early 1990s, innovation narratives were essentially absent beyond the lip service paid to technology transfer. This is not altogether surprising: studies on the specific impacts of IP were hard to find in the industrialized world and virtually nonexistent for the developing world. Negotiators put the policy cart before the empirical horse.

[1042]   See Daniel Gervais (ed.) *IP Calibration, in Intellectual Property, Trade And Development* (2nd edn, OUP 2014) 86.

and reproduce books in connection with educational activities.[1043] The
normative target can be defined in a fairly consensual manner. Developing
countries aim to develop both on the *human and economic fronts*. One
could largely posit this as the underlying normative underpinning of all
intellectual property regimes. As Amartya Sen noted:[1044]

> It is simply not adequate to take as our basic objective just the maximization of
> income or wealth, which is, as Aristotle noted, 'merely useful and for the sake
> of something else.' For the same reason, economic growth cannot sensibly be
> treated as an end in itself. Development has to be more concerned with enhanc-
> ing the lives we lead and the freedoms we enjoy.

This combination of human *and* economic development has in recent
years been translated into a series of objectives amenable in part at least
to the kind of metrics that evidence-based policy making might call for,
including the UN Human Development Index.[1045] Viewed positively,
development may be defined, in the words of Professor Okediji, as 'a
pseudonym for a complex network of benefits associated with economic
growth and human social capital'.[1046] Viewed negatively—that is, in
terms of factors that encumber development—one could mention income
inequality, discrimination, crime, education and a host of other factors.[1047]

Tying such broader objectives to intellectual property policy is complex
and determining with precision whether those objectives are achieved
remains hard. Each country is in a different posture:

> It should also be noted that not all developing countries are even. The stage of
> development of each country should not be measured with regard to an alien
> model as if the quality of that reference was sufficient to reflect the situation, as
> well as the perspective, of the developing country in question. On the contrary,
> the underdevelopment of a country cannot be objectively measured, but must

---

[1043]   Berne Convention (24 July 1971) App. See Chapter 2 and Appendix 2.

[1044]   Amartya Sen, *Development as Freedom* (OUP 1999) 14.

[1045]   See   <http://hdr.undp.org/en/content/human-development-index-hdi>
accessed 17 November 2016.

[1046]   Ruth L Okediji, 'History Lessons for the WIPO Development Agenda' in
Neil W Netanel (ed.), *Intellectual Property and Developing Countries* (OUP 2009)
140.

[1047]   Blending the attainment of the positive objective with ways to mitigate
the negative impacts that introducing higher levels of protection of IP may have,
Professor Chon has suggested an approach based on 'substantive equality' in this
context. See Margaret Chon, 'Substantial Equality in International Intellectual
Property Norm Setting and Interpretation' in Daniel Gervais (ed.), *Intellectual
Property, Trade and Development* (OUP 2007).

be considered on a case by case basis while taking into account the dynamics of the society and its cultural, educational and political status.[1048]

The main point is simple: merely measuring a country's aggregate economic output such as its Gross Domestic Product (GDP) as it may be affected by varying degrees of IP protection does not tell the whole development story. It does, however, tell *a* story, and one worth looking into.

Developing countries accepted the TRIPS Agreement (see Chapter 2) for a variety of reasons, ranging from ignorance to coercion to hard bargaining to a defence against the use of unilateral trade sanctions imposed bilaterally (by the US in particular).[1049] The TRIPS Agreement multilateralized the imposition of such trade sanctions and made the process more fair and transparent in two ways. First, the norms with which each WTO member must comply are contained in the text of TRIPS. Second, sanctions must be pre-authorized by the WTO before they can be imposed. The imposition trade-based sanctions follows the preparation by a panel of experts of a publicly available report on a dispute and, possibly, also by the WTO Appellate Body. The entire process is governed by the Dispute-Settlement Understanding adopted when the WTO was established in January 1995.[1050]

This bargaining-based explanation of TRIPS adds a key dimension to the analysis because they show that accepting TRIPS and implementing it

---

[1048]  Salah Basalamah, 'Compulsory Licensing for Translation: An Instrument of Development?' (2000) 40 IDEA 503, 513.

[1049]  Those sanctions were used to convince countries better to protect IP rights belonging to multinational companies headquartered in the US and other 'Western' nations. Indeed, before TRIPS the US used the Trade Act more frequently to threaten or apply trade sanctions against other nations that, in the judgment of the US Trade Representative (USTR), did not adequately protect US-owned IP rights. See Peter Drahos, 'Developing Countries and International Intellectual Property Standard-Setting' (2002) UK Commission on Intellectual Property Rights, Study Paper 8 (available at <www.anu.edu.au/fellows/pdrahos/reports/pdfs/UKCommIPRS.pdf> accessed 1 January 2016) 14. Compare s. 301 prior to the 1988 Trade Act—19 USC ss 2411–16 (1986) and s. 301 as amended by the 1988 Trade Act—19 USC ss 2411–20 (as amended by Pub L No 100-418, 102 Stat 1157 (1988). For a discussion of its application to cases of copyright infringement, see Antoinette M von Dem Hagen, 'Trade-Based Remedies for Copyright Infringement: Utilizing A 'Loss-Preventive' Synthesis' (1989) 12 *Hastings Communications and Entertainment Law Journal* 99.

[1050]  See World Trade Organization, *Understanding on Rules and Procedures Governing the Settlement of Disputes* (WTO 1994) (available at <www.wto.org/english/docs_e/legal_e/ursum_e.htm#Understanding> accessed 20 December 2015).

can be done with different foci: to comply to avoid WTO disputes,[1051] or to maximize innovation and creativity without endangering adequate access. Resulting policy choices are likely to be quite different. IP can be negotiated and traded against anything else with dollars as a common denominator but that does not necessarily make for optimal domestic innovation.

TRIPS crystallized the highest level of IP rights acceptable to the demanders (essentially Western Europe, Japan and the United States) as of December 1990. That is the year when a text close to the final one signed in Marrakech in 1994 was presented to the negotiators.[1052] For proponents of developmental theories based on historical accounts of how most industrialized countries got to where they are economically, namely by copying others first before adopting high IP standards, this was not good news.[1053] Indeed, the potential negative impact of TRIPS on development was recognized soon after the entry into force of the Agreement.[1054]

The etiology of the development of the innovative potential of developing countries is often anchored in, and negative welfare outcomes seen as offset by, transfers of knowhow and technology from more industrialized nations to developing ones. While this does not take account of all the dimensions of indigenous innovations,[1055] it leads to the conclusion that conditions for such transfers should be established. There is a related perception that technology transfers are more likely to happen if technologies are actually used by and not just sold to people in the developing world, that is, not imported as finished products. This is also not new for it spurred decades of discussions on forfeiture of patents and compulsory licenses for failure to 'work' an invention.[1056] One can see similar arguments in the discussions concerning Foreign Direct Investment (FDI) and

---

[1051] WTO disputes have since linked IP to both bananas and gambling, to take just two examples. See *European Communities – Regime for the Importation, Sale and Distribution of Bananas* (24 March 2000) WT/DS27/ARB/ECU; and *United States – Measures Affecting the Cross-Border Supply of Gambling and Betting Services* (21 December 2007) WT/DS285/ARB.

[1052] Gervais (n 98) 15–29.

[1053] Llewellyn Joseph Gibbons, 'Do As I Say (Not As I Did): Putative Intellectual Property Lessons for Emerging Economies from the Not So Long Past of the Developed Nations' (2011) 64 *SMU Law Review* 935–7.

[1054] Frederick M Abbott, 'The WTO TRIPS Agreement and Global Economic Development'(1996) 72 *Chicago Kent Law Review* 385.

[1055] Daniel Gervais, 'Traditional Innovation and the Ongoing Debate on the Protection of Geographical Indications' in Peter Drahos and Susy Frankel (eds), *Intellectual Property and Indigenous Innovation* (Austl Natl UP 2012).

[1056] Pedro Roffe and Gina Vea, 'The WIPO Development Agenda in Historical and Political Context' in Neil W Netanel (ed.), *The Development Agenda: Global Intellectual Property and Developing Countries* (OUP 2009) 79–110.

the hope that technology-focused FDI will do more for development than 'mere' trade.

The narrative according to which TRIPS (that is, the introduction of higher levels of IP protection and enforcement in developing countries) would spur innovation-based industrial development has been called into question especially when applied to least-developed countries (LDCs). As a result, the WTO has suspended most TRIPS obligations for LDCs.[1057]

## 13.2 DISTINCTIONS AMONG DEVELOPING COUNTRIES

Developing countries (other than LDCs) are obviously not all identical, far from it. The TRIPS Agreement essentially treats them all on the same footing, however. All developing countries other than LDCs had until 1 January 2000 to implement TRIPS—with up to five more years to apply full patent protection to pharmaceutical products for those, like India, that did not provide such protection. This seems to ignore many variables that directly affect how different developing countries were affected by TRIPS.

Developing countries can be grouped in various ways for purposes of this type of analysis. In previous work,[1058] I suggested that—again leaving aside LDCs for now—one could, in aggregate, distinguish developing countries where innovation benefits outweighed additional rent extraction made possible by TRIPS and those countries where additional rent extraction made possible by TRIPS outweighed innovation benefits. This 'net outcomes' approach led me and others to conclude that, if TRIPS is seen as a given, countries should move from the second to the first group by improving innovation outcomes but also adopting remedial actions (using the so-called TRIPS 'flexibilities') to reduce costs imposed by higher intellectual property protection.[1059]

---

[1057] See Council for Trade-Related Aspects of Intellectual Property Rights (Council for TRIPS), *Extension of the Transition Period under Article 66.1 for Least Developed Country Members* (11 June 2013) IP/C/64.

[1058] Daniel Gervais, 'TRIPS and Innovation: How Recent Developments Might Inform Canada's Foreign Technology Policy' (2013) 29 *Canadian Intellectual Property Review* 141–62.

[1059] Joseph Straus, 'A Marriage of Convenience: World Economy and Intellectual Property From 1990 to 2012' (2012) 40 *AIPLA Quarterly Journal* 633, 677–8; Lee Petherbridge, 'Intelligent TRIPS Implementation: A Strategy for Countries on the Cusp of Development' (2001) 22(4) *University of Pennsylvania Journal of International Law* 1029.

Professor Llew Gibbons proposed a taxonomy that I find helpful.[1060] He grouped developing countries according to three stages of development:

**Stage one** (which may be seen as including LDCs):

- foreign direct investment rare and usually limited to specialized sectors—often relating to the exploitation of natural resources or developing franchise service industries like a major international brand bottling company;
- unskilled, cheap labour;
- foreign businesses create the necessary infrastructure and invest in human capital;
- developing countries ideally investing in the training of skilled workers and junior managers—successfully developing a skilled workforce is a prerequisite to entering stage two.

**Stage two**

- economy now able to absorb technology, to imitate technology at some level, and to contribute minor improvements;
- well-educated workforce adapted to absorb new technology and incorporate it into the domestic economy;
- domestic research efforts primarily facilitative or associated with technology transfer. Focus shifts gradually to efforts on more innovative projects.

**Stage three**

- newly industrialized country producing its own intellectual property.
- nations very selective as to which intellectual property rights they zealously protect and of which rights they encourage (mis) appropriation.

This progression from imitation to absorption to innovation roughly tracks the innovation theorists' view of innovation following a path from imitation to adaptation to true global innovation.[1061] 'Stage 2' countries likely overlap the group identified previously, namely countries where innovation outcomes do not (yet) outweigh the additional rent extraction

---

[1060] Gibbons (n 1060) 932–3.
[1061] Gervais (n 1065) 161–2.

made possible by the implementation of TRIPS-compatible norms. As countries build innovation-focused industries, they typically develop, as Professor Gibbons rightly notes, more sophisticated and nuanced views of their IP policies. I had arrived at a similar conclusion.[1062] Simply put, they play the IP game better.

There is a widely held view that many developing countries possess negligible technological capacity, so that the points of departure for the progression vary enormously. The timing of the introduction of higher levels of IP matters correlatively. A number of developing countries 'have no meaningful prospects of attracting domestic innovations'.[1063] Benoliel and Salama mention only a handful of countries (BRICS +). Indeed, they opine that 'China and India are effectively the only developing countries that, aside from being scientifically proficient, are also able to produce technology-based products in patent-sensitive industries in large scale'.[1064] Cheng suggests along similar lines that China 'due to the size of its economy and its unique economic circumstances, should be treated as *sui generis*, and analysed separately from the remaining developing countries'.[1065] There are valid arguments for treating large emerging economies, such as some of the BRICS countries, as a special case, and perhaps China as special even among that group. In 2005, while developing countries accounted for only 23 per cent of worldwide research and development, this figure dropped to 14.8 per cent if China was excluded.[1066]

The brief discussion in the previous pages shows that differences among countries and their level of human and economic development matter. The next section considers other differences, namely those in the nature of the industries that each country has and can develop.

## 13.3   DISTINCTIONS AMONG INDUSTRIES

In the same way that it put every developing country in a more or less equal position, TRIPS also put all industries on the same footing. The

---

[1062]   Daniel Gervais, 'Intellectual Property and Development: The State of Play' (2005) 74 *Fordham Law Review* 505.

[1063]   Thomas K Cheng, 'A Developmental Approach to the Patent-Antitrust Interface' (2012) 33 *Northwestern Journal of International Law & Business* 1, 4.

[1064]   Daniel Benoliel and Bruno Salama,'Towards an Intellectual Property Bargaining Theory: The Post-WTO Era' (2010) 32 *University of Pennsylvania Journal of International Law* 265, 288–9.

[1065]   Cheng (n 1070) 9.

[1066]   Ibid.

costs and restrictions imposed by the 'one-size-fits all' approach of TRIPS means will be imposed on all other industries.[1067] As Professors Reichman and Lange noted:

> A chronic problem for policymakers even in the most developed countries is that the one-size-fits-all paradigms that underlie classical intellectual property law have proved especially inadequate to deal with the needs of innovators and borrowers in an information age. This problem is compounded many times over in the developing countries, where different players at different stages of development demand different and contradictory approaches to intellectual property rights in their respective fields of interest.[1068]

While a number of studies tend to support the view that the perception of stronger IP in LDCs and developing countries may increase the volume of FDI, Chen and Puttitanun also mention 'other variables including differences in size, age, political situation, economic freedom, natural resource allocation, technological absorptive capability, WTO accession, and level of development of LDC and developing countries, as well as small sample sizes, poor data collection, and regional instability'.[1069] Maskus, Fink and Primo Braga's work points in a similar direction.[1070] Maskus also notes that the 'multinational enterprises are more likely to transfer proprietary information to local affiliates or partners that are themselves engaged in adaptive R&D, suggesting that policies to encourage domestic innovation are complementary to inducing inward technology flows'.[1071] He

---

[1067]   Michael W Carroll, 'One Size Does Not Fit All: A Framework for Tailoring Intellectual Property Rights' (2009) 70 *Ohio State Law Journal* 1361.

[1068]   Jerome H Reichman and David Lange, 'Bargaining Around the TRIPS Agreement: The Case for Ongoing Public-Private Initiatives to Facilitate Worldwide Intellectual Property Transactions' (1998) 9 *Duke Journal of Comparative & International Law* 11, 50.

[1069]   Yongmin Chen and Thitima Puttitanun, 'Intellectual Property Rights and Innovation in Developing Countries' (2005) 78 *Journal of Development Economics* 474, 475–6; Garrett Halydier, 'A Hybrid Legal and Economic Development Model That Balances Intellectual Property Protection and Economic Growth: A Case Study of India, Brazil, Indonesia, and Vietnam' (2012) 14 *Asian-Pacific Law & Policy Journal* 86, n 64.

[1070]   Keith E Maskus, 'The Role of Intellectual Property Rights in Encouraging Foreign Direct Investment and Technology Transfer' (2004) 9 *Duke Journal of Comparative & International Law* 109, 138–52; Carlos A Primo Braga and Carsten Fink, 'The Economic Justification for the Grant of Intellectual Property Rights: Patterns of Convergence and Conflict' (1996) 72 *Chicago-Kent Law Review* 439, 444–54.

[1071]   Keith E Maskus, 'The WIPO Development Agenda: A Cautionary Note' in Netanel (n 1063), 171.

then observes that 'elasticity of FDI with respect to patent seems to rise with the abundance of local human capital'.[1072] This would explain why countries with very low absorptive capacity (such as many LDCs) do not show measurable gains when introducing higher levels of IP rules without a series of accompanying and parallel measures on several different fronts. To that extent, the pro-addition narratives used to support TRIPS' application to the developing world were woefully incomplete. Simply put, standard or mechanical TRIPS implementation with a view to avoiding WTO disputes was and is unlikely to produce net developmental benefits.

Countries implementing TRIPS should thus focus instead on a broad innovation strategy and set of policies to develop their innovation potential without having positives in that area outweighed by the higher costs imposed by foreign right holder's right to collect additional IP rents. This approach forms part of what I call the third phase of TRIPS, the calibration process. Dealing with IP rules and their enforcement without dealing with absorptive capacity (including human development and education) and entrepreneurship is unlikely to yield net positives in terms of domestic innovation.[1073] In other words, policy makers are dealing with a complex set of equations with multiple, interpolated considerations and variables.[1074] The word used, inter alia, by Michael Birnhack to describe the challenge and 'the meeting of the global and the local', is the 'glocal' situation'.[1075]

China has demonstrated its understanding of this need to be comprehensive in its approach to catch up and perhaps overtake the 'West'. It developed a national IP strategy.[1076] This includes a strong focus on human capital. There is, however, a debate as to whether the effort to push domestic industries to develop patent portfolios while slowly accepting enforcing rights belonging to foreign rights holders was deliberate or simply the result of a difficult transition.[1077]

The second phase ('subtraction or anti-IP') of TRIPS was incomplete

---

[1072] Ibid.

[1073] Lihong Li, 'Lessons from China's Experience with the TRIPs Agreement' in J deBeer (ed.) *Implementing the World Intellectual Property Organization's Development Agenda* (Wilfrid Laurier UP 2009) 118–30.

[1074] Daniel Gervais, 'A TRIPS Implementation Toolbox' in Gervais (n 1054) 527–45.

[1075] Michael D Birnhack, 'Trading Copyright: Global Pressure on Local Culture' in Netanel (n 1063) 397.

[1076] Straus (n 1066) 667.

[1077] Compare Jameson Berkow, 'Patent Dragon Awakes', *Financial Post* (Toronto, 7 November 2011) (available at <business.financialpost.com/2011/11/07/patent-dragon-awakes/> accessed 2 Jan 2016), and Peter K Yu, 'Five Oft-Repeated

in focusing solely on the need to reduce IP protection. While this was understandable in dealing with the major public health challenges facing LDCs unable to pay for necessary medicines, it led to the formation of an anti-intellectual property coalition that sees little good in any form of IP protection. An obvious problem with lowering protection across the board is that some industries are especially sensitive to certain IP protection and will simply not invest absent those rights (and proper enforcement).

This calls for alternative strategies and incentives, from awards and prizes to public funding of research. There are necessarily trade-offs in substituting public funding for private incentives.[1078] Clearly, however, just lowering IP levels is not a strategy. To quote Professor Maskus, 'governments should not view IPR flexibilities as a substitute for sound development policy'.[1079] Doing so (especially absent an overall strategy which might secure certain forms of 'compensation' for the removal or weakening of certain IP incentives) is likely to have negative impacts on FDI and local entrepreneurship. Limits on IP rights should be imposed carefully and with appropriate distinctions between types of issues and industries. Not all IP rights are the same, nor do all industries respond the same way to changes in IP protection.

In the field of copyright, it takes relatively little to generate growth in software and book publishing and even in music, where digital sales are picking up and allowing individually published songwriters and self-promoting artists to support a living outside of major 'record deals'. While it is important to bear in mind that many industries depend on proper limits to copyright, there is an effort in academic and certain NGO circles to jettison copyright for all online content. I find this troubling when the push includes an effort to destroy CMOs trying to support professionals in this area, as the following passage indicates: 'The entities that have the clearest interest in promoting the copyright dogma are collecting societies, who can bring the anti-competitive and the opportunistic motivations to perfection.'[1080] Fortunately, a number of developing countries, from Namibia to Nepal, have realized the need to support a fledgling professional 'creative class' and to build and supervise well-managed,

---

Questions About China's Recent Rise as a Patent Power' (2013) *Cardozo Law Review De Novo* 78, 97–199.

[1078] Carroll (n 1074) 1378–9.
[1079] Maskus (n 1078) 172.
[1080] Ariel Katz, 'The Orphans, the Market, and the Copyright Dogma: A Modest Solution for a Grand Problem' (2012) 27 *Berkeley Technology Law Journal* 1285, 1340. See Chapter 11.

transparent author collectives to represent them vis-à-vis major users. The need for local composers, songwriters and artists to get and remain involved in such collectives is key in ensuring that new collectives attain effectual levels of credibility (needed to license), transparency (needed for both licensing and to obtain and increase support from all stakeholders and 'sister' organizations in other territories and continued responsiveness to both authors and users).

Arguing that all online content should be free or that individual authors are better off negotiating on their own with the likes of Apple, Google or major broadcasters fails to make the necessary distinctions among types of copyright material and categories of authors, as explained in Chapters 6 and 8. Conflating all types of copyright material as mere 'content' is rhetorically useful to diminish its value—and the rights attached to it. It is also short-sighted, however. The normative case that, for example, scientific articles based on publicly funded research should be widely available, and especially so in developing countries, is easily convincing. Is it really the same point to argue that the latest song or novel should be freely available to all without payment of any kind because it is online?[1081] Policy decisions based on this type of distinction should emphasize both open access to scientific publication and educational materials but also proper mechanisms to facilitate monetization of digital content and to enforce copyright in cases of commercial-scale infringements. As developing countries think about copyright policy as part of their developmental strategy, two important changes can be expected in the relevant industries. First, as the majority of Hollywood's revenue now come from overseas markets, it is easy to foresee a future where most movies will be produced outside the US. India produces more films than Hollywood and many countries, including Nigeria, are increasing their production. There is fluidity in the market share(s) available for countries that play that game better. This will imply *appropriate* copyright protection. Second, while copyright is necessary for certain industries to prosper, it should be protected

---

[1081]   I do not wish to bring into the discussion the specialized formats such as Braille copies made available to people with print disabilities. My long-standing support for the recently concluded Marrakesh Treaty to Facilitate Access to Published Works for Persons Who Are Blind, Visually Impaired, or Otherwise Print Disabled (2013) is part of the public record. See 'Comment submitted by Professor Daniel Gervais to the United States Copyright Office' (available at   <www.copyright.gov/docs/sccr/comments/2009/comments-2/daniel-gervais-vanderbilt-university-law-school.pdf> accessed 2 January 2016). Conflating this and broad access to commercial works for free strikes me as unfair at best.

appropriately not excessively. This leads in turn to several important policy prescriptions that developing countries can consider.

As this book has tried to demonstrate, copyright needs fundamental rethinking and restructuring in the digital age. This presents opportunities for developing countries. Many industries flourish because there are appropriate limits on copyright protection such as fair use that allow them to use, make available and modify existing content in appropriate cases without authorization.[1082] This does not mean that 'it should all be free', but rather that a proper combination of a properly cabined but actually enforceable right, licensing and exceptions can make the system work best. Professional authors whose works are valued should have a way of being paid. If there is a silver lining to the systematic destruction of author CMOs in the West, it is that it may create an advantage for authors elsewhere. It also means that distribution systems allowing users to do what they want with digital content are likely to be more successful in the marketplace. This should allow software start-ups in many countries to win a share in the global intermediation game. What matters online is not scarcity or control of every copy as many rights holder-driven business models still try to enforce. It is axiomatic that online business models based on the use of copyright content work best not when enforcing scarcity but rather when connecting content with as many users who value it as possible.[1083] Local knowledge in each country and localized social networking could help launch this type of intermediation in several countries.

To achieve this objective, developing countries should be given a degree of flexibility. In the proposed redraft of the Berne Convention in the Epilogue that follows this chapter, I have suggested a simplified version of the flexibilities contained in the current Appendix to the Convention, which is almost unworkable administratively.

## 13.4  THE ROLE OF WIPO

The World Intellectual Property Organization (WIPO) has been retooling to face the demands of the developing world. It has adopted a Development Agenda, which is meant to infuse all of its activities

---

[1082]  Thomas Rogers and Andrew Szamosszegi, 'Fair Use in the U.S. Economy: Economic Contribution of Industries Relying on Fair Use' (CCIA 2010) (available at <www.wired.com/images_blogs/threatlevel/2010/04/fairuseeconomy.pdf> accessed 2 January 2016).

[1083]  See page 22.

with a normative direction pointing towards measurable developmental objectives.[1084] This 'entails a significant reform of WIPO'.[1085] The Organization seems to have responded, noting for example that:

> IP for Development is an emphatic articulation of the notion that IP is not an end in itself but rather is a tool that could power countries' growth and development. WIPO, as the lead United Nations agency mandated to promote the protection of intellectual property through cooperation among states and in collaboration with other international organizations, is committed to ensuring that all countries are able to benefit from the use of IP for economic, social and cultural development.[1086]

Even with a retooled WIPO, however, the multilateral future looks bleak. Partly because they were unhappy with WIPO's reshaped mandate, a number of rights holder groups have pushed national and regional governments to implement an agenda seeking to increase rights and enforcement not under WIPO's aegis. Efforts such as the Anti-Counterfeiting Trade Agreement (ACTA), and the more recent Comprehensive and Progressive Trans-Pacific Partnership (CPTPP) and the draft Transatlantic Trade and Investment Partnership (TTIP) are examples of this. ACTA was the first international, non-multilateral IP negotiation to be based not on geography but on like-mindedness. I described it as the 'country club' model in 2010, an expression I used to contrast this approach from the multilateral one.[1087] CPTPP and TTIP are broader negotiations that include copyright and other areas of IP. Their broad nature allows for bargains to be struck across sectors (farm subsidies for longer effective patent terms, etc.). There is a significant risk of overreach, however. Those negotiations are not necessarily informed by the latest evidence on the optimal scope of copyright protection. In addition, the secrecy involving the negotiation process is an obstacle for those who would want to inject such evidence into the policy discussions.

There are reasons to remain hopeful, however. First, secrecy is not a

---

[1084] Carolyn Deere, 'The Politics of Intellectual Property Reform in Developing Countries: The Relevance of the World Intellectual Property Organization' in Netanel (n 1063) 111–33.

[1085] Sisule F Musungu, 'The Role of WIPO's Leadership in the Implementation of WIPO's Development Agenda' in deBeer (n 1073) 75.

[1086] WIPO, 'Intellectual Property for Development' (available at <www.wipo.int/ip-development/en> accessed 2 January 2016).

[1087] Daniel Gervais, 'Country Clubs, Empiricism, Blogs and Innovation: The Future of International Intellectual Property Norm-Making in the Wake of ACTA' in Mira Burri and Thomas Cottier (eds), *Trade Governance in the Digital Age* (CUP 2012) 323–43.

fatal obstacle. As with ACTA, leaks will inevitably happen, and democratic institutions, including the European Parliament, should continue to try to obtain information on the process. While I understand the reasons for the secrecy, I continue to believe that in the end it produces more harm than good.[1088] A much better approach is to have a public process—with some side meetings where necessary. Second, to the ideology of 'more is always better', one should not respond with the ideology of 'less is always better'. It is too easy to disprove what are in the end just ideological claims. A better approach is to debate the desired outcome publicly using available evidence and analyses.

In the end, those regional and 'country club' agreements will not contain identical rules, which will leave us with a patchwork of rules. This is already true in some important respects—even at the multilateral level.[1089] This will increase international business costs, because companies will have to comply and live with different rules in different countries and their enshrinement in major trade agreements will decrease flexibilities going forward. On the positive side, however, it will also provide more empirical evidence to determine which policies are working best to promote innovation-based economic development. Variations among countries and regions will provide raw data and it will be up to scholars to parse causation.

## 13.5 CONCLUSION

From the Scylla of excessive copyright protection, one must not run to the Charybdis of insufficient protection. Excessive exceptions or recourse to compulsory licensing or antitrust restrictions are likely to discourage certain forms of FDI and may thus retard economic development. The focus should be on FDI transactions that include knowledge transfer and ideally a significant R&D component. A country with a large domestic market may have an easier time launching its own innovation-based enterprises, and be less dependent on favourable international trade rules. Countries with a larger population are also more likely to be more diversified. Yet, to translate innovation into commercial ventures requires a host

---

[1088]  Ibid.

[1089]  Consider e.g. Marrakesh Treaty to Facilitate Access to Published Works for Persons Who Are Blind, Visually Impaired, or Otherwise Print Disabled (2013) art. 11, which recognizes four different versions of the 'three-step test'. The text of the treaty is available at <www.wipo.int/meetings/en/doc_details.jsp?doc_id=241683> accessed 2 January 2016.

of factors that small countries can also provide.[1090] Indeed, sometimes it may be easier for them than for larger entities. Education, infrastructure, legal reforms and the formation of industry-specific clusters should be front and centre. A structured approach to designing exceptions and limitations was proposed in Chapter 9 and can be followed by developing countries taking account of their greater needs in certain areas such as education.

There is little doubt in my mind that the overarching objective of policy makers should be *endogenous growth* of their innovation potential within a balanced IP regime, that is, with an emphasis on innovation where there is a reasonable likelihood of success in the country concerned. Smaller countries may have fewer options to diversify. The policy framework should allow entrepreneurship to flourish, which may in turn require a hands-on approach in strategic areas where venture capital and various (e.g., legal) resources may be hard to find locally. Among those, one should not underestimate the role that the extremely limited availability of venture/ risk capital in many developing countries plays in retarding innovation-based entrepreneurship and development.[1091]

---

[1090]    See Susy Frankel, *Test Tubes for Global Intellectual Property Issues: Small Market Economies* (CUP 2015).

[1091]    Marco della Cava, 'A not-so-crazy goal to find, nurture talent' *USA Today* (16 July 2013) 4B. Interview with Linda Rottenberg, CEO of Endeavor Global, a company that has funded over 500 young companies around the world. She is quoted as saying: 'I think the next Steve Jobs or Oprah could come from emerging markets.' The juxtaposition of a tech entrepreneur and a media personality in her quote is also interesting.

# Epilogue—towards a New Berne Convention

This epilogue—perhaps it should have been called a coda—contains the rough partition for a re-orchestration of the Berne Convention in light of the ideas contained in this book. The Convention was last revised (on substance) in 1967, with an Appendix added in 1971 to offer developing countries a labyrinthine path to issue compulsory licenses for the translation and reproduction of books.[1092] The received wisdom is that the Convention can never be revised because unanimity is required to revise the substantive part of the Convention (Berne, art. 27(3)). The generally held view is that getting the current membership (176 countries as of September 2018) to agree to anything is simply impossible. This led to the elaboration in the 1980s and 1990s not of a new Act of the Convention but rather of a possible 'protocol' to the Convention (not requiring amendment), which in turn became the WIPO Copyright Treaty, signed on December 20, 1996.

The backdrop for the changes proposed in this book is the massive use of digital content, of course, and indirectly a recognition that copyright is ill-equipped to deal with mass online uses, that is where the potential 'licensee' is the end-user, not a distributor or other professional. The level of difficulty increases when that end-user becomes a creator of content in his or her own right.

As things stand, they hardly have a chance to get better. 'Pro-IP' lobbies push for ACTA, CPTPP, TTIP and other TRIPS-Plus agreements and national measures designed to elevate the level of protection. 'Copyleft' lobbies push for separate multilateral agreements to lower protection, for example on print-disabled users or libraries, as happened in 2013 with the Marrakech Treaty. Whether this 'ships passing in the night' approach currently used to advance international IP norms is the best way forward strikes me as highly doubtful.

The 'pro' and 'con' discourse is misguided. A true reform should include *both* higher and/or clearer protection of copyright where needed *and* new limitations to reflect changes since 1971 and inadequacies that need to be

---

[1092] See Chapter 2.

corrected. This would be both normatively balanced and politically much more palatable. The best way to 'impose' exceptions and limitations is *not* be to have a series of sector-specific treaties on exceptions and limitations.[1093] A comprehensive review of existing instruments, such as a new Act of the Berne Convention including additions to and revisions of the WCT and WPPT the Marrakech Treaty and new exceptions and limitations, would, I suggest, be a far preferable way forward by offering options to stakeholders.[1094] It would also be much more likely to be ratified by a large number of WIPO members due to its appeal to a much larger constituency.

There may not be a large number of exceptions and limitations that can be made *mandatory* in a new Act of the Convention. One way to find common ground on mandatory exceptions and limitations would be to inventory national existing laws, as was done in 2014 for libraries and archives, to identify widespread state practice.[1095] Making an exception or limitation permissive opens the door to bilateral pressure on individual countries not to use the exceptions and limitations of course.[1096] It also suggests, however, that such exception or limitation is viewed—at least by states adopting the treaty—as consistent with international legal norms such as the three-step test.

---

[1093]   This includes discussion concerning a possible exceptions and limitations instrument for libraries and archives. See WIPO Provisional working document towards an appropriate international legal instrument (in whatever form) on limitations and exceptions for educational, teaching and research institutions and persons with other disabilities containing comments and textual suggestions, document SCCR/26/4 PROV. (Apr. 13, 213).

[1094]   The adoption of a new Act of the Berne Convention would have to be accomplished by consensus, which admittedly is no simple feat with 168 member states (as of March 2015). Berne Convention, art. 27(3). Yet the World Trade Organization, which has 160 members (March 2015), operates largely by consensus. WTO rules permit even a single member state to block agreement. See Marrakesh Agreement Establishing the World Trade Organization, Apr. 15, 1994, 33 I.L.M. 1226, 1232 (1994). Yet it seems to function, presumably because actors see a systemic interest in making it work. *See* Joost Pauwelyn, 'The Transformation of World Trade' (2005) 104 *Michigan Law Review* 1, 26–9. The suggestion I am making here is to generate a similar systemic interest in a more comprehensive review of the Berne Convention.

[1095]   WIPO published a study of existing exceptions and limitations showing a variegated worldwide picture. See Kenneth Crews, 'Study on Copyright Limitations and Exceptions for Libraries and Archives' (Nov. 5, 2014), WIPO document SCCR/29/3 (available at <http://www.wipo.int/meetings/en/doc_details.jsp?doc_id=290457>.

[1096]   See Henning Grosse Ruse-Khan, 'The International Law Relation Between TRIPS and Subsequent TRIPS-Plus Free Trade Agreements: Towards Safeguarding TRIPS Flexibilities'? (2011) 18 *Journal of Intellectual Property Law* 325, 349.

To increase the chances of moving the multilateral reform effort, rhetorically the focus should be on consensus not 'unanimity'. While unanimity is seen as near impossible (per received wisdom), consensus is not, as the WTO, which essentially functions on that basis, demonstrates. A 'consensus reform' of Berne would imply a real negotiation, instead of the development of competing and sometimes incompatible norm sets. Admittedly it will not be easy because lobbies in this field have not won many medals for their ability to compromise.

I propose the draft below as a starting point for a global discussion on copyright reform. Both those who want less or more copyright as a matter of ideology will reject it. If that happens, perhaps it is a sign that this text is indeed the beginning of a compromise. The aims of this text are as follows:

- Simplify the right, exceptions and limitations of the Convention;
- introduce a new formulation for economic rights consistent with the approach in this book;
- update the language where this is useful and in some cases necessary. I have left terms of art which could be updated but where the change struck me such as mostly superficial;
- update the text to reflect points on which a consensus may be possible with respect to online uses;
- update the enforcement provisions, which were almost non-existent in Berne;
- jettison obsolete provisions; and
- align the Convention with key parts of the WIPO Copyright Treaty and Marrakech Treaty.

Leadership from major players will be required. The two major 'universalisms' that have dominated copyright history for close to a century and continue to do so—though the duopoly is weakening—will find something here. The US and its insistence on capitalism as the engine of growth should welcome a model that reflects commercial concerns of those who create and use content. Europe, and its post-nation-state universalism which attaches much importance to Culture—I am using this term with a capital C to illustrate a maximum use of the semiotic space and anthropological role that the term can capture—should welcome an approach that attempts to provide creators who wish to hone their skills and master their craft the ability to do so. Indeed, Europe and the US already agree on strong copyright protection in trade agreements and elsewhere, but for partly different reasons. US negotiators tend to see copyright as providing an incentive for private capital to invest in the production and dissemination of successful commercial products by US companies. The worldwide

success of American music, films, television, software and books supports
this view. Europeans see copyright as a tool to support the 'cultural
economy, and an indispensable facet of European humanist universalism'.
I am not arguing that either of those views are wrong. But, as the pages
that separate this epilogue from the table of contents have tried to demonstrate, the implementation of the ideology of 'strong copyright' based
on the current model is poorly adapted to this century; hence the need to
*restructure*. Last but not least, the proposal is meant to allow all countries
and regions—expressly incorporating developmental objectives—to calibrate their copyright regime to their situation.

# _____ Act of the Berne Convention for the Protection of Literary and Artistic Works (2018 revised version)

The Contracting Parties, being equally animated by the desire to protect in an effective and adequate manner the rights of authors in their literary and artistic works, have agreed as follows:

## Article 1

### Abbreviated Expressions

For the purposes of this Act, unless expressly stated otherwise:

(i) "Convention" means the Berne Convention for the Protection of Literary and Artistic Works, as last revised at Paris on July 24, 1971, and amended on September 28, 1979 or an earlier Act of the Convention when referred to in this Act, unless the context requires otherwise;

(ii) "Contracting Party" means any State or intergovernmental organization party to this Act;

(iii) "intergovernmental organization" means an intergovernmental organization eligible to become party to this Act in accordance with Article ___;

(iv) "Organization" means the World Intellectual Property Organization;

(v) "Director General" means the Director General of the Organization;

(vi) "International Bureau" means the International Bureau of the Organization

## Article 2

### Protected Works

(1) The expression "literary and artistic works" shall include every production in the literary and artistic domain, whatever may be the

mode or form of its expression, such as books, pamphlets and other writings; computer programs in source or object code, lectures, addresses, sermons and other works of the same nature; dramatic or dramatico-musical works; choreographic works; musical compositions with or without words; audiovisual works; works of drawing, painting, architecture, sculpture, engraving and lithography; photographic works; works of applied art; illustrations, maps, plans, sketches and three-dimensional works relative to geography, topography, architecture or science.

(2) It shall, however, be a matter for legislation in the countries of the Union to prescribe that works in general or any specified categories of works shall not be protected unless they have been fixed in a tangible medium of expression.

(3) Translations, adaptations, arrangements of music and other derivative works based on one or more pre-existing literary or artistic works shall be protected as original works without prejudice to the copyright in the original work or works.

(4) It shall be a matter for legislation in the countries of the Union to determine the protection to be granted to official texts of a legislative, administrative and legal nature, and to official translations of such texts.

(5) Compilations of data or other material, whether in machine readable or other form, which by reason of the selection or arrangement of their contents constitute intellectual creations shall be protected as such, without prejudice to the copyright subsisting in the data or material itself.

(6) The works mentioned in this Article shall enjoy protection in all countries of the Union. This protection shall operate for the benefit of the author and his successors in title.

(7) It shall be a matter for legislation in the countries of the Union to determine the extent of the application of their laws to works of applied art and industrial designs and models, as well as the conditions under which such works, designs and models shall be protected. Works protected in the country of origin solely as designs and models shall be entitled in another country of the Union only to such special protection as is granted in that country to designs and models; however, if no such special protection is granted in that country, such works shall be protected as artistic works.

(8) The protection of this Act shall not apply to ideas, procedures, methods of operation or mathematical concepts as such, nor to news of the day or miscellaneous facts having the character of mere items of press information.

# Article 3

**Possible Limitation of Protection of Certain Works**

(1) It shall be a matter for legislation in the countries of the Union to exclude, wholly or in part, from the protection provided by the preceding Article political speeches and documents used in the course of legal proceedings.

(2) It shall also be a matter for legislation in the countries of the Union to determine the conditions under which lectures, addresses and other works of the same nature which are delivered in public may be reproduced by the press and social media, broadcast, communicated to the public and made the subject of public communication when such use is justified by the informatory purpose.

(3) Nevertheless, the author shall enjoy the exclusive right of making a collection of his or her works mentioned in the preceding paragraphs.

# Article 4

**Criteria of Eligibility for Protection**

(1) The protection of this Act shall apply to:
   *(a)* authors who are nationals of one of the countries of the Union, for their works, whether published or not;
   *(b)* authors who are not nationals of one of the countries of the Union, for their works first published in one of those countries, or simultaneously in a country outside the Union and in a country of the Union.

(2) Authors who are not nationals of one of the countries of the Union but who have their habitual residence in one of them shall, for the purposes of this Act, be assimilated to nationals of that country.

(3) The expression "published works" means works published with the consent of their authors, whatever may be the means of dissemination of the copies, provided that the availability of such copies has been such as to satisfy the reasonable requirements of the public, having regard to the nature of the work. The performance of a dramatic, dramatico-musical, audiovisual or musical work, the public recitation of a literary work, the communication to the public or the broadcasting of literary or artistic works, the exhibition of a work of art and the construction of a work of architecture shall not constitute publication.

(4)   A work shall be considered as having been published simultaneously in several countries if it has been published in two or more countries within thirty days of its first publication.

(5)   It shall be a matter for legislation in the countries of the Union to determine the circumstances in which online availability of a work shall constitute publication.

# Article 5

### Criteria of Eligibility for Protection of Audiovisual Works, Works of Architecture and Certain Artistic Works

The protection of this Act shall apply, even if the conditions of Article 3 are not fulfilled, to:

*(a)*   authors of audiovisual works the maker of which is headquartered or has an habitual residence in one of the countries of the Union;

*(b)*   authors of works of architecture erected in a country of the Union or of other artistic works incorporated in a building or other structure located in a country of the Union.

# Article 6

### Rights Guaranteed

(1)   Authors shall enjoy, in respect of works for which they are protected under this Act, in countries of the Union other than the country of origin, the rights which their respective laws do now or may hereafter grant to their nationals, as well as the rights specially granted by this Act.

(2)   Subject to the provisions of Article 17, the enjoyment and the exercise of these rights shall not be subject to any copyright-specific formality; such enjoyment and such exercise shall also be independent of the existence of protection in the country of origin of the work. Consequently, apart from the provisions of this Act, the extent of protection, as well as the means of redress afforded to the author to protect his or her rights, shall be governed exclusively by the laws of the country where protection is claimed.

(3)   Protection in the country of origin is governed by domestic law. However, when the author is not a national of the country of origin

of the work for which he is protected under this Act, he shall enjoy in that country the same rights as national authors.

(4)   The country of origin shall be considered to be:

   *(a)*   in the case of works first published in a country of the Union, that country; in the case of works published simultaneously in several countries of the Union which grant different terms of protection, the country whose legislation grants the shortest term of protection;

   *(b)*   in the case of works published simultaneously in a country outside the Union and in a country of the Union, the latter country;

   *(c)*   in the case of unpublished works or of works first published in a country outside the Union, without simultaneous publication in a country of the Union, the country of the Union of which the author is a national, provided that:

      (i)   when these are audiovisual works the maker of which is headquartered or has an habitual residence in a country of the Union, the country of origin shall be that country, and

      (ii)   when these are works of architecture erected in a country of the Union or other artistic works incorporated in a building or other structure located in a country of the Union, the country of origin shall be that country.

# Article 7

## Moral Rights

(1)   Independently of the author's economic rights, and even after any transfer of the said rights, the author shall have the right to claim authorship of the work and to object to any distortion, mutilation or other modification of, or other derogatory action in relation to, the said work, which would be demonstrably prejudicial to the author's honor or reputation.

(2)   The rights granted to the author in accordance with the preceding paragraph shall, after the author's death, be maintained, at least until the expiry of the economic rights, and shall be exercisable by the persons or institutions authorized by the legislation of the country where protection is claimed. However, those countries whose legislation, at the moment of their ratification of or accession to this Act, does not provide for the protection after the death of the author of all

the rights set out in the preceding paragraph may provide that some of these rights may, after the author's death, cease to be maintained.

(3)  The means of redress for safeguarding the rights granted by this Article shall be governed by the legislation of the country where protection is claimed.

# Article 8

### Economic Rights

(1)  Authors of published literary and artistic works protected by this Act shall enjoy the exclusive right of using and authorizing others to use works protected under this Act throughout the term of protection in any way that demonstrably affects the author's ability to exploit an actual or reasonably predictable market for such works, subject to the provisions contained in the following articles.

(2)  Any non-transient reproduction or storage of a protected work in an electronic medium, its performance in public, its adaptation or its communication to a public by broadcasting or it being made available to the public in such a way that members of the public may access these works from a place and at a time individually chosen by them otherwise, of a work protected under this Act may be deemed to affect the author's ability to exploit an actual or reasonably predictable market for the work unless evidence to the contrary is adduced.

(3)  In the case of computer programs and phonograms, any commercial rental may be deemed to affect the author's ability to exploit an actual or reasonably predictable market for the work. This obligation does not apply to rentals where (a) the program itself is not the essential object of the rental; or (b) under that Contracting Party's law, rights are not granted to authors in respect of phonograms.

(4)  In the case of audiovisual works, any commercial rental to the public of originals or copies which has led to widespread copying of such works shall be deemed to affect the author's ability to exploit an actual or reasonably predictable market for the work.

(5)  Authors of unpublished literary and artistic works protected by this Act shall enjoy the exclusive right of first publication throughout the term of protection.

# Article 9

## Exceptions and Limitations in Domestic Law[1097]

(1) It shall be a matter for legislation in the countries of the Union to permit the use of works protected under this Act in certain special cases, provided that such reproduction does not conflict with a normal exploitation of the work and does not unreasonably prejudice the legitimate interests of the author.

(2) Where use is made of works in accordance with the preceding paragraph of this Article, mention shall be made of the source, and of the name of the author if it appears thereon unless those would be unreasonable or contrary to practice under the circumstances.

# Article 10

## Term of Protection

(1) The term of protection granted by this Act shall be the life of the author and [fifty][seventy] years after the author's death.

(2) However, in the case of audiovisual works, the countries of the Union may provide that the term of protection shall expire [fifty] [seventy] years after the work has been made available to the public with the consent of the author, or, failing such an event within [fifty] [seventy] years from the making of such a work, [fifty][seventy] years after the making.

(3) In the case of anonymous or pseudonymous work or other work, other than a work of applied art, the term of protection which is calculated on a basis other than the life of a natural person, the term of protection granted by this Act shall expire [fifty][seventy] years after the work has been lawfully made available to the public or, failing such lawful availability within 50 years from the making of the work, 50 years from the end of the calendar year of making. However, when the pseudonym adopted by the author leaves no doubt as to the author's identity, the term of protection shall be

---

[1097] *Agreed statement to Article 9.* The Contracting Parties agree that any exception or limitation consistent with the Marrakesh Treaty to Facilitate Access to Published Works for Persons Who Are Blind, Visually Impaired or Otherwise Print Disabled shall be considered consistent also with Article 9.

that provided in paragraph (1). If the author of an anonymous or pseudonymous work discloses his or her identity during the above-mentioned period, the term of protection applicable shall be that provided in paragraph (1). The countries of the Union shall not be required to protect anonymous or pseudonymous works in respect of which it is reasonable to presume that their author has been dead for [fifty][seventy] years.

(4) It shall be a matter for legislation in the countries of the Union to determine the term of protection of works of applied art in so far as they are protected as artistic works; [however, this term shall last at least until the end of a period of twenty-five years from the making of such a work].

(5) The term of protection subsequent to the death of the author and the terms provided by paragraphs (2), (3) and (4) shall run from the date of death or of the event referred to in those paragraphs, but such terms shall always be deemed to begin on the first of January of the year following the death or such event.

(6) The countries of the Union may grant a term of protection in excess of those provided by the preceding paragraphs.

(7) Those countries of the Union bound by the Rome Act of this Convention* which grant, in their national legislation in force at the time of signature of the present Act, shorter terms of protection than those provided for in the preceding paragraphs shall have the right to maintain such terms when ratifying or acceding to the present Act.

(8) In any case, the term shall be governed by the legislation of the country where protection is claimed; however, unless the legislation of that country otherwise provides, the term shall not exceed the term fixed in the country of origin of the work.

(9) The provisions of the preceding paragraphs shall also apply in the case of a work of joint authorship, provided that the terms measured from the death of the author shall be calculated from the death of the last surviving author.

(10) Countries of the Union shall provide authors with the possibility of terminating any assignment, transfer of license of the author's rights no more than 35 years after the date of such assignment, transfer or license. The means and conditions to exercise the rights granted by this Article shall be governed by the legislation of the country whose laws are applicable to the assignment, transfer or license.

*As of September 2018 this only applied to Lebanon.

# Article 11

## Broadcasting and Related Rights

(1) It shall be a matter for legislation in the countries of the Union to determine the conditions under which the rights mentioned in Article 8 may be exercised in respect of (i) the broadcasting of protected works or the communication thereof to the public by any other means; (ii) any communication to the public or by rebroadcasting of the broadcast of the work, when this communication is made by an organization other than the original one; and (iii) the public communication by loudspeaker or any other analogous instrument of the work, but these conditions shall apply only in the countries where they have been prescribed. They shall not in any circumstances be prejudicial to the moral rights of the author, nor to the author's right to obtain equitable remuneration which, in the absence of agreement, shall be fixed by competent authority.

(2) In the absence of any contrary stipulation, permission granted in accordance with paragraph (1) of this Article shall not imply permission to record, by means of instruments recording sounds or images, the work broadcast. It shall, however, be a matter for legislation in the countries of the Union to determine the regulations for ephemeral recordings made by a broadcasting organization by means of its own facilities and used for its own broadcasts. The preservation of these recordings in official archives may be authorized by such legislation.

# Article 12

## Musical Works

(1) Each country of the Union may impose for itself reservations and conditions on the exclusive right granted to the author of a musical work and to the author of any words, the recording of which together with the musical work has already been authorized by the latter, to authorize the phonogram of that musical work, together with such words, if any; but all such reservations and conditions shall apply only in the countries which have imposed them and shall not, in any circumstances, be prejudicial to the rights of these authors to obtain equitable remuneration which, in the absence of agreement, shall be fixed by competent authority.

(2) The previous paragraph does not apply to audiovisual works.

## Article 13

### Audiovisual works

Ownership of copyright in an audiovisual work shall be a matter for legislation in the country where protection is claimed.

## Article 14

### Public Domain

(1) The Contracting Parties recognize the importance of a rich and accessible public domain.
(2) The Contracting Parties shall provide authors and their successors in title the legal means to dedicate a work to the public domain. Such legal means shall include making the information about the author, the work and the date on which the dedication is effective available and searchable on a publicly-available online resource. A dedication may be limited to certain uses of a work. It shall not affect rights transferred or licensed before the effective date of the dedication.
(3) Where Contracting Parties allow a dedication referred to in paragraph 2 to be revoked, they shall provide the legal means for third parties who used the work after the effective date of its dedication to continue to do so, subject to fair practice.
(4) Contracting Parties may use an intergovernmental organization to make the information about dedicated works mentioned in paragraph 2 available.

## Article 15

### Obligations concerning Technological Measures

Contracting Parties shall provide adequate legal protection and effective legal remedies against the circumvention of effective technological measures that are used by authors in connection with the exercise of their rights under this Act and that restrict acts, in respect of their works, which are not authorized by the authors concerned or permitted by law.

# Article 16

## Obligations concerning Rights Management Information

(1) Contracting Parties shall provide adequate and effective legal remedies against any person knowingly performing any of the following acts knowing, or with respect to civil remedies having reasonable grounds to know, that it will induce, enable, facilitate or conceal an infringement of any exclusive rights or right of remuneration covered by this Act:
   (i) to remove or alter any electronic rights management information without authority;
   (ii) to distribute, import for distribution, broadcast or communicate to the public, without authority, works or copies of works knowing that electronic rights management information has been removed or altered without authority.
(2) As used in this Article, "rights management information" means information which identifies the work, the author of the work, the owner of any right in the work, or information about the terms and conditions of use of the work, and any numbers or codes that represent such information, when any of these items of information is attached to a copy of a work or appears in connection with the communication of a work to the public.

# Article 17

## Right to Enforce Protected Rights

(1) The author of a literary or artistic work shall be able to enforce rights in such work and to claim actual damages and an injunction without having to accomplish any prior copyright-specific formality. Prohibited formalities shall include registration of the work, an obligation to use or add a copyright notice, and deposit of a copy of the work.
(2) In order that the author of a literary or artistic work protected by this Act shall, in the absence of proof to the contrary, be regarded as such, and consequently be entitled to institute infringement proceedings in the countries of the Union, it shall be sufficient for his or her name to appear on the work in the usual manner. This paragraph shall be applicable even if this name is a pseudonym, where the pseudonym adopted by the author leaves no doubt as to his or her identity.

(3) The person or body corporate whose name appears on an audiovisual work in the usual manner shall, in the absence of proof to the contrary, be presumed to be the maker of the said work.

(4) In the case of anonymous and pseudonymous works, other than those referred to in paragraph (2) above, the publisher whose name appears on the work shall, in the absence of proof to the contrary, be deemed to represent the author, and in this capacity he shall be entitled to protect and enforce the author's rights. The provisions of this paragraph shall cease to apply when the author reveals his or her identity and establishes a claim to authorship of the work.

   *(a)* In the case of unpublished works where the identity of the author is unknown, but where there is every ground to presume that he or she is a national of a country of the Union, it shall be a matter for legislation in that country to designate the person or competent authority which shall represent the author and shall be entitled to protect and enforce the author's rights in the countries of the Union.

   *(b)* Countries of the Union which make such designation under the terms of this provision shall notify the Director General by means of a written declaration giving full information concerning the authority thus designated. The Director General shall at once communicate this declaration to all other countries of the Union.

# Article 18

## Enforcement

(1) Contracting Parties shall comply with Articles 41 to 61, being Part III of the Agreement on Trade-related Aspects of Intellectual Property Rights.

(2) It shall be a matter for legislation in the countries of the Union to determine the extent to which [online][Internet] intermediaries may be held liable for making works protected under this Act unlawfully available online.

(3) Contracting Parties where an exemption from liability is provided for under the preceding paragraph shall institute a notification system allowing authors to request that [online][Internet] intermediaries remove copies of their works protected under this Act that have been made unlawfully available online.

# Article 19

## Works Existing on Convention's Entry into Force

(1) This Act shall apply to all works which, at the moment of its coming into force, have not yet fallen into the public domain in the country of origin through the expiry of the term of protection.
(2) If, however, through the expiry of the term of protection which was previously granted, a work has fallen into the public domain of the country where protection is claimed, that work shall not be protected anew.
(3) The application of this principle shall be subject to any provisions contained in special conventions to that effect existing or to be concluded between countries of the Union. In the absence of such provisions, the respective countries shall determine, each in so far as it is concerned, the conditions of application of this principle.
(4) The preceding provisions shall also apply in the case of new accessions to the Union and to cases in which protection is extended by the application of Article 10 or by the abandonment of reservations.

# Article 20

## Developing Countries

Two options
A:
(1) Any Contacting Party regarded as a developing country in conformity with the established practice of the General Assembly of the United Nations which ratifies or accedes to this Act may, having regard to its economic situation and its social or cultural needs, designate a competent authority to issue translation and reproduction licenses for works published in printed or analogous forms, according to the conditions contained in the following paragraphs.
(2) After the expiration of a period of three years, or one year in the case of translations into a language which is not in general use in one or more developed countries which are members of the Union, if a translation of a work as described in paragraph 1 has not been published in a language in general use in that country by the owner of the right of translation, or with his authorization, any national of such country may obtain a license to make a translation of the work in the said language and publish the translation in printed or analogous

forms of reproduction. A license under the conditions provided for in this paragraph may also be granted if all the editions of the translation published in the language concerned are out of print.

(3)    After the expiration of a period of [three][five] years, if no copies of a work as described in paragraph 1 have been distributed in that country to the general public or in connection with systematic instructional activities, by the owner of the right of reproduction or with his authorization, at a price reasonably related to that normally charged in the country for comparable works, any national of such country may obtain a license to reproduce and publish the work for use in connection with systematic instructional activities.

(4)    A license under paragraphs (2) or (3) may be granted only if the applicant, in accordance with the procedure of the country concerned, establishes either that he or she has requested, and has been denied, authorization by the owner of the right to make and publish the translation or to reproduce and publish the edition at a price reasonably related to that normally charged in the country for comparable works, as the case may be, or that, after due diligence on his part, he or she was unable to find the owner of the right.

B:

Developing country Contracting Parties may avail themselves of the provisions contained in the Appendix of the Berne Convention.

# Article 21

### Access to Published Works for Persons Who Are Blind, Visually Impaired or Otherwise Print Disabled

Any Contracting Party taking appropriate measures to implement the Marrakesh Treaty to Facilitate Access to Published Works for Persons Who Are Blind, Visually Impaired or Otherwise Print Disabled of June 27, 2013, in accordance with the terms of said Treaty, shall be considered to be complying with its obligations under this Act.

# Article 22

### Laws

(1)    Laws and regulations, and final judicial decisions and administrative rulings of general application, made effective by a Contracting Party

pertaining to the subject matter of this Act shall be published, or where such publication is not practicable, made publicly available, in a national language, in such a manner as to enable governments, right holders and users to become acquainted with them.

(2) Contracting Parties shall notify all laws and regulations referred to in paragraph 1 to Director General as quickly as possible after their adoption.

# Article 23

### Berne Union Membership

The Contracting Parties shall be members of the same Union as the States party to the Berne Convention, whether or not they are party to the Berne Convention.

# Article 24

### Application of the Berne Convention

This Act alone shall be applicable as regards the mutual relations of States party to both this Act and the Berne Convention.

# [Additional Administrative Provisions]

# Appendix 1

## A primer on fair use and fair dealing

### A1.1 FAIR USE

Fair use finds its origins in the United States as a judicially created doctrine that permits some unauthorized uses of copyrighted works. It was codified in the 1976 revision of the US Copyright Act as section 107.[1098] It reads as follows:

> Notwithstanding the provisions of sections 106 and 106A, the fair use of a copyrighted work, including such use by reproduction in copies or phonorecords or by any other means specified by that section, for purposes such as criticism, comment, news reporting, teaching (including multiple copies for classroom use), scholarship, or research, is not an infringement of copyright. In determining whether the use made of a work in any particular case is a fair use the factors to be considered shall include —
> (1) the purpose and character of the use, including whether such use is of a commercial nature or is for nonprofit educational purposes;
> (2) the nature of the copyrighted work;
> (3) the amount and substantiality of the portion used in relation to the copyrighted work as a whole; and
> (4) the effect of the use upon the potential market for or value of the copyrighted work.
> The fact that a work is unpublished shall not itself bar a finding of fair use if such finding is made upon consideration of all the above factors.

Fair use is expressed as (a) a non-exhaustive list of purposes combined with (b) a seemingly exhaustive list of factors (4) to be considered by

---

[1098] For the reader interested in learning more, four of the best articles on fair use are written since 1976: Pierre N Leval, 'Toward a Fair Use Standard' (1990) 103 *Harvard Law Review* 1105; D Nimmer, 'Fairest Of Them All' and other Fairy Tales of Fair Use' (2003) 66 *Law and Contemporary Problems* 263; William W Fisher III, 'Reconstructing the Fair Use Doctrine' (1988) 101 *Harvard Law Review* 1659; and Wendy Gordon, 'Fair Use as Market Failure: A Structural and Economic Analysis of the Betamax Case and its Predecessors' (1982) 82 *Columbia Law Review* 1600.

courts on a case-by-case basis. Since the 1976 codification,[1099] there have been several decisions, including four by the US Supreme Court (*Sony Corp v Universal City Studios, Inc*;[1100] *Harper & Row, Publishers, Inc v Nation Enterprises*;[1101] *Campbell v Acuff-Rose Music, Inc*;[1102] and *MGM v Grokster*[1103]). We will consider those cases below but before doing so, a brief look at the pre-codification situation is in order.

The first pre-1976 case worth mentioning here is *Folsom v March*.[1104] Justice Story had to decide whether a book by Defendant March for school libraries which quoted excerpts from letters (to and from) George Washington most of which had only been published by Plaintiff Folsom was an infringement of copyright. In a famous dictum, he wrote the following:

> ...we must often, in deciding questions of this sort, look to the nature and objects of the selections made, the quantity and value of the materials used, and the degree in which the use may prejudice the sale, or diminish the profits, or *supersede the objects*, of the original work.[1105] (emphasis added)

The harm to plaintiff's market test is now generally referred to in US copyright doctrine as the 'Folsom test.'

While *Folsom* dealt with commercial reuse (though for education), other cases used similar criteria and applied them to other situations, including creation of new works for example, *Lawrence v Dana*,[1106] the first case to use the term 'fair use'. The court applied a test of substantial injurious appropriation to decide whether the reuse amounted to infringement.

The process that led to the adoption of the 1976 Copyright Act in the US and the codification of fair use included a number of reports and studies. A major report by the US Register of Copyrights published in

---

[1099]  Congress stated clearly that the purpose of s. 107 was to 'restate the present judicial doctrine of fair use, not to change, narrow or enlarge it in any way'. HR Rep No. 1476, 94th Cong, 2d Sess 66 (1976); S Rep No. 473, 94th Cong, 1st Sess 62 (1975).

[1100]  *(Sony v Betamax)* 464 US 417, 104 S Ct 774, 78 L Ed 2d 574, 220 USPQ (BNA) 665 (1984).

[1101]  471 US 539, 105 S Ct 2218, 85 L Ed 2d 588, 11 Media L Rep (BNA) 1969, 225 USPQ (BNA) 1073 (1985) [Harper & Row].

[1102]  510 US 569, 114 S Ct 1164, 127 L Ed 2d 500, 22 Media L Rep (BNA) 1353, 29 USPQ 2d (BNA) 1961 (1994).

[1103]  125 S Ct 2764, 2778–2779, 162 L Ed 2d 781, 33 Media L Rep (BNA) 1865, 75 USPQ 2d (BNA) 1001 (US 2005).

[1104]  9 F Cas 342, No 4901 (CCD Mass 1841).

[1105]  Ibid., 348.

[1106]  (1869) 15 F.Cas. 26.

1961 (*Report of the Register of Copyrights on the General Revision of the US Copyright Law*) cites examples of activities that courts have regarded as fair use:

> ...quotation of excerpts in a review or criticism for purposes of illustration or comment; quotation of short passages in a scholarly or technical work, for illustration or clarification of the author's observations; use in a parody of some of the content of the work parodied; summary of an address or article, with brief quotations, in a news report; reproduction by a library of a portion of a work to replace part of a damaged copy; reproduction by a teacher or student of a small part of a work to illustrate a lesson; reproduction of a work in legislative or judicial proceedings or reports; incidental and fortuitous reproduction, in a newsreel or broadcast, of a work located in the scene of an event being reported.

According to Judge Pierre Leval (judge on the Court of Appeals for the Second Circuit and the author of a number of important fair use decisions[1107]), the four factors are wrongly seen (and sometimes wrongly applied) as a simple 'scorecard'. In his opinion, and this is supported by the early cases, the first factor is the 'soul' of fair use. The question is, what is the purpose and character of the use—does it fulfil the principal objective of copyright law to stimulate creativity for public illumination? The second factor, the nature of the copyrighted work, implies that certain types of copyright material are more amenable to fair use than others. The third factor, the amount and substantiality of the use means that the use must be reasonable in relation to purported justification. The criterion is applied qualitatively not just quantitatively. For example, a quote of 100 per cent of short notes, poetry, or material not destined for publication (a matter for privacy law, not copyright) may be justified if necessary. The fourth factor parallels the second step of the three-step test. The effect on the market is the 'most important element' (*Harper & Row*). Because copyright is neither a natural right inherent in authorship nor 'ordinary' property (otherwise any taking is illegal), the impact must be assessed based on whether the fair use is a substitute ('supersedes the use of the original' from *Folsom*).

---

[1107]   *New Era Publications Intern, ApS v Henry Holt and Co, Inc*, 695 F Supp 1493, 1502, 15 Media L Rep (BNA) 2161, 8 USPQ 2d (BNA) 1713 (SDNY 1988), judgment aff'd, 873 F 2d 576, 16 Media L Rep (BNA) 1559, 10 USPQ 2d (BNA) 1561 (2d Cir 1989); *Salinger v Random House, Inc*, 811 F 2d 90, 97, 13 Media L Rep (BNA) 1954, 1 USPQ 2d (BNA) 1673, 87 ALR Fed 853 (2d Cir 1987), opinion supplemented on denial of reh'g, 818 F 2d 252, 2 USPQ 2d (BNA) 1727 (2d Cir 1987), quoted at *New Era Publications Intern, ApS v Henry Holt and Co, Inc*, ibid.

### A1.1.1 US Supreme Court cases since 1978

#### A1.1.1.1 Sony Betamax

In *Sony*, owners of audio-visual works sued a manufacturer of home videocassette recorders on the theory that their sale of equipment which the purchasers used for videotaping broadcasts of copyrighted material was contributory infringement,[1108] and that the manufacturer was vicariously liable[1109] for the damages suffered by the copyright holders as a result of the infringements committed by purchasers of the machines. Thus there were two issues for decision. First, whether the recording of copyrighted works by owners of videocassette recorders was an infringement. Second, if it was an infringement, whether vicarious liability for these infringements would be imposed on the manufacturing and distributing of these machines.[1110] In a hearing before Congress in 1982, two years before *Sony* made its way to the Supreme Court, Jack Valenti, the well-known former representative of the Motion Picture Association, had famously declared: 'I say to you that the VCR is to the American film producer and the American public as the Boston strangler is to the woman home alone.'[1111]

The trial court found that enforcement in private homes would be 'highly intrusive and practically impossible ... particularly ... when plaintiffs themselves choose to beam their programs into these homes' thus pitting copyright against privacy, not unlike in the Canadian *BMG* case.[1112] Another parallel may be drawn between *BMG* (P2P) and *Sony*:

> Although the majority opinion alluded to it only twice, and the dissent ignored it, perhaps the most salient and inescapable fact about the case was that the ownership and use of videocassette recorders had become widespread throughout the United States with a constantly growing base of installed machines. Consumer demand for video recorders was growing, and the market was far from saturated. To put it bluntly, the Court was faced with the prospect of criminalizing conduct which was engaged in on a regular and open basis by the

---

[1108] Contributory infringement requires: (1) knowledge of the infringing activity; and (2) assistance or inducement (the 'contribution') to the alleged piracy.

[1109] Vicarious liability, a form of indirect copyright infringement, is found where an operator has: (1) the right and ability to control users; and (2) a direct financial benefit from allowing their acts of piracy.

[1110] *Sony v Betamax* (n 1100) 418.

[1111] Home Recording of Copyrighted Works: Hearings on HR 4783, HR 4794, HR 4808, HR 5250, HR 5488, and HR 5705 before The Subcomm. on Courts, Civil Liberties, and The Administration of Justice of the House Comm. on the Judiciary, 97th Cong. 1–3(1982).

[1112] At the Trial Division: *BMG Canada Inc v John Doe*, [2004] 3 FCR 241 (FCTD).

American public, and which was seen by the vast majority of the public as both normal and desirable. The copyright holders were asking the Court to make a decision that could never realistically be enforced against the persons whose direct conduct was outlawed.[1113]

The Court of Appeals for the Ninth Circuit reversed the finding that copying on a VCR was prima facie reproduction and not fair use. In a very interesting and 'negotiated' decision,[1114] the Supreme Court essentially eliminated, for the first time, a requirement which had been present in the fair use doctrine since *Folsom*, namely that the use had to be productive/transformative. Noting that the case involved 'a difficult balance between the interests of authors and inventors in the control and exploitation of their writings and discoveries on the one hand, and society's competing interest in the free flow of ideas, information, and commerce on the other hand',[1115] the majority imposed on the right holders a burden to prove potential harm to the market (the fourth fair use criterion and a close equivalent to the second step of the three-step test) in the case of noncommercial use, adding that 'time-shifting merely enables a viewer to see such a work which he had been invited to witness in its entirety free of charge'.[1116] Otherwise its analysis of the fourth criteria is rather cursory, as was the review of precedents. It is worth mentioning that in respect of the fourth factor, the court noted that what was necessary 'is a showing by a preponderance of the evidence that some meaningful likelihood of future harm exist'. The court did *not* find that making libraries of films or distributing copies made on a VCR was fair use, nor that all private copying was fair use, noting that 'time-shifting merely enables a viewer to see such a work which he had been invited to witness in its entirety free of charge'.[1117]

On contributory infringement, the court imported from patent law the 'staple article of commerce doctrine' according to which manufacturers of devices capable of substantial non-infringing uses were not liable.

Ironically, had the rights holders been successful, one wonders whether there would be millions of VCRs and the technology that replaced them, the DVD player, and which now represents the second largest income market for pre-recorded and pay-per-view movies.

---

[1113]  Ibid.

[1114]  For a detailed account of the negotiation, see Jessica Litman, 'The Story of *Sony v Universal Studios*: Mary Poppins Meets the Boston Strangler', *in* Jane C. Ginsburg and Rochelle Cooper Dreyfuss (eds). *Intellectual Property Stories* (West, 2006).

[1115]  *Sony*, 464 US 417, 429.

[1116]  Ibid., 449–50.

[1117]  Ibid., 450.

Congress reacted by passing the Audio Home Recording Act[1118] which required a technical ban on multigenerational copying, imposed a levy on blank digital *audio* media but also banned lawsuits against consumers.

Professor Wendy Gordon[1119] published an economic analysis of fair use after *Sony.* She wrote that:

> [f]air use should be awarded to the defendant in a copyright infringement action when (1) market failure is present; (2) transfer of the use to defendant is socially desirable; and (3) an award of fair use would not cause substantial injury to the incentives of the plaintiff copyright holder. The first element of this test ensures that market bypass will not be approved without good cause. The second element of the test ensures that the transfer of a license to use from the copyright holder to the unauthorized user effects a net gain in social value. The third element ensures that the grant of fair use will not undermine the incentive-creating purpose of the copyright law.

In *Texaco,* the Second Circuit considered the impact of fair use on potential licensing revenues and noted: '[i]t is indisputable that, as a general matter, a copyright holder is entitled to demand a royalty for licensing others to use its copyrighted work, and that the impact on potential licensing revenues is a proper subject for consideration in assessing the fourth factor'.[1120] But 'were a court automatically to conclude in every case that potential licensing revenues were impermissibly impaired simply because the secondary user did not pay a fee for the right to engage in the use, the fourth fair use factor would always favor the copyright holder'.[1121]

### A1.1.1.2  Harper & Row

*The Nation* magazine had obtained an unauthorized copy of the soon-to-be published manuscript of the memoirs of ex-president Gerald Ford. It quoted 300 words from the memoirs. *The Nation* claimed that the relatively small taking was fair use. The district court found that the use of the material was infringing, which was reversed by a 2-1 decision of the Court of Appeals for the Second Circuit. The focus at the Supreme Court (based on Folsom) was on whether the use superseded the use of the original. The court noted that under ordinary circumstances, author's right to control

---

[1118] The Audio Home Recording Act of 1992 added Chapter 10, entitled 'Digital Audio Recording Devices and Media,' to title 17 of the US Code (the US Copyright Act). Pub L No 102–563, 106 Stat. 4237.

[1119] See Wendy Gordon, 'Fair Use as Market Failure: A Structural and Economic Analysis of the Betamax Case and Its Predecessors' (1982) 82 *Columbia Law Review* 1600.

[1120] Above note 298, 929.

[1121] Ibid., fn 17.

the first public appearance of his undisseminated expression will outweigh a claim of fair use. This is recognized in last paragraph of §107: 'The fact that a work is unpublished shall not itself bar a finding of fair use if such finding is made upon consideration of all the above factors.' Although news reporting is one of the purposes mentioned in the chapeau of section 107, and that _The Nation's_ claim was buttressed by free speech arguments (First Amendment), the court found that the use was infringing. The commercial nature of use weighed against fair use and free speech did not

> expand fair use to an extent that would destroy any expectation of copyright protection in the work of a public figure and thus diminish if not destroy the incentives to create or publish such works. Where an author and publisher have invested extensive resources in creating an original work and are poised to release it to the public, no legitimate aim is served by preempting the right of first publication.[1122]

For our purposes, the most important finding of _Harper & Row_ was that the fourth factor (effect of the use on the potential market for or potential value of the work) was 'undoubtedly the single most important element of fair use', adding that once a copyright holder had established 'with reasonable probability the existence of a causal connection between the infringement and a loss of revenue, the burden properly shifts to the infringer to show that this damage would have occurred had there been no taking of copyrighted expression'.

Lower courts in the US interpreted _Sony_ and _Harper & Row_ as establishing a presumption that commercial use was unfair.[1123]

### A1.1.1.3   Campbell v Acuff-Rose

The rap group '2 Live Crew' had recorded a rap version of Roy Orbison's 'Oh, Pretty Woman,' and rewritten the lyrics in rather dramatic fashion. The Supreme Court found that this use was comparable to a parody. The court went back to basics, as it were, finding that _Folsom_ had correctly 'distilled' the fair use doctrine.

Its analysis of the four factors was thus based on Folsom's teachings and briefly as follows:

- first factor: purpose and character of use. The court must consider the nature and objects of selections made;
  - ○ this factor is used to determine whether the new work supersedes the objects of the first or 'adds something new,

---

[1122]   _Harper & Row_, 471 US 539, 557.
[1123]   Abrams, §15.19.

with a further purpose or different character, altering the first
with new expression, meaning or message'. The court 'analysis to the extent the use brought something new to the audience rather than the emphasis of *Sony* and *Harper & Row* on
whether or not the use was commercial or non-commercial';[1124]

- ○ this is a statement of the 'transformative use' doctrine.
- second factor: nature of the copyrighted work. This is determined by measuring the value of materials used;
- third factor: amount and substantiality. The court must measure the quantity and quality of the material used. In the case of a parody, the factor applies somewhat differently because the parodist must draw upon recognizable elements of the parodied work;
- fourth factor: effect on market. Presented as the core of 'Folsom test', the Court defined it as 'the degree to which the use may prejudice the sale, or diminish the profits. . .of the original work'.

As Professor Abrams notes, the

> impact of *Campbell* on prior fair use analysis is immense. In specific terms,
> *Campbell* is significant for its minimization of the presumptions that arose from
> dicta in *Sony*. . . the question of whether the use is a transformative one, and the
> extent of any such transformation is now perhaps the most critical inquiry [. . .]
> *Campbell* is pellucidly clear that fair use analysis requires fact sensitive case-by-
> case analysis rather than mechanical application of presumptions.[1125]

In *Campbell*, the US Supreme Court essentially buried the fair use
findings of *Sony*, insisting that fair uses must be transformative or productive, leaving only the contributory infringement part of the *Sony* analysis,
which resurfaced in *Grokster*:

> Although such transformative use is not absolutely necessary for a finding of
> fair use, the goal of copyright, to promote science and the arts, is generally
> furthered by the creation of transformative works. Such works thus lie at the
> heart of the fair use doctrine's guarantee of breathing space within the confines
> of copyright and the more transformative the new work, the less will be the sig-
> nificance of other factors, like commercialism, that may weigh against a finding
> of fair use.[1126]

The focus is clearly on transformative, socially desirable reuse.

---

[1124] Abrams, §15.21.
[1125] Ibid., §15.26.
[1126] *Campbell*, 510 US 569, 579.

#### A1.1.1.4 MGM v Grokster

P2P technology (Internet file-sharing) is one of the many new possibilities opened up by Internet technology and the network effects it induces. In *Grokster*, the US Supreme Court had to decide whether the maker of one of the programs used to file-share was liable under either contributory or vicarious liability doctrines of infringement[1127] by P2P users.

A number of observers thought that Grokster and, more broadly, the legality of P2P technology would be 'saved' by the *Sony* doctrine because like the VCR in *Sony*, P2P technology is capable of substantial, noncommercial and/or non-infringing uses and the technology is present in millions of homes. This was a misreading of Sony and cases decided since. First of all, *Sony*'s fair use findings were all but buried in *Campbell*. Second, P2P is not 'private' in the same way as time-shifting. Third, infringing uses dwarf non-infringing ones. In *Sony*, while the test of non-infringing use was that of 'substantiality' (because that forms part of patent law's 'staple article of commerce' doctrine) the evidence showed that the overwhelming majority of VCR owners used them to time-shift (ie, a non-infringing use). Exchanging protected music or videos on P2P without a license is not transformative, at least not in a classical sense. It transforms markets and access to works, but not the works themselves. The format in which the musical and audio-visual works, performances and recordings are made available on P2P is functionally comparable to that of a CD or DVD.

Yet, while finding Grokster and other P2P providers liable, the majority (Justice Stevens who had penned the *Sony* majority opinion was in the dissent), did not openly reverse *Sony* but rather found as follows:

> The question is under what circumstances the distributor of a product capable of both lawful and unlawful use is liable for acts of copyright infringement by third parties using the product. We hold that one who distributes a device with the *object of promoting its use to infringe copyright,* as shown by *clear expression or other affirmative steps taken to foster infringement,* is liable for the resulting acts of infringement by third parties.

Essentially, liability was found under what we might refer to as the tort of inducement, which also forms part of Canadian intellectual property law,[1128] though its interface with the right to authorize found in section 3 *in fine* of the Copyright Act, which would apply to 'indirect' liability, is not clear. *Grokster* can be said to hinge on evidentiary matters: the P2P

---

[1127] See notes 1108 and 1109 above.
[1128] *Dableh v Ontario Hydro*, [1996] 3 FC 751 (CA).

operators had induced infringement by encouraging Napster users to switch after Napster was shut down.

While it now seems clear from the above cases that transformative use is often the principal criterion for a finding of fair use, one must not lose sight of the fact that a fair use is one that does not supersede the market for the original work. A copyright holder may not like a parody of her work, nor a fair use of another kind, but copyright is not pure property, and unauthorized uses are not trespasses in the ordinary sense. As a legal matter, the decoupling of copyright and, more broadly, intellectual property, on the one hand, and property or natural right justifications for copyright, on the other, was reinforced by the major displacement of international rule-making from the World Intellectual Property Organization (WIPO) to the World Trade Organization (WTO) during but also after the TRIPS negotiations. Put differently, by setting the IP table in the house of trade, the cloak of IP as a simple variation on the classic theme of property[1129] or even as a human right – notions essentially developed in the eighteenth and nineteenth century – was bound to fall. As a policy matter, however, the Government should retain as one of the main objectives of copyright the protection of authors, the objective from which natural rights justification were derived in the first place. As the US fair uses cases demonstrate, that is one of several objectives that need to be put in balance.

**A1.1.2  US Appellate Cases Dealing with 'Transformative' Use**

There are three appellate cases that deserve mention before leaving our overview of fair use. The first is the *Bill Graham Archives* (BGA) case.[1130] The biographer of the rock band *The Grateful Dead* used copies of promotional posters in his book. Those posters were still protected and actively licensed. The main focus was again on transformative use:

> In the instant case, DK's purpose in using the copyrighted images at issue in its biography of the Grateful Dead is plainly different from the original purpose for which they were created. Originally, each of BG's images fulfilled the dual purposes of artistic expression and promotion. The posters were apparently widely distributed to generate public interest in the Grateful Dead and to convey information to a large number people about the band's forthcoming concerts. In contrast, DK used each of BGA's images as historical artefacts to document and represent the actual occurrence of Grateful Dead concert events featured on Illustrated Trip's timeline.

---

[1129]  See generally William M Landes & Richard A Posner. *The Political Economy of Intellectual Property Law* (American Enterprise Institute Press, 2004).
[1130]  *Bill Graham Archives v Dorling Kindersley Ltd*, 448 F 3d 605 (2d Cir 2006).

...We conclude that ... uses fulfill DK's transformative purpose of enhancing the biographical information in Illustrated Trip, a purpose separate and distinct from the original artistic and promotional purpose for which the images were created.

The main reason to mention this case is the determination that *transformative markets* (improved access) provide benefits that exceed the cannibalization of the original one(s). This is similar to another case which takes the doctrine one step further, and perhaps a step too far, namely *Kelly v Arriba*.[1131] In that case, displaying search results as 'thumbnail' version of copyrighted pictures by search engine was said to be transformative use, because it 'serves an entirely different function' than the copyright holder's original images.[1132] The original images:

> are artistic works intended to inform and to engage the viewer in an aesthetic experience. [. . .] Arriba's use of Kelly's images in the thumbnails is unrelated to any aesthetic purpose. Arriba's search engine functions as a tool to help index and improve access to images on the internet and their related web sites. In fact, users are unlikely to enlarge the thumbnails and use them for artistic purposes because the thumbnails are of much lower-resolution than the originals.[1133]

In short, copyright holders may not pre-empt exploitation of transformative markets. A similar finding was made, again in the Ninth Circuit, in the *Perfect 10* case.[1134]

In those two cases, one could argue that a new work (a collection of thumbnail images) was created and was found to have little or no negative impact on the market for the original work and no demonstrable loss of income. Yet, a collection of all images found on the Internet or part thereof of even from another site is unlikely to be original, as the work is either automated and/or mechanical in nature (*CCH*). Additionally, the

---

[1131] *Kelly v Arriba Soft Corp*, 336 F 3d 811, 818–20 (9th Cir 2003), finding online search engine's use of thumbnail-sized images to be highly transformative.
[1132] Ibid., 818.
[1133] Ibid.
[1134] *Perfect 10, Inc v Amazon.com, Inc*, 487 F 3d 701 (9th Cir 2007), finding that a work is 'transformative', for purpose of inquiry into fair use factor that looks at the purpose and character of the use of a copyrighted work, when the new work does not merely supersede the objects of the original creation but rather adds something new, with a further purpose or different character, altering the first with new expression, meaning, or message; conversely, if the new work supersedes the use of the original, the use is likely not a fair use. In a parallel case (*Perfect 10, Inc v Visa Intern. Service Ass'n*, 83 USPQ 1144), the same Court decided that credit card companies that process payments for allegedly infringing material are not liable.

main purpose of the operators of the sites at issue in *Kelly* and *Perfect 10* was not to create works but to provide access. This is a stretch of the notion of transformative use but could be viewed as an application of the doctrine that takes account of the possibilities of Internet technology.

Fair use is often described as a tool to respond to market failures. When transaction costs are too high or permission unavailable (anti-dissemination motives) and/or social costs of relying on permission too high (e.g., vis-à-vis the positive externalities of teaching, scholarship, creation of new works and research), it acts as a safety valve.

Market failure is not or no longer necessarily the key driver. In the litigation opposing the Authors Guild of America and Google concerning Google's scanning and making available of millions of in-copyright books that became not just available (in fairly short 'snippets') but also word-searchable, the US Court of Appeals for the Second Circuit (New York) took the view that Google's use was fair, whether or not a licensing arrangement could have been negotiated.[1135] The Court stated that Google was not disseminating the protected expression but information about it:

> [P]recedents do not support the proposition Plaintiffs assert—namely that the availability of licenses for providing unprotected information about a copyrighted work, or supplying unprotected services related to it, gives the copyright holder the right to exclude others from providing such information or services.[1136]

The court, having noted that copyright 'is a commercial right, intended to protect the ability of authors to profit from the exclusive right to merchandise their own work',[1137] found that Goggle's snippets added 'important value to the basic transformative search function, which tells only whether and how often the searched term appears in the book'.[1138] The opinion again stretches the notion of transformativeness because, as in *Perfect 10*, it is not the expression of the original work that is (inherently) transformed, but rather the mode of access to it.

### A1.1.3  Fair Use in the Israeli Copyright Act

The Israeli Copyright Act,[1139] adopted in 2007 and which entered into force on 25 May 2008 contains a fair use provision that differs slightly

---

[1135]  *Authors Guild v Google, Inc*, No 13-4829 (2d Cir 16 October 2015).
[1136]  Ibid., 40
[1137]  Ibid., 16.
[1138]  Ibid., 23.
[1139]  2007 *Law Statutes of Israel*, at 34, November 25, 2007.

from the equivalent US provision.[1140] The English version reads as follows:

(a) Fair use of a work is permitted for purposes such as: private study, research, criticism, review, journalistic reporting, quotation, or instruction and examination by an educational institution.

(b) In determining whether a use made of a work is fair within the meaning of this section the factors to be considered shall include, inter alia, all of the following:

  (1) The purpose and character of the use;
  (2) The character of the work used;
  (3) The scope of the use, quantitatively and qualitatively, in relation to the work as a whole;
  (4) The impact of the use on the value of the work and its potential market.

(c) The Minister may make regulations prescribing conditions under which a use shall be deemed a fair use.[1141]

By comparison, the list of purposes in the US Act mentions criticism, comment, news reporting, teaching (including multiple copies for classroom use), scholarship, or research. The four criteria or factors are comparable except that the first US purpose specifically mentions 'whether such use is of a commercial nature or is for non-profit educational purposes'. Without further information, it seems that differences in the wording of the other factors may be attributable to the translation.

## A1.2  FAIR DEALING

### A1.2.1  Fair Dealing in the United Kingdom

It is possible that the roots of fair dealing lay in the preamble of the Statute of Anne of 1710, although this is not conclusive among academics.[1142] Broadly speaking, British copyright law aims to protect authors and

---

[1140] For a more thorough discussion, see Orit Fishman Afori, 'An Open Standard "Fair Use" Doctrine: A Welcome Israeli Initiative' (2008) 30(3) *European Intellectual Property Review* 85–6.

[1141] Israel, Copyright Act, 2007 (as amended to 2011), s. 19, translation from WIPO Lex.

[1142] M deZwart, 'A Historical Analysis of the Birth of Fair Dealing and Fair Use: Lessons for the Digital Age' (2007) 1 *Intellectual Property Quarterly* 60, 61. See also: M Handler and D Rolph, '"A Real Pea-Souper": The Panel Case and the Development of the Fair Dealing Defences to Copyright Infringement in Australia' (2003) 27(2) *Melbourne University Law Review* 381, 382–3.

creators from having their works, or any substantial part thereof, either produced or reproduced without their permission.[1143] However, this statutory right, if taken alone, only offers the reader half the story as it omits the true objective of historical British copyright law: to find a balance between the economic and moral rights of authors and those of the general public.[1144] As technology has developed, and the law of copyright in response, the rights of authors and creators have become better defined, though have done so at the peril of the rights of the general public.

### A1.2.1.1 Early cases

To understand the debate concerning fair dealing in the UK, one must distinguish between cases dealing with 'fair abridgement', on the one hand, and other uses considered legitimate (and legal) without the rights holder's permission.[1145]

Beginning in the year 1740, Lord Chancellor Hardwicke observed that copyright law was intended to prevent those from simply shortening the work of another, though this right could not go so far as to prevent another from making a 'fair' abridgement. The Lord Chancellor further held that the law did not grant authors a monopoly but was rather intended to remunerate them for their labours.[1146] A similar opinion was held by Willes, J in *Millar v Taylor*, which also examined the amount of the work taken in relation to an abridgement.[1147]

Shortly thereafter, the House of Lords issued a decision closer to what we now refer to as fair dealing. In *Donaldson v Beckett*, it held copyright as purely statutory. The decision has since been construed to mean the rights granted to authors therein are subject to the limits of public interest.[1148]

---

[1143] See, e.g., Copyright, Designs and Patents Act 1988, 1988 Chapter c. 48, s. 16(1) and (2) [CDPA].

[1144] Which echoes the US Supreme Court's majority opinion in *Sony*: '[t]he monopoly privileges that Congress may authorize are neither unlimited nor primarily designed to provide a special private benefit. Rather, the limited grant is a means by which an important public purpose may be achieved'. And later: [copyright] 'involves a difficult balance between the interests of authors and inventors in the control and exploitation of their writings and discoveries on the one hand, and society's competing interest in the free flow of ideas, information, and commerce on the other hand'.

[1145] See William F Patry *The Fair Use Privilege in Copyright Law* (Washington: BNA Books, 1985) 3–17.

[1146] *Gyles v Wilcox* (1740) 26 ER 489, 490. For a contrasting case, see: *Tonson v Walker* (1752) 36 ER 1017.

[1147] (1769) 98 ER 201, 205.

[1148] (1774) 98 Eng Rep 257. This view also coincides with the Preamble of the Copyright Act of 1842, 5 & 6 Vict., c.45, July 1, 1842 [Act of 1842]. See also

Other cases went on to consider issues inherent to fair dealing such as: the public interest in educational works;[1149] the promotion of science and public benefit;[1150] quantity taken for criticism or review;[1151] and the intended use of the new work.[1152] Though these cases dealt with basic notions inherent to the doctrine of fair dealing, it would not be until 1839 that the term 'fair use' was first used by the defendants in relation to their use of *The Topographical Dictionary of England*.[1153] It would take almost another 40 years before a judge would use the term.[1154]

### A1.2.1.2   Clarification of the purpose of copyright law

Shortly after the term 'fair use' was first heard in a courtroom in *Lewis v Fullarton*, Parliament enacted the Copyright Act of 1842. Although the term 'fair use' had not found its way into the new Act, it did clarify the law of copyright in the UK. Most importantly, the legislature ended any debate left by the Statute of Anne regarding the purpose of copyright law and ensured the law seek a balance between the rights of authors and the public. This was achieved by stating in the preamble: 'Whereas it is expedient to amend the law relating to copyright, and to afford greater encouragement to the production of literary works of lasting benefit to

---

A Drassinower, 'A Rights-Based View of the Idea/Expression Dichotomy in Copyright Law' (2003) 16 *Canadian Journal of Law & Jurisprudence* 3, para. 45. A similar view was also taken by the Supreme Court of Canada in *Compo Co Ltd v Blue Crest Music Inc*, [1980] 1 SCR 357, 372 where the court stated:

> [. . .] copyright law is neither tort law nor property law in classification, but is statutory law. It neither cuts across existing rights in property or contract nor falls in between rights and obligations heretofore existing in the common law. Copyright legislation simply creates rights and obligations upon the terms and in the circumstances set out in the statute.

[1149]   *Anonymous Case* (1774) 98 ER 913.
[1150]   *Cary v Kearsley* (1802) 170 ER 679.
[1151]   See, e.g., *Whittingham v Wooler* (1817) 36 ER 679 and *Mawman v Tegg* (1826) 38 ER 380.
[1152]   *D'Almaine v Boosey* (1835) 160 ER 117, 123.
[1153]   *Lewis v Fullarton* (1839) 48 ER 1080.
[1154]   In *Chatterton v Cave* (1878) 3 App Cas 483, Lord Hatherley held:

> Books are published with an expectation . . . that they will be criticised in reviews . . . and if the quantity taken be neither substantial nor material, if, 'a fair use' only be made of the publication, no wrong is done and no action can be brought.

See also: D Bradshaw, 'Fair Dealing as a Defence to Copyright Infringement in U.K. Law: An Historical Excursion from 1802 to the Clockwork Orange Case' (1995) 10(1) *Denning Law Journal* 67.

the world.'[1155] To this point in time, the notion of fair dealing remained in the realm of the common law and '[b]efore the coming into force of the Copyright Act 1911, there were no statutory fair dealing defences'.[1156]

### A1.2.1.3 Fair dealing as a statutory defence

The Copyright Act 1911 was introduced for three main reasons.[1157] First and foremost, as was pointed out by the Royal Commission of 1878, the law of copyright was 'wholly destitute of any sort of arrangement' as there were 22 Acts pertaining in some way or form to copyright. In direct response to this valid critique, the 1911 Act had the effect of repealing 18 of those Acts, amending four of them considerably and codified the common law.[1158] The second reason for the 1911 Act was imperial in nature. The UK Government sought uniformity throughout the colonies, which at that time included Australia, Canada and Newfoundland.[1159] Finally, the UK also desired to bring its national laws into conformity with the Berne, Paris and Berlin Conventions.[1160] Though not a primary reason for introducing the 1911 Act, the common law defence of fair dealing was codified in section 2 and provided for defences in relation to private study, research, review, criticism or newspaper summary.[1161]

The intention of the 1911 Act would be later commented upon in *Performing Right Society, Ltd v Hammond's Bradford Brewery Co.* In that case, the court stated: 'the Copyright Act, 1911, was passed with a single object, namely, the benefit of authors of all kinds, whether the works were literary, dramatic or musical'.[1162] This proposition is, prima facie, wholly consistent with the principle that authors and creators are entitled to protection for their works and the primary intention of the legislator.[1163]

---

[1155]   Act of 1842, note 1154 above. See also: deZwart, note 1148, 73.
[1156]   J. Griffiths, 'Preserving Judicial Freedom of Movement – Interpreting Fair Dealing in Copyright Law' (2000) 2 *Intellectual Property Quarterly* 164.
[1157]   1911, c. 46 [1911 Act].
[1158]   *Parliamentary Debates – Commons,* 4th Series, (London: HMSO, 1911), vol. 23, 2589.
[1159]   Ibid., 2590.
[1160]   Ibid., 2592.
[1161]   This section was introduced and adopted with little debate and less controversy, especially subsection (i) which pertains to the public interest—see Standing Committee A on the Copyright Bill with the Proceedings of the Committee, *British Sessional Papers – House of Commons,* (London: HMSO, 1911), vol. VI 725, 733–47.
[1162]   [1934] 1 Ch 121 [*Performing Rights Society*]. This was quoted with approval by the Supreme Court of Canada in *Bishop v Stevens,* [1990] SCR 467, para. 21.
[1163]   *Parliamentary Debates*, note 1158 above, 2588 where Mr Buxton says: '. . .

The effect of this statement, however, is that somewhere between the Act of 1842 and the 1911 Act, the dual intention originally contained in the preamble of the former has been ignored and this, as it will be argued, was not the intention of legislator.

In addition to stating that authors and creators alike deserve protection for their works, when introducing the 1911 Act, Mr Buxton also clearly enunciated:

> The general proposition of the Bill recognizes and endorses the principle that, *subject to the legitimate interests of the public*, the author is to be secured in the control and use of his work . . . that is the general basis of the law of copyright as we desire to apply it.[1164]

It therefore follows that the benefit of authors is not the single object of the 1911 Act as the legitimate interests of the public must also be considered. This proposition is both consistent with the preamble of the Act of 1842 and the method by which Parliament went about determining the term of protection.[1165] In summary, when enacting the 1911 Act, it can be argued that the intention of legislator remained unchanged from the Act of 1842 and both the rights of authors and the general public were to be considered. Despite the obiter dicta in *Performing Rights Society*, Parliament would again take a balanced approach when it next considered the law of copyright some 40 years later.

### A1.2.1.4    The Copyright Act of 1956

Due to such technological innovations as the television and photocopier, copyright was again the subject of much debate in the 1950s. In its Report published in October 1952, the Gregory Committee dealt carefully with the principle of fair dealing.[1166] More specifically, the Committee wanted to define and clarify what precisely constituted fair dealing and pay special attention to what it found as 'the actually and probably unintentionally restrictive wording of the proviso'.[1167] The Committee concluded that despite the wording, the fair dealing with any work shall be entitled to

---

that authors speaking of them in the largest sense of the term are entitled to ample protection for their works of creation. . .'.

[1164]   *Parliamentary Debates*, ibid., 2595 [emphasis added].

[1165]   *Parliamentary Debates*, ibid., 2596. See also Report of the Committee on the Law of Copyright, *British Sessional Papers – House of Commons* (London: HMSO, 1910), vol. XXI 241, 245.

[1166]   *Report of the Copyright Committee*, 1952, Cmnd. 8662 (Chair: Sir Henry Gregory).

[1167]   Ibid., para. 39.

full protection.[1168] Also of note is how, when considering the issue of photocopying in libraries, whether by librarians or students, the Committee adopted a balanced approach, and thus inferring that both authors and users or the public have rights.[1169]

When the Bill finally reached its second reading, the balanced approach had not been lost. As expressed by Mr. Peter Thorneycroft, the President of the Board of Trade:

> Each right given by the law of copyright is of interest to more than one section of the community. Therefore, each right has to be, in a sense, a compromise between conflicting claims. One must therefore consider not only those who benefit, but others, sometimes sections, sometimes the public at large, at whose expense the rights are given . . . The object of the Bill is to try to seek a fair balance between the authors, the composers, the librarians, the record makers, the broadcasting authorities, the purveyors of the general public, the readers, the students . . . and the millions who enjoy television in their own homes. Our attempt here has been to strike a balance between those rights.[1170]

From the above quotation, it is clear Parliament desired a balanced approach. However, when it attempted to better define fair dealing in light of the technological advances, it began with the general right which existed in the 1911 Act and divided it to reflect the different interests found within the public. The effect of Parliament's efforts was what once began as a shorter, more powerful general provision became diluted in an attempt to better take into account the interests of those directly concerned.[1171] In summary, Parliament attempted to take a balanced approach when considering copyright law in light of the invention of the television and photocopier and despite its efforts, the rights of the general public became a more detailed series of exceptions.

---

[1168] Ibid., para. 40.
[1169] Ibid., paras. 43–47.
[1170] *Parliamentary Debates – Commons, 5ᵗʰ Series*, (London: HMSO, 1956), vol. 553, 715–717. See also: Mr Irvine who states:

> I think the principle to which we should adhere in this matter is that of trying, as far as we can, to combine the maximum protection for the creator of an artistic or written work of the property in his work with the greatest possible circulation and diffusion of his work in the public interest. As far as the public interest is concerned, that can be very largely effected in my view by the fair dealing provisions.

Ibid., 772.
[1171] Copyright Act 1956, 1956 c. 74, ss 6 and 9 [*1956 Act*]. See also Standing Committee B, Official Report – Copyright Bill [Lords], *Standing Committees*, Session 1955–56 (London: HMSO, 1956), vol. II, 158–79.

### A1.2.1.5   From 1956 to the White Paper

Though the 1956 Act may be considered as the roots of present day copyright in the UK, and more specifically as the point in time in which the trend of transforming the public's rights into a series of exceptions began, it is not the biggest blow delivered to a user's rights based view of fair dealing.

When it became time to once again review the law of copyright, the Whitford Committee was assigned the task.[1172] First, from the public's perspective, the Whitford Committee deserves credit for making the following recommendation:

> We recommend a general exception in respect of 'fair dealing' which does not conflict with the normal exploitation of the work or subject matter and does not unreasonably prejudice the legitimate interests of copyright holders.[1173]

From this quotation, it would appear the Whitford Committee understood the effect of dividing the general principle of fair dealing into a series of exceptions when it suggested consolidating sections 6 and 9 of the 1956 Act, the former regarding fair dealing with respect to literary, dramatic and musical works and the latter with artistic works. However, such a presumption may have been premature, for the Whitford Committee began from the following premise: 'The Copyright laws of this and other countries have always accepted that certain dealings with copyright works should not infringe copyright. This view is supported by common sense.'[1174]

Although it may be true that such a view is supported by common sense, it completely ignores the issues surrounding the principle and thus also fails to consider them in depth. Had the Whitford Committee expressed itself differently, perhaps its recommendation of a more general fair dealing provision would not have been heavily criticized by later reports for its imprecision.[1175]

Prior to the enactment of the UK's current legislation on copyright, four subsequent reports were published after the Whitford Committee's, three Green Papers and one White Paper. The first two Green Papers, although on copyright reform, were more concerned with the

---

[1172]   Report of the Committee to consider the Law on Copyright and Designs, 1977, Cmnd. 6732.

[1173]   Ibid., para. 677.

[1174]   Ibid., para. 657.

[1175]   Especially by the following White Paper: Intellectual Property and Innovation, April 1986, Cmnd. 9712. See also: Griffiths, above note 1156.

technological innovations such as blank media formats and their impact on the authors' right than with the principle of fair dealing.[1176] The third and final Green Paper, while still discussing a levy for blank media, considered fair dealing to be an exception rather than a public right.[1177] More specifically, the Report claimed to consider the public interest then concluded: (a) authors and creators alike should be remunerated for uses which prejudice their legitimate interests; (b) there is no alternative to a compulsory levy system; and (c) once implemented, a levy scheme should then allow for private copying. Regarding the second finding, the Green Paper determined it was not feasible to allow an exemption either for individuals[1178] or for educational institutions[1179] despite any lawful use of the blank media they may have. In other words, the Green Paper refused to exempt families who were solely using blank media to record birthday parties and vacations just as it refused to exempt universities who were recording lectures from the proposed levy. The consequence of this, although the expense on each individual medium may be insignificant or inconsequential, is still that authors' rights become placed on a normative level above those of the public. In short, it was preferable to overly protect copyright than to under protect it. This view was upheld, albeit more subtly, in the White Paper published the following year.

The objective of the White Paper was stated clearly: in exploiting brain power and dealing with the changing times brought by innovation, it sought to accommodate new technology, strike a balance between competing interests and avoid any enforcement obstacles. Chapter 8 of the White Paper focuses on the principle of fair dealing, although it classifies fair dealing as an exception to infringement rather than a user's right.[1180] The Report also concludes that fair dealing should not be defined as that would benefit neither authors nor the public at large and commercial copying should be excluded from the defence.[1181] In that regard, the White Paper goes further than the previous Green Paper in protecting the interests of authors and creators at the expense of the public at large.

---

[1176] Green Paper: Reform on the Law relating to Copyright, Designs and Performers' Protection, July 1981, Cmnd. 8302; Green Paper: Intellectual Property Rights & Innovation, December 1983, Cmnd. 9117.

[1177] Green Paper: The Recording and Rental of Audio and Video Copyright Material, A Consultative Document, 1985, Cmnd. 9445.

[1178] Ibid., para. 7.8.

[1179] Ibid., paras. 8.1 and 8.2.

[1180] Ibid., at 46.

[1181] Ibid., at paras 8.12 and 8.13 respectively.

However, after five Reports in 11 years, Parliament was not prepared to accept all the recommendations contained in the White Paper.

### A1.2.1.6 The Copyright, Designs and Patent Act 1988[1182]

When the CDPA finally reached its second reading before Parliament, the stated objective of the legislation returned to more closely resemble that of previous copyright bills. As the Chancellor of the Duchy of Lancaster and Minister of Trade and Industry, Mr Kenneth Clarke, announced:

> Our overriding objective ... has been to ensure a fair balance between the need to encourage creativity by providing strong protection, and the justifiable desire of society and consumers to have access to and the use of the products of creativity ... The Bill seeks to provide the means for those with ideas to get a fair reward for their work, without placing unfair burdens on the public at large.[1183]

In line with the stated objective, the Bill did not contain a levy scheme on blank media as recommended by the Green Papers and the White Paper. Rather, the Minister of Trade and Industry stated that such a scheme would go beyond the law of copyright.[1184] However, the Bill did not completely tip the scales in favour of users or the public as it does leave fair dealing as an exception as opposed to a right and does not permit either commercial research under the fair dealing provisions or a private copying right. The current status of fair dealing is briefly outlined in the following paragraphs.

Under the CDPA, the defence of fair dealing is limited to three purposes, namely: research and private study;[1185] criticism and review;[1186]

---

[1182] See note 1143.

[1183] *Parliamentary Debates – House of Commons*, 6th Series, (London: HMSO, 1988), vol. 132, 526.

[1184] Ibid., 531. He would go on to say, 531–3: 'imposing a levy would go beyond the principle of the Bill, which is that we are passing legislation providing legal protection for the intellectual property of the creative artist ... It will provide a fair balance between the providers and users of intellectual property'.

[1185] CDPA, s. 29(1) and (1C) which only apply to literary, dramatic, musical or artistic work. See also: Catherine Colston and Kirsty Middleton, *Modern Intellectual Property Law* (2nd edn, Cavendish Publishing Ltd 2005), s. 11.2; and Lionel Bentley and Brad Sherman, *Intellectual Property Law* (2nd edn, OUP 2004), 193. It should also be noted that the CDPA has been amended to coincide with European Directives, though this is not the focus of this book.

[1186] CDPA, s. 30(1). See also: Colston and Middleton, ibid, and Bentley and Sherman, ibid.

and reporting of current events.[1187] Fair dealing may not exist outside these purposes.

To successfully invoke the defence of fair dealing in the UK, the defendant must be able to prove, in addition to fairness, that the dealing falls within one of the three categories.[1188] Specifically regarding the latter, should the defendant fail to do so, the plaintiff will succeed as 'it is irrelevant that the use might be fair for a purpose not specified in the Act, or that it is fair in general.'[1189] However, where the uncertainty lies is not in the wording of the CDPA, but rather by the fact the courts have interpreted the purposes of these dealings liberally,[1190] albeit from an objective standpoint.[1191]

Provided the defendant has established that the dealing belongs to one of three purposes, the court will move on to analyse its fairness. In assessing the fairness of the dealing, it has been established that the issue is of degree and impression.[1192] Thus, courts benefit from a certain amount of flexibility and may consider a variety of factors, some which may be of more relevance to a particular case than others. These factors include: the obtainment of the work;[1193] the quantity taken;[1194] the defendant's motives;[1195] the defendant's use of the work and consequences thereof;[1196] and the publication status of the work.[1197]

In the CDPA, there are also related exceptions which cover incidental

---

[1187]    CDPA, s. 30(2), though this excludes photographs. See also: Colston and Middleton, ibid, and Bentley and Sherman, ibid.

[1188]    *Newspaper Licensing Agency v Marks & Spencer plc* [1999] EMLR 369.

[1189]    Bentley and Sherman, note 1185 above, 193, s. 2.2.

[1190]    *Pro Sieben v Carlton UK TV* [1999] EMLR 109; *Newspaper Licensing Agency v Marks & Spencer plc* [2000] 4 All ER 239, 257; *Ashdown v Telegraph Group Ltd* [2002] Ch 149, 172. See also Bentley and Sherman, ibid. and W R Cornish and David Llewelyn *Intellectual Property: Patents, Copyright, Trade Marks and Alllied Rights 5ᵗʰ Edition* (5th edn, Sweet & Maxwell 2003) 11–38.

[1191]    *Hyde Park Residence v Yelland* [2000] EMLR 363, para. 21.

[1192]    *Hubbard v Vosper* [1972] 2 QB 84. See also: Colston and Middleton, note 1191 above, 11.2.2 and Bentley and Sherman, note 1185 above, 194, s. 2.3.

[1193]    *Beloff v Pressdram* [1973] 1 All ER 241. See also: Bentley and Sherman, ibid., s. 2.3.2.

[1194]    *Hubbard v Vosper*, note 1192 above, 1027. See also: Bentley and Sherman, ibid.

[1195]    *Pro Sieben v Carlton UK TV*, note 1190 above. See also: Bentley and Sherman, ibid., s. 2.3.5.

[1196]    See Bentley and Sherman, ibid., 195–6, ss 2.3.4. and 2.3.6.

[1197]    *Hyde Park v. Yelland*, note 1191 above, para. 34. See also: Colston and Middleton, note 1185 above, 11.2.2.

infringement,[1198] educational establishments (including reprography),[1199] libraries and archives,[1200] public administration,[1201] designs,[1202] typefaces[1203] and works in electronic form.[1204] Although these are not strictly speaking fair dealing defences, they are closely related and are often simultaneously considered as evidenced in Professors Cornish and Llewelyn's work.[1205]

### A1.2.2    Fair Dealing in Canada

*CCH* adopted a (non-exhaustive) list of six criteria to determine fairness:

(1)    the purpose of the dealing;
(2)    the character of the dealing;
(3)    the amount of the dealing;
(4)    alternatives to the dealing;
(5)    the nature of the work; and
(6)    the effect of the dealing on the work.

The Supreme Court of Canada specifically added that not all six criteria have to be applied in each and every case,[1206] thus avoiding the situation in the US where courts often go through each of the four statutory fair use criteria even when they are unlikely to be relevant.[1207] As a point of comparison, the four US criteria are as follows:

(1)    the purpose and character of the use, including whether such use is of a commercial nature or is for non-profit educational purposes;
(2)    the nature of the copyrighted work;

---

[1198]    CDPA, s. 31.
[1199]    CDPA, ss 32–36.
[1200]    CDPA, ss 37–44.
[1201]    CDPA, ss 45–50.
[1202]    CDPA, ss 51–53.
[1203]    CDPA, ss 54–55.
[1204]    CDPA, s. 56.
[1205]    Cornish and Llewelyn, note 1190 above, at 11–36, which is the beginning of their section relating to "Fair Dealing' and 'Like Exceptions".
[1206]    *CCH*, note 363 above, para. 53.
[1207]    The use of all four criteria seems to be mandated under 17 USC §107. The chapeau to this section states that 'in determining whether the use made of a work in any particular case is a fair use the factors to be considered *shall include. . .*' (emphasis added). The list is thus non exhaustive (though Pierre Leval has argued the opposite), but any fair use analysis must include the four criteria.

*Table A.1   Canadian and US criteria*

| Canada 'fair dealing' | United States 'fair use' |
| --- | --- |
| (1)  purpose of the dealing | Corresponds to above (1) in US list. However in the US the non-profit nature is relevant |
| (2)  character of the dealing | Corresponds to above (1) |
| (3)  amount of the dealing | Corresponds to below (3) except the substantiality |
| (4)  alternatives to the dealing | Corresponds to below (4) |
| (5)  nature of the work | Corresponds to above (2) |
| (6)  effect of the dealing on the work | Corresponds to below (4), although more specific as to the kind of effect |

(3)   the amount and substantiality of the portion used in relation to the copyrighted work as a whole; and

(4)   the effect of the use upon the potential market for or value of the copyrighted work.[1208]

If one compares the two 'lists' in Table A.1, one notes that five of the six Canadian criteria actually mirror the four US (and now Israeli) criteria, as follows:

Fair dealing in Canada is closely aligned with the United States' fair use doctrine. Canadian courts do, however, have more flexibility in that, first, they do not have to apply all criteria in each case; and, second, criteria (1) and (6) are defined in a more open fashion than the corresponding US criteria. An important distinction between the two systems is that for the dealing to be fair in Canada, it must be *for a designated purpose.* Yet, even on this point the two systems are fairly close. In *Harper & Row*, the US Supreme Court listed non-exhaustively the following purposes of fair use: 'criticism, comment, news reporting, teaching (including multiple copies for classroom use), scholarship, or research'.[1209] The net result of *CCH* is that, under Canadian law, there is a flexible list of six criteria to determine fairness but an exhaustive statutory list of acceptable purposes, while under the US fair use doctrine, there is a mandatory list of criteria to determine fairness but an open list of permissible purposes.

Given the high degree of parallelism between the criteria enunciated in *CCH* and the US fair use criteria, one may wonder whether US case law

---

[1208]   Ibid.

[1209]   *Harper & Row, Publishers, Inc. v. Nation Enterprises* (1985), 471 U.S. 539 at 560.

will be used to interpret the six Canadian criteria. Given the similarity of the wording used, the functional comparability of the two markets (except for their respective size), and the similarity of the legislative context in which the interpretive issue arises, this is certainly tempting. Yet, one should proceed with caution, because the origins and history of the two systems are distinct.[1210] One obvious difference is that, in the US, the Constitution itself not only gives Congress the power to adopt copyright legislation but states the purpose of that legislation, namely to 'promote the progress of Science and the Useful Arts'.[1211] While it is not possible to provide a full comparative analysis, a few key statements (Table A.2) can be juxtaposed.

US precedents on fair use could be used in appropriate cases, though caution would require filtering out any extraneous elements such as distinct constitutional arguments (e.g., based on the US Constitution's First Amendment), and elements based on a perception of the basic tenets of copyright law that seem alien to the Canadian approach. A proper guide to evolve those criteria is the three-step test (see Chapter 3) because it can ensure the harmonious development of Canadian law with that of our trading partners.

There are thus several positive elements in the US fair use doctrine. Its initial focus was transformative uses, which one could define as uses that add 'societal' value without significantly endangering the market for the work on which the new work is based, should be encouraged, whether in the form of parody or otherwise. This focus seems to have remerged in recent case law.

It is worth noting that fair dealing and fair use are being introduced or broadened in other jurisdictions.[1212] India expanded its fair dealing exception in the Copyright (Amendment) Act 2012 and Singapore

---

[1210]  The classic statement of 'caution' is found in *Compo Co v Blue Crest Music Inc*, [1980] 1 SCR 357, 367:

The United States Copyright Act, both in its present and earlier forms, has, of course, many similarities to the Canadian Act, as well as to the pre-existing Imperial Copyright Act. However, United States court decisions, even where the factual situations are similar, must be scrutinized very carefully because of some fundamental differences in copyright concepts which have been adopted in the legislation of that country

The statement is repeated in *CCH*, above note 363 at para. 22.

[1211]  US Const, art. I, § 8, cl. 8.

[1212]  See Richard J Peltz, Global Warming Trend? The Creeping Indulgence of Fair Use in International Copyright Law (2009) 17 *Texas Intellectual Property Law Journal* 267.

*Table A.2   Canada and US: comparative analysis, key statements*

| Canada | United States |
|---|---|
| [T]he purpose of copyright law was to balance the public interest in promoting the encouragement and dissemination of works of the arts and intellect and obtaining a just reward for the creator.[a] | [T]o promote the progress of science and useful arts. . .[b] |
| [W]hen an author must exercise skill and judgment to ground originality in a work, there is a safeguard against the author being overcompensated for his or her work. This helps ensure that there is room for the public domain to flourish as others are able to produce new works by building on the ideas and information contained in the works of others.[d] | [C]opyright's purpose is to promote the creation and publication of free expression.[c] |
|  | [I]n determining whether a fact-based work is an original work of authorship, [courts] should focus on the manner in which the collected facts have been selected, coordinated, and arranged. This is a straightforward application of the originality requirement. Facts are never original, so the compilation author can claim originality, if at all, only in the way the facts are presented.[e] |
| The Copyright Act is usually presented as a balance between promoting the public interest in the encouragement and dissemination of works of the arts and intellect and obtaining a just reward for the creator (or, more accurately, to prevent someone other than the creator from appropriating whatever benefits may be generated).[f] | [T]he Framers intended copyright itself to be the engine of free expression. By establishing a marketable right to the use of one's expression, copyright supplies the economic incentive to create and disseminate ideas.[g] |
| One of the purposes of copyright legislation has been to protect and reward the intellectual effort of the author.[h] |  |
| The Copyright Act 1911, was passed with a single object, namely, the benefit of authors of all kinds, whether the works were literary, dramatic or musical.[i] |  |
| See also Article 1 of the Revised Berne Convention. |  |

*Notes:*

[a]   *CCH*, at para. 23.
[b]   See note 1217.
[c]   *Eldred v Ashcroft*, (2003) 537 US 186.
[d]   *CCH*, at para. 23.
[e]   *Feist Publications v Rural Telephone Service*, (1991) 499 US 340, para. 39.
[f]   *Théberge*, (<http://scc-csc.lexum.com/scc-csc/scc-csc/en/item/1973/index.do?r=AAAAA QATQ2FuYWRhIEV2aWRlbmNlIEFjdAE> accessed 17 November 2016) para. 30.
[g]   *Harper & Row*, 558.
[h]   *Télé-Direct (Publications) Inc v American Business Information, Inc*, [1998] 2 FC 22.
[i]   *Performing Right Society, Ltd*, note 1168 above, 127.

has a fair use defence that is similar to section 107 of the US Act, but adds a fifth factor, namely 'the possibility of obtaining the work or adaptation within a reasonable time at an ordinary commercial price'.[1213]

---

[1213]  Singapore, Copyright Act (Ch. 63), s. 35(2)(e).

# Appendix 2

## The Berne Appendix unpacked

As noted in Chapter 2, a joint conference for the revision of the now obsolete Universal Copyright Convention (UCC) and the Berne Convention was held in Paris in July 1971 to overcome the crisis caused by the failure of the Stockholm Protocol that would have granted certain flexibilities to developing countries. That event was much more successful in that it led to the adoption of both a new UCC, and an Appendix to the Berne Convention which, when added to the Stockholm text (*sans* protocol) of Berne constitutes the Paris Act of that Convention (1971).[1214]

The UCC revisions and Appendix to Berne contain similar exceptions and limitations for developing countries inspired by the Stockholm text but modified to be more precise and to limit encroachment upon the rights of authors. Those provisions make compulsory licensing possible for translations and reproductions under certain conditions.

The changes made to the Stockholm text to make it acceptable as an Appendix to Berne in 1971 were designed to limit the scope of possible compulsory licenses. They thus protected copyright holders more than the draft protocol, for example in making it necessary to contact the right holder before issuing a license. As Olian explains:

> Licenses for translation, available for any purpose under the Protocol, may only be granted under the Paris Appendix 'for the purposes of teaching, scholarship or research.' Reproduction licenses, on the other hand, which had previously been available for any 'educational or cultural purposes' are now restricted to use 'in connection with systematic instructional activities.'[1215]

Provisions concerning payments were also strengthened when compared to the protocol. While the reference in the protocol to 'standards of payments made to national authors' would likely have allowed payment in nonconvertible local currency, the Appendix requires that countries 'make

---

[1214]  The new Act included the revised Convention text from 1967, administrative provisions of the (failed) protocol and the Appendix.
[1215]  Olian (n 110) 108.

all efforts, by the use of international machinery, to ensure transmittal in internationally convertible currency or its equivalent'.[1216]

As it now stands, the Appendix is a mixture of substantive rules on the imposition of compulsory licenses and detailed administrative provisions once a decision has been made to seek such a license. In summary, the Appendix:

- Defines 'developing country' as in the Stockholm protocol text using a member's standing in the UN. The criteria are rather vague, although in most cases accepting the status of a country as 'developing' should not pose a major problem;[1217]
- Includes an obligation to make a Declaration to the Director General of WIPO before a country can avail itself of the possibility of issuing compulsory licenses for translation or reproduction.[1218] Those are renewable every ten years;[1219]
- Generally, copies produced under a compulsory license cannot be exported except in limited cases, essentially to deal with country nationals living abroad;[1220]
- Just compensation must be paid;[1221] and
- Countries that had made reservation on the translation right can substitute those for use of the Appendix.[1222]

Specifically, with respect to *translation licenses*:

- The system is limited to published works,[1223] which would seem to exclude sound recordings and digital media;[1224] and licenses can only be granted for the purpose of teaching, scholarship or research;[1225]
- A license can be applied for by any national of a developing country no less than three years after publication if: (a) a translation has not been published in a 'language in general use' in the country in question (the place of publication need not be that country; only the

[1216] App., art. IV, para. (6)(a)(ii).
[1217] Ricketson and Ginsburg (n 17) s 14.51.
[1218] App., art. I(1).
[1219] App., art. I(2).
[1220] App., art. IV(a) and (c).
[1221] App., art. IV(5). See also above concerning currency issues.
[1222] App., art. V.
[1223] App., art. II(2)(a).
[1224] See Ricketson and Ginsburg, (n 17) s 14.61; and Mihály Ficsor, *The Law of Copyright and the Internet* (OUP 2001) 278.
[1225] App., art. II(5).

language is specified in the Appendix[1226]); or (b) if all editions are out of print;[1227]

- If the translation is into a language not in general use in one or more Berne member countries and from a language used in developing countries, the period can be shorted to one year.[1228] A similar reduction can be effected if countries where a language other than English, French or Spanish is in general use unanimously agree and notify the Director General [of WIPO];[1229]
- A translation compulsory license can be terminated if the owner of the translation price publishes a translation made available at a reasonable price, in the same language and gives reasonable advance notice;[1230]
- If an author can exercise her moral right to withdraw all copies of a work (right of repentance also known as *droit de repentir* or *droit de retrait*), that right in unaffected by the Appendix;[1231]
- A license can also be granted to a broadcaster if no translation is available provided it is not for commercial purposes, and is made from a lawful copy under the laws of the country where the translation is made.[1232]

*Reproduction* licenses can also be granted under the Appendix for 'systematic instructional activities'.[1233] However:

- Works covered are similar to those under translation except that some audio-visual works are included;[1234]
- One may apply after five years if no copies were distributed at a normal price charged in the country for comparable works;[1235] except that for works of natural and physical sciences the period is shortened to three years, and for works of fiction, poetry, music, art and drama, the period is increased to seven years;[1236]

---

[1226] At least, this is the view expressed by Ricketson and Ginsburg (n 17) s 14.64.
[1227] App., art. II(2)(a)–(b).
[1228] App., art. II(3).
[1229] App., art. II(3)(b).
[1230] App., art. II(6).
[1231] App., art. II(7).
[1232] App., art. II(9).
[1233] App., art. III(2)(a).
[1234] App., art. III(2). See also Ricketson and Ginsburg (n 17) s. 14.90.
[1235] App., art. III(2)(a).
[1236] App., art. III(3).

- If a work was distributed during that period, then a license can be applied to six months after the 'edition' in question is no longer available;[1237]
- There are procedural requirements including a notification to the right holder, which allows him or her to publish an edition but only within six months of the relevant administrative step (usually the notification followed by a 'denial' or the inability to find the right holder after due diligence);[1238]
- Works produced under the license cannot be sold at more than the 'normal price' referred to above.[1239]

The Appendix in an integral part of the 1971 Paris Act of the Berne Convention, and it was also incorporated into the TRIPS Agreement.[1240] The main critiques of the Appendix underscore the level and recurrence of formalities and administrative steps. Some of the substantive requirements and in particular the right of a copyright holder to terminate (or prevent a licence from being issued) after being notified may also be a significant disincentive to local translators and publishers. Indeed, the Appendix has been described exactly this way, but in reverse, in signalling its potential effect as an incentive for publishers to make their works available in developing countries.[1241] The latter issue (disincentive to use compulsory licenses) is political. The former (formalities) is designed to limit overall use of the Appendix but also provides some transparency. For example, imposing a renewal on the notification that one will use the Appendix opens up the possibility of bilateral pressure not to notify or not to renew an existing notification. Administrative complexities are a disincentive altogether. The system adopted at the WTO in 2003 known as 'paragraph 6' allowing the issuance of compulsory pharmaceutical license--now incorporated into TRIPS in Article 31*bis*—is, just in a way comparable to the Appendix.[1242] It was almost never used, perhaps due to the level of administrative complexities and, like the Appendix, it contains key restrictions on export of goods produced under a compulsory license. The stated objectives to prevent diversion and provide transparency are legitimate. One wonders whether a more general and less burdensome system could be devised, however.

---

[1237] App., art. III(2)(b).
[1238] App., art. III(4).
[1239] App., art. III(2)(a).
[1240] TRIPS Agreement, art. 9.1
[1241] See Ricketson and Ginsburg, (n 17) s. 14.106
[1242] See ibid.

# Index

354

358 *(Re)structuring copyright*

traditional knowledge 267
transaction costs 1, 20, 208, 228, 232, 233
  copyright management systems (CMS) 249
  fair use 325
  formalities 268
  three-step test 87, 88
Transatlantic Trade and Investment Partnership (TTIP) 292–3, 295
Transpacific Partnership (TPP) 199, 223, 292–3, 295
transparency 241, 244, 252, 254, 255, 290, 344
TRIPS Agreement 19, 30, 34, 35, 38, 56–8, 232, 323, 344
  Australia 77
  developing countries 57, 282–3, 284–9
  education 226, 227
  originality 112
  patents 181
  proposed reforms 213, 214
    formalities 266, 267, 269, 278
  three-step test 42, 57, 59, 61–2, 86, 91–2, 93, 180
    Australia 77
    fair use 65, 66
    legitimate interests of rights holder 68
    licensing schemes 90
    related rights 81
    WTO dispute settlement 64
TRIPS-Plus agreements 295
Twitter 198

unfair competition 98, 161–2, 200
unions 28
United Kingdom 19, 43, 61, 68
  adaptations 139–40
  Brexit 103
  CMOs 238, 255
  derivative right 147–8
  fair dealing 326–7
    Copyright Act 1956 330–31
    Copyright, Designs and Patent Act 1988 334–6
    early cases 327–8
    from 1956 to White Paper 332–4

    purpose of copyright law 328–9
    statutory defence 329–30
  formalities 259, 260
  higher education
    licensing schemes 90
  originality 100–103, 113, 118, 147–8
  science and copyright 91
  Statute of Anne (1709–10) 12–19, 33, 326
United States 19, 20, 36–7, 54, 170, 231, 233, 297–8
  Audio Home Recording Act 319
  Australia-US FTA 75
  California 17
  capture, regulatory 174
  CMOs 237, 238, 247, 251, 252, 253, 254
    ASCAP 238, 253, 254
  Constitution 175, 181–2, 205, 262, 338
  Copyright Act 35, 133, 338
    digital transmissions 164–5
    fair use 65–6, 314–15, 326, 340
    ideas 57
    originality 96, 112
    WTO dispute settlement 63–4, 65–6, 67, 68
  Copyright Clearance Center, Inc. 90–91, 229
  Copyright Principles Project (CPP) 177–8, 182, 186–7, 266, 273
  derivation 149, 150, 151, 152
  developing countries 282
  Digital Millennium Copyright Act (1998) (DMCA) 21, 23, 138, 197, 199, 202
  fair use 64–6, 89–90, 182, 187, 229, 314–16, 326, 340
    appellate cases: transformative use 134–5, 174, 323–5
    Copyright Principles Project 186, 187
    fair dealing in Canada and 336–9
    Folsom test 85–6, 315, 321
    Supreme Court cases since 1978 123, 134, 317–23
    transformative use 123, 134–5, 174, 323–5
    UGC: user-copied content 134–6
  fixation 94
  formalities 257–9, 260–62, 276